FOREWORD

Women of Unifarm proudly present the second edition of a classic country cookbook.

We have come a long way since 1928 when we first started our collection of farm women's favorite recipes. Who would have thought that 60 year's later our cookbook would still be in such demand? Our first edition was reprinted eleven times and sold more than 125,000 copies.

But how could we lose? We had treasured, tried and true recipes handed down from generation to generation of farm families. Recipes that filled our grandmothers' homes with mouthwatering aromas and lined their pantry shelves with pickles, jams and other preserves. We have chosen recipes that you will want to leave with your grandchildren.

This edition is a testimonial to the farm women, without whose fine contributions this book would not have been possible. It's a collection not only of their preserved traditions and creativeness, but also of their resourcefulness in day-to-day living. Along with the traditional favorites, *Country Classics* features more than 250 new recipes, many of them for microwave cooking.

We have assembled this book with love and present it to you, the reader, as a truly unique gift, to hold and treasure for all present and future generations of Canadians.

Dedication

To our pioneer farm women
for preserving their favorite recipes
so that we can share them
with our families today
and with all the generations of the future.

Table of Contents

Microwave

Barbecue

Time Saver

Low Calorie

APPETIZERS, DIPS & SPREADS

MEATBALL CANAPES

1 lb. lean ground round	1/4 tsp. pepper
1/4 tsp. garlic salt	1/4 cup wheat germ
1 medium onion, finely chopped	1 tbsp. oil
1 cup skim milk	16-oz. can tomato sauce
1 tsp. dry mustard	12-oz. bottle chili sauce
1/2 tsp. salt	3/4 cup grape jelly

Combine first eight ingredients and form into tiny meatballs. Heat the oil in a skillet and brown meatballs. Pour off fat and place in chafing dish. Combine the tomato sauce, chili sauce and grape jelly in saucepan. Heat until jelly is melted. Pour over meatballs and simmer 20 minutes.

Ellen Lunseth

SWEET-SOUR MEAT BALLS

1 onion, chopped fine	1 lb. ground beef, rolled
3/4 tsp. seasoned salt	into small balls
10 3/4-oz. can tomato soup	13 1/4-oz. can pineapple
3 tbsp. lemon juice	chunks, drained
1/4 cup brown sugar	

Combine onion, seasoned salt, tomato soup, lemon juice and brown sugar in a 9-inch square glass cake pan. Microwave for 7 minutes, stirring twice during this time. Place meat balls in this sauce, spooning some sauce over meat balls. Microwave 7 minutes, turning dish once during cooking period. Add drained pineapple chunks. Heat for 1 minute. Serve with toothpicks. NOTE: These meat balls are also good served as a main dish. Accompany with cooked rice or whipped potatoes, as desired.

Readymade Local

CRUNCHY CHICKEN WINGS

1/4 cup margarine	8 buttery crackers, rolled fine
3 lbs. chicken wings	1/2 cup parmesan cheese
2 tsp. parsley flakes	1/2 tsp. garlic powder
1/2 tsp. paprika	Dash of pepper

Microwave margarine in pie plate until melted. Layer chicken wings in plate. Combine remaining ingredients and pour over wings. Microwave 15 to 16 minutes on High.

Doris Barker

PINEAPPLE CHEESE BALLS

16 oz. pkgs. cream cheese
3 1/2-oz. can crushed pineapple
2 cups chopped walnuts

1/4 cup chopped green pepper
2 tsp. green onion
1 tsp. seasoning salt

Have cheese at room temperature and mix with beater until smooth. Gradually stir in drained pineapple, nuts, onions, green pepper and salt. Cover and chill overnight. Form into 2 or 3 balls quickly and roll in remaining nuts. Wrap in foil. Will keep two weeks in the refrigerator.

TOMATO CHEESE CUBES OR FINGERS

Bread fingers
Tomato soup

Grated cheese

Spread bread fingers with tomato soup from the can. Roll in grated cheese. Put under broiler to bake until golden brown. Serve hot.

CHEESE BALLS OR CROQUETTES

1/2 lb. grated cheddar cheese
2 cups soft bread crumbs
3 eggs, beaten
1 tsp. worcestershire sauce

Salt and pepper to taste
1 egg, slightly beaten
2 tbsp. water
1/2 cup dry bread crumbs

Mix cheese, bread crumbs, 3 eggs, worcestershire sauce, salt and pepper. Form into balls. Dip into slightly-beaten egg and water. Roll in bread crumbs and fry in hot fat until delicate brown. Drain and serve with tomato sauce.

PICKLED EGGS

• 1 1/2 tbsp. salt
1 tbsp. whole cloves
1 tbsp. pepper corns
1 1/2 cups water
3 cups vinegar

1 1/2 tbsp. celery salt **or**
2 tbsp. ginger root
12 hard boiled eggs
Sliced onion (optional)

Combine all ingredients but eggs and onion and boil for 3 minutes. Cool. Drop eggs and onion into solution. Let stand for a few days. NOTE: Beet pickle vinegar may be added for color.

Cheese should be kept in a covered container or wrapped in heavy wax paper or foil, and stored in the refrigerator. If the cheese is not covered, it will dry out and if stored in a warm place, some of the fat may melt and run out of the cheese.

Partially used cans or jars of pickles, olives, water chestnuts, pimentos, bamboo shoots and sauerkraut freeze well in their own liquid.

PICKLED MUSHROOMS

1 1/2 cups water	1/4 cup vinegar
1/2 cup olive oil	3/4 cup white wine
1 tsp. salt	1 tsp. mustard
1 tbsp. mustard seed	Few peppercorns
1/2 tsp. hot chili	2 tsp. paprika
Chopped parsley	Small button mushrooms

Combine all ingredients except mushrooms and bring to a boil. Simmer 2 to 3 minutes. Add mushrooms for 3 to 4 minutes and remove from heat. Let stand in solution for 24 hours.

STUFFED MUSHROOMS

12 large fresh mushrooms	1 tbsp. flour
3 tbsp. butter **or** margarine	1/2 cup heavy cream
Salt and pepper	1/4 cup chopped parsley
1/4 cup butter **or** margarine	1/4 cup grated Swiss cheese
1/3 cup finely-chopped onion	(optional)

Wipe mushrooms with a damp cloth. Carefully remove stems and set aside. In a small custard cup, melt 3 tbsp. of butter in microwave for 30 to 40 seconds. Brush mushroom caps with melted butter and place, hollow side up, in a baking dish. Sprinkle mushroom caps with salt and pepper. Finely chop the reserved mushroom stems. Melt 1/4 cup of butter in a medium-sized bowl in microwave for 30 to 40 seconds. Add onions and mushroom stems, stirring to combine. Heat, uncovered for 3 to 4 minutes or until onions and mushrooms are tender. Blend in flour until smooth. Gradually stir in heavy cream until smooth. Heat uncovered for 3 to 4 minutes or until thickened and smooth. Stir in chopped parsley. Fill each mushroom cap with some of the mushroom mixture. If desired, sprinkle a little grated cheese over each stuffed mushroom cap. Microwave uncovered for 3 to 4 minutes just before serving. If desired, mushrooms can be refrigerated until serving time. Increase heating time by 1 to 1 1/2 minutes. Yield: 6 servings.

PICKLED HERRINGS

3 - 4 herrings	2 - 3 tsp. sugar
1/2 cup vinegar	1 medium onion, sliced
1/2 cup water	

Soak herrings in water overnight. Clean, and remove skin and bone. Cut into tid-bit pieces and place in glass dish. Cover herrings with a dressing made of vinegar, 1/2 cup water, sugar and onion. Marinate a few hours or overnight.

Mrs. Anna Kobitzsch

NUTS AND BOLTS

1 1/2 cups butter **or** margarine **or**	2 tsp. celery salt
2/3 cup salad oil	1 lb. mixed salted nuts
1/4 cup worcestershire sauce	12 oz. Shreddies
1 tsp. liquid smoke	6 oz. crisp rice cereal
2 tsp. garlic salt	7 oz. Cheerios
2 tsp. onion salt	6 oz. small pretzel sticks

Heat oven to 200°. Melt butter in small saucepan. Add worcestershire sauce, liquid smoke and seasoned salts. Remove from heat and let stand for flavors to blend. Meanwhile combine nuts, cereals and pretzels in large roasting pan. Pour butter sauce over cereal mixture and mix lightly. Bake uncovered for 2 hours, stirring and tossing lightly every 15 to 20 minutes. Spread out on paper towels or brown paper to drain. Cool for several hours. Store in airtight container to keep crisp.

Laura Deyell

DIPS AND SPREADS

VEGETABLE DIP

1/2 cup cheese whiz	1/4 cup chili sauce
1 cup sour cream	2 tbsp. dry vegetable soup mix
1 cup mayonnaise	1/2 tsp. worcestershire sauce

Blend ingredients together and chill. Serve with any vegetables or use as a dressing for lettuce salad.

Phyllis McGhee

FRESH VEGETABLE DIP

1 1/2 cups mayonnaise	1 1/2 tsp. appetit
2 cups sour cream	1 1/2 tsp. onion flakes
1 1/2 tsp. dill weed	

Mix ingredients together and store in refrigerator.

Evelyn Bair Kurney

CHIP DIP

4 oz. cream cheese **or** 6 oz. cream-style cottage cheese	2 tsp. grated onion
	Dash of pepper
1 tbsp. canned milk **or** cream	1/8 tsp. dry mustard
1 tbsp. chili sauce	Dash of worcestershire sauce
1 tbsp. lemon juice	

Beat cheese until light and smooth. Add other ingredients and blend well. This is ideal for carrot or celery sticks, but more liquid may be added for chips.

EASY CHIP DIP

12 oz. creamed cottage cheese   1 env. onion soup mix
2 tbsp. milk

Beat cottage cheese with electric mixer until smooth and fluffy. Add milk and onion soup mix and blend well. Chill before serving.

HOT CHEESE SPREAD

3 cups grated sharp cheese   1/2 tsp. curry powder
1 small can ripe olives, chopped   Dash of garlic salt
1 medium onion, chopped   Dash of salt
1 cup mayonnaise   Dash of paprika

Mix cheese, olives and onions. Add mayonnaise, curry powder, garlic salt, salt and paprika. Store in refrigerator and use when needed on crackers or as a dip.

CHEESE AND BLACK OLIVE SPREAD

3 oz. chopped black olives   1/4 cup salad dressing
4 oz. old white cheddar cheese

Drain olives very well and combine ingredients. Keeps in refrigerator for two weeks.

CREAM CHEESE SPREAD

8 oz. cream cheese   1/2 jar seafood cocktail
Chopped onion   1 can lobster **or** crab meat
Garlic powder

Soften cheese; add onion and garlic powder. Line pie plate with mixture. cover with half a jar cocktail and lobster meat. Serve with crackers.

SHRIMP DIP

1 can shrimp, mashed   1/2 tsp. seasoning salt
2 cups sour cream   Dash of garlic salt
1 tsp. worcestershire sauce   Sweet cream (optional)
1 tbsp. finely-chopped green onion

Mix ingredients together and put in refrigerator for 1/2 hour before using. This is good as a raw vegetable dip.

CHIVE AND DILL DIP

12-oz. creamed cottage cheese   2 tbsp. chopped chives
Salt and pepper to taste   1 tsp. chopped dill herbs

Beat cottage cheese until creamed. Add salt and pepper, chives and dill. Mix well. 1 or 2 tbsp. lemon juice may be added if desired. This is also very good on baked potatoes.

DILL CREAM SAUCE DIP

1 cup sour cream
1 tbsp. lemon juice

1 tsp. grated onion
1/2 tsp. chopped dill

Blend all ingredients together. Salt and pepper may be added. Refrigerate. Yield: 1 cup.

SPINACH DIP

Round pumpernickel loaf
1 cup mayonnaise
1 cup sour cream

1 pkg. vegetable soup mix
1 can finely-sliced walnuts
1 tsp. onion flakes

Cut off lid of pumpernickel loaf and hollow out, cutting 1 inch from sides and bottom. Combine remaining ingredients and fill shell. NOTE: Make a day ahead for flavors to blend and allow shell to dry a little. To serve, circle loaf with cubes of bread for dipping.

SAUERKRAUT DIP

1 env. onion soup mix
2 cups sour cream **or**
   creamed cottage cheese

3 cups chopped sauerkraut
1 tbsp. chopped chives
1 tbsp. chopped parsley

Combine and blend ingredients until smooth. Chill before serving. NOTE: 1/2 cup chili sauce and chopped crisp fried bacon may be added.

MUSTARD SAUCE DIP

1 cup sour cream
2 tbsp. prepared mustard
1 tbsp. lemon juice

3 tbsp. dry onion soup mix
1 tsp. chopped fresh parsley

Combine all ingredients. Beat with rotary beater until well blended.

LEMON CHILI SAUCE DIP

1 cup chili sauce
2 tbsp. brown sugar

1 - 2 tsp. lemon juice
1/2 tsp. grated lemon rind

Combine all ingredients. Refrigerate. Yield: 1 cup.

Crisp potato chips, crackers or pretzels, etc. by heating about 1 minute on High in the microwave.

QUICK KABOBS: Marinate less tender cuts of meat and lean sea food several hours ahead of time, or wrap them in sliced bacon or salt pork to barbecue.

SOUPS & SANDWICHES

VEGETABLE SOUP

4 lb. soup bone, marrow exposed	1 tbsp. pepper
12 cups cold water	1/2 cup pot barley
1 tbsp. salt	

Boil bone, water, salt and pepper for 4 hours. Remove bone from kettle and scrape off any meat. Return meat to kettle and whatever marrow you can salvage. Discard bone. Add barley to liquid and return to boil. Meanwhile prepare:

3 tbsp. chopped green onion	1/2 cup green peas
1 cup carrots, cubed	1/2 cup potatoes, cubed
1 cup celery, sliced fine	1 tbsp. chopped parsley
1/2 cup cabbage, cut fine	1 whole bay leaf
1/2 cup green beans, cut up	

Add ingredients to liquid, along with more water if necessary and cook for 1 hour. Remove bay leaf and serve with or without tomato juice. Yield: 18 servings.

TOMATO SOUP

1 tbsp. chopped onion	3 tbsp. flour
28-oz. can tomatoes	2 cups milk
Salt and pepper to taste	1/8 tsp. soda
1 tbsp. melted butter **or** oil	

Cook onion, tomatoes, salt and pepper slowly. Blend butter and flour and all of milk. Add soda to tomatoes and stir well. Add flour mixture, stirring constantly while cooking.

CHICKEN NOODLE SOUP

1 chicken	1 tsp. thyme
Salt and pepper to taste	1 cup homemade noodles
1 onion, chopped fine	1 tsp. parsley, finely chopped
1 bay leaf	

Boil fowl with salt, pepper, onion, bay leaf and thyme until meat comes off bones. Remove fowl and set aside to cool. Add noodles and simmer until done. Add 1/2 cup of cooked fowl, chopped fine, and simmer another 5 minutes. Add parsley just before serving.

Women of Unifarm Local 213

HUNGARIAN CHICKEN SOUP

1 small boiling chicken
5 - 7 cups cold water
1 tbsp. salt **or** to taste
1 stalk celery with leaves
1 medium whole onion
1/2 clove garlic (optional)

1/2 tsp. whole black pepper **or**
  1/4 tsp. ground pepper
2 small carrots
2 medium parsnips
1/4 tsp. sweet paprika

Wash and cut up chicken. Add water, just covering chicken in pot. Add salt. Boil slowly, skimming foam from top. Add celery, onion, garlic and pepper. Add carrots and parsnips, both left whole. Simmer until chicken is tender. When chicken is tender, add paprika. Add cooked egg noodles or Italian Style Baby Shell Macaroni and simmer for 30 minutes.

Mrs. George Antal

HEARTY BEEF AND CABBAGE SOUP

1 lb. ground beef
1 onion, chopped
2 cups celery, diced
1 green pepper, chopped
2 tbsp. oil
2 tsp. salt
2 tbsp. sugar
1/2 tsp. pepper
1/2 tsp. paprika

1 tbsp. parsley flakes
28-oz. can tomato sauce
2 51/2-oz. tins tomato paste
1 can beef consomme
4 cups water
1 cup carrots, cubed
2 cups raw potatoes, cubed
6 cups coarsely-chopped
  cabbage

Sauté beef, onion, celery and green pepper in oil in a very large pot until meat is no longer red. Keep breaking up meat until it is in small pieces. Add remaining ingredients, except cabbage and simmer uncovered for 1 hour. Add cabbage and simmer for 1 more hour.

HAMBURGER SOUP

11/2 lbs. lean ground beef
1 medium onion, chopped fine
28-oz. can tomatoes
2 cups water
3 cans consomme
1 can tomato soup
4 carrots, chopped fine

1 bay leaf
3 sticks celery, chopped
Parsley, chopped
1/2 tsp. thyme
Pepper to taste
8 tbsp. pot barley

Brown meat and onions, draining well. Combine all ingredients and simmer 2 hours.

Miriam Galloway

To freeze garden fresh herbs such as parsley, thyme, dill, etc., pick before plant blooms. Blanch 15 seconds, chop ready for use and pack in small freezer bags. Use what you need and return to freezer.

BEEF BARLEY SOUP

Beef bone	1 bay leaf
Salt and pepper	Thyme
Onion	1/3 cup pearl barley

Boil bone for 2 to 2 1/2 hours with onion and seasonings. Remove bone. Add barley and cook until done. Diced fresh vegetables may be added with barley.

LENTIL SOUP

2 cups lentils	1/4 cup catsup
2 cups water	2 tbsp. worcestershire sauce
19-oz. can tomatoes	2 garlic cloves, crushed
1/2 tsp. sage	2 large onions, chopped
1/2 tsp. thyme	3 carrots, sliced
1/2 tsp. marjoram	4 stalks celery, sliced
2 tsp. salt	1 green pepper, chopped
1/3 cup vinegar	1 cup sliced mushrooms
2 tbsp. sugar	1 1/2 cup grated cheese

Rinse lentils before using and combine with all ingredients but cheese. Simmer about 20 minutes until tender. Add cheese. Yield: 10 cups. Freezes well.

AUSTRIAN SOUP

2 tbsp. oil	2 stalks celery, diced
1 lb. hamburger	2 springs parsley, chopped
1 chopped onion	1/4 cup macaroni
Garlic salt, to taste	1 tbsp. salt
1 medium can tomatoes	1/4 tsp. pepper
1 cup chopped cabbage	3 cups water
2 medium potatoes, diced	3 oxo bouillon cubes

Heat oil and add hamburger, onion and garlic salt. Brown. Add remaining ingredients and simmer for 1 hour.

CANADIAN PEA SOUP

1 cup dried peas	2 tbsp. lard
6 cups water **or** beef stock	2 tbsp. flour
1/2 lb. salt pork	Salt and pepper
2 tbsp. chopped onion	1 tsp. parsley

Soak peas overnight. Drain and add to the water, along with salt pork. Cook slowly until peas are tender. Sauté onions in lard and add the flour. Add to the soup mixture. Season to taste with salt, pepper and parsley. VARIATION: Use summer savory instead of parsley.

Women of Unifarm Local 213

PEA SOUP

1 cup dried peas
1/8 tsp. pepper
1 bay leaf

Sprig of thyme
1 tbsp. chopped onion
Salt pork, cubed

Wash peas. Let soak overnight. Next morning drain, add fresh water and cook with seasonings, onion and pork until soft. Put through sieve. Recover puree and liquid. Heat gently and serve at once. When serving, garnish with chopped parsley.

POTATO SOUP

7 cups water
6 medium potatoes,
2 onions, sliced
1 carrot, sliced
1/2 tsp. thyme
1 bay leaf

1 clove
1/2 cup milk, scalded
1/2 cup cream, scalded
1 1/2 tsp. salt
1/2 tsp. pepper

Bring water to a boil. Peel and slice potatoes. Add potatoes, onion, carrot, thyme, bay leaf and clove. Cook over low heat for 45 minutes. Force the mixture through sieve. Add milk, cream, salt and pepper and cook over low heat for 10 minutes. Serve hot.

SHRIMPS WITH RICE

1 medium onion, minced
3 tbsp. butter
1 cup rice

2 cups liquid
1 green pepper, minced
1 can small shrimp

Fry onion in butter until clear. Add rice and fry slightly. Do not brown. Add liquid from shrimp, plus water to make 2 cups. Bring to a boil, cover and let cook over low heat for 15 minutes. Sprinkle the pepper over the top of the rice, then the cleaned shrimp. Do not stir in. Cover and cook over low heat for 20 minutes. A heavy saucepan with a tight-fitting lid is the best type to use.

CHEESE SOUP

1 cup chopped onion
1/2 cup diced celery
3 tbsp. butter
1 tbsp. flour
1 tsp. dry mustard
1/4 tsp. pepper

1/8 tsp. paprika
1/2 tsp. salt
2 cups milk
2 cups grated cheddar cheese
3 slices bacon, fried and
    crumbled

Sauté onion and celery in butter about 5 minutes until onion is transparent. Blend in flour and seasonings. Gradually add milk and cook over medium heat about 5 minutes until smooth and slightly thickened. Stir constantly. Add cheese and stir until melted. Serve immediately, garnished with bacon. Yield: 4 servings.

CORN CHOWDER

4 slices bacon
1/2 cup chopped onion
3/4 cup chopped celery
1 cup diced potatoes
1 tbsp. pimento **or** tomato,
    chopped finely

1 tbsp. parsley
1/2 cup water
3 tbsp. flour
2 cups milk
1 can creamed
    or whole corn

Cut bacon and fry until crisp. Add onions, celery and potato and brown lightly. Add seasonings and water. Cover and simmer until vegetables are cooked. Beat flour and milk. Add to vegetables. Stir constantly until thickened. Add corn to soup shortly before serving.

Agnes Galloway

CLARE'S CORN CHOWDER

4 sliced of bacon, diced
1 onion, chopped
2 cups corn, fresh, frozen
    or canned
11/2 cups diced raw potatoes

10-oz. can cream of
    mushroom soup
3 cups milk
1/2 tsp. salt
1/8 tsp. pepper

Sauté bacon and onion in large pot until onion is limp. Add remaining ingredients and bring to boil. Cover and simmer until potatoes are cooked, stirring occasionally. Yield: 6 cups.

Clare Johnston

CREAM OF BROCCOLI SOUP

1 cup sliced celery
1 cup minced onion
1/4 clove garlic, cut fine
1/8 cup butter
6 cups chicken stock

3 lbs. fresh broccoli
2 cups light cream
Salt and pepper to taste
Parsley

Sauté celery, onions and garlic in butter in large pan. Cover and cook on low heat for 20 minutes. Add chicken stock. Cut broccoli stems into 1-inch pieces and add. Simmer for 15 minutes and add flowerettes. Cook an additional 15 minutes. Puree in blender or food processor, heat and stir in cream. Add salt and pepper and garnish with parsley. Yield: 12 servings.

Christina Smith

To dry herbs in the microwave, spread 1 cup of cleaned, dry fresh leaves on a double thickness of paper towel. Microwave on High 2 to 3 minutes until leaves are brittle. Let stand 15 minutes.

ZUCCHINI SOUP

1 onion, chopped	1/8 tsp. garlic powder
2 tbsp. margarine	1/8 tsp. celery salt
2 chicken bouillon cubes	Dash of pepper
2 cups boiling water	1/4 cup fresh chopped parsley
4 cups coarsely diced zucchini	**or** 1 tbsp. dried parsley
1/2 tsp. salt	

Sauté onion in margarine until tender. Add all remaining ingredients except parsley. Cook over medium heat about 5 minutes until zucchini is tender. Carefully pour into blender. Add parsley and whirl at high speed until smooth. Serve hot or cold. Can also be served with croutons on top. Yield: 4 to 6 servings.

Jean Leskow

MARY'S CLAM CHOWDER

1/2 cup chopped bacon	3/4 cup diced raw celery
1/4 cup chopped onion	1 cup diced raw potato
Salt and pepper	1 bay leaf
2 cups water	1 sprig thyme
1 cup diced raw carrot	15-oz. can minced clams

Fry bacon, add onion and fry lightly. Add salt, pepper, water, carrots, celery, potatoes, bay leaf and thyme. Let simmer 20 minutes. Add clams and liquid and let simmer another 15 minutes.

Mary Wright

CLAM CHOWDER

2 slices bacon	2 tbsp. flour
8-oz. can minced clams	1 1/3 cups milk
1 large potato, peeled and cubed	1/2 tsp. salt
1/4 cup chopped onion	Dash of pepper
1 medium carrot, sliced	

Place bacon in 2-qt. casserole. Cover with paper towel and microwave 1 1/2 minutes or until crisp. Remove towel and bacon, leaving drippings in pan. Add clam liquid, potatoes, onion and carrots to drippings. Cover and microwave 8 minutes until tender. Stir once. Mix flour with small amount of milk. Add to cooked mixture along with remaining milk, salt, pepper and clams. Microwave, covered for 3 minutes, stirring once at half time. Let stand 3 minutes and garnish with crumbled bacon and parsley.

Margaret Allan

To save space and freezer cartons, freeze soups in unlined pans. Once frozen, remove from pan like an ice cube and package in freezer bags.

SANDWICHES

BROILED CHICKEN SANDWICH

6 buns, halved
Butter **or** margarine
2 cups chopped, cooked chicken
1 tbsp. chopped onion
1/2 cup chopped celery
1/4 cup chopped green pepper
2 tsp. lemon juice
1/3 cup mayonnaise
1/2 tsp. salt
Dash of pepper
3/4 cup grated cheese

Toast buns and butter well. Blend chicken, onion, celery, green pepper, lemon juice, mayonnaise, salt and pepper together. Mix well. Spread on bun halves. Sprinkle with cheese. Place on broiler pan about 4 inches from heat until cheese is hot and bubbly. Serve hot.

CHICKEN A-LA-KING

1 1/2 cups cooked diced chicken
1/2 - 1 cup sautéed mushrooms
2 tbsp. chopped green pepper
1 1/2 cups white sauce

Heat ingredients together. Season to taste and serve on hot, buttered toast. Yield: 3 to 4 servings.

DEVILED HAMBURGERS

1 lb. ground beef, browned
1/3 cup chili sauce
1 1/2 tsp. worcestershire sauce
1 1/2 tsp. prepared mustard
1 1/2 tsp. horseradish
1 tsp. minced onion
1 tsp. salt
Dash of pepper

Combine ground beef will remaining ingredients, mixing well. Cut 4 buns in half, butter and spread with meat mixture. Place in broiler 5 to 7 inches from heat for 10 minutes. Yield: 8 servings.

SLOPPY JOES

1 lb. ground beef
2 tbsp. chopped green pepper
1 onion, chopped
1 tbsp. shortening
1 cup catsup
1 tsp. worcestershire sauce
3/4 tsp. celery seed
1/2 tsp. salt

Cook ground beef, green pepper and onion in skillet with shortening until brown. Stir in catsup, worcestershire sauce, celery seed and salt. Bring mixture to boil over full heat. Turn to simmer and cook 10 minutes. Spoon mixture onto hamburger buns. Yield: 6 to 8 servings.

Sandwich freezing tips: Never use mayonnaise or spread dressing on bread. Day old bread used for sandwiches to be frozen keeps better than fresh bread. Don't freeze green onions, chives or jelly.

HOT CREAMY TUNA BURGER

2 cans Albacore tuna
1 can cream of chicken soup
2 tbsp. green pepper, chopped
Dash of tobasco

1/4 cup hamburger relish
1 can cream of mushroom soup
2 tbsp. onion, chopped fine
Seasonings to taste

Combine all ingredients. Cut 18 hamburger buns in half, butter and spread with mixture. Wrap in foil and freeze. When ready to use, remove buns from freezer and bake at 400° for 30 minutes without unwrapping. Serve with greens and sliced tomato.

SALMON SANDWICH

8-oz. can salmon
3 hard-boiled eggs, ground
1 tbsp. grated onion

1 tbsp. mayonnaise
Salt and pepper to taste
2 - 3 gherkins, chopped

Mix salmon, eggs, onion, dressing and salt and pepper. Add gherkins.

BARBECUED CORNED BEEF SANDWICH

1 small onion, chopped fine
3 tbsp. oil

12-oz. can corned beef
1 cup catsup

Fry onion in oil. Chop corned beef and add with catsup. Cook slowly for 30 minutes. Spoon into hot, buttered hamburger buns. Yield: 4 to 6 servings.

DENVER SANDWICH

1 cup chopped, cooked meat
1 medium onion, chopped

4 eggs, well beaten
Pinch of salt

Combine ingredients and fry in hot greased pan until brown. Turn and brown well. Serve on buttered bread.

Verdie Stenson

CHEESE BOLOGNA BUNS

1 cup grated cheese
1/4 cup pickle relish
1/8 tsp. pepper
1 tsp. worcestershire sauce
1/4 cup salad dressing

1 1/2 cups bologna, chopped
1/4 tsp. salt
1 tbsp. grated onion
3 tbsp. catsup

Combine ingredients, mixing well. Split and butter 8 buns. Spread filling on each half. Place on broiler pan in oven about 3 inches from heat until browned slightly. Serve at once. Yield: 8 servings.

Poach chicken and turkey pieces in the microwave for use in sandwiches, salads and casseroles. More tender than roasting.

HOT CHEESE DREAMS

1 cup grated cheese	1 tbsp. melted butter
2 tbsp. milk	1 egg
1/2 tsp. mustard	1/4 tsp. paprika
Pinch of salt	

Mix all ingredients together into a smooth paste. Spread between slices of fresh buttered bread. Toast sandwiches on both sides or fry in butter. Serve hot.

CHEESE SANDWICH FILLINGS

Chopped cucumber	Chopped hard-cooked egg
Chopped crisp bacon	Seasonings, chili sauce **or**
Chopped green pepper and nuts	chopped pickle

Use one of the above with cheddar or process cheese.

Chopped green pepper and nuts	Cucumber
Onion juice **or** chopped chives	Pickle relish
Chopped dates and nuts	Chopped preserved **or**
Chopped nuts and raisins	candied ginger
Jams, jellies and marmalades	Maraschino cherries

Use one of the above with cream or cottage cheese.

CHEESE SPREAD

3/4 cup vinegar	1/2 tsp. salt
1/2 cup butter	1 cup grated cheese
4 eggs	1 small can pimento, chopped
2 tsp. dry mustard	8 large gherkins, chopped
1/3 cup sugar	1 medium onion, diced

Heat vinegar to boiling point. Melt butter in vinegar. Beat eggs thoroughly and add mustard, sugar, salt and cheese. Gradually pour hot mixture over eggs, stirring constantly. Cook in double boiler until thick. Remove from heat and add remaining ingredients. Store in sterilized glasses in cool place. Keeps well. Yield: 31/2 cups.

Cottage cheese, cream cheese and processed cream cheese are made from pasteurized milk but they are perishable. Like milk and cream, they should be kept refrigerated and used within a few days of purchase.

Bring cheese to room temperature for fuller flavor by microwaving on Warm for about 1 minute.

WELSH RAREBIT

2 tbsp. butter	1 1/2 cups grated cheddar
2 tbsp. flour	cheese
1/4 tsp. salt	1/4 tsp. mustard
Dash of pepper	1 egg, well beaten
1 cup whole **or** canned milk	

Melt butter. Add flour, salt and pepper, mixing well. Add milk slowly and bring to boiling point, stirring constantly. Add cheese, stir until melted and add mustard. Remove from heat. Pour sauce into egg, mixing well. Serve over hot toast.

BEAUTY SANDWICH FILLING

Boiling water	3/4 cup sweet pickle relish
1 cup raisins	1/3 cup mayonnaise
1 cup grated carrot	Salt and pepper

Pour boiling water over raisins. Let stand 5 minutes. Drain and chop finely. Combine with carrot, relish and mayonnaise. Salt and pepper to taste. Spread on buttered bread.

SANDWICH LOAF DELUXE

Remove crust from a loaf of unsliced bread. Slice lengthwise into 4 slices. Butter slices on both sides except top and bottom slices. Make fillings as follows:

RED FILLING: 1 cup finely chopped ham, 1 chopped pimento, mayonnaise.

YELLOW FILLING: 3 hard cooked, chopped eggs, salt, pepper, mayonnaise and yellow coloring.

GREEN FILLING: 1 pkg. cream cheese, 1 minced green pepper and green coloring.

Spread slice of buttered bread with fillings in order given. Soften two cups of cream cheese and mix with sweet cream. Spread all over outside of loaf. Chill for several hours. Garnish with chopped green pepper or olives and pimento.

SANDWICH SPREAD

1 can tomato soup	1 egg, well beaten
1 cup cream cheese, diced	

In double boiler, heat tomato soup and diced cheese. Add egg and cook until mixture is thick, stirring constantly. Remove from heat. Cool and bottle. Keeps well.

Wrap sandwiches in wax paper, foil or a dampened cloth to keep fresh.

SPREAD VARIATIONS

1/2 tsp. lemon juice

1/2 tsp. worcestershire sauce

1/2 tsp. dry mustard

1/2 tsp. grated onion

1/4 tsp. minced garlic

Beat 4 tbsp. butter until soft, and slowly add one or more of the above ingredients. Good additions to any of these mixtures are one of the following:

2 tbsp. chopped parsley

2 tbsp. chopped chives

2 tbsp. chopped watercress

1/4 cup soft **or** grated cheese

2 tbsp. horseradish

1 tbsp. finely-chopped olives

2 tbsp. catsup **or** chili sauce

1 tbsp. chutney

1/4 tsp. curry powder

2 tbsp. fish **or** seafood paste

Salt, pepper and paprika to taste as desired. Chill mixtures until they are a good spreading consistency.

PEANUT BUTTER SANDWICH VARIATIONS

Spread one slice of bread with peanut butter, the other slice with cream cheese. Top the cream cheese with thinly spread apple butter.

Mash one ripe banana. Blend with 1/2 cup peanut butter. Stir in 1/3 cup crumbled crisp bacon. Yield: 4 sandwiches.

Add contents of one 2 1/4-oz. can deviled ham to 2/3 cup peanut butter. Yield: 4 sandwiches.

Combine 2/3 cup peanut butter, 1/3 cup drained sweet pickle relish and 2 tbsp. mayonnaise. Yield: 4 sandwiches.

Combine 1 cup ground, cooked ham, 1/2 cup peanut butter, 6 tbsp. chopped sweet pickle and enough mayonnaise to make a paste the right consistency for spreading.

Combine equal parts of chopped olives, peanut butter and mayonnaise or any salad dressing.

Combine 1/4 cup finely chopped, salted peanuts, 1 tsp. lemon juice and 1/2 cup mashed bananas. Yield: 3/4 cup of spread.

SANDWICH QUANTITIES: One 40-oz sandwich loaf cut into approximately 46 1/4-inch slices requires 2 cups filling and 1/4 to 1/2 lb. butter.

CHECKERBOARD SANDWICHES: For each stack, alternate 2 slices of whole wheat and 2 slices of white bread and fill with one or more spreads. Cut each stack in 1/2-inch slices and put 3 alternating slices together using a butter or spread as filling. Chill for several hours.

SALADS
& SALAD DRESSINGS

LAYERED SALAD

1 large lettuce
1 cup chopped celery
4 hard-boiled eggs, chopped
10-oz. pkg. frozen peas
1/2 cup green pepper
1 onion, diced
Bacon bits
2 cups mayonnaise
Cheddar cheese

Cut lettuce into 13 x 9-inch pan. Spread with celery, eggs, frozen peas, green pepper and onion. Sprinkle with bacon bits. Cover with mayonnaise and sprinkle with cheddar cheese. Refrigerate 8 to 12 hours. This is best left overnight.

CABBAGE SALAD

1 head shredded cabbage
1 onion
1 green pepper
1 tsp. salt
1 1/2 cups boiling water
1/2 cup vinegar
1/2 cup water
1/2 cup sugar
1 tsp. celery seed **or**
   pickle spice

Mix cabbage, onion and pepper. Add salt and pour over boiling water. Cover. Let sit for 1 hour. Drain and squeeze out moisture. Boil remaining ingredients together, let cool and add. Left over vinegar from sweet pickles may be used instead of fresh vinegar. This salad will keep indefinitely in refrigerator.

Mrs. Hilda F. Comfort

MOLDED PATIO SALAD

3 env. unflavored gelatin
2 cups cold water
1/2 cup sugar
1 tsp. salt
1/3 cup vinegar
2 tbsp. lemon juice
1/2 cup salad dressing
1 1/2 cups shredded cabbage
1 1/2 cups chopped celery
1 cup grated carrot
1/2 cup green pepper, diced
2 pimentos, diced (optional)

Sprinkle gelatin over 1 1/2 cups of the water in saucepan. Stir, while heating slowly, until gelatin dissolves. Remove from heat. Stir in sugar and salt. Add remaining 1/2 cup water. Blend vinegar and lemon juice into salad dressing. Blend into gelatin mixture. Chill until mixture mounds slightly when dropped from a spoon. Stir in vegetables. Turn into a 6-cup mold. Chill until firm.

EVERLASTING SALAD

1 cabbage	1 tsp. mustard seed
5 carrots	1 tsp. celery seed
4 onions	2 cups sugar
4 peppers	2 cups vinegar
1/4 cup salt	

Grind vegetables, add salt and let stand 2 hours. Drain well and add other ingredients. Put into jars and keep refrigerated.

Mrs. Irene Benson

SUNSHINE SLAW

4 cups shredded cabbage	1/4 cup chopped green pepper
16-oz. can sliced peaches, drained	1 1/2 cups miniature marshmallows
1 cup celery, sliced	Salad dressing

Combine cabbage, peaches, celery, green pepper and marshmallows with enough salad dressing to moisten. Toss lightly. Chill. Yield: 6 to 8 servings.

VEGETABLE SOUFFLE SALAD

1 cup hot water	Dash of pepper
3 oz. pkg. lemon jello	1 cup fine, chopped cabbage
1/2 cup cold water	2 tbsp. minced green pepper
2 tbsp. vinegar	2 tbsp. sliced green onion
1/2 cup mayonnaise	1/2 cup chopped celery
1/4 tsp. salt	1/2 cup sliced radish

Pour hot water over gelatin. Stir until dissolved. Add next 5 ingredients and beat until well blended. Pour into freezer tray. Quick chill in freezer for 15 to 20 minutes or until firm about 1 inch from edges but soft in center. Turn mixture into bowl. Beat with hand beater until fluffy. Fold in vegetables. Pour into mold and chill until firm. Yield: 7 to 8 servings.

VITAMIN HEALTH SALAD

3-oz. pkg. lime jello	1/2 cup chopped celery
1 tsp. salt	1/2 cup chopped carrots
1 cup boiling water	1/2 cup salad dressing
1 cup chopped cabbage	

Dissolve jello in salt and water. Chill until syrupy. Fold in vegetables and add salad dressing.

Doreen Lyon

Honey and lemon juice are natural partners and are ideal in salad dressings.

SPINACH SALAD

1/2 lettuce	Chives
1/2 fresh bunch spinach leaves	Green onions
Radishes	Herbs

Combine lettuce and spinach. Add desired number of remaining ingredients, chopped fine. Prepare salad in usual way and toss in salad bowl. Serve with your favorite dressing.

CUCUMBER SALAD

1/2 cup sour cream	Salt and pepper to taste
1/4 cup sugar	1 cucumber, sliced thin
1/4 cup cider vinegar	1 Spanish onion, sliced thin

Mix all but vegetables and stir until dissolved. Pour mixture over cucumbers and onions. Refrigerate 4 hours before serving.

CUCUMBER CROWN SALAD

1 cucumber, sliced	1 tsp. vinegar
3-oz. pkg. lime jello	1 tsp. lemon juice
1 1/2 cups hot water	1 cup sour cream
Pinch of salt	

Line a ring mold with slices of cucumber. Dissolve jello in hot water. Add salt, vinegar and lemon juice. Pour just enough of the jello to cover the layer of cucumbers in mold. Chill. Refrigerate remaining jello until cool. Add the sour cream and rest of cucumber, cut in small pieces. Pour over crown and chill until firm. Unmold and serve on lettuce leaves and garnish as you desire.

Mrs. John Properzi

ONION PICKLE SAUCE

4 Spanish onions, sliced	4 eggs, beaten
1/2 cup sugar	2/3 cup vinegar
1 cup vinegar	1/3 cup water
1 cup water	Dash of salt
1 tsp. dry mustard	Dash of cayenne
1 tsp. sugar	Condensed milk

Soak onions in 1/2 cup sugar, 1 cup vinegar and 1 cup water for about 4 hours. Mix remaining ingredients except milk and cook in double boiler until thick. Cool. Add milk. Drain onions and add just enough sauce to coat thoroughly.

Mrs. Millie Babey

To remove onion flavor from hands, dampen hands and rub with dry mustard, then wash with water.

FIESTA ONION SALAD

6 Spanish onions	2 tsp. salt
1/2 cup water	1 1/2 cups mayonnaise
1/2 cup vinegar	3 tsp. celery seed
3/4 cup sugar	Salt and pepper to taste

Slice onions and soak for 3 hours in a brine of water, vinegar, sugar and salt. Drain well. Combine remaining ingredients to make the dressing and add to the onions.

Mrs. Muriel Shadlock
Darleen Wagstaff

BEAN SALAD

14-oz. can cut green beans	1/4 cup white vinegar
14-oz. can cut wax beans	1/2 cup salad oil
14-oz. can red kidney beans	1/4 tsp. ground pepper
14-oz. can lima beans	Pinch of garlic salt
1 cup celery	1 tsp. dry mustard
1/2 cup onion rings or chunks	1 tsp. thyme
1/4 cup green pepper	1/2 tsp. salt
Sprinkle of salt	1 tbsp. sugar

Drain beans well and mix with celery, onion rings, green pepper and salt. Set mixture in container. Mix remaining ingredients well and shake vigorously before pouring over salad. Let stand one day in refrigerator before serving. Turn upside down occasionally to make sure mixture is well marinated.

Irene Bennett
Mrs. Violet Kaun
Mrs. Violet Metzzer

FOUR BEAN SALAD

14-oz. can cut green beans	1/2 cup cooking oil
14-oz. can cut yellow beans	1/2 cup vinegar
14-oz. can red kidney beans	3/4 cup sugar
14-oz. can lima beans	1 tsp. salt
1/2 cup green pepper, cut thin	1/8 tsp. pepper
3/4 cup onion, sliced thin	1 tsp. celery seed
3/4 cup chopped celery	Celery salt to taste

Drain beans thoroughly and add green pepper, onion and celery. Heat oil and vinegar. Add sugar until dissolved and add remaining ingredients. Pour hot mixture over beans and store in a container with tight-fitting lid. Let stand overnight in refrigerator. Turn upside down occasionally to make sure bean mixture is well marinated. To serve, drain sauce from beans but keep this sauce. Any beans left may be returned to sauce and will keep for days in the refrigerator. Yield: 12 servings.

Mrs. Mary Heppler

GREEN BEAN SALAD

2 tbsp. lemon juice **or** vinegar
1 - 2 tbsp. salad oil
Salt and pepper to taste
1 tbsp. chopped chives **or**
   1 tbsp. minced onion
1 tsp. chopped parsley
1 tbsp. prepared mustard
1 can tomatoes, drained
4 cups cut cooked green beans

Mix lemon juice, oil, salt, pepper, chives, parsley, mustard and tomato juice. Add strained beans and marinate for 1 hour. Stir a few times. Arrange tomatoes on top and serve. Garnish with parsley.

POTATO SALAD

4 large potatoes, boiled
   in jackets and chilled
1 tsp. salt
1/4 tsp. pepper
4 hard-boiled eggs, cut up
1 cup mayonnaise
1 tbsp. chopped chives **or**
   green onion
1/2 cup celery, chopped fine
1/2 cup radish, cut fine

Peel and cube potatoes. Add salt, pepper, eggs and mayonnaise. Mix well. Refrigerate. Before serving, add onion, celery, radish and toss.

LEMON CHICKEN SALAD

6-oz. pkg. lemon jello
2 cups boiled chicken broth,
   all fat removed
2 cups diced chicken
2 cups diced celery
1 tsp. salt
Small onion, chopped fine
1 cup broken walnuts
Juice of 1 lemon
1 pint heavy whipping cream

Dissolve jello in boiling chicken broth. Chill. When it begins to set add all ingredients except whipping cream. Set aside a bit longer. Then add whipped cream, mixing well. Set aside to set again. Serve on lettuce leaves with salad dressing.

Mrs. Earle Murray

CUCUMBER CHICKEN SALAD

5 cups diced cooked chicken
5 cups diced celery
8 hard-cooked eggs, chopped
2 cups mayonnaise
1 cup drained pineapple cubes
1 tsp. salt
3 cups diced cucumber
1 1/2 cups toasted, blanched
   almonds, chopped
3 heads lettuce

Combine all ingredients, except lettuce. Chill and serve on lettuce. Yield: 30 small servings.

Mollie Leonhardt

To remove onion flavor from a paring knife, plunge the blade into the soil at the edge of a potted house plant.

JELLIED CHICKEN SALAD

1 pkg. chicken noodle soup
2 cups boiling water
3-oz. pkg. lemon jelly powder
1/2 tsp. salt
1/2 cup diced celery

1 cup diced cooked chicken
or pork
1/2 cup diced apple, skin on
2 tbsp. chopped green onion

Prepare chicken noodle soup according to directions, using boiling water. Stir in jelly powder and salt until dissolved. Stand until partially set. Add remaining ingredients. Pour into oiled mold. Chill until firm. Unmold on salad greens. Serve with mayonnaise. Yield: 6 to 8 servings.

Mrs. J.L. Samga

CHICKEN SALAD WITH GRAPES

2 cups cooked chicken, diced
1/2 cup velveeta cheese
1 cup pineapple tidbits, drained

1 cup chopped celery
1 cup seeded red grapes,
halved

Mix ingredients in salad dressing to desired consistency. Spoon onto lettuce-lined salad bowl, or serve in individual plates on lettuce leaves.

FISH, CELERY & APPLE SALAD

4 tsp. lemon juice
1 tsp. salt
4 tsp. salad **or** olive oil
2 cups flaked salmon **or** tuna
1 cup diced celery

1 1/2 cups diced tart apples
3 shelled hard-boiled eggs
1/4 cup mayonnaise
Lettuce leaves

Combine lemon juice, salt and oil. Mix fish, celery and apple and let stand in oil mixture for 20 minutes. Add chopped eggs and mayonnaise. Serve on lettuce leaves and garnish with carrot slices.

R.C. Healing

JELLIED SALAD

3-oz. pkg. lemon jello
1 cup hot water
1/2 cup salad dressing
1 tbsp. vinegar
1/2 tsp. salt
1/2 lb. can lobster, salmon
shrimp, crab, etc.
2 cups diced celery

1/4 cup stuffed olives
2 hard-cooked eggs, chopped
1 tsp. green onion, cut fine
1/4 lb. pimento cream cheese,
diced
1/2 cup whipping cream,
whipped

Combine jello and hot water. Cool. Combine with remaining ingredients. Pour into mold and chill.

Mrs. W.C. Taylor

TACO SALAD

1 - 2 lbs. hamburger
1 env. seasoned taco mix
1 small lettuce, shredded
3 tomatoes, diced
1 onion, chopped
1 can kidney beans, drained

2 cups grated cheddar cheese
Corn, tortilla **or** taco chips
1 cucumber, chopped
2 - 3 stalks celery, chopped
1 green pepper, diced
Fresh mushrooms

Cook hamburger in fry pan until crumbly and no longer pink. Season with taco mix. Drain well and cool. In a large bowl mix the hamburger with remaining ingredients. Toss well. A dressing made of oil, lemon juice and salt can be poured on and tossed, or use a dressing of your choice just before serving. This mixture can also be put into taco shells.

Irene Wagstaff

TOMATO ASPIC

48-oz. can tomato juice
3 3-oz. pkg. lemon jello powders
Worcestershire sauce to taste
2 tsp. salt
2 tbsp. vinegar

Celery salt to taste
1/2 cup celery, chopped fine
1 onion, chopped fine
Sliced olive
Salad dressing to taste

Heat juice to boiling point and combine with jello powders to dissolve. Add worcestershire sauce, salt, vinegar and celery salt. Chill until thick and syrupy. Add celery, onion, olive and fold in salad dressing.

CARROT & PINEAPPLE SALAD

3-oz. pkg. lime **or** lemon jello
1 cup hot water
8 - 10 ice cubes
1 cup grated carrot

1 cup crushed pineapple, drained
1 pkg. Dream Whip

Dissolve jello in hot water, add ice cubes and stir until mixture thickens. Add the carrot and drained pineapple. Beat the Dream Whip according to directions on package and fold into mixture. VARIATION: Chilled Mandarin oranges may be substituted for pineapple.

PINEAPPLE & CUCUMBER SALAD

2 pkgs. gelatin
1/4 cup cold water
1 cup boiling water
1/4 cup sugar
1/2 tsp. salt

1/4 cup vinegar
2 tbsp. lemon juice
1 cup diced cucumber
1 cup crushed pineapple, drained

Soak gelatin in cold water for 5 minutes. Dissolve in boiling water. Add sugar, salt, vinegar and lemon juice and stir until dissolved. Chill until partially set. Add cucumber and pineapple. Turn into mold. Chill. Unmold on lettuce and garnish with radish roses. Yield: 8 servings.

PINEAPPLE MINT FREEZE SALAD

20-oz. can crushed pineapple
1 env. unflavored gelatin
10-oz. jar mint jelly

Dash of salt
1 cup whipping cream
1 tsp. icing sugar

Drain pineapple and reserve syrup. Soften gelatin in syrup in saucepan. Add mint jelly and a dash of salt. Heat and stir until gelatin is dissolved and melted. If needed, beat to blend jelly. Stir in pineapple. Chill until mixture is thick and syrupy. Whip cream with sugar and fold into thickened gelatin mixture. Tint with green food coloring. Spoon into loaf pan 81/2 x 41/2 x 1/2 inch. Freeze until firm. Let stand at room temperature 10 to 15 minutes before serving. Unmold, slice and place on lettuce-lined salad plates. Garnish with mint sprigs. Yield: 8 servings.

Mrs. Grace Gore

LIME APPLE MOLD

131/2-oz. can crushed pineapple
3 oz. pkg. lime jello
1 cup evaporated milk
3/4 cup red apples, cut up

1/2 cup fine, chopped nuts
1/2 cup mayonnaise **or**
  salad dressing
1 tbsp. lemon juice

Drain pineapple and reserve juice. Add enough water to juice to make 1 cup, then heat. Dissolve gelatin in hot juice. Cool slightly, then stir in milk. Chill until as thick as unbeaten egg whites. Fold in pineapple bits, apple, nuts, mayonnaise and lemon juice. Pour into 51/2 cup mold. Chill until firm. Unmold on lettuce leaves. Yield: 10 to 12 servings.

Mrs. Lorna Hug

MARSHMALLOW SALAD

1 pkg. Dream Whip
1/2 tsp. vanilla
1 cup sour cream
2 cups miniature marshmallows

1 can pineapple chunks
  drained
1 can mandarin oranges,
  drained

Beat Dream Whip and vanilla. Add sour cream. Stir in marshmallows, pineapple and oranges. Refrigerate. This is best if left overnight.

QUEEN CHARLOTTE SALAD

3-oz. pkg. lime jello
3-oz. pkg. raspberry jello
3 cups boiling water
3 cups miniature marshmallows

1 cup drained, crushed
  pineapple
1 cup thick cream, whipped

Prepare jellos individually, using 11/2 cups boiling water for each. Pour into 2 loaf pans and chill overnight. Combine marshmallows, pineapple and jello cut up in 1-inch cubes. Fold in whipped cream and chill for 1 hour or longer.

Mrs. Audrey Thompson

PINEAPPLE JELLO SALAD

3-oz. pkg. pineapple jello
13/4 cup hot water
1/2 cup cottage cheese

1/2 cup salad dressing
1/2 cup grated carrot
1/2 cup chopped celery

Dissolve jello in hot water. When chilled, add remaining ingredients and refrigerate until set.

Mrs. Paul Young

CRANBERRY, PINEAPPLE SALAD

3-oz. pkg. cherry jello
1 env. plain gelatin
1 cup sugar

1 cup hot water
1 cup pineapple syrup
1 tbsp. lemon juice

Dissolve jello, gelatin and sugar in hot water. Add pineapple syrup and lemon juice. Chill until partly set. Then add:

1 orange, chopped
1 cup drained, crushed pineapple

1 cup ground raw cranberries
1 cup chopped celery

Chill until firm and serve.

Mrs. D. Campbell

CRANBERRY SALAD

19-oz. can pineapple
Hot water
11/2 pkg. pineapple jelly powder
1 qt. cranberries

2 cups apples
11/8 cup sugar
1 cup whipping cream, whipped

Drain and reserve juice from pineapple and add sufficient hot water to make 11/2 cups liquid. Combine with jelly powder and stir until dissolved. Let cool until partially set, then add cranberries and apple which have been put through food chopper. Add sugar, drained pineapple and whipped cream. Cool until well set. Serve with cold chicken or turkey.

Mrs. Les Bartley

CRANBERRY ARCTIC FREEZE

8-oz. cream cheese
2 tbsp. sugar
2 tbsp. mayonnaise
16-oz. can cranberry sauce

1 cup well-drained crushed
   pineapple
1/2 cup cream, whipped

Cream cheese and sugar. Stir in mayonnaise. Fold in cranberry sauce, pineapple and cream. Pour into a 9 x 5 x 3-inch loaf pan. Freeze until firm. Cut in squares and serve on lettuce.

Dry fresh bread for croutons or crumbs in the microwave.

GINGERALE FRUIT SALAD

2 env. unflavored gelatin	1/4 cup lemon juice
1/4 cup cold water	2 cups fruit cocktail
1/2 cup hot water	1 cup seedless grapes, halved
2 tbsp. sugar	1/2 cup chopped walnuts
1/8 tsp. salt	1 cup ginger ale

Soften gelatin in cold water for 5 minutes and dissolve in hot water. Add sugar, salt, lemon juice and syrup from fruit cocktail. Chill until partially set. Add remaining ingredients. Pour into greased mold or individual molds. Chill until firm. Unmold on crisp lettuce. Yield: 8 to 10 servings.

Mrs. Mary L. Roberts

SPICY JELLY FOR MEATS

1 can peas	3-oz. pkg. strawberry jello
1 can tomato juice	

Drain peas and boil tomato juice. Make jelly using tomato juice instead of water. Add peas, pour into mold and put in refrigerator to set.

Mrs. E. Aasen

JELLIED FRUIT SALAD

3-oz. pkg. lemon jelly powder	Juice of 1 lemon
2 bananas, sliced	2 tbsp. flour
2 firm red apples, diced	Juice of 1 orange
4 slices pineapple, diced	1 cup pineapple juice
2 eggs	1/2 cup whipping cream
2/3 cup sugar	

Prepare lemon powder according to package directions. Refrigerate. Mix the fruit and place in a cold, wet mold or separate dishes. When jelly begins to thicken, pour it over the fruit. Beat eggs until light. Add sugar, lemon juice and flour and mix until smooth. Add orange and pineapple juice and cook in double boiler until thick. When cool, fold in whipped cream and use as topping on fruit salad.

Mrs. Johanna Cossins

LOW CALORIE FRUIT SALAD

2 cups low-calorie canned fruit cocktail	1 cup cold water
2 env. unflavored gelatin	4 tbsp. lemon juice

Drain fruit cocktail and add enough water to juice to make 2 1/2 cups. Heat liquid. Soften gelatin in cold water. Add hot fruit juice and lemon juice. Stir until dissolved. Chill until slightly thicker than consistency of unbeaten egg whites. Beat gelatin mixture with egg beater until light and fluffy. Fold in fruit cocktail. Pour into mold. Chill until firm and unmold. Yield: 6 servings.

SPRING SALAD

3-oz. pkg. lemon gelatin
1 cup hot water
4 small, whole green onions,
chopped

1/4 cup chopped crisp radishes
2/3 cup salad dressing
1 cup cottage cheese
1 cup chopped celery

Dissolve gelatin in hot water. Chill until it starts to set. Combine remaining ingredients and add to gelatin. Pour into 9-inch square dish. Chill until firm and cut into squares. Serve on lettuce.

Mrs. Dorothy Cowell

GREEN SALAD

15-oz. can apple sauce
3-oz. lime jello powder
8 **or** 10-oz. bottle 7-Up

1 can mandarin orange
sections, drained
Whipped cream (optional)

Heat apple sauce in pan over low heat. Stir in jello powder. Mix until dissolved. Add 7-Up. Mix well and add oranges. Chill. Unmold on lettuce leaves and garnish with whipped cream.

Mrs. Marina Vannatta

SPRINGTIME SALAD

3-oz. pkg. lime jelly powder
3/4 cup boiling water
1/4 tsp. salt
3 tbsp. lemon juice **or** vinegar
1/2 cup chopped celery

1 cup chopped apple
1/4 cup chopped sweet pickle
2/3 cup evaporated milk,
well chilled

Dissolve jelly in boiling water. Add salt and lemon juice and chill until mixture begins to set. Then add celery, apple and pickle. Whip evaporated milk until stiff and fold into jelly mixture. Turn into mold. Chill until set.

Mrs. C. Blair

FRUIT SALAD

2 eggs, well beaten
4 tbsp. vinegar
4 tbsp. sugar
2 tbsp. butter
1 cup cream, whipped
2 oranges, cut in pieces
1 can fruit salad, drained

1 can crushed pineapple,
drained
2 bananas
2 cups colored miniature
marshmallows **or** whole
marshmallows, quartered

Put eggs in double boiler. Add vinegar and sugar. Beat constantly until thick and smooth. Add butter. Cool. Fold whipped cream into first mixture. Add fruit and marshmallows. Place in cooler for 24 hours. Serve on lettuce leaves topped with cherries. Yield: 12 to 14 servings.

Mrs. Glenys Ewing

OVERNIGHT SALAD

1 pkg. lemon pie filling
1 pkg. Dream Whip
1/2 pkg. miniature marshmallows

1 can fruit cocktail, drained
1/2 cup seedless grapes

Mix and cook pie filling according to instructions and let cool. Make up Dream Whip according to directions and fold in. Add marshmallows and fruit. Refrigerate overnight.

Mrs. Alice Murray

24-HOUR SALAD

1 cup or more grapes, halved
and pitted
1 can crushed pineapple, drained
1 can oranges, drained

1 can fruit cocktail, drained
2 cups miniature marshmallows
1 cup cream
1/2 cup salad dressing

Combine fruit and marshmallows. Whip cream and add salad dressing. Add to fruit and store in refrigerator for 24 hours before serving.

Mrs. Mary Spornitz

JELLO & COTTAGE CHEESE SALAD

3-oz. pkg. lime jello
1 cup boiling water
1/2 cup mayonnaise
1/2 cup canned milk
1 cup cottage cheese
1/2 cup walnuts, chopped

1 cup drained, crushed
pineapple
2 tsp. horseradish
Walnuts
Pineapple **or** olives

Combine jello and boiling water and let mixture get syrupy. Add mayonnaise and milk, which have been beaten together. Add cottage cheese, 1/2 cup walnuts, pineapple and horseradish and mix. Garnish top with walnuts and pineapple. Refrigerate.

Mrs. Leulla Callies

WALDORF WHIP SALAD

3-oz. pkg. lemon jelly powder
1 cup hot water
3 tbsp. lemon juice
1/2 cup mayonnaise

1 cup chopped celery
1/2 cup chopped walnuts
1 1/2 cups chopped apples
2/3 cup evaporated milk

Dissolve jelly powder in hot water. Cool. Add 1 tbsp. lemon juice, mayonnaise, celery, nuts and apples. Mix well. Chill until mixture is consistency of unbeaten egg whites. Chill milk in refrigerator tray 10 to 15 minutes until soft ice crystals form around edges. Whip until stiff. Add remaining lemon juice, whip very stiff. Fold whipped evaporated milk into jello mixture. Spoon into mold. Chill until set. Unmold on salad greens and garnish with walnuts and raw apple slices. Serve as dessert or salad.

Mrs. Elsie Hasse

SHRIMP DINNER SALAD

4 cups shell macaroni
1/2 cup french dressing
2 cups raw cauliflowerettes
1 cup thinly-sliced scallions
1 tsp. salt

1/4 tsp. pepper
2 5-oz. cans shrimp, drained
1 cup mayonnaise
1/2 cup chili sauce
Lettuce leaves

Cook and drain macaroni as directed on package. Put into a large bowl, toss with french dressing and chill 1 hour. Add cauliflowerettes, scallions, salt, pepper and shrimp. Blend mayonnaise and chili sauce. Pour over salad. Toss and chill. Serve in lettuce-lined bowl. Yield: 10 servings.

Georgina Taylor

MAY'S MACARONI SALAD

2 cups cooked macaroni
4 eggs, chopped
2 green onions, chopped

Few radishes, chopped
1 can shrimp
1 cup celery **or** peas

Mix with salad dressing and garnish with tomatoes and olives. Serve on lettuce.

Mrs. May Smith

APPLE MACARONI SALAD

2 cups macaroni, uncooked
6 apples, peeled and cubed
1 can cubed pineapple, drained
1 cantaloupe, cubed (optional)
Grapes (optional)

4 whole eggs
1/2 cup lemon juice
2 cups icing sugar
1 cup cream

Cook macaroni until tender, drain and blanch with cold water. Add the fruit to the macaroni. In double boiler, beat eggs until very light and add lemon juice and icing sugar. Cook until thick like pudding. Cool. Pour over macaroni and fruit. Mix well. Let stand overnight in refrigerator. Just before serving, whip 1 cup unsweetened cream and fold in salad. Serve with a cold supper.

Mrs. Eddie Jackson

Save cheese from mold, etc. by wrapping in small pieces in wax paper, then aluminum foil to freeze. Defrost completely in refrigerator. Cheese becomes crumbly after freezing and tends to mold faster so defrost only in amounts needed. Freshly grated cheese keeps well in the freezer and is handy to have.

MACARONI SALAD

1 1/2 cups cooked macaroni
2 eggs, hard boiled and chopped
1/4 cup celery, cubed
1 tbsp. sugar

2 tomatoes, cut in eighths
2 tsp. onion, chopped fine
Salt and pepper to taste

Mix with salad dressing and serve.

Mrs. Glenys Ewing

TUNA MACARONI SALAD

1/2 cup mayonnaise
3 tbsp. French dressing
1 1/2 tsp. salt
1/2 tsp. pepper

7-oz. can flaked tuna, drained
1 cup chopped celery
1/2 cup chopped sweet pickle
3 cups cooked shell macaroni

Combine mayonnaise, French dressing, salt and pepper. Toss in remaining ingredients. Mix lightly. Spoon in mound shapes onto chilled plates. Yield: 6 to 8 servings.

Ruth White

SALAD DRESSINGS

DAWN'S DRESSING

1/3 - 1/2 cup sugar
3/4 cup vinegar

1/2 cup oil
1 1/2 tsp. salt

Put all ingredients into a small jar or shaker. Shake well. This dressing will store in the refrigerator very well for months. Just shake again before using.

Judy Pimm

FAVORITE FRENCH DRESSING

10-oz. can tomato soup
3/4 cup brown sugar
2/3 cup vinegar
Crushed garlic **or** garlic powder
   to taste
1 tsp. salt

2 tsp. prepared mustard
1/2 cup oil
2 tsp. grated onion **or**
   onion powder
2 tbsp. worcestershire sauce

Put ingredients in quart jar and shake. Keep refrigerated. This is nice with salad, spaghetti or used in barbecuing meat.

Maisie Jacobson

LOW-CALORIE FRENCH DRESSING

3/4 cup water
2 tsp. cornstarch
2 tbsp. salad oil
3/4 tsp. salt
1/4 tsp. pepper
1/4 tsp. dry mustard

1/4 cup catsup
1 tsp. worcestershire sauce
1/2 tsp. monosodium glutamate
1/4 tsp. paprika
1/4 cup lemon juice
1/4 tsp. non-caloric sweetener

Mix water and cornstarch in saucepan and bring to boil. Reduce heat and cook 5 minutes or until thick and clear. Cool, add all other ingredients and beat until well-blended. Store covered in refrigerator. Shake well before using. Yield: 1 1/4 cups dressing. 18 calories per tablespoon.

HONEY FRENCH DRESSING

10-oz. can tomato soup
1/2 cup vinegar **or** lemon juice
1 tsp. salt
1/2 tsp. black pepper
1/4 tsp. garlic salt
1/4 cup honey

1/4 cup oil
1 tsp. dry mustard **or**
  1 tbsp. prepared mustard
1/4 tsp. onion salt
1 tsp. barbecue sauce

Put ingredients in large jar and cover tightly. Shake vigorously until very well blended. Keeps very well in refrigerator. NOTE: When available, chopped green onions and finely chopped fresh parsley enhance the color and flavor of this.

Lucie St. Andre

WONDERFUL FRENCH DRESSING

1/4 cup sugar
Dash of paprika
5 tbsp. catsup

3 tbsp. grated onion
1 tsp. salt
3/4 cup salad oil

Combine ingredients in a glass jar and shake vigorously to blend well. Store in refrigerator. Yield: 1 1/2 cups.

Frances Redmond

LIGHT FRENCH DRESSING

6-oz. can tomato sauce
4 tbsp. lemon juice

1 tbsp. chopped green onion
1 tsp. chopped, fresh parsley

Put ingredients in a jar. Shake vigorously. 5 calories per tablespoon.

The juice from cut-up tomatoes will thin salad dressing, so avoid adding them to tossed salad. Prepare the tomatoes separately and use as a garnish.

ITALIAN DRESSING

1/4 cup vinegar
1/4 tsp. garlic powder
1 tsp. sugar
Pinch of pepper
1 cup salad oil

1/2 tsp. salt
1/4 tsp. cayenne
1/2 cup mayonnaise **or**
    salad dressing

Add all ingredients and beat thoroughly to blend. Store in covered jar in refrigerator. Shake well before using.

QUICK MAYONNAISE

1 egg
1 tbsp. prepared mustard
Salt and pepper to taste
Dash of garlic salt

2 tbsp. lemon juice
2 tbsp. vinegar
5 cups salad oil

Break egg into mixing bowl. Add mustard, seasonings, lemon juice, vinegar and beat with electric mixer at high speed while gradually adding oil. When thick, pour into a jar and store in refrigerator until required for use on cold meats or in sandwich fillings. NOTE: Use equal amounts of *Quick Mayonnaise* with honey for use on fruit salads.

SOUR CREAM DRESSING

1 cup sugar
1 tbsp. cornstarch **or** 2 tbsp. flour
1/2 tsp. dry mustard
1/2 tsp. salt
2 eggs, slightly beaten

1/2 cup water
1/2 cup vinegar
1 tbsp. butter **or** margarine
1 cup sour cream

Combine sugar, cornstarch, dry mustard and salt in saucepan. Add eggs. Heat the water and vinegar and stir into the egg mixture. Cook and stir over low heat until thick and smooth. Add butter. Cool. Add sour cream. Serve with fruit and vegetable salads.

UNCOOKED SOUR CREAM DRESSING

1/2 tsp. salt
1/2 tsp. mustard
1 tbsp. sugar
Dash of paprika

2 tbsp. lemon juice
1 egg, well beaten
1 cup thick sour cream

Add salt, mustard, sugar, paprika and lemon juice to egg. Whip the sour cream until thick. Add egg mixture to cream and blend until creamy. This salad dressing has a delightful tang. Excellent with cabbage salad.

When a recipe calls for liquid honey and all you have is granulated honey, it may be liquefied by placing honey in a container in hot water for a few hours or microwaving uncovered on High for a few minutes.

COLE SLAW DRESSING

1 tbsp. sugar
1 tsp. salt
1/2 tsp. dry mustard
1/4 tsp. pepper
1/4 cup vinegar
1 tbsp. oil

Mix dry ingredients together in a small saucepan. Add vinegar and oil. Bring to boil. While hot, pour over 3 cups finely-shredded cabbage. Chill in refrigerator at least 1 hour before serving.

LOW CALORIE SALAD DRESSING

1 tbsp. flour
2 tbsp. sugar
1 1/4 tsp. salt
Pinch cayenne pepper
1 tsp. prepared mustard
1 tbsp. oil
1 cup water
2 eggs
1/4 cup vinegar

Blend first 7 ingredients together. Cook slowly until slightly thickened. Beat eggs until light, gradually adding vinegar. Add half the hot mixture to the egg mixture. Return to stove and cook until mixture coats a spoon. 14 calories per tablespoon.

SWEET MILK SALAD DRESSING

1 cup sugar
1 tbsp. mustard
2 tbsp. flour
1 tsp. salt
4 eggs, beaten
1 cup sweet milk
1 cup vinegar

Mix dry ingredients well. Add eggs and milk. Heat vinegar, add and beat well with beater. Cook until thick, stirring constantly. Thin with cream when used.

May Huddlestun

UNCOOKED SALAD DRESSING

1 can sweetened condensed milk
1 cup vinegar
Pinch of salt
1 tsp. dry mustard
1 egg, beaten

Add milk, vinegar, salt and mustard to egg. Continue beating until well blended. Keep in refrigerator.

EGG YOLK SALAD DRESSING

1 cup sugar
1 tsp. mustard
1/2 cup flour
1 tsp. salt
1 tbsp. butter
1/2 cup vinegar
Pinch of turmeric
1/2 cup water
6 egg yolks, well beaten

Combine all ingredients but yolks and bring to boil until clear. Add this to egg yolks but do not boil again. This will keep in refrigerator.

SALAD DRESSING

1 cup sugar	1/2 tsp. pepper
2 tbsp. flour	3/4 cup vinegar
1 tsp. dry mustard	3/4 cup water
1 tsp. salt	3 eggs, well beaten

Mix sugar, flour, mustard, salt, pepper, vinegar and water in top of double boiler. Add the eggs. Cook over boiling water until thick.

Mrs. V. Johnson
Mrs. Edith Shantz

PREPARED MUSTARD DRESSING

3 tbsp. dry mustard	1 tsp. turmeric
1/2 tsp. salt	1 egg, well beaten
1 tbsp. cornstarch	1 cup vinegar
1 tbsp. sugar	2 tbsp. butter

Mix dry ingredients with egg and beat well until smooth. Add vinegar and cook over low heat until thick and creamy, stirring constantly. Remove from heat and add the butter.

LOW CALORIE MUSTARD SALAD DRESSING

2 tbsp. cornstarch	1 cup vinegar
2 tsp. dry mustard	2 tbsp. liquid non-caloric
1 tsp. salt	sweetener
3/4 tsp. white pepper	4 eggs, well beaten

Mix dry ingredients together in double boiler. Add vinegar and liquid sweetener. Heat until mixture is hot. Reduce heat and add eggs, stirring constantly. When thickened, beat vigorously until smooth. Pour into jar. Cool and refrigerate. Yield: 2 cups. 13 calories per tablespoon.

To keep whipped cream stiff, add 1/2 cup miniature marshmallows to 1 cup whipping cream. Allow to stand at least 2 hours in refrigerator before whipping.

Microwave tomatoes on High for 30 seconds for easy peeling.

To reduce calories in salad dressings, substitute plain yogurt for sour cream or use cottage cheese instead of mayonnaise.

BEVERAGES, SAUCES & BUTTERS

BEVERAGES

LEMON SYRUP (for cold drinks)

4 lemons
1 qt. boiling water

8 cups sugar
3 oz. tartaric acid

Pare off lemon rind so thinly that it is yellow on both sides. Place in bowl, cover with boiling water and allow to stand until cold. Put sugar and water in saucepan and dissolve. Strain through a muslin cloth into basin. When the syrup is quite cold, add strained juice of 4 lemons and the tartaric acid blended with a little of the syrup. Add water from the rinds. Stir thoroughly and bottle. Use about a tablespoonful in a glass of water.

Peggy Woferstan

MINT LEMONADE

2 cups sugar
2 1/2 cups water
Grated peel from 1 - 2 oranges

Juice of 6 lemons
1 cup mint leaves

Cook sugar and water for 5 minutes. Cool. Add grated peel and lemon juice. Pour over mint leaves, cover and let stand 1 hour. Strain. Store in refrigerator. Use 1/3 cup of the syrup for each glass and fill with crushed ice and water. Yield: 10 to 12 servings.

ORANGEADE

8 cups sugar
4 large **or** 6 small whole oranges,
    cut in small pieces

6 cups boiling water
2 oz. citric acid

Mix the sugar and oranges. Pour boiling water over them and let stand several hours or overnight. Strain and add the citric acid just before bottling. Put a small amount in a glass and fill with cold water. Chipped ice improves it. This will keep indefinitely.

Mrs. A.E. Hobbs

For a special occasion, fill freezer trays with punch or fruit juice. Slip a sprig of mint, twist of lemon or orange, or a strawberry into each compartment before freezing. Add to punch before serving. Freeze fruits or holly in a ring or mold of fruit punch and float in the punch bowl.

LEMON ORANGEADE

4 oranges, grated
3 lemons, grated
6 cups sugar

1 1/2 oz. citric acid
8 cups boiling water

Cut oranges and lemons in small pieces and mash to get all the juice. Add sugar, acid, boiling water and boil. Seal jars. Use 1/3 cup of syrup for each glass of water.

Mrs. A.L. Pearce

GRAPE TINGLE

1/4 cup unsweetened grape juice
1 - 2 tbsp. lemon **or** lime juice
3 - 4 ice cubes

Low calorie lemon **or** lime beverage

Measure grape juice and lemon juice into tall glass. Add ice cubes and low calorie beverage. Stir. Yield: 1 serving.

FANCY SUMMER BEVERAGE

1 1/2 cups sugar
1 cup water
3-oz. pkg. lime jello

Juice of 2 lemons
4 cups milk
Lemon-lime soft drink to taste

Combine sugar and water and bring to boil. Stir in jello. Cool. Stir in lemon juice and milk. Mix well and freeze in shallow pan. When ready to serve, beat with beater until soft and mushy. Add lemon-lime soft drink.

Mrs. Don Antal

CHILLED TOMATO BOUILLON

1 cup hot water
2 bouillon cubes
1 tsp. sugar
1/2 tsp. salt
Few grains pepper
1/8 tsp. cloves

3 cups tomato juice
2 tsp. lemon juice
1 tsp. Worcestershire sauce
1/2 cup chopped green pepper
1/2 tsp. monosodium glutamate
1/2 clove garlic

Put hot water and bouillon cubes into 2-qt. saucepan. Add all other ingredients except garlic clove. Cover and simmer for 6 to 8 minutes until green pepper is tender. Strain. Add garlic clove. Chill for about 3 hours. Remove garlic before serving. Yield: 5 servings. 36 calories per serving.

COLD TEA

4 tsp. tea
4 cups water
1/4 - 1/2 cup sugar

Juice and rinds of 3 oranges
Juice and rind of 1 lemon

Prepare tea with water. Combine with sugar and add the fruit juices and rinds. Refrigerate.

Mrs. Lorena R. Sime

BLACK CURRANT TEA

1 tbsp. black currant jam **or** jelly   2 cups boiling water
Juice of 1/2 lemon   Sugar to taste

Simmer ingredients together for 15 minutes. The hotter the drink the better it is.

Mrs. Appleby

ICED COFFEE

Add 1 tsp. honey to each cup of coffee. Mix well and cool. Serve ice cold with whole milk or cream and top with a tsp. of vanilla ice cream.

COCOA SYRUP

1/2 cup cocoa   1/8 tsp. salt
1 cup cold water   2 tsp. vanilla
1 1/2 cups sugar

Stir cocoa and cold water over direct heat until smooth. Add sugar and salt, stirring until dissolved. Boil 3 minutes. Flavor with vanilla and pour into glass jar. Yield: 1 pint. Keep in cold place. Use 1 or 2 tsp. to a glass of hot or cold milk.

Mrs. Rita Carveth

MILK-ALE

10-oz. can of gingerale   2 cups milk
  or orangeade

Add gingerale to milk. Mix and chill well before serving.

LOW CAL MILKSHAKE

8 oz. ice cold water   3 whole strawberries, frozen
1/4 cup instant skim milk powder   Artificial sweetener

Put water in blender. Add milk powder, whole frozen strawberries and sweetener. Blend for 15 seconds. VARIATION: Use 1 heaping tbsp. jello powder for different flavors. Do not add any sweetener with jello.

HONEY PEANUT SHAKE

1/4 cup liquid honey   5 cups cold milk
1/4 cup smooth peanut butter

Beat honey and peanut better with rotary beater or electric mixer until well blended. Gradually beat in 1/2 cup milk. Pour in remaining milk. Mix well and pour into tall glasses. Yield: 6 servings.

Use the microwave to increase the amount of juice from fresh fruit. Before cutting, microwave fruit on High for 20 to 25 seconds or until slightly warm to the touch.

MOCHA FLOAT

3 cups milk	1 tbsp. sugar
2 1/2 tsp. instant coffee	Dash of salt
6 tbsp. chocolate syrup	3 scoops vanilla ice cream

Combine all ingredients except ice cream in blender or shaker. Pour into glasses and top with ice cream. Yield: 3 large servings.

Mrs. M. Parcels

BANANA EGGNOG

1 egg	1 banana, peeled
1 cup milk	Dash of nutmeg

Mix ingredients in blender. Pour into glasses and sprinkle a little more nutmeg on top.

HONEY EGGNOG

1 egg	1 tbsp. brandy
1 tbsp. honey	Dash nutmeg
2 cups milk	Dash cinnamon

Blend ingredients together until light and frothy. Yield: 2 to 3 servings.

HURRY-HURRY BREAKFAST

1/2 cup chilled orange juice	1 tbsp. honey
1 egg	1 tsp. lemon juice

Blend ingredients well and serve at once.

RHUBARB JUICE DRINK

2 lbs. rhubarb	3 tbsp. dry white wine
1 lemon	12 cups boiling water
1 1/2 cups sugar	

Slice rhubarb and lemon and combine. Add sugar, wine and boiling water. Put in cool place for 24 hours. Strain. To serve, add ice to 5 oz. water and 1 oz. of juice.

Doris Barker

RHUBARB PUNCH

1 1/4 cups boiling water	1/2 cup sugar
1 cup rhubarb, finely cut	1/2 cup water
1 tsp. lemon **or** orange juice	

Pour the boiling water over the rhubarb and add lemon juice. Sweeten to taste with syrup made by boiling together the sugar and 1/2 cup water. Serve cold.

PUNCH

12-oz. can frozen lemonade	Orange slices
2 cups orange juice	Cherries
2 large bottles gingerale	Ice
26-oz. bottle vodka	1 qt. orange sherbert

Mix all ingredients but sherbert in large punch bowl. Add sherbert 5 minutes before serving.

TROPICAL PUNCH

1 cup Tahiti fruit juice	1 cup sugar
1 cup pineapple juice	2 cups water
1 cup frozen pink lemonade	2 bottles gingerale

Mix first 5 ingredients. Add gingerale immediately before serving.

HOLIDAY PUNCH

8 oz. honey	16 oz. cranberry cocktail juice
32 oz. hot water	6-oz. can frozen lemonade
8 oz. apple juice	

Mix ingredients together. Let cool. When ready to serve, add:

28 oz. ginger ale	ice cubes with 1
1 qt. red dry wine (optional)	green cherry in each

Lucie E. St. Andre

RECEPTION FRUIT PUNCH

2 cups water	1 pint grape juice
4 cups sugar	12 cups ice water
2 1/2 tbsp. tea	2 cups pineapple juice
1 qt. boiling water	8 cups gingerale
1 pint orange juice	1 large can crushed pineapple
1 pint lemon juice	**or** 1 cup thin orange slices

Bring 2 cups water and sugar to a boil. Steep the tea in boiling water. Combine strained tea and syrup. Add orange juice, lemon juice, grape juice, ice water and pineapple. When ready to serve, add the gingerale. Garnish with thin orange slices. Yield: 30 large glasses of punch.

MULLED WINE

2 cups apple juice	1 unpeeled lemon, thinly sliced
4 cups dry red wine **or**	4 whole cloves
cranberry juice	4 allspice berries
1/2 cup honey	2 cinnamon sticks

Combine all ingredients and heat without boiling. Strain. Serve very hot. Yield: 12 servings.

Elizabeth Durie

GINGER BEER

1 lemon, peeled and sliced
3 cups sugar
4 tbsp. cream of tartar

3 tbsp. ginger
5 qts. boiling water
1 yeast cake, if desired

Add lemon to sugar. Add cream of tartar and ginger and pour the boiling water over all. When nearly cold, add the yeast. Let stand for 12 hours, then strain and bottle.

Mrs. J. Porter

SLUSH

2 cups sugar
7 cups water
26-oz. bottle vodka

12-oz. can frozen lemonade
12-oz. can frozen orange juice

Boil sugar and water together and cool. Add lemonade, orange juice and vodka. Stir every few hours the first day and keep in the freezer. Serve with gingerale.

KAHLUA LIQUEUR

2 cups sugar
2 cups water
1 cup instant powdered coffee
1 cup water

4 cups vodka
1 vanilla bean
1 tsp. glycerine

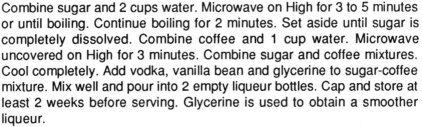

Combine sugar and 2 cups water. Microwave on High for 3 to 5 minutes or until boiling. Continue boiling for 2 minutes. Set aside until sugar is completely dissolved. Combine coffee and 1 cup water. Microwave uncovered on High for 3 minutes. Combine sugar and coffee mixtures. Cool completely. Add vodka, vanilla bean and glycerine to sugar-coffee mixture. Mix well and pour into 2 empty liqueur bottles. Cap and store at least 2 weeks before serving. Glycerine is used to obtain a smoother liqueur.

Elleline Ansell

LIQUEUR

8 oz. of rye
1 pt. whipping cream
3 tsp. instant coffee

1 can condensed milk
3 eggs
4 tsp. chocolate syrup

Combine ingredients and blend on low speed for 45 seconds. Keeps for 3 weeks in the refrigerator.

Freeze egg nog in its original container. It will keep for up to two months. Thaw in refrigerator. Shake before using.

SAUCES

BASIC WHITE SAUCE

1 tbsp. butter	1/2 tsp. salt
1 tbsp. flour	1 cup milk

Melt butter, add flour and salt and stir well. Add milk. Stir and cook until there is no taste of raw starch. This makes a thin sauce. NOTE: Use 2 tbsp. flour for a medium sauce and 3 tbsp. flour for a thick sauce. When using less butter than flour, milk must be warm and added very gradually. For a rich sauce, double the amount of butter or use cream instead of milk. For a brown sauce, use twice as much flour as for a white sauce. Brown flour or flour and butter before adding milk. VARIATION: Combine a pinch of dry mustard and 1 cup basic white sauce. Just before serving, stir in 3/4 cup shredded cheddar cheese and stir until melted.

CHEESE SAUCE

1/4 cup butter	1/8 tsp. pepper
1/4 cup flour	1/2 tsp. dry mustard
1/2 tsp. salt	2 cups milk
1/8 tsp. paprika	1 cup grated cheddar cheese

Melt butter and blend in flour and seasoning. Gradually stir in milk. Cook over medium heat until mixture thickens, stirring constantly. Stir in cheese. Beat well just before serving. Use with vegetables, hard-cooked eggs, fish or macaroni. Yield: 2 cups.

LEMON SAUCE

1/3 cup sugar	2 tsp. butter
1 tbsp. cornstarch	1 1/2 tbsp. lemon juice
Pinch of salt	1/2 tsp. grated lemon rind
1 cup boiling water	

Combine sugar, cornstarch and salt. Slowly add boiling water and cook until there is no taste of raw starch. Remove from heat and add butter, lemon juice and rind. Serve over puddings, cakes or custards.

Mrs. Rhoda Fossen

MEAT LOAF TOMATO SAUCE

2 tbsp. butter **or** oil	2 tbsp. flour
1 tbsp. chopped onion	1 can tomatoes
Salt and pepper	

Melt butter, add onion and fry until light brown in a heavy pan. Add salt, pepper and flour, stirring constantly. Gradually mix in tomatoes, stirring gently until cooked. Serve over meat loaf, fried liver, etc.

TOMATO SAUCE

2 8-oz. cans seasoned
   tomato sauce
1/4 tsp. salt
1 tsp. worcestershire sauce

1/2 cup chopped onion
Pepper to taste
1 tbsp. vinegar
Dash of tabasco sauce

Combine ingredients. Cover and simmer 30 minutes until onions are tender. This keeps well in refrigerator. Good for basting barbecued steaks, hamburgers and wieners.

FABULOUS BARBECUE SAUCE

1 cup strong coffee
1 cup catsup
1/2 cup worcestershire sauce
1/3 cup vinegar

1/2 cup brown sugar
1/2 cup butter **or** margarine
Juice of 1/2 lemon

Combine ingredients and simmer 5 minutes. Cool. Store in covered jar in refrigerator. Yield: 4 cups. Use to marinate steaks, chops or chicken and basting steaks, hamburgers, chicken, etc. when barbecuing.

SOUPER BARBECUE SAUCE

1/3 cup chopped onion
1/3 cup chopped celery
1 small garlic clove, minced
2 tbsp. oil
10 1/2-oz. can tomato soup

2 tsp. mustard
2 tbsp. worcestershire sauce
2 tbsp. brown sugar
2 tbsp. lemon juice **or** vinegar
1/4 tsp. tabasco (optional)

Cook onion, celery and garlic in hot oil until soft. Blend in remaining ingredients and simmer 10 minutes.

SUPER BAR-B-CUE SAUCE

1/4 cup vinegar
2 tbsp. sugar
1 1/2 tsp. salt
1/4 tsp. cayenne
1/4 cup butter
2 tbsp. worcestershire sauce

1/2 cup water
1/2 tsp. pepper
1 tbsp. lemon juice
1 onion, chopped
1/2 cup catsup
1 1/2 tsp. liquid smoke

Combine all ingredients, bring to boil and simmer 20 minutes. This will store in refrigerator. Thin with a little water if it becomes too thick.

QUICK KABOBS: Alternate cubes of canned luncheon meat, green pepper squares and pineapple chunks on skewers. Brush with barbecue sauce. Broil 3 to 4 inches from heat until lightly brown, turning once.

THIN BARBECUE SAUCE

1 cup butter **or** margarine
1 cup water
2 tbsp. chopped onion
1 1/2 tsp. sugar
3/4 cup tomato catsup
Juice of 1/2 lemon

1/2 cup vinegar
1 tsp. dry mustard
1 clove garlic
1/2 cup worcestershire sauce
1/2 cup chili sauce

Mix all ingredients together and simmer one hour to blend seasonings. Remove garlic clove. For a hot sauce, add 1/2 tsp. cayenne pepper. This sauce may be made in advance and stored in refrigerator.

HURRY-UP BASTE

16-oz. can frozen lemonade
2 tsp. salt
4 tbsp. chili sauce **or** catsup
1/4 cup vinegar
1/2 tsp. garlic powder

1/4 cup salad oil
1/2 tsp. pepper
1 tsp. worcestershire sauce
1 tsp. basil
2 tsp. dry mustard

Combine all ingredients and shake well before using.

WINE MARINADE

1 1/2 cups oil
1/2 cup soya sauce
2 tbsp. worcestershire sauce
1 tbsp. dry mustard
1 1/2 tsp. salt

3/4 tsp. pepper
2 tsp. parsley, chopped
1/3 cup fresh lemon juice
1 cup dry, red wine

Put all ingredients in a jar and shake vigorously. Marinade may be drained from steaks and reused. It may also be frozen. It is a good meat tenderizer. Let tough meat marinate at least 5 to 6 hours or overnight before cooking. This is also very good for wild meats of any kind.

MARINATING SAUCE

1 clove garlic
1/2 cup vinegar
1/4 tsp. pepper
2 tsp. worcestershire sauce

1 cup salad oil
1 tsp. salt
2 tsp. dry mustard
1/4 tsp. tabasco sauce

Slice garlic clove into container. Add remaining ingredients and blend well. Pour carefully over meat to marinate.

Sauces will not be runny if you squeeze the seeds out of tomatoes.

Remove the last drop of catsup or barbecue sauce by microwaving on High for 15 to 30 seconds. Remove metal lid or cap.

SAVORY CHICKEN SAUCE

1/2 cup salad oil
2 tbsp. chopped onion
1 1/2 tsp. sugar
1 tsp. chili powder
1 tsp. pepper
Dash cayenne
1 tsp. worcestershire sauce

1 1/4 cups water
1 clove garlic, crushed
1 tsp. salt
1 tsp. paprika
1/2 tsp. dry mustard
2 tbsp. vinegar
1 tsp. tabasco sauce

Combine all ingredients and simmer for about 30 minutes. Brush on broiling chicken frequently.

CHINESE SAUCE

1/2 cup soya sauce
1 garlic clove, crushed
1 tsp. brown sugar

1/2 cup sherry wine
1 tsp. powdered ginger

Mix ingredients together, blending well. Good for chicken, pork, shrimp or spareribs. Yield: 1 cup.

SWEET & SOUR SAUCE

10-oz. can crushed pineapple
2/3 cup white wine vinegar
2 tbsp. salad oil
2 tbsp. oxo concentrate
1 tbsp. lemon juice
1 small clove garlic, minced

1/2 tsp. dry mustard
3 tbsp. honey
1 small onion, chopped
1 tbsp. cornstarch
Salt and pepper

Combine all ingredients in a saucepan, bring to a boil and simmer 10 minutes.

CHILI SAUCE

1 can ripe tomatoes
3 onions, chopped
2 - 3 stalks celery, chopped
1 large apple, chopped
1 cup vinegar
1 1/4 cups sugar

Salt to taste
1 tsp. allspice
1 tsp. cinnamon
1 tsp. cloves
1 tsp. ginger

Combine ingredients in a saucepan and cook for 1/2 hour.

APRICOT HONEY GLAZE

1 cup brown sugar
1/2 cup honey

1/4 cup canned apricot nectar

Combine ingredients in saucepan. Heat and stir until sugar dissolves. Yield: 1 1/2 cups.

HAM GLAZE

Glazing takes 15 minutes in a 425° oven. When the ham is almost cooked, remove the rind and score the fat diagonally, cutting about 1/4 inch deep with a sharp knife, to make diamonds. Stick a whole clove in the center of each diamond. You can use almost anything sweet for the glaze. Just baste the ham with honey, maple syrup, melted jelly or sweetened fruit juice, etc. A little mustard is good added to any of these. To make an old-fashioned brown sugar glaze, mix 1 cup brown sugar with 2 tsp. dry mustard and 3 tbsp. each of flour and vinegar. This brown sugar glaze spreads more easily if it is put on before the meat is studded with cloves. For a very large ham, double the glaze recipe.

EASY HONEY GLAZE FOR HAM

1/2 cup apple juice   1/2 cup honey
1 tbsp. prepared mustard

Boil ingredients together for 1 minute, blending well. Spoon over ham.

ZIPPY MARINADE FOR HAM

1/4 cup prepared mustard   1 cup catsup
1/4 cup honey

Stir ingredients together and baste the ham during the last 30 minutes of baking.

BUTTERS

LEMON HERB BUTTER

1/2 cup soft butter   1 tbsp. grated lemon rind
1/2 tsp. dried basil   1/2 tsp. chopped chives
1 tsp. parsley

Blend ingredients well. Refrigerate. Spread on hot vegetables or fish.

HONEY BUTTER SPREAD

Combine equal amounts of honey and butter. Store honey-butter in refrigerator ready for toast, hot rolls or spicy upside-down cake.

GARLIC BUTTER

1 clove garlic, crushed **or**   1/2 cup butter
   garlic salt to taste

Blend garlic and butter well. Spread on a loaf of French bread that has been cut in half. Wrap in aluminum foil and heat in oven or on grill. VARIATION: Use butter and sprinkle with parmesan cheese.

VEGETABLES

MIXED VEGETABLE CASSEROLE

10-oz. can peas
10-oz. can corn
10-oz. can carrots
1 onion, sliced

1 pkg. stove top dressing
1 cup mayonnaise
1 cup grated cheese

Stir ingredients together and bake at 350° for 45 minutes.

Doreen Sexty

SUMMER MEDLEY

1 small head cauliflower **or**
  2 large stalks broccoli
1/4 cup butter **or** margarine

1/2 tsp. salt
1 cup sliced green onion
5 cherry tomatoes, halved

Break cauliflower into small flowerettes. Microwave butter to melt in 2-qt. casserole. Add cauliflower and salt, tossing to coat. Microwave covered, on High for 5 to 6 minutes, stirring twice. Stir in onion and tomato. Microwave covered 2 to 3 minutes or until vegetables are tender-crisp. Yield: 4 to 6 servings.

Elizabeth Durie

BARBECUED CREAMY VEGETABLES

Potatoes, thinly sliced
Carrots, thinly sliced
Onions **or** wax beans

Salt and pepper to taste
Carnation milk

Combine vegetables and put individual servings on squares of aluminum foil. Add salt and pepper. Add 1 tbsp. of milk. Do not seal. Put on top of barbecue for 15 minutes, until milk bubbles. Seal foil around vegetables and continue to barbecue for 30 minutes. Slit open foil and peel back to serve.

VEGETABLE STEW

2 tbsp. chopped bacon
Salt and pepper to taste
1 1/2 cups chicken broth
1 cup cut-up celery

1 cup cup-up carrots
1 cup cut-up beans
1 cup cut-up leeks
Potatoes (optional)

Fry bacon until crisp and drain. Add salt, pepper, broth and vegetables. Simmer lightly until done. Potatoes may be put on top to steam and cook. This is lovely with roast beef, lamb or chicken.

STIR FRY VEGETABLES WITH MEAT

1 tbsp. oil	1 cup carrots, sliced diagonally
1 tbsp. butter	1 cup broccoli flowerettes
2 onions, quartered	1 cup cauliflower flowerettes
lengthwise	1 stalk celery, sliced diagonally
1 small green pepper, cut in	1/2 cup cooked meat
1/4-inch strips	1/2 cup sliced mushrooms

Place oil, butter and onions in 2-qt. glass casserole. Microwave uncovered on High for 3 minutes until hot. Stir in the green pepper, carrots, broccoli, cauliflower and celery, mixing well. Microwave on High, covered, for 4 minutes. Thinly slice meat and add along with mushrooms and continue to microwave uncovered for 4 to 6 minutes more. Yield: 6 to 8 servings. Variation: Shrimp or cooked chicken can be substituted for meat.

Florence Trautman

STIR FRY VEGETABLES

1/2 cup shredded cabbage	1/4 cup chopped peppers
1/4 cup chopped onions	1/2 cup chopped bacon
1/2 cup chopped zucchini	1 can mushrooms
Salt and pepper	

Combine ingredients. You can include any vegetables you prefer. Put in electric frying pan with a little water. Fry until cooked.

Stella Pimm

SKILLET CHOP SUEY

1 1/2 cups celery strips	1 cup cold water
1 onion, cut in 8 wedges	1 tbsp. soya sauce
1 green pepper, cut in strips	7-oz. can flaked tuna **or**
1 clove garlic, minced	1 cup cooked chicken
3 tbsp. cornstarch	1 tsp. salt

Sauté celery, onions, green pepper and garlic until light brown but still crisp. Blend cornstarch with a little cold water. Add remaining cold water and soya sauce to vegetables. Gradually stir in cornstarch mixture. Add tuna and salt. Cook and stir until liquid thickens and vegetables are glazed. Serve with rice.

Irene Wagstaff

Use canned whole onions and canned potatoes for kabobs. Baste vegetables with melted butter or margarine. Give mushrooms and peppers a boiling water bath for a minute to keep them from falling apart when skewering. To avoid overcooking, string vegetables such as tomatoes, on their own skewer.

CAMPFIRE VEGETABLES

Place one block frozen vegetables on a square of aluminum foil. Season with salt and pepper. Top with butter or margarine. Bring edges of foil up and, leaving a little space for expansion of steam, seal tightly with double fold. Place package on grill or right in the hot coals for about 10 to 15 minutes. Turn occasionally. This may also be done in oven at 450° for about 15 to 20 minutes. When doing potatoes, foil-wrap whole potato. Tomatoes, peppers, zucchini, eggplant, onions, corn on the cob, any block of frozen vegetables may be done in this manner, placing foil package on grill. Potatoes and yams may be placed in the coals. To speed their cooking, spear with aluminum spikes or "potato" nails.

POTATOES SUPREME

6 potatoes	1 cup diced Velveeta cheese
1 cup milk	1 egg, beaten

Boil, drain and mash potatoes. Add milk gradually until potatoes are creamy. Fold in cheese and egg. Pile into greased 2-qt. casserole. Cover and bake at 350° for 40 to 45 minutes. Uncover during last 10 minutes to brown lightly.

Edna Dempsey

POTATO SOUFFLE

1 egg, separated	Parmesan cheese
1 1/2 - 2 cups mashed potatoes	Sour cream **or** sweet cream

Beat egg white until stiff. Mix egg yolk into well-seasoned cooled mashed potatoes. Fold in egg white and spread in small buttered baking dish. Sprinkle cheese on top and dab or drizzle with cream. Bake at 400° for 15 minutes.

QUICK SCALLOPED POTATOES

4 medium potatoes, sliced thin	1/4 tsp. pepper
1/2 cup chopped onion	2 tbsp. butter **or** margarine
2 tbsp. flour, if using milk	2 tbsp. shredded cheddar
1 1/2 cup milk **or** light cream	cheese (optional)
1/2 tsp. salt	Paprika **or** parsley flakes

Alternate potato and onion in a 2-qt. casserole dish. Mix flour, milk, salt and pepper into a 4-cup measuring pitcher. Microwave 2 minutes on High, stirring well. Microwave 1 minute on High until hot. Dot potatoes with butter and pour milk mixture over potatoes. Cover tightly to prevent over-boiling of milk. Microwave 10 minutes on High and stir. Cover loosely and microwave 10 minutes on High. Sprinkle on cheese, paprika or parsley. Let stand 5 minutes. Yield: 4 to 5 servings. If using left-over boiled potatoes, cut the cooking time by 10 minutes.

Spring Valley Local

SCALLOPED POTATOES

1 1/2 tbsp. flour
3/4 tsp. salt
Dash of pepper
3 1/2 cups pared potatoes

1/4 cup thinly-sliced
   peeled onion
1 1/2 tbsp. butter
2 1/2 cups milk

Mix flour, salt and pepper. Slice potatoes 1/8 inch thick and arrange with onion in layers in an oiled casserole. Sprinkle each layer with a little flour mixture. Dot with butter and pour 1 1/2 cups of milk over potatoes. Bake at 300° for 1 hour. Heat remaining cup of milk and add slowly. Return to oven and continue baking for 1 hour longer.

POTATOES AU GRATIN

8 potatoes
4 tbsp. butter
4 tbsp. flour
2 cups milk

1/2 lb. cheese, finely shredded
1 tbsp. onion flakes
Salt and pepper to taste
Bread crumbs

Boil or bake potatoes with skins on. Cool. Peel and slice or dice. Melt butter in saucepan, add flour and cook 1 minute. Add milk and reduce heat to medium. Stir until sauce is smooth and thickened. Add cheese, potatoes, onion, salt and pepper. Stir gently and turn into casserole. Sprinkle with crumbs. Dot with additional butter. Bake at 375° for 30 to 35 minutes or until nicely browned. Leftover boiled potatoes may be used as well.

Mrs. James Gaschnitz

BUD'S SPUDS

6 potatoes
1/2 cup butter **or** margarine
2 cups shredded cheddar cheese
1/4 cup chopped onion

1 1/2 cups sour cream
1 tsp. salt
1/4 tsp. pepper

Boil potatoes in jackets, cool in refrigerator and peel. Grate coarsely and gently mix with remaining ingredients. Bake in oiled shallow 3-qt. casserole at 350° for 30 minutes.

Miriam Galloway

MICROWAVE CHEESY POTATOES

4 cups thinly sliced potatoes
3/4 cup chopped onion
3/4 tsp. salt
1/2 cup milk

10-oz. can condensed cheddar
   cheese soup
1 1/2 tsp. worcestershire sauce

Layer 1/3 of the potatoes, onion and salt in a buttered 2-qt. casserole. Heat soup, milk and worcestershire sauce and layer with 1/3 of mixture. Repeat three times. Microwave on High for 30 to 40 minutes.

Margaret Erickson

MICROWAVE POTATOES

6 - 8 potatoes
1 grated onion
1/2 tsp. salt

1/2 tsp. pepper
1 can mushroom soup
1/2 can milk **or** water

Peel and grate potatoes and add to onion, salt and pepper in large dish. Add mushroom soup diluted with milk. Cover and microwave 20 minutes on High, stirring once. Let stand 5 minutes. Yield: 4 to 5 servings.

Mary Wright

HOT POTATO SALAD

6 potatoes
4 strips bacon cut in 1/2-in. squares
1/4 cup chopped onion
1/4 cup chopped celery
1/4 - 1/2 cup vinegar
1/4 cup water
1/2 tsp. sugar

3/4 tsp. salt
Few grains pepper
1/8 tsp. paprika
1/4 cup chopped sweet
   cucumber pickle
2 - 3 hard-boiled eggs,
   chopped

Boil potatoes with skins on. Meanwhile fry bacon pieces until crisp, then remove from pan. Sauté onion and celery in drippings, until barely transparent. Add vinegar, water, sugar, salt, pepper and paprika. Bring to boil. Keep mixture hot but not boiling. Peel and dice potatoes into 1/2 inch cubes. Pour vinegar mixture over potatoes. Add bacon and pickles, then combine. Sprinkle with egg and serve immediately. Yield: 6 servings.

OVEN FRIED POTATOES

Cut potatoes into 3/8 inch strips. Dry thoroughly between towels. Spread one layer deep in a greased shallow pan. Pour 1/4 cup oil over potatoes, turning to coat. Bake at 400° about 30 minutes. Turn twice to brown evenly. Drain on paper towels and salt to taste.

MICRO HASH BROWNS

2 tbsp. butter, melted
1 chopped onion
1 can cream of mushroom soup
1 cup sour cream
1 lb. frozen hash browns
1/2 tsp. salt

1/4 tsp. pepper
1 cup grated cheese
1 cup crushed cornflakes
1/4 cup melted butter
Parmesan cheese

Microwave 2 tbsp. butter and onion on High for 3 minutes. Mix all but last three ingredients together and place in dish. Combine cornflakes and 1/4 cup butter and cover hash browns. Cover with parmesan cheese. Microwave on Medium for 15 minutes.

Florence Trautman

BAKED POTATO BALLS

3 cups hot mashed potatoes
3 tbsp. butter
Salt and pepper to taste
Cayenne to taste

2 eggs, well beaten
Diluted beaten egg
Crushed cornflake crumbs

Mash potatoes with butter and seasonings. Add eggs and mix well. Roll into small balls. Dip in diluted egg. Roll in cornflake crumbs. Place on greased cookie sheet. Bake at 400° for 20 minutes or until brown.

Mrs. Elis Kocsis

POTATO DUMPLINGS

2 cups flour **or** 1 cup flour
    and 1 cup graham flour
1 tsp. baking powder
1 tsp. salt

4 cups grated raw potatoes
Beef broth **or** chicken broth
1/2 lb. diced fresh or salt pork

Sift flour, baking powder and salt together. Add potatoes and broth. Shape into balls with hands, putting a piece of pork in the center of each ball. Add enough flour to keep them from sticking to hands. Drop into boiling broth, cover and boil 1 hour, stirring occasionally to prevent sticking. Remove from broth as soon as done and serve with butter.

Muriel Sletton
Gina Hagen

LEMON POTATO CASSEROLE

4 cups potatoes, thinly sliced
1/4 cup melted butter
1 tbsp. lemon juice

1 tsp. salt
1/8 tsp. paprika

Put potatoes into shallow baking dish. Combine butter, juice and seasonings. Pour half over potatoes. Cook 30 minutes in moderate oven. Add remaining butter mixture. Bake another 15 to 20 minutes.

SWEET POTATO CASSEROLE

6 medium sweet potatoes **or**
    yams, cooked and mashed
2 tbsp. butter
1/2 tsp. grated lemon peel

2 tbsp. lemon juice
1 tsp. salt
1/2 cup brown sugar
1/2 cup walnuts **or** pecans

Put potatoes in casserole. Add butter, lemon peel and juice. Add salt and half the brown sugar. Mix well. Top with remaining brown sugar and sprinkle nuts on top. Bake at 375° for 20 to 25 minutes.

Mary Stimson

To prevent curdling of scalloped potatoes, slice potatoes and cover with water. Bring to a boil, drain and proceed from there.

ORANGE GLAZED CARROTS

Carrots, enough for 10 servings
4 tbsp. butter

3 tbsp. strained orange
marmalade

Drain hot cooked carrots. Add butter and marmalade. Toss, stir lightly and heat thoroughly.

HONEY GLAZED CARROTS OR BEETS

3 tbsp. butter
2 tbsp. honey
1 tbsp. brown sugar

Salt and pepper to taste
2 - 3 cups cooked diced,
drained vegetables

Lightly brown butter in skillet. Add honey, sugar, salt and pepper. Simmer mixture for 2 minutes. Add vegetables and cook over low heat about 5 minutes until well glazed. Yield: 4 to 6 servings.

MARINATED CARROTS

5 - 6 cups carrots, cut round
1 sliced green pepper, optional
1 sliced onion
1 can tomato soup
1 tbsp. worcestershire sauce
1/2 cup salad oil

1 tsp. salt
1 tsp. prepared mustard
3/4 cup vinegar
1/4 tsp. black pepper
3/4 cup sugar

Boil carrots in lightly-salted water until tender. Drain and cool. Combine with green pepper and onion in container. Mix and heat remaining ingredients until sugar is dissolved. Pour over carrots and marinate at least 24 hours. This will keep in refrigerator for 2 to 3 weeks.

Christina Smith

GOLDEN CARROT LOAF

3/4 cup raw, grated carrot
1 onion, minced
2 tbsp. chopped parsley
1 celery stalk, diced with leaves
1/2 cup chopped nuts
2 tbsp. dry whole wheat
bread crumbs

2 tbsp. cream
1 egg, slightly beaten
11/2 tsp. vegetable salt
2 tsp. golden oil
Whole wheat bread crumbs
2 tsp. margarine

Mix all ingredients thoroughly except the last three. Coat the inside of a loaf pan with oil and dust oiled surfaces with remaining bread crumbs. Pack mixture into loaf pan, dot with margarine, cover pan and bake in moderate oven about 35 minutes. Invert on serving platter. Serve with your favorite sauce.

Cook cheese at a moderate temperature. High temperatures toughen the protein of cheese. When making cheese sauce, the cheese should be added last and cooked only until melted.

SCALLOPED CORN WITH MUSHROOM SOUP

1 1/2 cups whole kernel corn
3/4 cup condensed cream of
    mushroom soup
2 tbsp. butter
2 tbsp. flour

1 tsp. salt
Dash of pepper
2 eggs, beaten
1/2 cup bread **or** cracker crumbs

Drain the liquid from the corn and add liquid to the soup. Melt the butter, add flour and seasonings and mix until well-blended. Add the soup gradually, stirring constantly until smooth and thickened. Combine the corn and eggs and add to the sauce. Pour into a baking dish and top with the crumbs. Place dish in pan of water and bake at 350° for about 30 minutes or until set. Yield: 6 servings.

Mrs. Howard Stevenson

SCALLOPED CORN

1 can cream style corn
1 can whole kernel corn
1 cup soda cracker crumbs

5 1/2-oz. can evaporated milk
1 egg, slightly beaten
2 tbsp. butter **or** margarine

Combine corn, crumbs and milk in 1-qt. casserole. Mix well. Stir in egg. Dot with butter. Cover with wax paper. Microwave 10 minutes on Medium High (80%) power, stirring once.

Edith Galloway

BAKED CORN

2 tbsp. butter
1 1/2 tsp. flour
1 cup milk
2 cups cooked **or** canned corn

1 tbsp. sugar
1 tsp. salt
1/8 tsp. pepper
2 eggs, well beaten

Melt butter, add flour and mix well. Add milk gradually and bring to the boiling point, stirring constantly. Add corn, sugar, salt and pepper and heat thoroughly. Remove from heat, add eggs and pour into greased baking dish. Bake at 350° for 25 minutes.

Mrs. Beulah Burger

CORN DELIGHT

1 tbsp. butter
1/3 cup onion
1 tbsp. chopped red and
    green pepper

Salt and pepper to taste
1 cup warm milk
1 tbsp. sugar
3 1/2 cups frozen kernal corn

Fry butter, onion and pepper lightly. Add salt, pepper, milk, sugar and corn. Stir until well-blended and sugar is dissolved. Pour into baking dish, cover and bake 1 hour at 350°.

BARBECUED CORN ON THE COB

Pull back husks but leave attached. Remove silk. If desired, soak in salted ice water for 20 minutes. Drain well. Brush with soft butter. Sprinkle with salt and pepper. Bring husks up around corn. Wrap each ear in double thickness of heavy-duty foil. Twist ends to seal. Cook on grill over coals for 20 minutes, turning occasionally. Or cook directly on coals, turning often for 10 minutes.

CORN TIMBALES

10-oz. can creamed corn
2 eggs, beaten
1/4 tsp. salt
1 tbsp. sugar

1/4 tsp. mustard
Few grains cayenne
1/8 tsp. paprika

Combine ingredients and pour into greased baking dish. Bake at 375° for 25 minutes.

Mrs. George Sime

CURRIED KERNEL CORN

Drop few pieces of butter into hot drained kernel corn, sprinkle generously with curry powder and lightly with fine-snipped green onion tops. Toss, keep hot.

PIQUANT MINTED PEAS OR GREEN BEANS

Adds bits of butter and a generous sprinkle of drained mint sauce to hot drained peas or beans. Reheat thoroughly. Keep covered to retain color.

WAX BEANS SUPREME

1 tbsp. chopped bacon
11/2 tsp. chopped green pepper
1 tbsp. chopped onion

2 - 3 cups cooked wax beans
1 cup stewed tomatoes

Fry bacon. Add green pepper and onion and cook until soft. Add beans, tomatoes and simmer for 15 to 20 minutes before serving. Yield: 4 to 6 servings.

HERBED GREEN BEANS

1/4 cup chopped onion
1/4 cup chopped celery
2 - 3 tbsp. butter
3 cups cut, cooked green beans

1 clove garlic, minced
1/2 tsp. rosemary
1/2 tsp. basil
Salt and pepper to taste

Fry onion and celery in butter. Add remaining ingredients and simmer for 10 minutes. Yield: 4 to 6 servings.

CANNED PORK AND BEANS

3 qts. navy beans
1/2 lb. bacon trimmings
3 onions, finely chopped
1 tbsp. mustard
1/2 cup molasses

1/2 cup beef bouillon
48-oz. can tomato juice
1 tbsp. salt
1 tsp. pepper
24 cups warm water

Clean and sort beans. Wash and soak in plenty of water overnight. Drain and rinse in cold water. Cut bacon into small pieces and mix with onions, mustard, molasses, bouillon, tomato juice, salt and pepper. Add beans. Fill jars 2/3 full with bean mixture. Add the warm water to collar. Seal and process 4 hours in hot water bath or 1 hour under 18 lb. pressure in pressure cooker-canner.

Lucie C. St. Andre

OLD-TIME BAKED BEANS

1 lb. dry navy beans
6 cups cold water
1 tsp. salt
1/3 cup brown sugar
2 tsp. salt

1 tsp. dry mustard
1/4 cup molasses
1/4 lb. salt pork
1 medium onion,
    chopped finely

Wash and pick over beans. Add cold water. Simmer 2 hours **or** add beans to water and soak overnight. Add 1 tsp. salt, cover and simmer about 1 hour until tender. Drain, reserving liquid. Measure 13/4 cup bean liquid, adding water if necessary. Combine with brown sugar, 1 tsp. salt, mustard and molasses. Cut salt pork in half. Score one-half and set aside. Grind or finely chop the remainder. Alternate layers of beans, chopped onion, chopped pork and sugar mixture in 2-qt. bean pot or casserole. Repeat layers. Top with scored salt pork. Cover. Bake at 300° for 5 to 7 hours, adding more liquid if needed. Yield: 8 servings.

SPEEDY BAKED BEANS

4 slices bacon
1 onion, diced
1 green pepper (optional)
19-oz. can pineapple tidbits

2 14-oz. cans pork and beans
2 tbsp. worcestershire sauce
1/2 cup brown sugar
3/4 cup catsup

Fry bacon until crisp, then add onions and green pepper. Cook until onions are clear. Drain off excess fat. Stir into remaining ingredients in a casserole. Bake uncovered at 325° for 30 to 45 minutes.

Minnie Blair

Always microwave fresh vegetables covered, except those cooked with their skins on. A fitted glass lid or plastic wrap stretched tightly over the dish hastens cooking.

SWEET-SOUR BEANS

3 slices bacon, diced
1 tbsp. chopped onion
Salt and pepper to taste

2 - 3 cups cut, cooked beans
1 cup bean liquid
3 tbsp. sweet pickle juice

Fry bacon until crisp. Drain off fat. Add onion and fry. Add salt and pepper. Add beans and liquid. Add pickle juice and let simmer for 15 to 20 minutes to blend flavor. If you use yellow beans, sprinkle with herbs and serve. If using green beans, chopped red pepper may be added with chopped onion. Yield: 4 to 6 servings.

LUAU BEANS

1/2 lb. sliced bacon
2 onions, sliced
4 16-oz. cans pork and beans
1 cup crushed pineapple

1/4 cup chili sauce
2 tbsp. molasses
1 1/2 tsp. dry mustard
1/2 tsp. salt

Fry bacon until crisp. Remove and drain. Save drippings. Cook onion in drippings. Crumble bacon and combine in Dutch oven with onions, beans, pineapple, chili sauce, molasses, mustard and salt. Mix well. Cover and bake on grill over medium hot coals for 1 1/2 hours. Remove cover and cook 25 minutes longer. Stir occasionally. Yield: 10 to 12 servings.

BEET GREENS

4 - 6 cups cut up beet tops
2 tbsp. chopped bacon
1 clove garlic, minced

Salt and pepper
2 cups water

Wash and pick over beet tops and cut into 1-inch pieces. Place bacon in frying pan. Add garlic, salt, pepper and water. Add greens. Cook until done, turning over a few times to cook evenly. Swiss Chard leaves are also very good this way.

GREENS CASSEROLE

4 cups beet tops **or**
  spinach leaves
1 tbsp. chopped bacon
1 tbsp. chopped onion
1 cup lean ground beef
Salt and pepper to taste

1/2 tbsp. beef bouillon
1 cup cooked rice **or**
  mashed potatoes
Grated cheddar cheese
1/3 cup bread crumbs

Wash and cut up beet tops fairly fine so there is 4 cups well packed. Set aside. Fry bacon, add onion, meat, salt and pepper. Cook slowly, mixing well until done. Add bouillon, stirring well. Add rice and greens and mix well. Pour into baking dish. Sprinkle with grated cheddar cheese and 1/3 cup bread crumbs. Cover and bake at 350° about 30 minutes or until done.

BEETS IN ORANGE SAUCE

1 cup orange juice
1/3 cup raisins
3/4 tsp. salt
1/4 cup sugar
1 tbsp. cornstarch

2 tbsp. beet liquid
1 tbsp. lemon juice
1 tbsp. butter
2 - 3 cups drained,
  chopped beets

Boil the orange juice and raisins. Combine salt, sugar, cornstarch and beet liquid. Add this to the orange-raisin juice and cook until thick. Add lemon juice, butter and beets. Serve hot. Yield: 4 to 6 servings.

Mrs. Eddie Jackson

SAVORY BEETS

1 tbsp. margarine
1 large onion, diced
1 tbsp. sugar
1/2 tsp. curry powder

3 tbsp. cider vinegar
1 tsp. salt
1/4 tsp. ground cloves
2 - 4 cups diced cooked beets

Melt margarine in saucepan. Add onion, sugar and curry powder. Cook over medium heat until onion is soft. Add vinegar, salt and cloves. Heat five minutes. Add beets and simmer until hot.

Janey Hayworth

HARVARD BEETS

1 tbsp. butter **or** margarine
1 tbsp. flour
2 tbsp. boiling water
3 tbsp. brown sugar
2 tbsp. vinegar

1/4 tsp. salt
Dash of pepper
Dash of mace
Dash of powdered cloves
1 1/4 cups cooked, diced beets

Melt butter in double boiler, blend in flour and let bubble 3 minutes. Add boiling water slowly. Stir until smooth, then add brown sugar, vinegar, seasonings and spices. Blend well. Add beets and cook over boiling water until hot. Yield: 4 servings.

Pansy Molen

HARVARD BEETS WITH RAISINS

2 20-oz. cans sliced **or**
  diced beets
1/3 cup raisins
2 tbsp. brown sugar

2 tbsp. cornstarch
2 tbsp. vinegar
2 tbsp. butter

Drain juice beets into saucepan. Add raisins. Cover and simmer 10 minutes. Combine brown sugar, cornstarch and vinegar and add to raisin mixture. Cook until smooth and clean, then add beets and butter. Season to taste.

TASTY BEETS

1 garlic clove, minced
1 tbsp. butter
Salt and pepper to taste
1 tbsp. prepared mustard

2 - 3 tbsp. vinegar
1/2 cup water
4 - 6 cups frozen, diced beets

Fry garlic in butter in saucepan. Add salt, pepper, mustard, vinegar, water and beets. Let simmer until done. NOTE: Frozen beets are always sweeter than canned beets, so sugar is not necessary. Garlic gives beets a much finer flavor than onion, so if no fresh garlic is available, you may use a bit of garlic salt. If you like a sauce, add more water and thicken with a bit of cornstarch.

CAULIFLOWER VINAIGRETTE

3 tbsp. vinegar **or** lemon juice
3 tbsp. butter

Freshly boiled cauliflower

Gradually add vinegar to lightly-browned butter. Pour over cauliflower. Brussels sprouts, boiled cabbage, leeks, cut-up boiled celery stalks or Swiss chard stalks are also very delicious this way.

BROCCOLI - LIGHT

4 - 6 cups cut-up frozen broccoli
  or cauliflower
2 cups grated cheddar cheese

1 cup bread crumbs
Salt and Pepper
1/2 cup milk

Layer broccoli with cheese and bread crumbs, ending with cheese layer. Season with salt and pepper. Just before you put on the last layer of cheese, sprinkle milk over broccoli. Bake at 325° for 3/4 to 1 hour .

BAKED ONIONS

Small-sized onions, peeled
1 tbsp. butter
Salt and pepper to taste

3 tbsp. tomato catsup
3 tbsp. water

Parboil the onions in water for about 20 minutes and place in casserole. Combine catsup and water and pour over onion. Dot with butter, salt and pepper and bake at 350° for 20 minutes.

A.F. Schnee

SCALLOPED TOMATOES

28-oz. can stewed tomatoes
2 cups dried crumbled bread
Salt and pepper to taste

Pinch of thyme
1 tsp. sugar
4 tbsp. butter

Butter baking dish. Combine bread with seasonings and sugar. Alternate layers of tomatoes, bread mixture and dotted butter. Bake at 375° for 20 minutes.

TOMATO ENTREES

Firm ripe tomatoes
1 cup fine cut lettuce
1 tbsp. celery, chopped fine
1 1/2 tsp. green onion, chopped
1 can shrimp, broken and drained

1 tsp. chopped green parsley
1/4 cup mayonnaise **or**
   salad dressing
1 tbsp. lemon juice

Scoop out tomatoes. Toss vegetables, shrimp and parsley to mix well. Combine mayonnaise and lemon juice and add enough to moisten thoroughly. Repack tomatoes. Garnish with dash of parsley and serve before a meal.

STUFFED GREEN OR RED PEPPERS

Green **or** red peppers
1 tbsp. chopped bacon
1 tbsp. chopped onion
1 cup lean ground beef

Salt and pepper to taste
1 cup cooked rice **or**
   mashed potatoes
Chicken broth **or** bouillon

The large, sweet type of pepper is best to use. Wash peppers well and cut in half to remove seeds. Fry bacon, add onion and fry lightly. Add ground meat, salt and pepper. Cook slowly until done, mashing and stirring so it will not be lumpy. Add rice and stuff into pepper halves. Arrange in baking dish. Add chicken broth to about half way up to top of peppers. Cover and bake at 375° for 3/4 to 1 hour or until done. Onions can also be done this way.

HOT SLAW

1/2 head cabbage, finely sliced
Salt and pepper
2 tbsp. lard
2 cups water

1 cup cream
1/2 cup vinegar
2 tbsp. sugar
1 tbsp. flour

Place cabbage, lard and seasoning with water in skillet and cook until cabbage boils dry. Combine remaining ingredients, cook and pour over cabbage before serving.

RED CABBAGE

1 red cabbage,
   finely sliced
1/4 cup margarine
3 tbsp. brown sugar
1/4 cup finely-chopped onion

2 firm apples, peeled and sliced
2 tbsp. vinegar
1/3 tsp. salt
1/8 tsp. pepper
1/4 cup grape jelly

Sauté the cabbage in the margarine for about 5 minutes, turning occasionally. Add the brown sugar, onion and apples. Add remaining ingredients. Cover and simmer slowly for 20 minutes, stirring occasionally.

Frieda Boelman

SCALLOPED GREEN CABBAGE

1 medium cabbage, sliced	1 1/2 cups sour cream
Salt and pepper to taste	1 cup tomatoes **or** diluted
2 tbsp. chopped onion	tomato soup
2 tbsp. flour	

Place cabbage in greased casserole. Add salt, pepper and onion; sprinkle with flour. Pour enough sour cream over the cabbage to cover , then add tomatoes. Mix well. Bake at 400° for 30 minutes or until cabbage is tender.

SWEET & SOUR CABBAGE

4 tbsp. butter	1/2 cup water
2 onions, chopped	1 cup vinegar
12 cups shredded cabbage	2 tbsp. sugar

Cook butter and onion until tender. Add remaining ingredients. Cook for 20 minutes. Pack in jars and seal.

Mary Stott

FRESH SAUERKRAUT

Shred cabbage finely into large pan. Sprinkle with coarse salt at the rate of 1/2 tsp. per quart of cabbage. Rub between hands briskly and mash with hands until plenty of juice runs out freely. Pack in stone crock. Weight down and cover lightly to ferment in warm place until done. Wash and it is ready to use in your favorite dish, or for cakes. If you wish, you may also pack washed sauerkraut in sealers and process 30 minutes for pints or 1 hour for quarts. Test for seal when cold and store in cool place for later use.

DILLED TURNIPS

Turnips	Cream
Salted skim milk	Salt to taste
1/2 tsp. dill seed **or** 2 bay leaves	1 - 2 tbsp. brown sugar
Butter	

Simmer turnip in small amount of milk with dill seed until tender. Drain. Mash well. Whip in butter and enough cream to moisten. Add salt. Add brown sugar when mashing.

TURNIP PUFF

2 tbsp. flour	1 1/2 tbsp. butter
1/2 tsp. baking powder	2 cups hot mashed turnip
1/2 tsp. salt	1 egg, separated

Add dry ingredients and butter to turnips. Beat until light, add beaten egg yolk and cool. Beat egg whites and fold in. Place in greased baking dish. Bake at 375° for 20 minutes.

PARSNIP CAKES

1 cup mashed parsnips	1 egg
1/2 tsp. salt	2 tsp. baking powder
1 cup flour	3/4 cup milk

Combine and stir ingredients to smooth batter. Fry in 1/2 inch of hot fat.

Mrs. Kathleen Teague

MUSHROOM ZUCCHINI

1 onion, chopped	Chopped parsley **or**
4 tbsp. butter	parsley flakes
2 unpeeled sliced zucchini	Salt and pepper
1 can sliced mushrooms, drained	Garlic salt
Chopped celery	1 small can tomato paste
Dash of oregano	

Sauté onion in butter. Add remaining ingredients and cook on low heat for 10 to 15 minutes.

Hilda Thornton

ZUCCHINI SQUASH CASSEROLE

6 cups zucchini	1 cup shredded carrots
1/4 cup chopped onion	8-oz. pkg. herb seasoned
10-oz. can cream of chicken soup	stuffing mix
1 cup sour cream	1/2 cup melted butter

Cook zucchini and onion in boiling water for 5 minutes. Drain. Combine soup, sour cream and carrots. Fold in zucchini and onions. Combine stuffing mix and butter. Spread half in dish, fill with zucchini mixture and top with remaining stuffing. Bake at 350° for 25 to 30 minutes.

RUTABAGA PUFF

6 cups rutabaga	1 tsp. baking powder
4 tbsp. butter	1/4 tsp. salt
2 eggs	1 tsp. pepper
3 tbsp. flour	1 tsp. nutmeg
1 tbsp. brown sugar	1/2 cup fine bread crumbs

Cook rutabaga and mash with 2 tbsp. butter and eggs. Combine flour, sugar, baking powder and seasonings and add. Combine bread crumbs and remaining butter and sprinkle over top. Bake at 375° for 25 minutes.

Doris Barker

Frozen vegetables are more tasty and nutritious if baked in a greased casserole. Top with butter or margarine, and season. Add 2 tbsp. milk to cauliflower and 2 tbsp. water to lima beans. Cover vegetables tightly and bake 40 to 50 minutes at 350°. Stir half-way through cooking time.

MEAT,
FISH & POULTRY

BEEF

POT ROAST

4 - 5 lb. pot roast
1/4 cup fat
Salt to taste
2 tbsp. water

Pepper to taste
Vegetables, cut in half
   lengthwise

Brown meat well on both sides in fat in roasting pan on top of stove. Add water. Season meat with salt and pepper. Cover pan and roast at 325° for 30 to 35 minutes per pound. Add vegetables of your choice approximately 1 1/4 hours before meat is cooked. More water might have to be added at this time so vegetables will cook evenly. Baste occasionally. Use liquid in pan for gravy.

ROUND STEAK SUPREME

2 1/2 lbs. round steak
1/2 cup flour
2 eggs
1/2 cup milk
1 cup fine bread crumbs
1/2 cup parmesan cheese
1/2 tsp. pepper
1 tsp. garlic salt

1/4 cup parsley flakes
1 tsp. onion salt
3 tbsp. oil
Fresh ripe tomatoes **or**
   firm, canned and drained
1/2 cup water
Salt and pepper to taste

Cut meat into 1-inch squares and coat with flour. In a pie plate, beat eggs and milk. In a second plate, combine crumbs, cheese and seasonings. Dip meat into egg mixture, then roll in crumbs. Brown meat in hot oil. Place in 2-qt. baking dish. Arrange sliced tomatoes over meat. Stir water into drippings in skillet. Bring to boil, scraping brown bits from pan. Pour over the meat. Salt and pepper lightly. Cover and bake at 325° for 1 1/2 hours.

Edna Dempsey

Use paper towel to keep microwave cooking dry. Use plastic wrap for moist cooking, wrapping loosely and allowing air vents.

SWISS STEAK

1 round steak	1 can mushrooms
2 large onions	1 can tomatoes
1 1/2 cups water	Salt and pepper to taste

Cut steak into serving pieces. Brown well and place in casserole. Cut and fry onions for approximately 1 minute in same frying pan. Add water, using more if needed, depending on the amount of juice you want. Bring to a boil. Pour onions on steak. Add mushrooms, tomatoes, salt and pepper. Cover. Bake at 350 to 375° for 2 hours.

Paula Jasman

STEAK AND MUSHROOMS

2 lbs. round steak	2 tbsp. dehydrated onion flakes
1/2 cup canned mushrooms, drained	2 tbsp. water
	Salt and pepper to taste

Trim fat from steak. Center steak on large piece of aluminum foil and sprinkle with remaining ingredients. Fold foil over to make a leak-proof container. Place on shallow pan and bake at 350° for 2 hours. Yield: 4 to 5 servings.

Mrs. Adelaide G. Adie

BEEF STROGANOFF

1/4 cup butter **or** margarine	2 - 2 1/4 lb. boneless beef round
4 medium onions, thinly sliced	steak, cut into thin strips
1 tbsp. dry mustard	8-oz. can mushroom stems and
1 tbsp. sugar	pieces, drained
2 tsp. sugar	1 cup sour cream
2 tsp. salt	Hot buttered noodles
1 tsp. pepper	

Combine butter, onion, mustard, sugar, salt and pepper in 3-qt. glass casserole. Cover with plastic wrap. Microwave on Roast (70% power) for 6 minutes or until onion is partly cooked. Stir in beef, recover and microwave on High for about 16 minutes or until no longer pink. Stir in mushrooms. Cover and microwave on Simmer (50% power) for 20 minutes. Mix in sour cream, cover and continue on Simmer for 4 to 5 minutes or until heated through. Let stand, covered, 5 minutes before serving. Serve with buttered noodles. Yield: 6 to 8 servings.

Miriam Galloway

Microwave food with the thickest portion to the outside of dish. Boney parts, sugar, fats and faster-cooking pieces should be placed towards the center. Arrange food of equal size in a ring, leaving center empty.

BEEF HAWAIIAN

2 tbsp. cooking oil
2¹/2 - 2³/4 lb. boneless beef round
  steak, cut into thin strips
1 tbsp. soy sauce
1 tsp. salt
1/2 tsp. pepper
1/2 cup packed brown sugar

1/4 cup vinegar
3 tbsp. cornstarch
14-oz. can pineapple chunks,
  undrained
1 medium green pepper, cut
  into thin strips
2 tomatoes, cut into wedges

Measure oil into 2-qt. casserole. Microwave on High for 2 to 3 minutes. Stir in beef and cook for about 6 minutes until no longer pink. Stir in soy sauce, salt, pepper, sugar and vinegar. Cover and microwave on Simmer for 20 minutes. Blend cornstarch and pineapple juice and stir into mixture. Mix in pineapple chunks, green pepper and tomatoes. Cover and cook on Simmer for 8 to 10 minutes until hot and meat is fork tender. Let stand, covered, 5 minutes before serving. Yield: 4 to 6 servings.

Miriam Galloway

FLANK STEAK ORIENTAL

1 lb. flank steak
1/3 cup soy sauce
1/3 cup dry white wine **or**
  apple juice
1 tsp. sugar

2 tbsp. cornstarch
1 medium sliced onion
2 cups sliced, fresh mushrooms
1/2 cup sliced green pepper
1 pint cherry tomatoes

Cut steak across grain into thin strips. Place in 2-qt. glass casserole. Combine soy sauce, wine and sugar. Pour over meat. Mix lightly to coat evenly. Allow to marinate 1 to 2 hours. Stir in cornstarch, onion, mushrooms and pepper. Cover and microwave 8 to 10 minutes, until sauce is thickened. Stir halfway through cooking time. Add tomatoes. Microwave covered about 1 minute until tomatoes are heated. Yield: 5 servings.

Readymade Local

ROAST BEEF CHART

Boned and Rolled	Approximate Time	Internal Temperature
Rare	30 min./lb.	140°
Medium	35 min./lb.	160°
Well Done	40 min./lb.	170°
Bone in		
Rare	22-25 min./lb.	140°
Medium	27 min./lb.	160°
Well Done	32 min./lb.	170°

CHOP SUEY

1 lb. beef **or** pork strips
1/2 cup sliced onions
1/2 cup sliced green pepper
1 cup sliced celery
1 tbsp. cornstarch
1 cup water

1 can drained bean sprouts
1 can water chestnuts, sliced
1 can sliced mushrooms
2 tbsp. soya sauce
1/2 tsp. salt

Brown meat in oil over high heat, stirring constantly. Add onion, green pepper and celery and cook for 3 minutes. Mix the cornstarch in the water and add. Cook until it thickens. Add bean sprouts, chestnuts, mushrooms, soya sauce and salt. Cook about 3 minutes until these last vegetables are warmed thoroughly. Serve with fried or steamed rice.

Mrs. Carsin E. Stukart

MAULL'S CHINA GARDEN CHOP

1 lb. lean beef, pork, veal **or**
    chicken, cut in small squares
2 tbsp. cooking oil
3 tbsp. soya sauce
1/4 tsp. salt
1 cup sliced onions
1 cup soup stock
1 can Chinese vegetables

1 - 2 cups carrots, thinly sliced
2 cups edible podded peas **or**
    1 cup shelled peas
1 cup slivered celery (optional)
2 tbsp. butter
3 tbsp. cornstarch
1/2 - 1 cup slivered almonds
Shredded cabbage (optional)

Fry meat in oil. Add 1 tbsp. soya sauce, salt, onions, soup stock, Chinese vegetables, carrots, peas, celery, cabbage and 2 tbsp. soya sauce. Mix well, cover and cook. Mix cornstarch in cold water and add to mixture to thicken. Brown almonds in butter and scatter over top.

Diane Maull

DEVILED VEAL CUTLET

2 lbs. thin veal cutlets
2 tbsp. flour
1 tsp. salt
1 tsp. paprika
1 cup minced onion
2 tbsp. butter **or** margarine

1 bouillon cube
1 cup boiling water
1 tsp. prepared mustard
2 tsp. horseradish
1/2 cup commercial sour cream

Cut cutlets into serving-sized pieces and roll in flour, salt and paprika. Sauté onion and butter in skillet. Set aside. Brown veal pieces well in same skillet. Dissolve bouillon in boiling water and pour over veal. Add sautéed onion, mustard and horseradish. Simmer, covered, for 25 minutes or until tender. Remove meat to serving dish. Gradually stir the sour cream into the gravy and spoon over meat. Serve at once. Yield: 6 servings. 326 calories per serving.

Miss Stefanie Fodchuk

WESTERN STEW

2 lb. top, round **or** chuck beef
Flour
1/4 cup fat
4 cups water
1 bay leaf

1 tsp. salt
Dash of pepper
1 cup celery, chopped
2 - 3 cups sliced carrots
1 onion, chopped

Cut meat into 1-inch cubes and roll in flour. Melt fat in Dutch oven and add meat. Sear thoroughly to retain juices. Add approximately 4 cups water and seasonings. Cover pan and simmer for 11/2 hours or until meat is tender. Add more water if necessary. Add vegetables and cook 1/2 hour longer. Thicken with paste of 1/4 cup flour and 1/4 cup cold water. Stir constantly until mixture thickens. Simmer a few minutes longer. NOTE: Stew tastes much better if it is made the day before. Reheat to boiling and simmer gently a few minutes just before serving.

BARBECUED BEEF PIE

11/2 lbs. ground beef
3/4 cup chopped onion
1/2 cup sliced celery
1/2 cup catsup
2 tsp. salt
1 tsp. paprika
19-oz. can tomatoes

3/4 cup chopped green peppers
1/2 cup pickle relish
1 tbsp. worcestershire sauce
1 - 2 tsp. chili powder
1/4 tsp. pepper
10-oz. pkg corn bread mix

Brown ground beef. Add remaining ingredients except corn bread mix. Simmer 20 minutes. Pour in 9-inch square baking dish. Prepare cornbread mix according to directions. Spoon evenly over meat mixture. Bake at 425° for 15 minutes or until corn bread is golden.

Mrs. Rita Cannard

MEATBALLS

1 egg
1/2 cup milk
1/4 cup bread crumbs
1 lb. ground beef
1/2 cup grated carrot
1/3 cup grated onion
1/2 tsp. salt
1/8 tsp. pepper

Flour
Fat for frying
3 tbsp. drippings
3 tbsp. grated onion
1 can mushroom soup
1 can water
Salt and pepper to taste

Beat egg and milk together, add bread crumbs and stir. Add next five ingredients and blend well. The mixture should be moist and soft. Coat a spoonful at a time in flour, then brown quickly in fat on all sides. Remove to a casserole. Cook 2 tbsp. flour and drippings until brown. Stir in onion. Add soup and water and simmer a few minutes. Season with salt and pepper and pour over the meatballs. Bake at 350° for 30 minutes.

Geneva Miller

BEEF BALL STROGANOFF

2 eggs	1/4 cup cooking oil
1 1/2 cups milk	2 large onions, chopped
3/4 cup fine bread crumbs	1 can sliced mushrooms,
1 tbsp. salt	drain and save liquid
1 tsp. black pepper	2 tbsp. paprika
3 tbsp. parsley (optional)	6 tbsp. flour
3 lbs. ground beef	1 bouillon cube

Beat eggs slightly. Add milk and bread crumbs. Stir and let sit for a few minutes. Add salt, pepper, parsley, ground meat and mix. Melt oil in frying pan. Form meat into small meatballs and fry until golden brown. Remove to side dish and add more oil if needed. Add onion and mushrooms. Cook until light brown. Add paprika and sprinkle with flour. Stir. When slightly brown add liquid from mushrooms. Dissolve bouillon cube in some hot water and add to mushrooms. Stir well and when thickened, add meat balls. Cover and cook for 20 minutes at low heat.

Mrs. Mary L. Properzi

SPEEDY SPAGHETTI & MEATBALLS

1 lb. ground beef	1 cup evaporated milk
1/2 cup fine, dry bread crumbs	2 tbsp. flour
1 1/2 tsp. onion salt	2 tbsp. shortening
1/4 tsp. marjoram	2 10-oz. cans spaghetti sauce
1/4 tsp. pepper	4 cups cooked spaghetti

Mix beef, bread crumbs, seasonings and evaporated milk until well blended. Shape into about 20 small balls. Roll in flour. Melt shortening in frying pan. Brown meat balls on all sides. Pour sauce over meat. Cook over low heat 15 minutes. Serve with spaghetti and parmesan cheese.

MICROWAVE MEAT BALLS

1 1/2 lbs. ground beef	1/4 tsp. pepper
1/2 cup bread crumbs	2 tbsp. cooking oil
1/2 cup chopped onions	2 tbsp. flour
1 egg, beaten	1/4 cup water
1/4 cup milk	1/2 cup red wine
4 tsp. garlic powder	Chopped parsley
1/2 tsp. salt	

Combine ground beef, bread crumbs, onion, egg. milk and seasonings. Shape into small meatballs. Preheat browning pan for 4 minutes on High with oil. Cover and microwave meat balls 3 minutes on High. Turn meatballs and microwave for 3 minutes. Remove meatballs and. Keep warm. Combine flour, water and wine. Cook in browning dish and pan drippings for 3 minutes on High. Return meatballs to sauce. Cover and microwave 5 minutes. Sprinkle with parsley. Serve over noodles.

Mary Wright

MEATBALL CASSEROLE

1 egg plus milk
2 lb. ground beef
1 1/2 cups bread crumbs
1 1/2 tsp. salt

1 tsp. pepper
1/4 cup beef drippings
10-oz. can cream of celery soup
2/3 cup milk

Beat egg and add milk to make 1 cup. Add to beef with 1 1/4 cups bread crumbs, salt and pepper. Mix well. Form into 12 meatballs and roll in remaining crumbs. Melt drippings in skillet. Brown meatballs and place in casserole. Combine soup and 2/3 cup milk and pour into casserole. Cover and bake at 300° for 1 1/2 hours. Yield: 6 servings.

BEEF & RICE KRISPIE CASSEROLE

1 1/2 lbs. ground beef
1 small onion, chopped
1/2 cup celery, chopped
1 can chicken rice soup

1 can cream of celery soup
1 can cream of mushroom soup
5 1/2 cups rice krispies

Combine and brown ground beef, onions and celery. Add soups and simmer. Pour into casserole dish and stir in rice krispies. Bake at 350° for 45 minutes.

Georgina Taylor

MEATLOAF

1 1/2 lb. ground beef
3/4 cup chopped onion
1/2 cup fine bread crumbs
1 egg
1 tsp. prepared mustard

1 tbsp. catsup (optional)
1 cup milk
1 tsp. salt
1/4 tsp. pepper
1/8 tsp. paprika

Mix ingredients together and put in a loaf pan. Spread 2 tbsp. catsup over top. Microwave at Medium-High for 25 to 30 minutes.

Clare Johnston

CHEESY MEATLOAF

1 1/2 lbs. ground beef
1 egg
1 1/4 cups soft bread crumbs
8-oz. can tomato sauce
1 cup shredded cheese
1/2 cup finely-chopped onion

1/4 cup finely-chopped
green pepper
1/2 tsp. dried thyme leaves
or oregano
1/2 tsp. salt
1/4 tsp. pepper

Combine ingredients in a mixing bowl. Blend thoroughly. Spread mixture evenly in a glass loaf dish. Cover with wax paper. Microwave at Power Level 7 for 23 to 29 minutes or until center is no longer pink. Let stand covered for 5 minutes before serving. Yield: 6 servings.

Lena Haywood

DANISH FRICADELLIN

2 lbs. beef and pork mixture, finely ground
2 medium onions, finely chopped
6 tbsp. flour
2 1/2 cups milk
2 eggs, well beaten
2 tsp. salt
1/2 tsp. pepper
1/2 tsp. cloves

Combine all ingredients and mix well. Drop by tablespoonful into hot oil in frying pan. Fry slowly until well-browned on all sides.

SAUCY LITTLE MEAT LOAVES

1 1/2 lbs. ground beef
3/4 cup rolled oats
1 1/2 tsp. salt
1/4 tsp. pepper
1/4 cup chopped onion
1 egg, beaten
3/4 cup milk
1/3 cup catsup
1 tbsp. brown sugar
1 tbsp. mustard

Combine beef, oats, salt, pepper, onion, egg and milk. Top with catsup, sugar and mustard. Bake at 350° for 35 minutes for 6 small loaves, 1 hour for 1 large loaf or 25 minutes for muffin tins.

Georgina Taylor

HAMBURGER LOAF

1 lb. minced beef
1 tsp. salt
1/4 tsp. pepper
2 stalks celery with leaves, cut up
1 can tomato soup
1 cup rolled oats
Pinch of garlic salt
1 onion, minced
1 egg, slightly beaten
1 tbsp. vinegar
1 tbsp. mustard
1 tbsp. water

Mix beef, salt, pepper, celery, tomato soup, rolled oats, garlic salt, onion and egg and press into loaf pan. Mix the vinegar, mustard and water into a paste and spread on top. Bake at 300° for 1 1/2 hours. Serve hot or cold.

Shirley W. Steward

MEAT LOAF

2 lbs. ground beef
1 cup cracker crumbs
1 1/2 tsp. salt
1 tbsp. catsup
1 egg
2 tbsp. chopped onion
1 tsp. dry mustard
1 can mushroom soup

Combine all ingredients except soup. Mix half can of soup with the meat and the other half with equal parts of water and pour over the loaf before baking. Bake at 350° for 1 hour or more.

VEGETABLE MEAT LOAF

2 lb. ground beef	1 tbsp. worcestershire sauce
1 beaten egg	1 can vegetable soup
1/2 cup bread crumbs	1 chopped onion
1 tbsp. prepared mustard	1 tsp. salt

Combine the ingredients and mix thoroughly. Pack into loaf pan and bake at 350° for 1 hour .

BEEF & PORK MEAT LOAF

1 1/2 lb. ground beef	5 slices bread, broken up
1/2 lb. skinless pork sausage	1/4 cup milk
2 eggs	1/2 cup catsup
2 chopped onions	1 tsp. worcestershire sauce
1/4 tsp. celery	1 tsp. salt and pepper, mixed

Combine the ingredients thoroughly and shape into a loaf. Bake at 375° for 2 hours.

Mrs. Ida Schonberner

HAMBURGER CASSEROLE

1 lb. ground beef	1 onion, sliced
Salt and pepper	3 cups sliced potatoes
1/2 cup rice, uncooked	1 can tomatoes

Season ground beef with salt and pepper and place in bottom of 2-qt. casserole. Layer rice, onions and potatoes over meat. Pour can of tomatoes over all. Bake at 350° for 1 1/2 to 2 hours or until done.

Mrs. Rhoda Fossen

HAMBURGER & RICE CASSEROLE

2 lbs. ground beef	19-oz. can tomatoes
1 onion, chopped fine	Salt and pepper
1 cup cooked rice	1 small can tomato juice

Partially cook ground beef. Combine with onion, rice, tomatoes, salt and pepper. Mix well. Add tomato juice and bake at 350° for 1 hour.

Mrs. Lee Herbert

SYLVIA'S HAMBURGER CASSEROLE

1 lb. ground beef	1/2 tsp. sage
1/2 cup chopped onions	1 cup milk
1 tsp. salt	2 eggs
Pepper	1 cup bread crumbs
1/4 tsp. dry mustard	1 can tomato soup

Mix all but soup together and put in casserole dish. Pour the soup over top. Do not stir. Bake at 350° for 1 hour.

Sylvia Haldenby

ONE DISH DINNER

1/4 cup uncooked rice
1 lb. ground beef
3 cups shredded cabbage
1 cup carrots
1 cup peas
1 cup sliced celery

1 medium-sized onion, sliced
1 tbsp. chopped green pepper
Salt and pepper to taste
Dash of chili powder
1 tbsp. gravy mix
1 can tomato soup

Precook rice. Brown ground beef in deep skillet. Add cabbage, carrots, peas, celery, onion, green pepper, rice and enough water to keep mixture moist. Add salt, pepper and chili powder. Cook until vegetables are tender. Add gravy mix and soup shortly before serving. Keep plenty of moisture in skillet. Stir often.

Mrs. Frances A. Chambers

HASTY HAMBURGER MEAL

2 lbs. ground meat
1 tsp. salt
1/4 tsp. pepper
Onion salt **or** garlic powder

1 can vegetable soup **or**
1 can mixed vegetables
Biscuit mix

Brown meat in skillet. Add salt, pepper and onion salt to taste. Add vegetables and enough water to cover meat. Thicken gravy. Put in casserole and top with prepared biscuit mix.

Mrs. Romona Koch

HEKKA

1 lb. ground beef
1 onion
Salt and pepper, to taste
2 - 3 carrots, cut in strips

4 - 5 celery stocks, cut in strips
1/2 cup shredded cabbage
1/2 cup **or** less soya sauce
1/4 cup water

Brown ground beef and onion. Add salt and pepper. Add carrots, celery, cabbage and soya sauce. Add water to vegetables. Cover, stirring often and cook 20 minutes. Do not overcook.

Mrs. M. Rains

CHINESE AMERICANA

1 - 2 onions, chopped
1 cup chopped celery
1 tbsp. oil
1 lb. ground beef
1 can cream of mushroom soup

1/8 cup soya sauce
1 can chicken noodle soup
2 cups water
1/2 cup uncooked rice

Cook onion and celery in oil until light brown. Cook meat until brown and crumbly. Blend in remaining ingredients. Put into large casserole. Cook at 350° for 1 1/2 hours with cover on, removing cover for the last 1/2 hour.

Mrs. Geraldine Shadlock

HONG KONG HAMBURGER

Bread slices	2 tbsp. cornstarch
1 lb. ground beef	1/3 cup brown sugar
1 egg, beaten	1 tbsp. soya sauce
1/2 tsp. salt	1 tbsp. worcestershire sauce
Dash pepper	3 tbsp. vinegar
1/3 cup pineapple syrup	Pineapple slices

Spread bread on cookie sheet. Combine ground beef, egg, salt and pepper. Spread over bread. Broil until done. Combine pineapple syrup with cornstarch and brown sugar. Add soya sauce, worcestershire sauce and vinegar. Cook and stir mixture until it boils and thickens. Spread half of mixture over broiled meat. Top with pineapple slices and remainder of glaze. Return to broiler for 2 to 3 minutes to brown slightly. NOTE: If you use a thick layer of meat, it is advisable to cook it a bit before broiling so you do not have raw meat on the bottom.

ORIENTAL BEEF CASSEROLE

1 lb. ground beef	1/4 cup light cream **or** milk
1 tbsp. cooking oil	1 can cream of celery soup
1 small green pepper, slivered (optional)	1 tbsp. soya sauce
	1/4 tsp. pepper
2 cups thinly-sliced celery	1/2 cup fine bread crumbs
3 green onions, sliced	1 tbsp. melted butter
10-oz. can mushrooms, drained and sliced	1/2 cup slivered almonds

Brown beef in oil. Place in well-buttered 1 1/2-qt. casserole and top with green pepper, celery, onion and mushrooms. Combine cream, soup, soya sauce and pepper and pour over. Combine crumbs, butter and almonds and sprinkle over all. Bake at 375° for 35 to 40 minutes.

Mrs. Bertha Webber
Mable Hall

CHILI-CON-CARNE

1 1/2 lbs. lean ground beef	1 can mushrooms
2 tbsp. vegetable oil	1 tsp. worcestershire sauce
1/2 cup chopped onions	2 tbsp. vinegar
1/2 cup chopped celery	2 tbsp. brown sugar
1/3 cup chopped green pepper	Salt and pepper to taste
1 can tomatoes	2 bay leaves
2 cans red kidney beans	Chili powder to taste
2 cans pork and beans	

Brown meat in oil and add onions, celery and peppers. Mix well. Add remaining ingredients and bring to a boil. Simmer for 30 to 45 minutes. This freezes well.

Mrs. Evelyn Davey

MEXICAN SHORTCAKE

1 lb. ground beef	1 cup milk
1 cup flour	1/4 cup soft margarine
4 tsp. baking powder	10-oz. can cream corn
1 cup corn meal	1/4 tsp. pepper
1/2 tsp. salt	1 onion, sliced **or** chopped
1/4 cup sugar	1/2 lb. cheese, sliced **or** grated
1 egg	

Brown meat and drain off fat. Salt lightly and set aside. Sift flour, baking powder, cornmeal and salt together. Add sugar, egg, milk and margarine. Beat until smooth. Stir in corn and pepper. Pour half of batter into ovenproof greased skillet. Add meat and top with layer of sliced onion, then a layer of grated cheese. Cover with remaining batter. Bake at 350° for 45 minutes. Yield: 5 to 7 servings. NOTE: This recipe can be doubled but use a 14-oz. can of corn.

Maisie Jacobson

STUFFED HAMBURGER ROLL

1/4 cup chopped onions	1/2 tsp. salt
1/3 cup water	1/4 tsp. sage
2 1/2 cups bread cubes	Dash of pepper
1 1/2 lb. ground beef	1 cup sharp process cheese,
1 egg	shredded

Combine onions and water and simmer 5 minutes. Add toasted bread cubes and toss. Combine meat, egg and seasoning. On waxed paper, pat meat into 14 x 8 inch rectangle. Spread bread mixture over. Sprinkle with 3/4 cup of the cheese. Roll meat mixture. Place seam side down in 8 1/2 x 4 1/2 x 2 1/2-inch loaf dish. Bake uncovered at 350° for 70 minutes. Top with remaining cheese. Bake until melted. Yield: 6 servings.

SUPPER MEAT PIE

2 cups flour	2 tbsp. minced parsley
3/4 tsp. salt	1 clove minced garlic
2/3 cup shortening	1 1/2 tsp. salt
4 - 6 tbsp. cold water	1/4 tsp. pepper
1 1/2 lbs. ground round, chuck	2 tbsp. salad oil
or cooked roast beef	10-oz. can tomato soup
4 tbsp. minced onion	

Combine first 4 ingredients for crust. Set aside. Combine remaining ingredients except soup and brown in oil in frying pan. Add tomato soup. Roll out dough for a 2-crust pie. Add filling and bake at 350° until crust is golden.

Mrs. Emily Bibby

SHEPHERD'S PIE

1/2 cup chopped onion	2 cups cut-up beef
3 tbsp. margarine	10-oz. pkg. frozen peas and
3 tbsp. flour	carrots, thawed
1/2 tbsp. parsley	2 cups hot mashed potatoes
1 1/2 cup beef broth	Paprika

In 2-qt. casserole, microwave onion and butter for 2 to 2 1/2 minutes on High or until onion is tender. Stir in flour and parsley. Gradually add broth. Heat 2 to 3 minutes until gravy is thickened, stirring once. Stir in beef, peas and carrots. Heat 7 1/2 to 8 1/2 minutes on Medium-High or until heated through, stirring once. Spoon potatoes on top of casserole and sprinkle with paprika. Heat, if necessary, 2 to 3 minutes.

Barbara Ziebler

HAMBURGER CUPCAKES

16 - 18 slices of bread	1/4 cup chopped onion
Butter	1 egg, beaten
1 lb. lean ground beef	1/2 cup bread crumbs
1 cup mushroom soup	Salt and pepper

Trim crusts off bread. Butter one side and place buttered side down in muffin pans and shape. Combine remaining ingredients and fill bread. Bake at 350° for 40 minutes. These freeze well and can be warmed in the microwave.

BEEF CASSEROLE

1 cup uncooked rice	1 cup chopped onions
1 lb. ground beef, browned	1 can sliced mushrooms
1 tsp. salt	1 large can tomatoes
1/2 tsp. pepper	1 can cream of mushroom soup

Place rice, beef, salt, pepper, onions in a casserole dish. Drain mushrooms, reserve liquid and add mushrooms. Combine tomatoes, mushroom juice and soup. Pour over, cover and bake at 325° for 2 hours.

Ruby Prior

POOR MAN'S STROGANOFF

1 lb. ground beef	1/2 tsp. instant beef bouillon,
1 small onion, chopped	beef **or** onion in a mug
10 3/4-oz. mushroom soup	1 cup sour cream **or** sour
1 can mushrooms with juice	light cream

Crumble beef into 1 1/2-qt. casserole. Add onion. Microwave uncovered for 6 minutes, stirring once. Drain off fat. Add remaining ingredients, stirring well. Cover. Microwave 7 to 8 minutes until heated through. Serve over noodles or rice. Yield: 4 to 5 servings.

SUPPER ON SLICE OF BREAD

1 1/2 lb. ground beef
2/3 cup evaporated milk
1/2 cup bread **or** cracker crumbs
1 beaten egg
1/2 cup chopped onion
1 tbsp. prepared mustard

1 1/2 tsp. salt
1/2 tsp. pepper
2 cups grated process cheese
Loaf of French bread, cut
   in half lengthwise

Combine ingredients and spread evenly on each half of bread. Wrap in tin foil around crust side of each half. Leave top uncovered. Place on cookie sheet and bake at 350° for 25 minutes. Garnish with strips of cheese. Bake 5 minutes more. Cut slices across and serve hot.

Mrs. Peter Kellar

TOMATO-CHEESEBURGER PIE

1 cup flour
1/2 tsp. salt
2 tbsp. lard
3 tbsp. butter
3 tbsp. milk
1 lb. lean ground beef
3/4 cup chopped onion
4 eggs, slightly beaten

1/2 cup milk
1 cup shredded cheese
1 tsp. salt
1 tsp. oregano
1 tsp. pepper
8-oz. can pizza sauce **or**
   tomato soup
6 triangles cheddar cheese

Make a crust with the flour, salt, lard, butter and milk and place in a 9-inch pie shell. Bake at 400° for 10 to 15 minutes. Brown meat with onion and pour off excess fat. Add remaining ingredients and put in the baked shell. Bake at 325° for 40 to 45 minutes. Take out and spread with pizza sauce and cheese triangles. Return to oven for another 10 minutes. Yield: 6 servings.

Mrs. Jean Stanley

CABBAGE ROLL CASSEROLE

1 lb. ground beef
1 onion, chopped
10-oz. can tomato soup
3 tbsp. rice
1 tsp. salt
Pepper

Garlic powder to taste
1 cup water
3 cups coarse, shredded
   cabbage
Grated cheese **or** cheese
   slices

Crumble ground beef into cold casserole. Cover and microwave 4 minutes on High. Stir to break up the meat. Add the onion. Cook 2 minutes on High. Drain excess fat. Add soup, rice, seasonings and 1/2 cup water. Line 2-qt. casserole with cabbage. Pour meat mixture over the cabbage. Pour remaining water on top. Microwave for 5 minutes on High. Microwave for 25 minutes on Medium. Top with cheese during last minute. To prevent ground beef from sticking, start with a cold pan.

Spring Valley Local

SLOPPY JOES

1 1/2 - 2 lbs. lean ground beef	Small can tomato paste
1 small onion, diced	1 1/4 cups water
1 small green pepper, diced	1 cup grated cheddar cheese
1 pkg. sloppy joe mix	(optional)

In large casserole, mix beef, onion and green pepper. Microwave on High for 7 to 9 minutes, stirring once after 4 minutes. Drain well. Add sloppy joe mix, tomato paste and water. Microwave on High for an additional 5 to 7 minutes. Add cheese if desired and serve on buns.

Nettie Connolley

WITCHES BREW

1 lb. ground beef	1 tsp. pepper
1 medium onion, chopped	1/2 tsp. oregano
3 stalks celery, chopped	14-oz. can red kidney beans
1 tsp. salt	14-oz. can spaghetti sauce

Brown beef, onion and celery in frying pan. Add salt, pepper, oregano, kidney beans and spaghetti sauce. Simmer 1/2 hour. Serve with potatoes, noodles or rice. Yield: 4 to 6 servings.

Lydia Goosen

SAVORY HASH

1 cup onion, chopped coarsely	1 1/2 tsp. salt
1 cup celery, chopped coarsely	1/4 tsp. pepper
1 cup green pepper,	1/2 tsp. oregano
chopped coarsely	3/4 cup raw rice
1/4 cup cooking oil	2 cups tomatoes
1 1/2 lbs. lean ground beef	Garlic powder to taste

Sauté onion, celery and green pepper in cooking oil. Remove and cook ground beef until no longer pink. Add salt, pepper, oregano, rice and tomatoes. Sprinkle with garlic powder. Add sautéed vegetables and bake covered at 325° for 1 hour. Stir occasionally. Dumplings may be dropped on top of meat during last portion of cooking period.

Mrs. Mary E. Hoke

MOO BURGERS

1 1/2 lbs. ground beef	1 tbsp. chopped onion
1 cup sour cream	1 1/2 tsp. salt
1/4 cup worcestershire sauce	1 1/2 cups cornflakes

Combine ground beef, sour cream, worcestershire sauce, onion and salt. Crush cornflakes and stir into meat mixture. Shape into patties about 3/4-inch thick. Barbecue in wire toaster over slow coals for 5 minutes. Turn. Cook 3 to 4 minutes more or until done. Yield: 8 burgers.

CHILI BURGERS

1 cup evaporated milk	1 tsp. dry mustard
1 egg	1/4 cup finely-chopped onion
11/2 lb. ground beef	1/4 cup chili sauce **or** catsup
1/2 cup fine cracker crumbs	1 tsp. prepared mustard
1 tsp. salt	1 tsp. chili powder
1/4 tsp. pepper	

Thoroughly combine first 8 ingredients and form into 8 patties. Mix chili sauce, mustard and chili powder. Place meat patties on grill or on folding wire broiler. Cook over glowing coals 4 to 5 minutes on each side or until done as desired, brushing several times with chili mixture.

POCKET GOLD BURGERS

Ground beef	1 tbsp. pickle relish
1 tbsp. shredded cheese	1 tbsp. melted margarine

Roll out thin patties of ground beef between sheets of wax paper to a little over 1/4-inch thick. In center of half the patties, place 1 tbsp. shredded cheese and pickle relish. Top with meat lids. Press around edge to seal. Brush with melted margarine. Barbecue, turning once. Season with salt and pepper.

HAMBURGERS WITH SWEET & SOUR SAUCE

2/3 cup evaporated milk	Pineapple syrup and water
11/2 lb. ground beef	1/4 cup vinegar
2/3 cup cracker crumbs	2 tbsp. cornstarch
1 tsp. salt	1/4 cup brown sugar
15-oz. can pineapple chunks	2 tbsp. soya sauce

Combine milk, beef, crumbs and salt and form into four 4-inch patties. Brown patties in small amount of fat. Drain pineapples and add enough water to syrup to make 1 cup of liquid. In saucepan, mix syrup mixture with other ingredients. Cook, stirring until thick and clear. Pour excess fat off burgers. Cover with sauce and pineapple chunks. Cover and simmer over low heat for 5 minutes.

Mrs. Carol Stinson
Mrs. Faye Knitel
Mabel Gaetz

DISAPPEARING CASSEROLES: Line dish with aluminum foil, leaving enough to extend from top of dish to fold over to top after cooking. When food is frozen, remove from casserole and fold aluminum foil securely over top. Label and store. To defrost, remove from freezer about 1 hour before time to bake. Remove foil and place in original casserole. Bake at 350° for 1 to 11/4 hours, or remove foil, place in original casserole and defrost 8 hours in refrigerator. Heat until bubbling.

FORTIFIED BEEF BURGERS

1 lb. lean chopped beef	2 tbsp. chopped onions
2 tbsp. wheat germ	2 tbsp. chopped parsley
1/4 cup water	1 tbsp. chopped celery
13/4 tbsp. non-fat dry milk	

Mix all ingredients and make into 4 flat patties. Cover bottom of heavy skillet with 1/2 tsp. oil. Brown patties quickly on both sides. Beefburgers may also be broiled on a slightly-greased rack, but make patties 3/4-inch thick for broiling.

GERMAN BEEF BURGERS

1 cup grated raw carrots	1/2 cup chopped celery
1 cup grated whole potatoes	1 beaten egg
2 tbsp. chopped onion	1/4 cup milk
2 tbsp. chopped parsley	1/4 cup wheat germ
1 lb. ground lean beef	2 tsp. vegetable salt

Mix all ingredients together, form into patties and place on lightly-oiled shallow pan. Bake at 400° for 20 minutes.

GLAZED PORK LOIN

4 lb. pork loin roast	1/2 cup water
1/3 cup brown sugar	1/2 tsp. whole cloves
1/3 cup molasses	1/4 tsp. cinnamon
1/4 cup vinegar	2 cups cranberries

Place loin roast fat side up on rack in roasting pan. Season with salt and pepper. Roast uncovered 40 to 45 minutes per pound at 325°. To make glaze, combine sugar, molasses, vinegar, water and spices. Bring to boil, add cranberries and simmer 15 minutes. To make a smooth glaze, press mixture through sieve or blender and pour over roast. Bake at 425° for about 15 minutes, basting occasionally.

PORK CHOPS MILANAISE

6 pork chops,1-inch thick	2 tbsp. water
1/4 cup flour	1/2 cup dry bread crumbs
1 tsp. salt	1/3 cup grated
1/4 tsp. pepper	parmesan cheese
1 egg, slightly beaten	1/4 cup fat

Snip fat edge of chops and dip in flour seasoned with salt and pepper, then in combined egg and water and finally in crumbs mixed with cheese. Brown in fat 1 to 2 minutes each side. Arrange in baking dish and bake uncovered at 325° for 30 to 40 minutes until tender. Serve with spaghetti and tomato sauce. Yield: 6 servings.

PORK CHOPS SUPREME

1 cup hot catsup	6 pork chops, 1/2-inch thick
6 tbsp. honey	1 large lemon, sliced

Blend catsup and honey. Pour over each pork chop. Top each chop with slice of fresh lemon. Bake uncovered at 325° for 1 hour or until done. This same honey sauce is delicious over chicken pieces.

COATING FOR PORK CHOPS

Pork chops	1 cup flour
2 eggs	1 tsp. salt
1 tbsp. vegetable oil	1/4 tsp. pepper
2 tbsp. milk	2 tsp. season salt
2 cups dry bread **or**	2 tbsp. celery salt
cracker crumbs	

Pound pork chops with tenderizing hammer. Mix liquid ingredients and beat well with a fork. Mix all dry ingredients in separate bowl. Dip and coat each pork chop thoroughly in liquid and then the dry mixture. Fry until brown on both sides. This method may also be used for chicken or fish.

Mrs. Jean Leskow

GOURMET PORK CHOPS

10 - 12 pork chops	Salt and pepper to taste
1 tbsp. chopped onion	10-oz. can cream of
Dash garlic salt **or**	mushroom soup
1 clove garlic, chopped	1 qt. canned apricots

Fry pork chops and set side by side in baking dish. Drain off excess fat from frying pan and add onion, garlic salt, salt and pepper, frying lightly. Add soup, stirring constantly over low heat. Drain apricots and add juice, mixing well. Boil 1 minute and remove from heat. Arrange apricot halves over meat. Pour sauce over and keep warm until ready to serve.

PORK CHOP SUPPER DISH

6 lean pork chops, browned	1/2 tsp. pepper
6 potatoes, thinly sliced	10-oz. can mushroom soup
3 green onions, thinly sliced	1/2 cup milk
2 tsp. salt	

Arrange chops in bottom of baking dish. Add the potatoes and green onions. Combine the salt, pepper, mushroom soup and milk. Pour this mixture over chops. Bake at 350° for 1 hour. Yield: 6 servings.

Cover whole or quartered ham with cold water and soak 2 to 3 hours before baking. This draws the excess salt out and produces a more tender ham.

COSMOPOLITAN STEW

2 lbs. fresh pork butt
3 qts. water
1 tsp. salt
1 tsp. pepper
1 tbsp. worcestershire sauce

1 tbsp. hot chili sauce
1 tsp. ginger
Garlic to taste
1/2 cup green pepper
1/2 cup celery

Defat the pork and cut into cubes. Boil it in the water. Add salt, pepper, worcestershire sauce, hot chili sauce, ginger and garlic. Bring the green peppers and celery to boil in some of the broth. Pour into meat when meat is almost done. Continue to cook until almost dry. Stir often. Serve with a combination of buttered noodles and finely-sliced green onions.

Pearl Hodgson

PORK HOCKS WITH SAUERKRAUT

6 pork hocks
8 cups hot water
1/2 cup chopped onion
1 tbsp. salt

1/4 tsp. pepper
1/4 tsp. sage
3 whole cloves
28-oz. can sauerkraut, drained

Cover pork hocks with water. Add onion and seasonings. Cover and simmer approximately 2 hours until tender. Skim off fat and strain cooking liquid. Add 1 cup cooking liquid and sauerkraut to pork hocks and simmer 10 minutes. Yield: 6 servings.

GLAZED SPARE RIBS

5 lbs. spareribs
Salt and pepper
1 1/2 cups honey
5 cloves garlic, cut fine

1 1/2 cups tomato catsup
1/2 cup soya sauce
1 tsp. tabasco

Rub spare ribs with seasoned salt and pepper. Bake covered at 325° for 1 hour. Mix honey, garlic, catsup, soya sauce and tabasco to make glaze. Brush on both sides of spareribs. Bake uncovered for 3 to 4 minutes. NOTE: Put on lots of glaze.

SPICEY BARBECUED SPARERIBS

1/2 cup catsup
1 cup water
1 1/2 tsp. salt
1/4 tsp. worcestershire sauce
1/2 tsp. chili powder

1/2 tsp. dry mustard
1/4 cup brown sugar
Spareribs
Onions, sliced

Mix all ingredients but spareribs and onions together. Place a layer of spareribs in the bottom of a deep baking dish. Cover with a layer of onions, then pour on some of the sauce. Repeat the three layers. Cover tightly and bake at 325° for 2 hours, uncovering during the last half hour. VARIATION: Substitute pork steaks and bake 1 1/2 hours.

BARBECUED SPARERIBS

3 lbs. spareribs
1 tsp. salt
1/4 tsp. pepper
1 tbsp. butter
1/4 cup onion, chopped
8-oz. can tomato sauce
1 tbsp. vinegar
1 tbsp. lemon juice

2 tbsp. brown sugar
1 tsp. salt
1 tsp. dry mustard
1/2 tsp. tabasco sauce
1 bay leaf
1 garlic clove
1/2 cup water

Place ribs in a shallow pan and sprinkle first with salt and pepper. Bake uncovered at 350° for 45 minutes. Combine butter and remaining ingredients. Bring to a boil and simmer for 5 minutes. Spoon half the sauce over ribs and bake one hour longer. Baste twice with the remaining sauce. Time: 1 hr. 45 minutes. Yield: 4 generous servings.

SPARERIBS A LA PAYSANNE

3 lbs. back spareribs
1/2 cup chopped onion
1/2 cup chopped celery
1/4 cup butter
4 cups toasted bread cubes
2 cups diced peeled apples

2 tbsp. chopped pasrley
1/2 tsp. salt
1/8 tsp. pepper
1/2 tsp. sage
2 tbsp. brown sugar

Place one piece sparerib, hollow side up, on rack in shallow roasting pan. Sauté onion and celery in fat until onion is transparent. Mix remaining ingredients, add sautéed vegetables and toss together lightly. Fill hollow in ribs with stuffing and cover with second piece of ribs, hollow side down. Tie ribs together and sprinkle with additional salt and pepper. Cover and bake at 350° about 1 1/2 hours, until almost tender. Uncover and continue baking about 40 minutes, until tender and crisp. Yield: 4 to 6 servings.

SWEET & SOURS

2 lbs. spareribs, cut small
1 small onion
1 tbsp. fat **or** cooking oil
1 tsp. salt
3/4 tsp. pepper

1/2 cup water
3/4 cup brown sugar
1/4 cup catsup
1/4 cup vinegar
3 tbsp. soya sauce

Brown spareribs and onions in fat. Add salt, pepper and water. Cover saucepan and simmer 1 hour. Combine sugar, catsup, vinegar and simmer for 5 minutes. Add soya sauce and add to spareribs. Simmer for 20 to 30 minutes. Pineapple chunks may be added. Serve with rice. Yield: 4 servings.

SPARERIBS WITH APPLE AND SQUASH

4 lbs. spareribs, cut in rib portions	3 tbsp. brown sugar
Salt and pepper	11/2 tsp. cinnamon
2 tbsp. butter **or** margarine	2 tbsp. cornstarch
1/2 cup minced onion	2 acorn squash, peeled
3 cups apple juice	4 large apples
1/2 cup cider vinegar	

In a large, shallow roasting pan, place ribs meaty side up. Sprinkle with salt and pepper and bake at 400° for 45 minutes until brown. In a saucepan, cook onions in hot butter until golden. Stir in 23/4 cups apple juice, vinegar, brown sugar, cinnamon and salt. Heat to boiling point. Combine cornstarch with remaining apple juice and thicken hot liquid with it. When ribs are browned, reduce oven heat to 350°. Drain fat from pan, then pour apple juice mixture over the ribs and bake about one hour. Cut squash in wedges and apples in half, discarding cores and seeds. Add to the ribs, spooning liquid over them. Cover and bake for another hour or until all is tender.

Emma Innocent

CHINESE SPARERIBS

2 lbs. spareribs	1/2 cup vinegar
11/2 tsp. salt	3/4 cup cold water
2 tbsp. shortening **or** cooking oil	1 can pineapple chunks, drain and reserve liquid
2 tbsp. gravy thickener	1 onion, thinly sliced
2 tbsp. cornstarch	1/2 green pepper
3 tbsp. brown sugar	1 cup sliced celery
1 tbsp. soya sauce	

Cut ribs into single pieces and put in a saucepan. Add salt and cover with boiling water, simmer covered about 1 hour, until pork is almost tender. Drain thoroughly. Heat shortening or cooking oil, add cooked spareribs and brown on all sides. Combine gravy thickener, cornstarch, brown sugar, soya sauce, vinegar, cold water and pineapple juice. Pour over spareribs. Cook, stirring until sauce comes to a boil. Add onions, green pepper cut into thin strips, celery and pineapple. Cover and simmer about 10 minutes. Yield: 4 to 6 servings.

Since it is fast and simple to microwave each food separately, and since food retains heat very well, a meal is usually microwaved in the following sequence: 1) warm or cool dessert, 2) meat dish, 3) slower cooking vegetables such as baked potatoes, 4) faster cooking vegetables, and 5) hot dessert can be microwaved during main course.

ISLAND SPARERIBS

1/2 cup soya sauce
1/2 cup catsup
3 tbsp. brown sugar
2 tsp. dry ginger

1 tsp. monosodium glutamate
1 tsp. salt
1/4 cup sugar
4 lbs. spareribs

Mix soya sauce, catsup, brown sugar, ginger and monosodium glutamate together and let stand overnight in refrigerator. Rub spareribs on both sides with the mixture of salt and white sugar. Let stand about 2 hours. Brush with the chilled sauce and let stand at least another hour. Grill well on both sides, brushing well with sauce. Yield: 8 or 9 servings.

HAM STEAKS CANADIENNE

12 whole cloves
2 ham steaks, 1/2- inch thick
3/4 cup brown sugar
2 tbsp. flour
2 tsp. dry mustard

3 tbsp. vinegar
1/2 cup apple juice
3 apples, cored and peeled
Tart red jelly

Press cloves into fat side of each steak and snip fat between cloves. Mix dry ingredients and blend in vinegar and apple juice. Cut 6 apple rings 1/4-inch thick to garnish top. Slice remaining apples thinly. Place one steak in greased baking dish, cover with sliced apples and pour 1/4 cup apple juice mixture over them. Place second steak over apples and garnish top with apple rings. Cover and bake at 325° for 30 minutes. Remove cover and pour remaining apple juice mixture over steaks. Continue baking uncovered about 30 minutes, basting occasionally. Place 1 tsp. of tart red jelly in center of each apple ring before serving. Yield: 6 servings.

HAM IN PINEAPPLE ASPIC

11/2 lbs. canned ham
1 envelope unflavored gelatin
2 tbsp. granulated sugar

1 cup pineapple juice
1 tbsp. lemon juice
2 drops yellow food coloring

Have canned ham at room temperature. Remove bottom of can with ordinary can opener. Do not use the key. Remove ham and drain juices. Wash, dry and lightly grease can on both sides and top, which now becomes the bottom. Trim sides of ham so that it is slightly smaller and put back in can. Combine gelatin and sugar in saucepan, add pineapple and lemon juices. Heat until gelatin dissolves, stirring constantly. Stir in food coloring. Pour over ham and chill in can until firmly set. To unmould, loosen around edges with knife. Remove bottom with can opener and push ham out of container.

SOUPER SUPPER

1 can cream of mushroom soup	1 1/2 cups cooked broccoli
1 soup can water	4 cheese slices
1 soup can rice	1 1/2 cups cooked ham

Combine first 3 ingredients in casserole and mix together. Cut up remaining ingredients and add. Cover and bake at 350° for 30 minutes. Yield: 6 servings.

Nettie Connolley

HAM BAKED IN MILK

Slice of ham, 1- inch thick	2 tbsp. brown sugar
1/2 tsp. cloves	Milk to cover

Mix sugar and cloves and rub well into both sides of ham. Let stand several hours. Cut into serving-sized pieces, place in a casserole, cover with milk and bake at 350° for 1 hour.

HAM SURPRISE

6 slices boiled ham	1/4 tsp. dry mustard
2 tbsp. butter	Salt, pepper and paprika
1 tbsp. vinegar	

Brown ham in butter. Remove from pan. Blend remaining ingredients for sauce, stir and cook 2 minutes. Pour over ham slices. Serve at once.

CORN-HAM SHORTCAKE

1/4 cup chopped onion	1/4 tsp. salt
2 tbsp. margarine	Pepper
1 can cream corn	1 cup diced ham
1/2 cup milk **or** cream	1/3 cup sliced ripe olives

Cook onion in margarine. Add corn, milk and seasoning. Add ham and olives. Heat thoroughly. Serve over cornmeal cake. Yield: 6 servings.

Mrs. Elwyn A. Grobe

HAM PATTIES

2 cups ground ham	1 tsp. prepared mustard
1 cup cold mashed potatoes	Salt to taste
2 eggs, beaten	Bread crumbs **or** cereal crumbs
1/4 tsp. sweet basil	

Put leftover ham through a grinder, using a medium blade. Combine all but crumbs and shape into patties. Roll in crumbs and fry.

Honey enhances the flavor of many foods such as pork and poultry and sweetens fruit without masking the fresh flavor.

TOURTIERE (PORK PIE)

1 small onion, chopped	2 tbsp. chopped celery and
3 lbs. minced pork	parsley leaves
2 tsp. salt	Pinch of cloves
1/2 garlic crushed **or** garlic salt	2 cups meat stock **or** water

Cook onion until tender. Add meat and remaining ingredients. Cook slowly over low heat for 30 minutes, stirring occasionally. When cooked, let cool at least 35 minutes. Prepare pastry, same as for pie. Roll out pastry to line 9-inch pie plate. Fill it with meat mixture. Top with another crust. Bake at 425° for 15 minutes, reduce heat to 375° and continue baking for 25 minutes. NOTE: Frozen unbaked tourtiere turns out deliciously crisp and piping hot if baked at 400° for 25 minutes, then reduced to 350° for 40 minutes. VARIATION: Use half minced pork and half minced veal.

CRETONS

3 lbs. fresh ground pork	1/2 tsp. cinnamon
1 medium onion, chopped fine	1/2 tsp. nutmeg
2 cups water	1/2 tsp. cloves
1 tsp. salt	

Place ground pork, onion, water and salt in saucepan. Let simmer gently about 1 1/2 hours. Add cinnamon, nutmeg and cloves. Simmer about 5 minutes until spices are well blended. Pour into moulds and let cool overnight. Serve cold with fresh homemade bread.

SWEET & SOUR PORK BALLS

1 1/2 lbs. minced lean pork	1/4 tsp. ground ginger
1/2 cup finely chopped onion	1 egg, beaten
1 tsp. salt	2 tbsp. cooking oil
1/8 tsp. pepper	

Mix pork, onion, seasoning and egg. Form into balls about 1 1/2-inch in diameter. Fry in hot oil until brown on all sides. Remove and drain.

1/2 cup chopped onion	1 tbsp. soya sauce
1 cup sliced celery	1 cup chicken bouillon
2 tbsp. cornstarch	10-oz. can peaches, drain and
1/4 tsp. ginger	reserve 1/2 cup syrup
2 tbsp. sugar	1/4 cup vinegar

Drain all but 1 tbsp. of fat from pan. Add onion and celery and sauté about 2 minutes until onion is transparent. Combine remaining ingredients except peaches. Add to pan and stir about 2 minutes until thickened and clear. Add meat balls and peaches. Cover and simmer gently 10 minutes. Serve with rice or noodles. Yield: 6 servings.

Harriet Flaade

DANISH MEAT BALLS

1 lb. ground pork	2 tsp. salt
3/4 cup flour	Small onion, chopped
1 egg	3/4 cup milk
1 tsp. pepper	

Combine the ingredients and mix well. Form into balls and fry for about 5 minutes on each side.

Irene Skaaning

CABBAGE ROLLS

1/2 cup onion, chopped	2 lbs. lean ground pork
4 tbsp. butter	2 heads cabbage
2 tbsp. catsup	1/2 large can sauerkraut
Salt and pepper	1 small can tomato soup
Seasoning salt to taste	2 cups tomato juice
1 1/2 cups rice, cooked	

Fry onion in butter until soft. Add catsup, salt, pepper and seasoning salt. Add rice and pork. Mix well. Blanche cabbage heads, removing hard core in each leaf. Drain. Roll 1 tbsp. of meat and rice mixture in each leaf. Arrange some of the sauerkraut and some cabbage leaves on bottom of dish, add rolls, more sauerkraut and cabbage. Pour soup and juice over rolls. Bake in slow oven 2 to 3 hours until done. These can also be simmered on top of stove until done. Yield: 26 rolls.

Mrs. J. Androkovich

CHEESE AND SAUSAGE PIE

1/2 lb. sausages, cut up	2 eggs, slightly beaten
1 medium onion, diced	3/4 cup milk
1 tbsp. butter	2 cups grated sharp cheddar
6-oz. can tomato paste	cheese
1/8 tsp. oregano	

Fry sausages and onion in butter. Drain off fat and spread mixture into bottom of 9-inch unbaked pastry shell. Spread with tomato paste and sprinkle with oregano. Combine eggs, milk and cheese. Pour into shell. Bake in hot oven at 425° for 10 minutes, then reduce heat to 350° and bake 35 minutes longer, or until set. Yield: 4 to 6 servings.

SAUSAGE CASSEROLE

1 lb. sausage	1/4 cup chopped green pepper
2 cups cooked lima beans **or**	1 cup tomato sauce
small onions	1/2 cup shredded cheese

Brown sausage and place in casserole with lima beans and green pepper. Pour sauce over this mixture and sprinkle with cheese. Bake at 350° for 25 minutes.

SAUSAGE SUPPER SQUARES

11/2 lb. link sausage	12-oz. can kernel corn
13/4 cups sifted flour	Milk
11/2 tbsp. sugar	1/2 cup all bran cereal
4 tsp. baking powder	3 eggs
1 tsp. salt	

Cook sausage slowly in frying pan until thoroughly done and well browned. Drain well, reserving 1/4 cup drippings. Sift the flour, sugar, baking powder and salt together. Set aside. Drain corn, reserving liquid. Add milk to liquid to measure 11/2 cups. Combine milk mixture, drippings, bran, corn and eggs and beat well. Add sifted dry ingredients and continue beating until smooth. Pour into greased 151/2 x 101/2-inch baking pan. Place browned sausage links in batter, arranging in uniform pattern. Bake at 450° for 20 minutes. Cut into squares. Serve with hot syrup or hot seasoned cream sauce.

Mrs. Helen Krahn

RICE AND SAUSAGE CASSEROLE

1/2 cup cracked wheat cereal	2 tsp. sugar
11/2 lb. sausage meat **or**	2 tsp. salt
lean hamburger	1/4 tsp. pepper
Flour	1/2 tsp. worcestershire sauce
2 cups cooked tomatoes	1 tsp. chili powder
1/4 cup catsup	1 cup uncooked rice
1 onion, chopped fine	11/2 cups water

Combine cereal and meat. Make into patties, roll in flour and brown in small amount of fat. Drain off excess fat. In separate bowl, combine tomatoes, catsup, onion, sugar, salt, pepper, worcestershire sauce and chili powder. Spread rice in well-greased baking dish. Arrange meat patties and cover with tomato mixture. Add water and cover tightly. Bake at 375° for 11/4 hours or until rice is tender.

Mrs. T. Marchand

SNAPPERONI FRANKS

6 frankfurters	1/4 cup catsup
12-oz. can pork and beans	2 tbsp. sweet pickle relish
1/2 cup diced pepperoni	6 frankfurter buns

Heat frankfurters. Mash beans slightly with fork in saucepan. Blend in pepperoni, catsup and relish. Cook and stir until mixture is heated thoroughly. Place franks on buns which have been split and toasted. Spoon pepperoni and bean mixture over franks. Yield: 6 sandwiches.

BOLOGNA CUPS WITH SPANISH RICE

8 slices bulk bologna
3 tbsp. shortening
2 tbsp. chopped onion
2 tbsp. diced celery
2 tbsp. flour

1 1/2 cups tomato juice
1/2 tsp. salt
1/4 tsp. pepper
2 1/2 cups cooked rice
Grated cheese

Broil or parboil bologna slices. Do not remove plastic casing. The edge will curl up and form a cup. Place these on a greased baking sheet. Melt the shortening in a heavy pan and brown the onion and celery. Blend in flour, tomato juice, salt and pepper. Cook until thick, stirring constantly. Add rice and cook 5 minutes more. Place this mixture in bologna cups. Sprinkle with cheese. Bake at 375° for 10 minutes, or until cheese is melted and lightly browned. VARIATION: Fill cups with potato salad and sprinkle with paprika.

SMOKIES IN A BLANKET

8 lasagna noodles
8 smokies

Cheese

Cook lasagna noodles. Split smokies lengthwise and boil 5 minutes to remove fat. Fill centers with cheese. Wrap one noodle around each smokie. Place in a 10 x 13 pan, cover with spaghetti sauce and bake at 350° for 1/2 hour.

FISH

DEEP FRIED FISH

Season fish with salt and cut into serving size portions. Make one of the following batters. Dip fish into batter and deep fry in hot oil at 375° about 3 to 4 minutes until golden brown. Drain and serve immediately.

TENDER BATTER

1 1/2 cups flour
1 tbsp. baking powder
1 tsp. salt

2 eggs
1 cup milk

Mix and sift dry ingredients. Beat eggs and add milk. Add liquid to dry ingredients and stir until smooth. Yield: Batter for 2 lbs. of fish.

CRISPY BATTER

1 cup flour
2 tsp. baking powder
1 1/4 tsp. salt

2 tsp. sugar
1 tbsp. salad oil
1 cup water

Mix and sift dry ingredients. Add oil to water. Make a well in dry ingredients and slowly pour in liquid, stirring until well-blended. Yield: Batter for 2 lbs. of fish.

BAKED FISH WITH DRESSING

Fish prepared for stuffing	1 medium ripe tomato
1 cup bread crumbs	1 tbsp. oil
Chopped green peppers	Flour
1 clove minced garlic	Salt and pepper to taste
1 cup mashed potatoes	Juice of 1/2 lemon
1/2 cup chopped celery	Parsley

Slit skin on sides of fish at intervals. Combine next 6 ingredients and stuff fish. Tie and place in oiled pan to bake. Brush top with oil, sprinkle with flour, salt and pepper and bake 30 minutes. Turn fish and repeat above, baking for only 15 minutes. Sprinkle with lemon juice and parsley when done and serve with fresh salad.

SMOKED FISH

8 cups water	2 tsp. onion salt
1/2 vinegar **or** lemon juice	1 tsp. garlic salt
1 cup pickling salt **or**	Dash of tabasco sauce
dairy salt	Fresh fish fillets
1 cup brown sugar	

Bring water to a boil and add all ingredients but fish. Clean fish and put in large container. A plastic five-gallon pail is good. Pour brine over fillets and soak for 5 hours. Pat the fish dry and place flesh side down on racks in smoker with clean paper on floor to catch brine. Smoke until flesh is golden brown. Finish at cooking temperature or remove from smoker and finish in moderate oven for 30 minutes.

Christina Smith

CREAMED SCALLOPS

3 tbsp. butter	1/3 cup white wine
4-oz. jar sliced mushrooms	1 lb. raw scallops
2 green onions, sliced	1/4 cup dairy half & half
1/4 cup chopped celery	1 egg yolk, beaten
2 tbsp. flour	2 tbsp. butter
1/2 tsp. salt	1/4 cup fine dry bread crumbs
Dash of ground ginger	2 tbsp. parmesan cheese
1 tbsp. chopped pimentos (optional)	

In 2-qt. casserole, place butter, mushrooms, onion and celery. Microwave 2 to 3 minutes on High , stirring after 1 minute. Stir in flour, salt, ginger and pimento well, then add wine and scallops, stirring again. Microwave 5 to 6 minutes on High, stirring after 3 minutes, until thickened. Stir in half & half and egg yolk and microwave 3 to 4 minutes on Medium, stirring after 2 minutes. Mix the butter, crumbs and cheese together and spread on scallops. Microwave 1 minute on Medium. Yield: 4 servings. Microwave time: 17 to 20 minutes.

Joyce Templeton

FILLETS IN LEMON BUTTER

1 lb. sole **or** haddock fillets
1/2 - 1 tsp. salt
1/8 tsp. pepper
1/2 cup butter

1/2 cup chopped fresh parsley
1 tbsp. lemon juice
1/2 cup buttered cracker crumbs
1/2 tsp. paprika

In 12 x 8 x 2-inch dish, arrange fillets with thickest meaty areas to outside edges of dish. Sprinkle with salt and pepper. Melt butter on High for 1 to 2 minutes. Blend in parsley and lemon juice and pour over fish. Top with crumbs and sprinkle on paprika. Microwave for 9 to 11 minutes, rotating half turn after five minutes, until fish flakes easily with a fork.

Sherrie Rude

SOLE WITH LEMON PARSLEY BUTTER

3 tbsp. lemon juice
1/2 cup butter **or** margarine
2 tbsp. cornstarch **or**
   tapioca starch
1/2 tsp. parsley flakes

1/8 tsp. celery salt
1/4 tsp. salt
Dash of pepper
2 lbs. thawed sole fillets

Blend lemon juice, butter, cornstarch, parsley flakes, celery salt, salt and pepper. Mix well. Dip each fillet into seasoned butter. Arrange fillets in a round 9-inch dish, with thick edges towards the outside of dish. Cover with wax paper and microwave 6 to 8 minutes on High or until fillets flake easily. Let stand, covered for 5 minutes. This works equally well with cod.

Spring Valley Local

FILLET OF SOLE IN ALMOND BUTTER

1/3 cup sliced almonds
1/3 cup butter **or** margarine
2 tsp. lemon juice
2 tsp. white wine

1/2 tsp. dill weed
1/2 tsp. salt
1 lb. fresh **or** frozen sole

In 2-qt. glass baking dish, combine almonds and butter. Microwave uncovered for 5 minutes or until butter and almonds are golden brown. Stir in lemon juice, wine, dill and salt. Arrange fillets in butter mixture, spooning sauce over fillets. Cook, covered with wax paper, 5 minutes or until fish flakes easily. Let stand, uncovered for 2 minutes before serving. If desired, garnish with lemon slices. Yield: 4 servings. NOTE: If using frozen fillets, thaw first.

Louise Van Camp

A batter made with water will be crisp, while a batter made with milk will be tender.

SALMON CASSEROLE

1 1/2 cups instant rice
1 can salmon
10-oz. can mushroom soup
1/2 cup milk

1 tbsp. lemon juice
Salt to taste
1/2 cup finely chopped onion
Buttered crumbs

Cook rice in 1 1/2 cups boiling water. Add the rice to the salmon, mushroom soup, milk, lemon juice, salt and onion. Mix thoroughly and cover with buttered crumbs. Bake at 350° for 25 to 30 minutes until crumbs are browned.

SALMON CELERY CASSEROLE

10-oz. can cream of celery soup
1/2 cup milk
1 can flaked salmon

1 1/4 cups crushed cheese
crackers **or** soda crackers
1 cup cooked green beans

Place soup in casserole, add milk and mix well. Add salmon, 1 cup of crackers and beans to soup, stirring well. Sprinkle top with remaining 1/4 cup crackers. Bake at 350° for about 20 to 25 minutes. Yield: 4 servings.

SALMON STEAKS WITH SMOKY SAUCE

2 tbsp. salt
1 cup water
2 lbs. salmon steak
1/2 cup catsup
3 tbsp. lemon juice
2 tbsp. liquid smoke
1 tsp. salt

1/2 tsp. grated onion
1 clove garlic, fincly chopped
1/4 cup cooking oil
2 tbsp. vinegar
1 tsp. worcestershire sauce
1/4 tsp. paprika
1/4 tsp. tabasco sauce

Add 2 tbsp. salt to 1 cup water to make brine. Soak fish in brine for about 3 minutes. Turn and soak other side for 3 minutes. Drain. Make sauce with remaining ingredients. Place fish in well-greased hinged grills and grill over hot coals for 7 to 10 minutes, or until lightly brown around edges. Baste well with the sauce. Turn and cook other side, basting well with sauce. Fish is done when it flakes easily when lifted with a fork.

SALMON LOAF

1 large can salmon
2 eggs, beaten
1/4 tsp. pepper
1 tsp. lemon juice

2 cups soft bread crumbs
2 cups milk
1/2 tsp. salt
2 tbsp. finely-chopped onions

Remove the skin from fish if desired. Crush salmon. Add remaining ingredients. Place in a greased loaf pan and dot with butter. Bake at 350° for 45 to 50 minutes until firm and brown. VARIATION: Substitute tuna, shrimp or other canned fish for salmon.

Dorothy Lunty

SALMON & CELERY LOAF

2 cups dried bread crumbs **or**
   3 cups fresh bread crumbs
1 cup milk
1 env. gelatin
2 cups celery, chopped fine

1 lb. can salmon
2 eggs
2 tsp. salt
1/2 tsp. pepper
Dash of paprika

Soak bread crumbs in 1/2 cup milk. Soak gelatin in other 1/2 cup milk. Add celery to salmon. Mix together all ingredients and put in loaf pan or casserole and bake at 350° for 1 hour. Serve hot or cold.

TUNA CRISP CASSEROLE

3 cups crushed potato chips
1 can cream of mushroom soup
61/2-oz. can tuna, drained
4-oz. can sliced mushrooms,
   drained

1/4 cup pimento-stuffed sliced
   olives
1/2 cup shredded cheddar
   cheese
11/2 tsp. dried onion flakes

Mix 2 cups potato chips and remaining ingredients in a 11/2-qt. casserole. Microwave 4 to 6 minutes on High until heated, stirring every 2 minutes. Top with remaining chips. Yield: 4 servings.

Georgina Taylor

TUNA CASSEROLE

5 medium potatoes
7 oz. solid tuna **or** salmon
1 can cream of mushroom soup

1 cup milk
2 tbsp. minced onion
Salt and pepper to taste

Slice potatoes into 2-qt. casserole and cover with layer of tuna. Repeat procedure. Mix soup, milk and onion. Add salt and pepper and pour over potatoes and tuna. Bake at 375° for 1 hour.

Phyllis Elmer

TUNA MUSHROOM PIE

6 oz. cooked noodles
7-oz. can tuna
1/4 cup chopped celery
2 chopped hard-boiled eggs
1 can mushroom soup

1/8 tsp. pepper
1 tsp. worcestershire sauce
1/4 cup grated cheese
1/2 cup crushed potato chips

Arrange border of cooked noodles in oiled casserole baking dish. Flake fish into center. Sprinkle fish with celery and eggs. Blend soup, pepper and worcestershire sauce and pour over fish. Sprinkle cheese and chips over casserole. Bake at 350° for 30 minutes.

TUNA NOODLE CASSEROLE

1 can tuna
1 can peas (optional)
1 can mushrooms (optional)
1 can mushroom soup
1 can milk

1 cup diced celery
1 can chow mein noodles
1/2 cup diced onion
Crushed potato chips

Mix all ingredients together except chips. Place in buttered casserole. Top with chips. Bake at 325° for 1 hour.

HALIBUT STEAKS WITH SAUCE

1/4 cup oil
1/2 clove garlic
1/4 cup chili sauce
1/2 tbsp. worcestershire sauce

1/2 cup vinegar
1/4 tsp. chili powder
1/2 tbsp. chopped onion
2 tbsp. brown sugar

Combine ingredients until blended. Season steaks and marinate in sauce for one hour or longer, turning occasionally. To barbecue the steaks, put in well-greased rack or directly on greased grill. Grill over moderately hot coals for about 7 to 10 minutes or until lightly brown. Baste with sauce. Turn and cook other side and baste. Test by flaking fish from bone with fork. Do not overcook.

2 tbsp. instant coffee
1/4 cup butter
1/2 tsp. salt

2 tbsp. lemon juice
1 tsp. onion salt

Mix ingredients well. Brush on halibut steaks while cooking on barbecue.

OYSTER FRITTERS

1 1/4 cups flour
2 tsp. baking powder
1/4 tsp. salt
1 egg, beaten

2/3 cup milk **or** oyster liquid
1 pint oysters
1 tbsp. lemon juice

To make batter, mix and sift dry ingredients. Beat egg and milk together, and combine mixtures. Beat until smooth. Chop oysters and season with lemon juice. Add to batter. Fry. Oysters may be left whole if desired.

OYSTER STEW

2 tbsp. butter **or** margarine
8-oz. can oysters and liquid
2 cups milk
1/4 tsp. paprika
1/4 tsp. salt.

1/4 tsp. pepper
Dash of cayenne
1/4 tsp. seasoning salt
1/4 tsp. worcestershire sauce

Combine all ingredients and heat thoroughly. Do not boil. Yield: 3 to 4 servings.

SHRIMP CREOLE

3 tbsp. vegetable oil
1 medium onion, chopped
1/2 green pepper, chopped
1 stalk celery, sliced
1 clove garlic, finely minced
14-oz. can tomatoes,
    drained and chopped

1 bay leaf
1 tsp. paprika
1 tsp. salt
Few drops of tabasco
1 lb. medium raw shrimp,
    peeled

Combine oil, onion, green pepper, celery and garlic in large casserole dish. Cover with plastic wrap, venting one corner. Microwave on Full Power for 5 to 7 minutes, until vegetables are softened. Uncover and stir in remaining ingredients except shrimp. Cover with plastic wrap and microwave on Medium Power for 8 to 10 minutes. Uncover and stir in shrimp. Recover and microwave another 4 to 5 minutes on High, until shrimp turns pink. Discard bay leaf and serve on steamed rice. Yield: 4 to 6 servings.

Mary Belanger

POULTRY

CHICKEN SUPREME

2 frying chickens
Oil
2 large cans tomatoes
2 tsp. seasoned salt
3/4 cup brown sugar

3/4 cup chopped onion
2 tsp. worcestershire sauce
1 cup chopped celery
3/4 cup vinegar
2 bay leaves

Cut chicken into serving pieces. Brown in oil. Mix tomatoes with remaining ingredients. Remove chicken from skillet and put into roasting pan. Pour the tomato mixture over chicken and bake at 350° for about 1 hour or until tender. Serve with rice and green salad.

Annie Ronning

BAKED CHICKEN

Salt and pepper
1/2 cup flour
5 tbsp. butter, melted

1 chicken
1 cup boiling water

Lightly sprinkle roasting pan with salt and pepper. Add enough flour to the butter to make a paste that will spread easily. Season with salt. After spreading paste on chicken, lightly sift again with flour. Add the boiling water and bake at 350° to 375° about 2 hours until tender .

Margaret Gould

BAKED BARBECUED CHICKEN

1 chicken	1 cup catsup
1/3 cup fat **or** oil	1/4 cup lemon juice
2 tbsp. worcestershire sauce	1/2 cup chopped celery
2 tbsp. brown sugar	1 onion, chopped
2 tsp. salt	1 tsp. pepper
Dash of tabasco	1 tsp. prepared mustard

Cut chicken into serving-size pieces. Cook in fat until well-browned on all sides. Combine remaining ingredients and simmer on stove for 10 minutes. Place browned chicken in shallow pan and pour sauce over. Bake at 350° for about 45 minutes and baste occasionally with sauce. Add small amount of water if sauce becomes too thick. Serve chicken with the sauce.

Mrs. Lars Hagenson

NAPA VALLEY BARBECUED CHICKEN

1 - 3 lb. broiler-fryer, cut up	1/2 cup sherry
1/4 cup flour	1/3 cup water
1/4 cup butter, margarine **or** bacon drippings	2 tbsp. lemon juice
	1 minced onion, medium sized
1/3 tsp. pepper	1 tbsp. worcestershire sauce
1 tsp. paprika	2 tbsp. melted butter **or** margarine
3/4 tsp. salt	
1 cup catsup	1 tbsp. brown sugar

Coat chicken with seasoned flour and cook until evenly brown in 1/4 cup butter in large skillet. Remove to 2-qt. casserole. Combine remaining ingredients in saucepan. Bring to boil and pour over chicken. Cover and bake at 325° for 11/4 hours until tender. Yield: 4 servings.

Mrs. Frances Redmond

CHICKEN CASSEROLE

1 chicken, cut up	1 pkg. onion soup
1 pkg. cream of mushroom soup	11/2 cups milk
1 cup long grain rice	

Place chicken in greased casserole dish. Mix all ingredients and pour over chicken. Bake 1 hour uncovered, and one more hour covered with tin foil.

Mrs. Elizabeth Kocsis

Speedy seasoning for chicken: Roll cut-up chicken in seasonings from your favorite rice mix . Use only the contents of envelope of mix. Pour melted butter on pieces and cook.

CHICKEN IN CREAM

1 chicken	1 onion
4 cups water	1/4 tsp. salt
3 cups dairy half & half	1/8 tsp. pepper

Cut chicken into small pieces. Cover with water and boil 45 minutes. Drain stock, add cream, onions and seasonings. Boil again until meat is tender. Serve with new potatoes and young green peas.

Mrs. K. Drapaka

ENGLISH CHICKEN PIE

1 chicken **or** fowl	Salt and pepper to taste
4 hard-boiled eggs, quartered	1 cup stock
1/2 lb. bacon **or** ham, diced	

Boil chicken until meat comes off the bones. Reserve broth. Cut chicken into small pieces. Place chicken, eggs and bacon in layers in deep dish, seasoning each layer. Fill 3/4 full with stock. Cover with your favorite short-crust or flaky pastry. Bake at 325° for 1 to 1 1/2 hours until pastry has risen and set, then at about 200° for 30 minutes.

MODERN OVEN-FRIED CHICKEN

1/2 cup golden oil	1/2 tsp. sweet paprika
1 tsp. salt	2 1 1/2-lb. broilers, quartered
1 clove garlic, crushed	1/2 cup wheat germ

Mix the oil, salt, garlic and paprika. Apply to the chicken pieces with a pastry brush. Roll chicken in wheat germ and place, skin side down, in a shallow baking dish coated with the remaining oil mixture. Bake at 350° for approximately 1 1/2 hours. Turn skin side up after 45 minutes.

MARY ANN'S FRIED CHICKEN

1 broiler-fryer, cut up	2 tsp. onion powder
3 cups water	1/2 tsp. chives
1 tbsp. salt	1/4 tsp. pepper
1 tbsp. parsley	1 tsp. instant chicken broth
1/2 tsp. tarragon	1 cup flour
2 tsp. seasoned salt	Oil for frying

Cover chicken with water and salt and chill for 1 hour. Mix seasonings, chicken broth and flour in plastic bag. Remove chicken pieces from water. Coat individually in flour mixture while still wet. Add 1 inch of oil in frying pan. Heat to 375°. Fry chicken pieces, turning once, 5 minutes on each side. Drain on paper towels. Drain oil from frying pan. Add 1 cup chicken broth to pan. Return chicken pieces. Cover skillet. Cook 15 minutes or until tender. Chicken Broth: After chicken has soaked in salt water, use water in saucepan and add chicken giblets, neck, onion slices and cut celery tops. Cover and simmer 30 minutes. Yield: 3 cups.

FRIED CHICKEN

1 chicken	1/4 cup unsalted butter
Salt	1/2 cup flour
1/4 cup lard	

Cut a young chicken into serving-sized pieces. Sprinkle with salt and put in refrigerator until well-chilled. Heat lard and butter in frying pan. Roll each piece of chicken in flour and lay in hot fat. Cover with lid. Fry rather quickly until golden brown, on all sides. Reduce heat and cook slowly for 1/2 hour.

SESAME FRIED CHICKEN

1 frying chicken, cut up	2 tsp. paprika
1/2 cup milk	1 tsp. baking powder
1 egg, well beaten	1/4 cup chopped nuts
1 cup flour	2 tbsp. sesame seeds
2 tsp. salt	1/2 cup butter
1/4 tsp. pepper	

Dip chicken pieces into milk and egg mixture, then into mixture of flour, salt, pepper, paprika, baking powder, nuts and sesame seeds. Melt butter in shallow baking dish in hot oven. Put floured chicken pieces into hot dish, turn to coat with butter, then bake skin side down in a single layer. Bake at 350° for 30 minutes on each side, or until done.

Chris A. Smith

SAILOR'S RAISIN CHICKEN SCRAMBLE

8 small chicken pieces	1/2 tsp. oregano
3 tbsp. shortening	1 tsp. paprika
1 onion, chopped	1/4 tsp. pepper
1 cup rice	1 can stewed tomatoes
2/3 cup dark seedless raisins	2 tbsp. chicken stock
1 tsp. garlic salt	1 1/2 cups water

Brown chicken slowly in shortening. Remove chicken to keep warm. Add onion and cook to soften. Add remaining ingredients. Stir to mix well and distribute chicken throughout the rice. Cover tightly and simmer about 45 minutes until chicken is tender and rice has absorbed all the liquid. Yield: 4 servings.

Christina Smith

When frying in butter, use unsalted butter as it does not burn as easily.

CAROL'S CHICKEN-RICE CASSEROLE

1 cup long grain rice
1 chicken, cut up
Paprika
1 env. onion soup mix

10-oz. can cream of
mushroom soup
1 can water
Parsley

Sprinkle rice in buttered baking dish and place chicken on top. Sprinkle with paprika and onion soup. Combine mushroom soup and water and pour over chicken. Sprinkle with parsley. Bake covered at 300° for 2 hours.

Carol Stott

PHYLLIS' PINEAPPLE CHICKEN

1 cup flour
1/2 tsp. baking soda
1/2 cup cornstarch
1 tsp. baking powder
1 cup water
1 chicken **or** 2 chicken breasts
Salt and pepper to taste
1/3 cup water
2 carrots

1 green pepper
Cooking oil
1 cup pineapple juice
3 tbsp. brown sugar
3 tbsp. vinegar
15-oz. can pineapple chunks
1 tsp. soya sauce
1 1/2 tbsp. cornstarch
1/3 cup water

Make batter of flour, baking soda, 1/2 cup cornstarch, baking powder and 1 cup water. Skin and debone chicken and cut into bite-sized pieces, sprinkle with salt and place into batter. Cut carrots thinly. Place in 1/3 cup water and cook with lid off. Cut green pepper. Heat cooking oil in skillet and when hot, lift chicken pieces from batter and deep fry until golden brown. Put pineapple juice in pan with the sugar and vinegar. Heat. Add carrots and pineapple chunks, then the green pepper. Add soya sauce. Bring to boil and add the 1 1/2 tbsp. cornstarch mixed in the 1/3 cup water. Put chicken on platter and pour the vegetables and sauce over.

Phyllis Manning

PINEAPPLE CHICKEN

1 fryer, cut up
Oil
1 small can pineapple tidbits
3/4 cup uncooked rice
3 tsp. salt

1/4 tsp. poultry seasoning
1 tbsp. soya sauce
2 chicken bouillon cubes
1 1/2 cups boiling water
1 cup diced celery

Brown chicken in oil in frying pan. Drain pineapple, reserving liquid. In large casserole, combine rice, pineapple juice, salt, seasoning and soya sauce. Combine bouillon and boiling water to make stock and add. Place browned chicken pieces on top and cover. Bake at 350° for 1 1/2 hours. Uncover for last 15 minutes of baking and add the pineapple tidbits and celery. Serve with hot buns or baking powder biscuits.

Elizabeth Pedersen

SPANISH-STYLE CHICKEN

21/2-3 lb. broiler-fryer
1 tsp. salt
1/4 tsp. pepper
1/2 tsp. monosodium glutamate
3 tbsp. shortening
1/2 cup chopped onion

1 garlic cove, minced
1 cup tomato juice
2 cups chicken broth
1 cup uncooked long grain rice
10-oz. pkg frozen peas

Cut chicken into bite-sized pieces and season with salt, pepper and monosodium glutamate. In skillet, brown chicken in hot shortening. Add onion and garlic. Cook until onion is tender but not brown. Add tomato juice and 1 cup chicken broth. Cover and simmer for 20 minutes. Add rice and remaining broth. Simmer covered for 20 minutes. Add peas and simmer for 5 minutes more or until peas are tender, stirring once or twice. Yield: 4 servings.

Carol Laun

ORIENTAL CHICKEN

1 cup soya sauce
1 cup grapefruit juice
1 tsp. sugar

1 fryer, cut up
1/2 tsp. ginger
1/4 cup cooking oil

Mix the soya sauce, grapefruit juice, sugar and ginger in large shallow dish. Add chicken pieces, turning to coat both sides. Cover and marinate in refrigerator for several hours. Turn occasionally. Remove chicken from marinade and brush with oil. Grill or broil about 6 inches from source of heat. Brush with marinade, turning frequently until brown and tender. Yield: 4 servings.

ALMOND CHICKEN CHOW MEIN

11/2 cup coarsely chopped onion
3 tbsp. cooking fat **or** oil
2 tbsp. cornstarch
1 tsp. salt
1 tbsp. sugar
2 cups broth **or** bouillon
2 - 3 tbsp. soya sauce

3 cups diced, cooked chicken
2 cups sliced celery
1 medium green pepper
1/2 lb. mushrooms **or**
　1 can sliced mushrooms
1 can bean sprouts (optional)
Sliced almonds

Sauté onions in hot fat 3 to 5 minutes. Mix cornstarch, salt and sugar. Blend to a smooth paste with some of the broth. Add remaining broth and soya sauce to the pan. Stir in cornstarch mixture and cook until thickened and clear, stirring constantly. Add chicken, celery, green pepper cut in 1/4-inch strips, and drained mushrooms. Cover and cook gently 5 to 8 minutes, stirring occasionally. Add drained bean sprouts. Add sliced almonds as garnish on top when done.

Gladys Van Petten
Mrs. Gwynver

CHICKEN WITH RICE

1 1/2 cups rice
1 frying chicken, cut up
1 env. onion soup mix

2 cans cream of chicken soup
2 soup cans of milk

Put rice in greased 9 x 13-inch pan. Lay chicken on rice and sprinkle with soup. Mix soup with milk and pour over. Bake at 350° for 1 1/2 hours.

Georgina Taylor

HOT BAKED CHICKEN SALAD

2 cups cubed cooked chicken
1/4 cup chopped almonds
1 1/2 cups diced celery
2 tsp. chopped onion
1 tsp. grated lemon rind

1 tbsp. lemon juice
1/8 tsp. pepper
2/3 cup salad dressing
1 cup grated cheddar cheese
1 cup crushed potato chips

Place chicken, almonds, celery, onion, lemon rind, lemon juice and pepper in mixing bowl. Add salad dressing and toss. Add salt and pepper to taste. Put mixture in casserole. Sprinkle cheese on top and arrange crushed chips over cheese. Bake at 375° for 25 minutes or until thoroughly heated and cheese is melted. Yield: 4 servings.

HAWAIIAN CHICKEN BREASTS

1 tbsp. oil
2 whole chicken breasts,
  halved and skinned
14-oz. can pineapple tidbits
1/4 cup brown sugar

1/8 tsp. ginger
2 tbsp. cornstarch
1 tsp. soy sauce
2 tbsp. cider vinegar

Preheat a large browning dish in microwave for 6 minutes on High . Add oil. Place chicken breasts in dish with meat side down. Microwave for 1 minute on High. Remove from oven and set aside. Drain juice from pineapple and add enough water to make 3/4 cup. Stir in sugar, ginger, cornstarch, soy sauce and vinegar. Bring to boil on high, stirring twice. Pour sauce over chicken. Cover and microwave for 10 minutes on Medium . Stir in pineapple. Let stand 5 minutes, then serve over rice. 1 serving - 322 calories. Yield: 4 servings.

M. Belanger

BARBECUED CHICKEN

2 fryer chickens
Melted butter

Halve chickens, wash and dry. Dip into melted butter. French or Italian dressing or a vinegar-butter-water mixture may be used. Salt and pepper to taste. Have fire burned down to a bed of coals. Place chicken skin side away from heat to start. Turn, baste with additional butter or sauce every 5 to 10 minutes. Allow about 1 1/2 hours for a 2 1/2 lb. chicken. When hip joint moves easily, it is done. Serve with a mushroom sauce.

TURKEYS LAST ROUND-UP

2 cups cooked, ground turkey
1 can chicken **or** mushroom soup
12 slices of bread

3 eggs, well beaten
1/2 cup milk
Salt and pepper

Mix turkey with soup. Spread between slices of bread and dip these sandwiches in combined egg and milk. Sprinkle with salt and pepper. Sauté in butter until well browned on each side. Serve hot with turkey gravy. Yield: 6 servings.

Mrs. E. Holland

TURKEY STROGANOFF

1/4 cup green pepper, chopped
2 tbsp. onion
2 tbsp. margarine
10-oz. can cream of
  mushroom soup

1/2 cup sour cream
1/4 cup milk
1/2 tsp. paprika
2 cups cooked noodles
11/2 cups cubed cooked turkey

Brown green pepper and onion in margarine, and combine all ingredients into a casserole dish. Bake at 350° for 35 minutes.

Doris Barker

GOLDEN TURKEY CASSEROLE

1 pkg. chicken noodle soup
3 cups water
4 tbsp. butter
4 tbsp. flour
1/2 cup heavy cream, whipped
1 cup peas

10-oz. can mushrooms
3/4 cup cooked turkey
  or chicken, diced
3/4 cup buttered bread crumbs
3 tbsp. grated cheese

Cook soup in water. In saucepan, melt butter and blend in flour. Stir in hot soup. Simmer 3 minutes. Remove from stove. Fold in cream. Stir in peas, mushrooms and chicken. Season to taste. Place in 2-qt. casserole. Top with buttered bread crumbs and sprinkle with cheese. Bake at 350° for 20 minutes. Yield: 6 to 8 servings.

CREAMED TURKEY NOODLE

6 oz. broad noodles
2 cups chopped onion
2 cups chopped celery
2 tbsp. butter **or** margarine
4 cups cooked turkey

1 can cream of mushroom soup
1 can cream of chicken soup
10-oz. can sliced mushrooms
1 tsp. salt
1/4 tsp. pepper

Cook noodles according to package directions. Drain. Sauté onion and celery in butter until limp. Add to noodles. Add turkey, soups, mushrooms, salt and pepper. Pour into large casserole. Bake uncovered at 350° for 35 minutes. Yield: 6 to 8 servings.

Donna Bon

POTATO BASKETS WITH CREAMED TURKEY

2 eggs
1 tsp. salt
3 tbsp. butter
3 tbsp. milk
3 cups hot mashed potatoes

2 tbsp. butter
2 tbsp. flour
2 cups heated milk
2 cups diced cold turkey

Beat eggs well. Add salt and beat in 3 tbsp. butter and 3 tbsp. milk. Blend in potatoes and mix thoroughly. Shape into baskets, leaving the center hollow and brown in hot oven. Meanwhile, melt 2 tbsp. butter and blend in flour. Add heated milk and turkey, stirring until thickened. Fill hollows and serve.

Mrs. J. Harink

RICE STUFFING

1/2 cup butter
2 cups chopped celery
21/4 cups chopped onion
1 green pepper, chopped fine
Giblet, liver and heart,
   chopped **or** ground
1 tbsp. salt
1 tsp. marjoram

1 tsp. sage
1/2 tsp. savory
1/2 tsp. thyme
1/4 tsp. pepper
8 cups cooked rice
1 cup chopped pecans
1/2 cup chopped celery leaves
2 eggs, well beaten

Melt butter and sauté celery, onion, green pepper, liver, heart and giblets until thoroughly cooked. Add salt, marjoram, sage, savory, thyme, pepper, rice, nuts and celery leaves. Stir in eggs and mix thoroughly. Loosely stuff turkey. Yield:12 cups.

Iris Humble

DRESSING FOR FOWL

8 cups stale bread crumbs
1/2 tsp. salt
1/4 tsp. pepper
1 tsp. sage

1 medium onion, chopped
1/4 - 1/2 cup melted butter
1 cup water

Prepare crumbs. Add seasoning and onion. Stir in butter and moisten with hot water.

Mrs. E.V. Stanley

NOVA SCOTIA DRESSING FOR FOWL

2 qts. mashed potatoes
1 cup bread crumbs
1/4 cup sugar
1/2 cup butter

1 onion, chopped fine
2 tsp. cinnamon
Salt and pepper to taste

Combine ingredients and stuff fowl.

DRESSING FOR TURKEY

1 tsp. baking soda
1/2 lb. sausage meat
1 cup chopped walnuts
7 1/2 cups old bread crumbs
1 1/2 tsp. poultry spice **or** dressing
Pepper to taste

1/2 tsp. ginger
1/2 cup chopped onions
2 tbsp. melted butter
1/2 cup hot water
1/2 tbsp. salt

Rub inside of turkey with baking soda. Combine sausage meat with walnuts and cook until crisp in frying pan. Add remaining ingredients and stuff turkey.

CHRISTMAS TURKEY DRESSING

8 cups oven-toasted bread cubes
2 cups diced apple
1/2 cup onion, chopped fine
1/3 cup cold water
2 tsp. salt

1 cup mayonnaise
3/4 cup thinly sliced celery
1/2 cup chopped walnuts
1 tsp. sage
Dash of pepper

Combine all ingredients. Mix lightly until well-blended. Enough for a 10 to 12 lb. turkey.

GIBLET GRAVY

Turkey giblets and neck
1 qt. water
1/3 cup flour

1 tsp. accent
Salt and pepper

Cook giblets and neck in water for 1 hour or until tender. Drain. Chop meat, saving broth. Leave about 1/2 cup fat in pan after removing chicken or turkey. Stir in flour and accent. Gradually add cool broth and enough cold water to make smooth, thin gravy. Cook for 5 minutes, stirring constantly. Add chopped giblets. Season to taste with salt and pepper.

WILD DUCK AU VIN

3 clean dry ducks
Flour
1/2 cup chopped bacon
3 tbsp. chopped onion
1 clove garlic, minced

Salt and pepper to taste
1 cup chicken broth **or** bouillon
1/2 cup red wine
1 sprig thyme
1 bay leaf

Soak fowl in cool water with salt and some vinegar overnight. Cut fowl in pieces and dredge completely in flour. Fry bacon until crisp. Remove from pan and save. Fry pieces of dredged meat in bacon dripping until brown and arrange in bottom of pot or oven dish. Fry onion and garlic in remaining drippings, adding more oil if necessary. Combine salt, pepper, chicken broth, wine, thyme and bay leaf. Pour over duck pieces and simmer gently about 1 1/2 to 2 hours until done. The flour from the dredged meat will thicken the gravy as it cooks.

DUCK AU GRAND MARNIER

1 large **or** 2 small ducks
1 large orange
Salt and pepper to taste
1 1/2 cups water

1 1/2 cups orange juice
1/2 cup honey
1/2 cup Grand Marnier

Stuff duck with unpeeled orange, cut in quarters. Sprinkle salt and pepper and rub in skin. Pierce skin if fat. Make broth with gizzard, liver and neck. Mix 1/2 cup of the orange juice and honey to baste duck. Roast duck at 375° for 15 minutes, then lower heat to 325° until cooked. After duck is cooked, remove excess fat from pan. Add 1 cup broth, remaining orange juice and Grand Marnier in pan and boil down. Pour a little over roasted duck and serve the rest in a pitcher.

FRIED PRAIRIE CHICKEN

1 young prairie chicken
Salt and pepper to taste
Flour
1 tbsp. butter
3 tbsp. oil

1 tbsp. chopped onion
2 cups water
1/2 cup wine
1 bay leaf

Clean prairie chicken, dress and cut into serving pieces. Plunge into cold water. Drain thoroughly but do not wipe dry. Season with salt, pepper and dredge thickly with flour. Fry slowly in butter and oil until brown and tender. Add onions and brown lightly. Add 2 cups water, wine and bay leaf and simmer gently for 10 minutes. Yield: 3 to 4 servings.

STUFFED PARTRIDGE

3 partridges
Bread stuffing
Salt and pepper to taste
Flour
3 tbsp. oil
1 tbsp. onion, chopped

1/2 cup red wine
1 tsp. barbecue sauce
2 cups water
1 bay leaf
6 slices bacon

Clean, dress and stuff partridges. Salt, pepper and dredge with flour heavily and fry in hot oil until brown. Put breast side up into small roaster or large baking dish. Add onions to fat in frying pan and brown lightly. Pour over partridges in baking dish. Add wine, barbecue sauce, water and bay leaf. Lay 2 slices of bacon on each partridge. Cover and let cook at 350° approximately 2 hours until done. Roast duck or wild goose may be done in exactly the same way as the stuffed partridge, but do not dredge in flour or fry. Roast directly in oven. If birds are fat, omit bacon; otherwise drain off excess fat before adding water and wine.

RICE,
PIZZA & PASTA

RICE

CHINESE FRIED RICE

3 cups cooked rice
31/2 tbsp. butter **or** oil
11/2 cups ham, chicken **or** shrimp
1/2 cup chopped parsley
1 tsp. salt
1/4 tsp. pepper
3/4 cup chopped bean sprouts
  or green onion
2 eggs, well beaten
2 tbsp. soya sauce

Steam and cook the rice the usual way. To make this dish successfully, cook rice a day ahead and refrigerate covered overnight. Add oil to frying pan and add cooked rice. Stir constantly until light golden brown. Do not overcook. Add chopped meat, parsley, salt, pepper and bean sprouts. Mix with rice. Make a hole in the center. Add the eggs and stir until it begins to cook. Mix all together. Add soya sauce.

SPANISH RICE

2 tbsp. rice
1 tbsp. chopped onion
1 tbsp. celery
1 tbsp. green pepper
11/2 tsp. oil
1/2 cup tomatoes
3 tbsp. water
Few grains salt
1/4 tsp. sugar

Sauté rice, onion, celery and green pepper in oil in frying pan until they are tender. Combine the tomatoes, water, salt and sugar and bring to a boil. Pour into casserole with rice and tomatoes. Bake at 350° for about 1 hour.

Janet Hagstrom

QUICK SPANISH RICE

1/2 cup chopped onion
11/2 cups cooked rice, cooled
1/4 cup salad oil
1 cup bouillon **or** beef broth
14-oz. can tomato sauce
11/2 cup diced cooked beef
Salt and pepper to taste

Sauté onion and rice in salad oil, stirring until lightly browned. Add broth, tomato sauce, beef and seasonings. Bring to a boil, reduce heat and simmer uncovered for 5 minutes. Yield: 4 servings.

Irene Wagstaff

PERFECT FLUFFY RICE

1 cup long grain rice   1 tbsp. butter **or** margarine
1/2 tsp. salt   2 cups hot tap water

Measure rice into 2-qt. casserole. Add salt and butter. Stir in hot water. Cover with lid or plastic wrap, rolling back one edge slightly. Microwave 5 minutes on High . Stir. Reduce power to Medium and microwave for 11 to 15 minutes. Stir. Let stand covered 2 to 4 minutes. Fluff with fork before serving. Yield: 4 servings. Cooking time: 16 minutes.

Rita Cannard
Georgina Taylor
Spring Valley Local

RICE PILAF

1/4 cup butter **or** margarine   1/8 tsp. pepper
1 onion, finely chopped   1/3 bay leaf
1/2 cup diced celery   1/8 tsp. thyme
11/2 cup uncooked rice   101/2-oz. can condensed
1/4 cup parsley   chicken broth
1/4 tsp. salt   11/3 cups water

Combine butter, onion and celery in a 2-qt. casserole. Microwave 3 to 4 minutes or until onion is transparent. Add rice, parsley, salt, pepper, bay leaf, thyme, broth and water. Cover and microwave 5 to 6 minutes on High. Stir. Microwave16 to 18 minutes on Low until rice is tender. Let stand 3 to 5 minutes covered. Yield: 6 servings.

Edith Galloway

HOLUPCHI

1 medium sized cabbage, cored   Salt and pepper
1/4 cup vinegar   1 medium onion
1/2 lb. rice   1 qt. canned tomatoes
1/4 lb. bacon **or** other smoked pork

Scald cabbage in water and vinegar long enough to wilt leaves. Remove leaves and slice off heavy midrib so that they won't break when rolled. Wash rice. Boil hard for 10 minutes in salted water and drain. Dice bacon finely and fry until crisp. Add bacon, salt, pepper and onion to rice, mixing well. Spread spoonful of mixture on each cabbage leaf and roll tightly. Line large baking dish with boiled cabbage leaves and place rolls closely together on them. Pile on top of the other until dish is full. Pour on the tomatoes and seasoning. Cover with more cabbage leaves. Bake at 375° for 11/2 hours, then cover and bake another 30 minutes. Serve hot.

Mrs. W.B. Ogilvie

LAZY CABBAGE ROLLS

2 cups rice	3 onions
4 cups water	1 - 2 cups sauerkraut
Salt and pepper to taste	3 tbsp. cooking oil
Pinch of paprika	1/2 cup rolled oats

Wash rice and cook in salted boiling water. Do not overcook rice, it should be quite moist. Add salt, pepper and paprika. Sauté onions and sauerkraut individually in cooking oil, then add to rice. Toss lightly. Add rolled oats and again toss lightly. Place in baking dish. Cover and bake at 250 to 300° for 1 to 11/2 hours.

PIZZA

BASIC PIZZA DOUGH

1 cup warm water	2 tbsp. oil **or** shortening
1 pkg. active dry yeast	1/4 tsp. salt
1 tsp. sugar	2 cups sifted flour

Put warm water, yeast and sugar in large bowl and let stand 10 minutes until yeast is dissolved. Stir in oil and salt, gradually adding flour. Mix well. Transfer dough to a well-floured board and knead until smooth. Place dough in oiled bowl, cover and let rise in warm spot about 1 hour until double in size. Punch down and divide into two. On lightly-floured surface, roll each half into a 13-inch circle. Give the dough a light sprinkle of oil and spread with pizza sauce. Choose your toppings, arrange on top of sauce and bake for 25 to 30 minutes at 350°.

Lena Morin

BASIC PIZZA SAUCE

2 tbsp. oil	1 tsp. salt
1 onion, coarsely chopped	Dash of pepper
28-oz. can tomatoes	1 tsp. sugar
1 bay leaf	1/2 tsp. thyme
Garlic salt	Dash of monosodium glutamate

Heat oil in saucepan. Cook onion until soft. Add tomatoes and remaining ingredients. Cover and cook slowly for about 30 minutes or until sauce is slightly thick. Freezes well.

Lena Morin

EASY PIZZA SAUCE

1 can tomatoes	2 tbsp. oil
Salt and pepper	1 tsp. oregano
1 cup cubed sharp cheese	1 tbsp. chopped parsley
1 cup cubed and chopped salami **or** sausage	1 tbsp. chives

Drain and chop tomatoes. Combine remaining ingredients and pour on the basic pizza dough which has been brushed with olive oil. Bake at 450° for 20 minutes.

Mrs. Bert Friend

PIZZA

1 cup flour	1/2 - 1 cup grated mozzarella cheese
1 1/2 tsp. baking powder	1 cup canned tomatoes
1/2 tsp. salt	1/4 tsp. oregano
2 tbsp. shortening	Dash of pepper
1/3 cup milk	1/2 tsp. salt
Melted butter	1/2 - 1 clove garlic, minced

Sift flour, baking powder and salt together. Cut in shortening, add the milk and mix well. Divide dough in half and pat into circles on 2 pie plates or on a pizza pan, making a slight ridge around the edge. Brush lightly with melted butter. Sprinkle crust with half the cheese. Add remaining ingredients to the tomatoes and spoon the mixture over the cheese and top with the rest of the cheese. Bake at 425° for 15 minutes. Reduce heat to 350° and continue baking for 15 minutes.

PIZZA TOPPINGS

CHEESE: Mozzarella cheese in thin slices. Arrange on top of sauce.
ONION: Cut 2 medium onions in thin slices. Arrange on top and sprinkle with 1 cup grated parmesan cheese.
SAUSAGE: Slice garlic sausage or pepperoni. Arrange on top of sauce. Cover with cheese.
ANCHOVY: Drain 2-oz. can of anchovy fillets. Arrange on top and then cover with thin slices of mozzarella cheese.
GREEN PEPPER: Sprinkle 1 cup chopped green pepper over pizza.
HAM: Spread with 2 cups cooked, chopped ham, 1 cup finely-chopped lean bacon and 2 tbsp. chopped onion.

Lena Morin

Turn leftover catsup into a sauce. Remove metal cap from bottle, add a spoonful or two of leftover red wine, cream, orange juice or Madeira, and a square of butter. Heat 3 to 4 minutes in oven. Cover bottle. Shake well until catsup no longer sticks to bottom of bottle.

SAUSAGE PIZZA

2 cups biscuit mix
1/2 cup milk
1 can tomato sauce **or**
   1 cup canned tomatoes
1 tsp. sugar
1 tsp. minced onion
2 tsp mustard
1/4 tsp. oregano

1 lb. pork sausage meat **or**
   1/2 lb. ground beef and
   1/2 lb. sausage meat
1 cup shredded cheddar
   cheese
2 tbsp. shredded parmesan
   cheese

Knead biscuit mix and milk for 1 minute. Roll out to fit pizza pan and prick surface. Bake at 425° for 5 to 7 minutes. Boil tomato sauce, sugar, onion, mustard and oregano for 8 to 10 minutes. Cook and drain sausage. Spread sauce and sausage over partially-cooked crust. Sprinkle cheddar and parmesan cheese over filling and bake pizza until cheese melts.

Lena Morin

STIR 'N ROLL PIZZA

2 cups flour
2 tsp. baking powder
1 tsp. salt

2/3 cup milk
1/4 cup salad oil
2 tbsp. salad oil

Heat oven to 425°. Measure flour, baking powder, salt, milk and 1/4 cup salad oil into a bowl. Stir vigorously until mixture leaves sides of bowl. Gather together and press into a ball. Knead dough in bowl 10 times to make smooth. Divide dough in half. On lightly-floured board roll each half into a 13-inch circle. Place on pizza pan or baking sheet. Turn up edge 1/2-inch and pinch or pleat. Brush with 2 tbsp. oil. Layer cheese, tomato sauce and pizza toppings and bake 20 to 35 minutes. Cut into wedges to serve. This recipe can be made in a food processor.

Irene Wagstaff

PASTA

EGG NOODLES

1 dozen eggs
2 tsp. salt

Flour to make stiff dough

Beat the eggs with salt. Then add flour and knead until stiff. Roll out with rolling pin to paper thin, dredging well with flour. Roll up like a jelly roll and slice across roll. Unwind each roll. Dredge with more flour. Let dry completely. Break into pieces, shake off all loose flour and store in airtight container until required for use. Cook in boiling salted water. Season and serve.

NOODLES

5 cups flour	6 eggs, beaten
1/4 tsp. salt	2 - 3 tbsp. water

Combine flour and salt and add to eggs and water. Mix flour to a very stiff dough. Roll and cut into four pieces, using plenty of flour to roll them. Cut 1/8-inch wide and plunge in boiling water for 2 or 3 minutes and stir. Drain and serve.

Mary Wright

NOODLES ROMANOFF

6-oz. wide egg noodles	1 tsp. monosodium glutamate
1 qt. boiling salted water	11/2 tsp. worcestershire sauce
3 tbsp. chopped onion	Dash of tabasco
1 cup creamed cottage cheese	1/4 cup dry, fine bread crumbs
1 cup sour cream	1/2 cup grated parmesan
1/4 tsp. garlic powder	cheese
1/2 tsp. celery seed	Paprika

Grease a 11/2-qt. casserole. Cook noodles in boiling salt water. Drain and rinse in hot water. Combine noodles with onions, cottage cheese, sour cream, garlic powder, celery seed, monosodium glutamate, worcestershire sauce and tobasco. Mix thoroughly. Pour into greased casserole. Sprinkle with bread crumbs and cheese. Bake at 350° for 25 minutes or until brown. Sprinkle with paprika. Serve hot. Yield: 6 servings.

Clara Link

COTTAGE CHEESE CASSEROLE

2 tbsp. margarine	4 cups elbow macaroni
1/2 cup chopped mushrooms	2 tsp. salt
1/2 cup chopped onions	1 tsp. sugar
1/2 cup chopped celery	1/4 cup parsley, chopped
1 clove garlic, minced	2 cups cottage cheese
1/4 tsp. marjoram	1/3 cup grated parmesan
41/2 cups water	cheese
3/4 cup tomato paste	

Sauté margarine, mushrooms, onions, celery and garlic in large skillet. Stir in marjoram, water, tomato paste, macaroni, salt and sugar. Simmer about 25 minutes until macaroni is tender. Put half of macaroni mixture in a greased 2-qt. casserole dish. Top with half of parsley, cottage cheese and parmesan cheese. Repeat layers. Bake at 350° for 40 minutes.

Mary Parsons

TOMATO MACARONI BAKE

1/4 cup chopped onion
2 tbsp. butter
1 can tomato soup
1/2 cup water

3/4 cup grated cheese
2 cups cooked macaroni
1/4 cup grated cheese
2 tbsp. buttered bread crumbs

Lightly brown onion in butter in a saucepan. Stir in soup, water and 3/4 cup cheese. Heat until cheese melts. Blend with macaroni. Pour into greased casserole. Sprinkle with 1/4 cup grated cheese and bread crumbs. Bake at 350° for 30 minutes or until brown and bubbly. Yield: 4 to 6 servings.

Mrs. Geraldine Shadlock

MACARONI PIZZA

1 1/2 cups uncooked macaroni
2 eggs, beaten
1 cup milk
Salt and pepper to taste
1 lb. ground beef

19-oz. can tomato sauce
Onion salt to taste
Garlic salt to taste
Dash of oregano
Grated cheese

Cook macaroni and add eggs, milk, salt and pepper. Bake in 9 x 13-inch greased pan at 400° for 10 minutes until it looks like soft custard. Brown beef. Add tomato sauce to macaroni mixture. Season ground beef with onion salt, garlic salt and oregano and add. Sprinkle cheese on top. Return to oven until cheese is melted. Cut in squares and serve hot.

Georgina Taylor

LASAGNA

1 lb. ground beef
3/4 lb. sausage meat
16-oz. can tomato sauce
4-oz. can mushroom pieces
2 tsp. dried oregano **or**
    basil leaves
2 cloves pressed garlic
1 tsp. salt

1/2 tsp. pepper
1/2 lb. lasagna noodles, cooked
1 cup cream style cottage
    cheese **or** ricotta
6-oz. pkg. sliced mozzarella
    cheese
2/3 cup grated parmesan
    cheese

Put beef and sausage into a 1 1/4-qt. glass casserole. Cover and microwave at Power Level 10 for 7 to 9 minutes or until meat is lightly browned, stirring 3 times. Drain off fat. Stir in tomato sauce, drained mushrooms, oregano, garlic salt and pepper. In a 2-qt. glass casserole, layer one-third of noodles, one-half of sauce, cottage cheese and mozzarella cheese. Add second layer. Sprinkle with parmesan cheese. Cover. Microwave at Power Level 8 for 29 to 35 minutes or until lasagna is hot in the center. Let stand covered for 5 minutes before serving. Yield: 4 servings.

QUICK LASAGNA

1/2 lb. ground beef
1 cup chopped onions
2 large cloves garlic, minced
2 tsp. crushed oregano
2 cans tomato soup
1/2 cup water

2 tbsp. vinegar
1/2 lb. plain lasagna noodles,
  cooked and drained
1 pint cottage cheese (optional)
1/2 lb. mozzarella cheese, sliced
  thinly

Brown beef; add onion, garlic and oregano. Mix well. Add soup, water and vinegar. Simmer 30 minutes, stirring occasionally. In a shallow 12 x 8-inch pan, arrange 3 alternate layers of noodles, cottage cheese and meat sauce. Top with mozzarella cheese. Sprinkle with parmesan cheese, if desired. Bake at 350° for 30 minutes. Let stand 15 minutes.

Lena Kopp

PEROGIES

4 cups flour
1/2 tsp. salt

2 cups warm water
2 tbsp. melted butter

Combine flour and salt. Combine water and butter. Make a well in the dry ingredients and pour in liquids. Mix as much as possible in bowl. Turn out onto floured board. Knead until dough is soft and smooth. You may have to add a sprinkle of flour. Cover. Let dough stand several hours to absorb flour. Roll out thin. Cut in circles or squares. Place filling in center. Fold over and pinch edges tightly. Place on floured board or tea towel. Bring water to a boil and add 1 tsp. salt. Drop into the water, stirring with a wooden spoon. Cook 8 minutes for fresh and 10 minutes for frozen perogies. Remove into colander and drain well. Place in bowl, pour 3 tbsp. melted butter over it, cover and toss lightly to grease. Yield: 4 to 5 dozen. Serve with: sour cream, onions sautéed in butter, bacon, cubed and fried, mushrooms and gravy. Perogies are very good browned and served with eggs and bacon the next day.

POTATO FILLING

3 cups mashed potatoes
1 tbsp. finely-chopped onion

Salt and pepper to taste
3 tbsp. butter

Mash well and set aside to cool.

POTATO AND CHEESE FILLING

2 cups mashed potatoes
1 cup dry cottage cheese

1 tbsp. finely-chopped onion
2 tbsp. butter

Mix ingredients well and cool. You can also use cheeze whiz. Add 1/2 cup cheese to 2 cups mashed potatoes. Season to taste.

SAUERKRAUT FILLING

2 cups sauerkraut
1 onion, chopped

1 tbsp. butter
Salt and pepper to taste

Scald and drain sauerkraut. Fry onion in butter and add sauerkraut. Fry quickly. Add salt and pepper and cool before using.

Beth Belik

EGGS, PANCAKES & WAFFLES

LIQUID BREAKFAST

1 beaten egg   1/2 - 3/4 cup juice, chilled

For a nourishing liquid breakfast, combine an egg with orange, vitaminized apple, grapefruit or tomato juice in blender.

SCRAMBLED EGG AND ONION

1 cup chopped onion   2 tbsp. milk
2 tbsp. bacon fat **or** butter 1/8 tsp. pepper
4 eggs   1/2 tsp. salt

Fry chopped onion in the fat slowly. Mix the eggs, milk and seasoning until just blended. Pour mixture over onion and cook slowly, lifting occasionally from the bottom of the pan. When just firm, remove quickly from heat and serve on toast.

SCRAMBLED EGG AND BACON

1 tbsp. chopped bacon   1 tbsp. milk
1/2 tsp. chopped onion   Salt and pepper to taste
1 egg, slightly beaten

Fry bacon, add onion and fry lightly. Add egg, milk, salt and pepper. Cook gently, stirring lightly. Just before removing from pan, add 1 tbsp. grated cheddar cheese if desired.

COUNTRY BREAKFAST

6 slices bacon   2 tbsp. milk
4 cups cooked potatoes, cubed   1/2 tsp. salt
3 tbsp. chopped onion   1/8 tsp. pepper
1/3 cup melted butter   1 cup shredded cheese
4 eggs   Tomato wedges
1/2 cup creamed cottage cheese   Parsley

Fry bacon until crisp, drain and crumble. Cook potatoes and onions in butter in large skillet until lightly browned. Beat eggs in mixing bowl and stir in cottage cheese, milk, salt and pepper. Fold into potato mixture in skillet over low heat. Turn portions of mixture with spatula as it begins to thicken. Do not overcook. Sprinkle bacon over potato and egg mixture and top with shredded cheese. Cover skillet and heat until cheese is melted. Garnish with tomato wedges and parsley and serve immediately. Yield: 4 to 6 servings.

Georgina Taylor

GREEN EGGS AND HAM (Kid's recipe)

4 eggs	Blue food coloring
1/4 cup milk	1/2 cup chopped ham
1/4 tsp. salt	4 tsp. butter

Break eggs into a jar with a tight lid. Add milk and salt. Put the lid on and shake very well. Add blue food coloring one drop at a time. Cover and shake after each addition. When a "lovely" green shade is reached. Add the ham. Microwave butter in a small casserole dish 30 seconds to melt. Add the eggs. Microwave 3 to 4 minutes, stirring very often after the first minute. Cook until barely set. The eggs will continue to cook and firm up after being removed from the microwave. Yield: 2 to 4 servings.

Witla-Seven Persons

CHEESE OMELET

2 tbsp. butter	Salt and pepper to taste
1 onion, diced	3/4 cup grated cheese
4 tbsp. milk	6 eggs

Melt butter in frying pan and fry onions. Add milk, seasoning and grated cheese to eggs. Pour mixture over onions. Using spatula, lift edge of omelet to allow uncooked mixture to run under the cooked portion. Fold over when cooked. VARIATION: Before folding over, spread jelly on half the egg.

RECIPE TERMS

Eggs, slightly beaten: *beaten with a fork just enough to blend whites and yolks.*

Eggs, well beaten: *eggs beaten until light and frothy.*

Egg yolks, well beaten: *beaten until thick and light colored.*

Egg whites, beaten stiff: *beaten until they stand in peaks when beater is lifted out. The points of these peaks droop over a bit and the surface is still moist and glossy.*

Egg whites, beaten very stiff: *beaten until peaks stand upright without dropping when beater is removed and the surface looks dry.*

Fold into beaten egg whites: *it is usually recommended that a heavy mixture is folded into beaten whites rather than the whites into the mixture as less air is forced out of entire mixture in the process. Gradually add mixture to stiffly-beaten egg whites with an up, over and down movement of spoon or wide rubber or plastic scraper. If mixture is stirred into whites, the air is driven out and the whites collapse.*

Adding slightly beaten yolks to hot mixture: *always blend a spoonful or more of hot mixture into yolk, then stir into remaining hot mixture. Egg yolk will blend more evenly and won't lump.*

FRENCH OMELET

1 tbsp. butter	1/2 cup milk
1 tbsp. chives	1 tsp. chopped parsley
6 eggs, slightly beaten	Salt and pepper to taste

Fry butter and add chives. Cook until soft. Add eggs and milk. Sprinkle with parsley, salt and pepper. Lift gently with fork, cooking at medium low heat.

MAGIC QUICHE

1/2 lb. bacon	1/4 tsp. pepper
1 cup grated cheese	1/4 tsp. nutmeg
1/2 cup finely-chopped onion	1/2 cup biscuit mix
4 eggs	2 cups milk
1/4 tsp. salt	

Grease pan. Cook bacon. Drain and crumble and combine with cheese and onion. Spread in casserole. Blend remaining ingredients and pour over top. Bake at 350° for 50 to 55 minutes.

Doris Barker

HAM OR BACON QUICHE

1 1/4 cups flour	3 tbsp. cold water
6 tbsp. butter	3 tbsp. light cream

Sift flour into a bowl. Cut in butter with knife or pastry blender until mixture looks mealy. Make a well in the center and pour the water and cream into it. Work the pastry with a fork until it can be formed into a ball. Chill thoroughly. Roll out to fit 9-inch pie plate. Flute edge, prick bottom and sides of crust with fork. Microwave on Roast setting for 4 minutes.

1/2 lb. bacon **or** ham	1/4 tsp. nutmeg
3 eggs	1/2 tsp. salt
1 cup half & half	1/8 tsp. pepper
1/4 cup finely chopped onion	2 cups shredded cheese
or green onions	1 baked 9-inch pastry shell

Place bacon between 2 layers of paper toweling and microwave on full power for 8 to 9 minutes or until crisp. Crumble bacon or ham into pastry shell. In bowl, beat eggs, cream, onion, nutmeg, salt and pepper until well mixed. Stir in cheese. Pour mixture into baked pastry shell. Heat, uncovered on Simmer for 10 minutes. Move cooked eggs toward center and continue to microwave on Simmer for 20 minutes or until knife inserted in center comes out clean. Let stand at room temperature 4 to 5 minutes to finish cooking.

When microwaving, pierce foods such as egg yolks, potatoes and liver to prevent bursting.

CHEESE SOUFFLE

1 1/2 cups milk	4 eggs, well beaten
2/3 tsp. salt	1 1/2 cups bread crumbs
1 cup grated cheese	1 tbsp. butter

Combine ingredients in baking dish. Place dish in pan of water in oven at 350° about 45 minutes to bake until set.

LIGHT CHEESE SOUFFLE

4 tbsp. butter	1 1/2 cups grated cheese
4 tbsp. flour	4 egg yolks, slightly beaten
1 cup milk	4 egg whites, stiffly beaten
Salt, pepper and paprika to taste	

Make a white sauce of the butter, flour and milk. Add seasoning. Add cheese and stir until melted. Add egg yolks, remove from heat and fold in whites. Turn into greased baking dish. Bake at 325° about 45 minutes.

SWISS EGGS

1/4 lb. cheese	3/4 cup table cream
8 eggs	Salt and pepper to taste

Coat a pie plate generously with butter. Grate half the cheese well over the surface. Break eggs evenly over the cheese. Coat surface of eggs with table cream. Grate remaining cheese liberally over surface. Season with salt and pepper and bake at 350° until eggs are done.

QUICK EGG SUPPER

1 egg	1/4 cup chopped ham
1/2 tsp. flour	1/4 tsp. chili powder
2 tbsp. milk	Salt to taste
1/4 cup shredded cheddar cheese	1/2 sliced tomato

Beat egg. Add flour, milk, cheese, ham and seasonings, blending well. Pour into greased individual casserole dishes. Microwave on Medium for 4 minutes. Arrange tomato slices on top. Microwave 1 to 2 minutes to complete cooking. Serve hot with salad. Yield: 1 serving.

Georgina Taylor

Suggested Uses For Egg Yolks Only: Add to rice or mashed potatoes to make potato croquettes or Duchesse potatoes. Cook yolks in salted water below boiling point until hard, press through sieve and use in sandwiches or as garnish on soup, salads or vegetables. Use in custard sauce or cup custard, egg yolk sponge cake, French toast, gold cake, layer or cup cakes, Hollandaise sauce, mayonnaise, orange cake frosting, breading food for frying and to thicken cooked sauces.

EGG NESTS

2 slices hot buttered toast	2 eggs, separated
2 slices fried ham	1/4 tsp. salt
2 slices process cheese	1 tsp. butter

Place toast on baking sheet. Top each slice with ham and cheese. Beat egg whites and salt until stiff but not dry. Dividing equally, pile whites on toast slices. Make an indentation in the center of each pile with the back of a spoon. Carefully slip an egg yolk into each indentation. Place 1/2 tsp. butter on top of each yolk. Bake at 350° for 12 to 15 minutes until whites are lightly browned and yolks are set to desired degree. Serve at once. Yield: 2 servings.

Irene Wagstaff

FREEZING EGGS

Whole eggs, yolks or whites, may be frozen for later use. Freeze in quantities suitable for family use or in amounts for specific recipes.

Yolks, frozen alone or with whites, must be blended with corn syrup, sugar or salt to prevent them becoming gummy during storage. Allow 1 tbsp. syrup or sugar or 1/2 tsp. salt per cup of yolks. It is not necessary to add syrup, sugar or salt to egg whites before freezing. Prepare quickly and freeze promptly.

To freeze whole eggs, break into a bowl. Stir slowly to blend yolks and whites. Do not beat.

Press egg whites and blend through medium-mesh strainer or food mill.

If eggs are to be used in desserts, cakes, cookies, etc. add 1/2 tbsp. corn syrup or sugar per 8-oz. cup. If eggs are to be used as omelettes, scrambled or in main courses, etc., add 1/2 tsp. salt per cup. Mix syrup, sugar or salt in thoroughly.

Freeze eggs in moisture-vapor proof cartons or glass sealers. Leave 1/2 inch head space to allow for expansion during freezing. Whole eggs, yolks or whites, may also be prepared as directed above and then frozen in one or two egg portions in custard cups or ice cube trays. Remove from containers and package in moisture-vapor proof bags and store as usual. Will retain quality for up to 9 months.

Thaw in refrigerator only the amount of eggs needed at one time. An 8-oz. container will thaw overnight in refrigerator. Use any left-over thawed eggs within 24 hours.

Use frozen eggs in cooked dishes only, not in uncooked icings, egg nogs, etc.

Left over egg yolks or whites will keep for several days if stored properly. Cover yolks with water in small tightly sealed container. Store whites in covered container.

EGGS IN NESTS

1 tbsp. butter **or** chopped bacon   1 cup cooked tomatoes
1 tbsp. chopped onion   2 cups cooked rice
Salt and pepper to taste   6 eggs

Melt butter over low heat. Add onion and fry lightly. Add salt, pepper, tomatoes and rice. Mix well and put into baking dish. Break fresh eggs, one by one, in saucer and place in a well in rice dish, using one well for each egg. Sprinkle with salt and pepper. Bake at 350° until eggs are done. Serve hot. VARIATION: Cut macaroni may be substituted for rice.

EGG McMUFFINS

1 egg   1 slice cheese
1 tsp. milk   1 large bun **or** English muffin,
1 slice ham   buttered

Put egg and milk in small round dish. Mix well and microwave on High for 60 seconds. Place ham slice, egg and cheese between bun halves. Microwave on High for 20 to 25 seconds.

Nettie Connolley

EGG FOO YONG

1/4 cup butter   1/2 tsp. salt
1 green pepper, chopped   1/4 tsp. pepper
1 onion, chopped   15-oz. can water chestnuts,
2 cups bean sprouts, drained   drained and chopped
2 41/2-oz. cans shrimp, drained   Vegetable oil
6 eggs

Combine all ingredients but oil. Form into cakes using 1/3 cup of mixture to form each cake. Fry cakes in hot vegetable oil until golden brown on each side. As cakes are fried, put in oven to keep warm. When all cakes are fried, return to skillet, add following sauce and heat thoroughly.

21/2 cups water   2 tbsp. cornstarch
1/4 cup soya sauce

Combine ingredients in saucepan, cook until clear and pour over cakes.

Suggested Uses For Egg Whites Only: Add to eggs before scrambling or making omelette, angel cakes or cup cakes, Baked Alaska, baked custard, butter icing, Divinity fudge, fruit whips, meringues (coconut kisses), meringue shells, meringue topping for cake or pie, sea-foam candy, seven-minute frosting or other cake frosting, soft custard or sauce, thickening cooked sauces, breading foods for frying, various cookies.

BUTTERMILK PANCAKES

1/4 cup flour	2 tbsp. sugar
1 tsp. baking powder	2 tbsp. cooking oil
1/4 tsp. salt	1 1/2 cups buttermilk
1 cup graham flour	1 egg, well beaten
1/2 tsp. baking soda	Fresh fruit (optional)

Mix dry ingredients. Add cooking oil, buttermilk and egg to make a smooth batter. Stir in fruit. If using electric frying pan, set temperature at 360°. Yield: 7 or 8 pancakes. VARIATION: Omit cooking oil for fat-free pancakes. Beat mixture until smooth.

Leon Van Petten
Mrs. Doreen Sexty

FLUFFY PANCAKES

2 cups flour	2 egg yolks, well beaten
2 tbsp. sugar	2 cups milk
4 tsp. baking powder	2 tbsp. melted butter
1 tsp. salt	2 egg whites, beaten stiff

Measure flour, without sifting, into mixing bowl. Add sugar, baking powder and salt. Stir well to blend. Combine egg yolks, milk and butter. Add to blended dry ingredients. Beat with rotating beater until smooth. Fold in beaten egg whites. Pour 1/3 cup batter for each pancake on hot griddle. Grease griddle lightly for first pancake only. Bake until puffy and bubbly. Turn before bubbles break and cook other side. Serve hot with maple or fruit syrup. Yield: 10 to 12 pancakes. VARIATIONS: add any of the following: 1 cup chopped, cooked sausage, 1 cup grated nippy cheese, 1 cup fresh, frozen or drained canned blueberries, 1 cup coarsely grated apple.

FRENCH PANCAKES

1 cup light cream	3 tbsp. icing sugar
1 tsp. salt	1/2 cup flour
4 eggs	

Place ingredients in mixing bowl. Beat until smooth with rotary mixer. Batter will be thin. Cook on lightly-greased pan — about 2 tbsp. batter per pancake. When browned on one side, roll up and serve.

Mrs. Anna Kobitzch

Suggested Uses For Yolks Or Whites: Mix with a little water and use as a dip when breading foods for frying, salad dressing (raw yolk keeps French dressing from separating), in butter icings, to replace all or part of a liquid and add smoothness, cooked and used for sandwich fillings, mixed with celery, nuts or other crunchy ingredients.

GRANDMA'S HOT CAKES

2 cups buttermilk
2 tsp. soda
3/4 tsp. salt
1/2 cup sour cream
2 eggs

1/2 cup rolled oats
1 cup plus 2 tbsp. flour
2/3 cup sugar
3/4 tsp. baking powder
1/2 cup cornmeal

Pour buttermilk into mixing bowl. Add soda and salt. Stir in sour cream until mixture foams. Add eggs and beat with spoon. Add oatmeal. Sift flour, sugar, baking powder and cornmeal into mixture and beat until flour lumps are out. Heat greased griddle. Pour on large hot cakes. When deep brown on one side, turn over and brown on the other side. Yield: 4 to 6 servings.

KLONDIKE FLAPJACKS

1 cup milk
1/4 cup shortening
2 tbsp. sugar
1 tsp. salt

1 pkg. dry yeast
1/4 cup warm water
1 egg
1 cup flour

Scald milk with shortening. Stir in sugar and salt. Cool to lukewarm. Dissolve yeast in warm water. Stir in milk mixture. Beat in egg and flour. Cover and let rise in warm place about 1 hour until very light. Stir batter down and bake on hot griddle. Yield: 10 to 12 pancakes.

Mrs. James Baschnitz

HENRICI'S EGG PANCAKE

1/2 cup milk
3 eggs
1/2 cup whole wheat flour

3 tbsp. powdered milk
2 tbsp. oil
1/2 tsp. salt

Mix all ingredients in a bowl or blender and pour into oiled cold pie plate. Bake at 400° for 10 minutes. Lower heat to 350° and bake another 10 minutes. Pancake will puff up.

POTATO PANCAKES

1 egg
2 tbsp. chopped onion
1/4 cup flour
3/4 tsp. salt

2 1/2 cups grated raw potato,
   soaked in cold water
1/4 cup lard

Combine egg, onion, flour and salt. Drain potatoes and add to first mixture. Melt lard in skillet. Spoon potato mixture onto hot griddle. Spread lightly and fry until underside is crisp and brown. Turn and brown other side. Serve hot.

WAFFLES

21/4 cups flour	2 egg yolks, slightly beaten
3/4 tsp. salt	21/4 cups milk
4 tsp. baking powder	1/2 cup cooking oil
11/2 tbsp. sugar	2 egg whites, stiffly beaten

Sift together dry ingredients. Combine egg yolks, milk and cooking oil. Stir into dry ingredients. Fold in egg whites. Do not overmix. Bake in preheated waffle baker. Yield: 6 servings.

Mrs. Francis Blue

YEAST WAFFLES

11/2 cups milk	2 tsp. sugar
1/3 cup sugar	2 env. active dry yeast
2 tsp. salt	2 eggs, well beaten
1/2 cup butter **or** margarine	2 tsp. vanilla
1/2 cup lukewarm water	2 cups flour

Scald the milk and stir in sugar, salt and margarine. Cool to lukewarm. Combine water and 2 tsp. sugar into a bowl and sprinkle the yeast over. Let stand 10 minutes. Stir well. Stir in the lukewarm milk mixture. Stir in eggs, vanilla and flour. Beat until smooth. Batter should be very thin. Cover bowl with damp cloth. Let rise about 40 minutes until double in bulk. Stir down batter. Bake in heated waffle iron at medium heat about 5 minutes until golden brown and serve with butter and hot syrup.

CALORIE-TRIMMERS FRENCH TOAST

4 eggs	6 slices slightly dry bread
1/2 cup skim milk	2 tbsp. butter **or** margarine
Dash of salt	4 tbsp. honey

Beat eggs slightly with milk and salt in pie plate. Dip bread slices one at a time into egg mixture, turning to coat both sides well. Sauté slowly in 1 tbsp. of the butter, turn once and add more butter as needed, in heated large frying pan 3 to 4 minutes, or until golden. Cut each slice in half diagonally. Arrange the triangles on serving plates and drizzle with 1 tbsp. honey. Yield: 4 servings. 296 calories per serving. Weight watchers serving: 11/2 slices bread and 1 tbsp. honey.

CREPES

8 eggs	1/2 cup flour
1/2 tsp. salt	1 pint milk

Beat egg and salt until light. Gradually add flour and mix well. Add milk and blend well. In a well-greased cast iron pan, spread a spoonful of this mixture so it will line bottom of pan. Fry on one side, turn over. When done, sprinkle with brown sugar or your favorite jam and roll up.

OLD FASHIONED BROWN SUGAR SYRUP

1 1/2 cups brown sugar
3/4 cup water

1/2 tsp. vanilla **or**
1/4 tsp. cinnamon

Combine sugar and water, stirring until dissolved. Boil 2 to 3 minutes until syrup is of preferred thickness. Add flavoring and store covered in jar in the refrigerator, or serve hot at once with griddle cakes or French toast. Yield: 1 cup.

YORKSHIRE PUDDING

1 cup flour
1 cup milk
1 tsp. salt

2 - 3 eggs
1/2 cup sultana raisins
3 0 4 tbsp. hot drippings

Beat flour, milk and salt until smooth. Add eggs separately, beating until smooth after each egg. Add raisins and beat. Let stand. Put 3 or 4 tbsp. drippings from roast beef in 8 x 12-inch baking pan and heat in oven until it smokes. Pour batter into pan and bake at 350° for 30 minutes. Cut into squares and serve with gravy and roast.

Mrs. E. Kelly

STANDARD FRITTER BATTER

2 eggs
1/2 cup milk
1 cup flour

1 tsp. baking powder
1 tsp. salt
2 tsp. melted shortening

Put eggs into small bowl and beat until light. Add milk. Stir together flour, baking powder and salt and add to milk mixture. Add shortening and beat until blended. Use batter for coating fish, poultry or fruit, then deep fat fry in hot oil.

APPLE FRITTERS

Pare, core and slice apples. Dip into standard fritter batter. Cover each slice with batter. Fry for 5 minutes in hot oil at 375°. Serve with icing sugar or maple syrup.

EGG VOLUME EQUIVALENTS

4 large, 5 medium, 6 small whole eggs = approximately 1 cup
14 large, 17 medium, 19 small egg yolks = approximately 1 cup
7 large, 8 medium, 9 small egg whites = approximately 1 cup

BREADS, BISCUITS
& DOUGHNUTS

BREAD

WHITE BREAD

1/2 cup warm water
1 tsp. sugar
1 env. active dry yeast
11/2 cups water
1/2 cup milk

3 tbsp. margarine
3 tbsp. sugar
2 tsp. salt
51/2 - 61/2 cups flour

Combine warm water and 1 tsp. sugar. Sprinkle with yeast. Let stand 10 minutes. Stir well. Combine 11/2 cups water, milk and margarine. Heat until liquids are warm and margarine melts. Stir in 3 tbsp. sugar and salt. Add yeast. Beat in 2 cups of flour until smooth. Stir in additional flour to make a soft dough. Turn onto floured board. Knead until smooth and elastic. Place in greased bowl. Cover. Let rise about 1 hour until double in bulk. Punch dough down. Turn onto floured board. Cover. Let rest for 15 minutes. Divide dough in half and shape into loaves. Place in greased loaf pans. Cover. Let rise about 1 hour until double in bulk. Bake at 375° for 45 minutes. Remove from pans and cool on wire racks.

COLD DOUGH WHITE BREAD

1 cup warm water
2 tsp. sugar
2 env. active dry yeast
11/2 cups water

1/2 cup margarine
2 tbsp. sugar
1 tbsp. salt
6 - 7 cups flour

Measure warm water into a bowl. Stir in sugar and yeast. Let stand 10 minutes. Stir well. Combine 11/2 cups water and margarine, heat over low heat until liquid is warm and margarine melted. Stir in 2 tbsp. sugar and salt. Add liquid to yeast. Beat in 21/2 cups flour until smooth. Stir in remaining flour to make soft dough. Turn onto floured board and knead about 8 to 10 minutes until smooth and elastic. Cover with plastic wrap and a towel. Let rest 20 minutes. Punch dough down. Divide in half and shape into loaves. Place in greased 9 x 5 x 3-inch loaf pans and brush with cooking oil. Cover pans loosely with plastic wrap. Refrigerate up to 24 hours. Uncover dough carefully and let stand uncovered for 10 minutes. Puncture any gas bubbles with greased toothpick. Bake at 400° about 30 to 40 minutes or until done. Remove from pans and cool on wire racks.

SOUR DOUGH BREAD

1/2 cup warm water	1 tbsp. sugar
1 tsp. sugar	1 tbsp. salt
1 env. active dry yeast	13/4 cups flour
2 cups warm water	

To make starter, measure 1/2 cup warm water in bowl. Stir in 1 tsp. sugar and yeast. Let stand 10 minutes and stir. Combine 2 cups warm water, 1 tbsp. sugar and salt. Add liquid to the dissolved yeast. Add flour and beat vigorously until smooth. Cover. Let stand at room temperature for 4 days. Stir down daily. NOTE: To re-use starter for next baking, add 1 1/2 cups warm water, 3/4 cups flour and 1 1/2 tsp. sugar to the unused starter. Beat well for about 1 minute. Cover. Let stand until ready to make bread again. Stir down daily.

1/2 cup warm water	2 tbsp. sugar
1 tsp. sugar	1 tsp. salt
1 env. active dry yeast	1 1/2 cups starter
1 cup milk	5 - 6 cups flour
2 tbsp. margarine	

Measure the warm water in bowl. Stir in 1 tsp. sugar and sprinkle yeast over. Let stand 10 minutes. Stir well. Combine milk and margarine in saucepan. Heat until margarine melts. Stir in 2 tbsp. sugar and salt. Add liquid to dissolved yeast. Add starter and 1 1/2 cups flour. Beat until smooth. Stir in remaining flour to make soft dough and turn onto floured board. Knead until smooth and elastic. Place in greased bowl. Cover. Let rise about 1 hour. Punch dough down and turn onto floured board. Let rest 15 minutes. Divide dough in half. Shape each half into loaf. Place in two greased loaf pans. Cover. Let rise about 1 hour until double in bulk. Bake at 400° for about 30 minutes. Cool.

CINNAMON BREAD

White bread recipe dough	1/3 cup sugar
Melted butter **or** margarine	3 tsp. cinnamon

Punch dough down. Turn onto floured board. Divide dough in half. Roll half the dough into a 12 x 8-inch rectangle. Brush lightly with melted margarine or butter. Combine the sugar and cinnamon and sprinkle half over the dough. Roll tightly from the 8-inch side as for jelly roll. Seal edges firmly. Seal ends of loaves and fold underneath. Place each seam side down in a greased 9 x 5 x 3-inch loaf pan. Cover and let rise in warm place about 1 hour until double in bulk. Bake at 350° about 30 minutes or until brown. Cool on wire racks when done.

Freezing does not injure color or flavor of honey and prevents granulation. Refrigeration hastens granulation.

WHOLE WHEAT BREAD

2 env. active dry yeast	3 tbsp. molasses
2 tsp. sugar	4 tsp. salt
1/2 cup lukewarm water	4 tbsp. shortening
2 cups milk	5 cups flour and 5 cups
2 cups cold water	whole wheat flour **or**
4 tbsp. sugar	10 cups whole wheat flour

Dissolve yeast with 2 tsp. sugar and lukewarm water. Let stand for 10 minutes. Scald milk, add cold water and cool to lukewarm. Add sugar, molasses, salt and shortening. Measure flour, make hollow in center and add liquid. Stir yeast and add. Stir until flour is dampened. Mix and knead about 8 minutes. Place in greased bowl. Cover. Let rise until double in bulk. Punch down. Divide into 4 loaves. Let rise in pans. Bake at 375° for 40 to 50 minutes.

Mrs. Leona Ost

100% WHOLE WHEAT BREAD

1 cup warm water	6 tbsp. margarine
1 tsp. sugar	1/2 cup honey
2 env. active dry yeast	4 tsp. salt
1 cup water	8 - 9 cups whole wheat flour
1 1/2 cups milk	

Measure the warm water into a bowl. Stir in sugar and yeast. Let stand 10 minutes. Stir well. Combine 1 cup water, milk, margarine and honey in saucepan. Heat until liquids are warm and margarine melts. Add to dissolved yeast. Add salt and 4 cups flour. Beat until smooth. Stir in an additional 5 cups flour to make soft dough. Turn onto floured board. Cover dough and let rest 10 minutes. Knead until smooth and elastic. Place in greased bowl. Cover. Let rise about 50 minutes until double in bulk. Punch dough down. Turn onto floured board. Divide dough in half. Shape each half into a loaf. Place in two greased loaf pans. Cover. Let rise in warm place about 50 minutes until double in bulk. Bake in moderate oven at 375° about 35 to 40 minutes. Remove from pans and cool on wire racks.

To soften hardened brown sugar, add a slice of apple or bread, cover and microwave 1 minute on High or until soft.

Bread freezes well. After bread or rolls are thoroughly cooled, wrap in aluminum foil or airtight plastic bags. Seal tightly. A double layer will keep wrap from tearing. Do not frost or decorate breads before freezing. Quick-freeze bread.

HIGH FIBER OAT BREAD

1 potato, enough to yield 1 1/2 cups mashed	1 tsp. cream of tartar
2 tbsp. honey	1/2 tsp. salt
1 cup unbleached flour	1 cup whole wheat flour
2 1/2 tsp. baking soda	3/4 cup rolled oats
	1/2 cup currants **or** raisins

Peel and slice potato and cover with enough water to cover. Cook until tender. Drain, reserving 3/4 cup liquid, and mash potatoes. Add 1/2 cup mashed potato and honey to potato water, stirring well. Sift together unbleached flour, soda, cream of tartar and salt into medium bowl. Add whole wheat flour and mix. Stir in oats and currants. Make a well in the center of dry ingredients and add potato mixture. Stir until a soft dough forms. Knead 1 minute with floured hands. shape into a ball and place into an 8-inch round pan that has been oiled. Flatten and slash an X on top with a sharp knife. Bake at 350° for 30 minutes. Slice when cool.

Jean Leskow

ROLLED OAT BREAD

1/2 cup lukewarm water	2 tbsp. sugar
2 tsp. sugar	2 tsp. salt
1 env. active dry yeast	2 tbsp. oil
2 cups hot water	2 tbsp. molasses
2 cups rolled oats	Flour

Combine lukewarm water, sugar and yeast and let stand for 10 minutes. Combine hot water, rolled oats, 2 tbsp. sugar, salt, oil and molasses. Add yeast mixture. Cool to lukewarm. Add 1 cup flour. Beat until smooth and elastic. Work in about 2 3/4 cups flour. Knead until smooth. Place in a greased bowl, cover and let rise about 1 1/4 hours until double in bulk. Punch down and knead again. Divide into two portions. Let stand for 10 minutes. Shape into loaves and place in pans. Let rise about 40 minutes until double in bulk. Bake at 400° for 45 to 50 minutes.

CASSEROLE BREAD

3/4 cup milk	3/4 cup lukewarm water
1/4 cup sugar	2 tsp. sugar
2 tsp. salt	1 egg, well beaten
1/4 cup shortening	3 cups flour
2 env. active dry yeast	

Scald milk and stir in the sugar, salt and shortening. Cool to lukewarm. Add yeast to lukewarm water and sugar. Let stand 10 minutes and stir into the lukewarm milk mixture. Stir in egg and flour. Mix well until batter is smooth and elastic. Cover with damp cloth. Let rise in warm place until double in bulk. Stir down and turn into greased 6-cup casserole. An 8-inch tube pan may also be used. Bake at 400° for 45 minutes.

LOW CHOLESTEROL BREAD

1/2 cup warm water	1 tbsp. margarine
1 tsp. sugar	1 tbsp. sugar
1 env. active dry yeast	2 tsp. salt
21/2 cups water	61/2 - 71/2 cups flour

Measure warm water into bowl. Stir in 1 tsp. of sugar and yeast. Let stand 10 minutes and stir well. Combine 21/2 cups water and margarine in saucepan and heat over low heat until liquid is warm and margarine melts. Stir in 1 tbsp. sugar and salt. Add liquid to dissolved yeast. Add 23/4 cups flour. Beat until smooth. Stir in additional 41/4 cups flour to make soft dough. Turn onto lightly-floured board. Knead about 8 to 10 minutes until smooth and elastic. Place in greased bowl, turning to grease top. Cover. Let rise in warm place about 1 hour until double in bulk. Punch dough down. Turn out onto lightly-floured board and divide dough in half. Shape each half into loaf. Place in two greased 9 x 5 x 3-inch pans and cover. Let rise in warm place about 1 hour until double in bulk. Bake at 400° about 40 to 45 minutes or until done. Remove from pans and cool on wire racks.

RYE BREAD

1/2 cup warm water	1 tbsp. salt
1 tsp. sugar	1 tbsp. caraway seeds, optional
1 env. active dry yeast	21/2 cups rye flour
3/4 cup water	21/2 cups white flour
1 cup milk	1/4 cup corn meal
2 tbsp. honey	1 egg white
1 tbsp. margarine	2 tbsp. water
2 tsp. sugar	

Measure 1/2 cup warm water in bowl, stir in 1 tsp. sugar and sprinkle with yeast. Let stand 10 minutes and stir well. Combine 3/4 cup water, milk, honey and margarine in saucepan. Heat over low heat until liquids are warm and margarine melts. Stir in 2 tsp. sugar, salt and caraway seeds. Add liquid to dissolved yeast. Combine flours and add 2 cups to liquids. Beat until smooth. Stir in additional 3 cups flour to make soft dough. Turn onto lightly-floured board. Knead about 8 to 10 minutes until smooth and elastic. Place in bowl and grease top. Cover. Let rise in warm place about 1 hour. Punch dough down. Turn onto floured board. Divide dough in half. Form each piece into smooth ball. Cover. Let rest 10 minutes. Flatten each piece slightly and roll lightly on board to form tapered ends. Sprinkle two greased baking sheets with corn meal. Place breads on baking sheets. Combine egg white and 2 tbsp. water and brush breads. Let rise uncovered about 35 minutes. Bake at 375° for 40 to 45 minutes. Remove from baking sheets and cool on wire racks.

RAISIN CASSEROLE BREAD

2/3 cup boiling water
1/2 cup sugar
11/2 tsp. salt
1/4 cup shortening
1/2 cup lukewarm water

2 tsp. sugar
2 env. active dry yeast
1 egg, well beaten
3 cups flour, approximately
1 cup seedless raisins

Combine boiling water, sugar, salt and shortening. Cool. Combine lukewarm water and sugar. Stir and sprinkle with yeast. Let stand 10 minutes and stir well. Stir into the lukewarm water mixture. Add egg, flour and raisins. Blend well. Cover with damp cloth. Let rise about 1 hour until more than double in bulk. Stir down batter. Turn into greased 6-cup casserole and bake uncovered at 400° for 40 to 45 minutes.

CHERRY PUFF LOAVES (Yeast Bread)

1 cup milk
1/3 cup sugar
1/2 cup margarine
1/2 cup warm water
1 tsp. sugar

1 env. fast-rising yeast
2 eggs, well beaten
5 cups flour
1 cup chopped glaze cherries

Scald milk; add sugar and margarine. Cool. Combine warm water and sugar and sprinkle with yeast. Let stand 10 minutes. Stir well. Combine yeast and lukewarm milk mixture. Add eggs. Add 2 cups flour and mix until smooth. Mix cherries into1 cup flour, coating well. Add to batter, mix well and continue adding remaining flour. Turn out onto floured board and knead until smooth and elastic. Place in greased bowl and cover with cloth. Let rise about 1 hour until double in bulk. Punch down. Turn onto board and divide into three pieces. Form into balls and place in three well-greased 48-oz. juice cans. Let rise about 11/2 hours. Bake at 350° for 35 to 40 minutes. Cut, butter and serve with cheese slices.

BASIC SWEET DOUGH

1/2 cup milk
1/2 cup sugar
11/2 tsp. salt
1/4 cup shortening
1/2 cup lukewarm water

2 tsp. sugar
2 env. active dry yeast
2 eggs, well beaten
4 cups flour
Melted shortening

Scald the milk and stir in 1/2 cup sugar, salt and shortening. Cool to lukewarm. Mix 1/2 cup lukewarm water and 2 tsp. sugar. Stir well. Sprinkle with yeast and let stand 10 minutes. Stir well. Stir into lukewarm milk mixture. Add eggs and stir in 2 cups flour. Beat until smooth. Add the additional flour and continue mixing. Turn dough onto floured board and knead until smooth and elastic. Place in greased bowl. Brush top with shortening. Cover. Let rise about 1 hour until double in bulk. Punch down. Turn onto floured board and shape into buns. Place on greased pans and let rise until double in bulk. Bake at 375° about 25 minutes.

CINNAMON BUNS

Basic Sweet Dough recipe   Cinnamon
Butter **or** margarine   1/2 cup raisins (optional)
1/2 cup brown sugar

Make the basic sweet dough. Let rise. Punch down. Turn out on lightly-floured board. Divide in two portions. Roll each portion in a rectangle. Spread with butter and sprinkle with the brown sugar. Sprinkle well with cinnamon and raisins. Roll up like a jelly roll. Cut into 3/4 inch slices. Place in a pan which has been well-greased with butter and sprinkled with brown sugar. Let rise. Bake at 350° for 20 to 25 minutes, or until light brown. Invert pan immediately when taken from oven. Remove buns. Bottom of buns will be glazed. Serve warm or cold.

CLOVER LEAF ROLLS (Basic Sweet Dough)

Make the basic sweet dough. Halve the dough and cut each half into 9 equal pieces. Cut each piece into three and form into small smooth balls. Place three balls in each section of greased muffin pans. Brush lightly with melted butter or margarine. Cover. Let rise in warm place until double in bulk. Bake at 400° for 15 to 20 minutes.

PAN ROLLS

Basic Sweet Dough   1/4 cup melted butter

Make the basic sweet dough. Halve the dough and form each half into 12-inch roll. Cut each roll into 12 equal pieces. Form into smooth balls. Place in greased 8 or 9 inch layer cake pans or 8-inch square cake pans. Brush with butter. Cover. Let rise until double in bulk. Bake at 375° about 25 minutes. Yield: 24 rolls.

WHITE BATTER ROLLS

3/4 cup milk   1/2 cup lukewarm water
3 tbsp. sugar   2 tsp. sugar
1 tsp. salt   2 env. active dry yeast
1/4 cup shortening   2 cups flour

Scald the milk and stir in the 3 tbsp. sugar, salt and shortening. Cool to lukewarm. Measure warm water and 2 tsp. sugar into a bowl and sprinkle the yeast over. Let stand 10 minutes. Stir well. Stir in the lukewarm milk mixture and add the flour. Stir until well blended. Cover with damp cloth. Let rise in warm place about 40 minutes until double in bulk. Stir down batter. Fill greased average-sized muffin pans about 3/4 full. Bake at 400° for about 20 to 25 minutes.

Frozen foil-wrapped bread may be thawed and warmed at 375° for 20 minutes. Unwrap bread the last 5 minutes to crisp the crust.

BATTER BUNS

1 cup warm water	1/2 cup whole wheat flour
1 tbsp. sugar	11/2 - 13/4 cups white flour
1 env. active dry yeast	2 tbsp. melted margarine
1 tsp. salt	1 egg

Mix water, sugar and yeast together. Let stand 10 minutes. Combine remaining ingredients and add to yeast mixture. Cover and let rise 30 minutes. Spoon into muffin tins and let rise for 30 minutes. Bake at 400° for 12 to 15 minutes. Yield: 14 muffins.

Doris Barker

AIR BUNS

1/2 cup warm water	2 tsp. salt
1 tsp. sugar	31/2 cups warm water
1 tbsp. Quick-Yeast	1 tbsp. vinegar
1/2 cup sugar	Pinch of mace
1/2 cup cooking oil	6 cups flour

Mix the warm water, sugar and yeast. Let stand 10 minutes. Combine 1/2 cup sugar, cooking oil, salt and warm water in a bowl. Stir to smooth batter. Add yeast, vinegar and mace. Continue adding flour until soft, not sticky, dough is formed. Knead well. Place in well-greased bowl and set in warm place to rise about 2 hours. Punch down and set to rise again to double in bulk. Form into buns or rolls and let them rise to double their size. Bake at 400° for 15 minutes or until brown. Yield: 5 dozen buns.

Mrs. G.L. Stewart

OVERNIGHT BUNS

1 env. active dry yeast	2 tsp. salt
1 tsp. sugar	1/2 cup cooking oil
1/2 cup water	21/2 cups warm water
4 eggs, well beaten	10 cups flour
3/4 cup sugar	

The night before, dissolve yeast in the sugar and 1/2 cup water. Let stand about 12 minutes. Beat eggs, sugar and salt with cooking oil, add the warm water and stir into yeast mixture. Work about 10 cups flour into this, mixing well until medium stiff. Let rise about 1 hour. Punch down at one hour intervals (after the first hour and twice more). Let dough rise overnight. Form into buns and bake at 375° for about 12 minutes. Yield: 90 to 100 buns. Preparation time: 31/2 hours.

Mrs. Pearl Liebelt

For best results in yeast baking, use warm water (105° to 115°). When tested on inside of wrist, water feels warm, not hot.

HOT CROSS BUNS

1 env. active dry yeast	3/4 cup sugar
1 cup lukewarm water	1/2 cup seeded raisins
1 tbsp. sugar	1/8 cup currants
1 cup milk	1/2 cup mixed peel
4 cups flour	1 egg yolk
1 tsp. salt	2 tbsp. milk
2 eggs, well beaten	1 egg white
1/2 cup butter	1/2 cup sugar

Soak yeast in lukewarm water and add 1 tbsp. sugar. Scald and cool milk and add to flour and salt, mixing well. Add the eggs, butter and 3/4 cup sugar creamed together, raisins, currants and mixed peel. Beat hard and add enough flour to make a fairly stiff dough. Knead well and place in greased bowl. When dough is double in bulk, knead again, and shape into buns. Place in well-greased pans and let rise in a warm place. With a sharp knife or razor blade, cut a cross in each bun. Brush with egg yolk beaten in 2 tbsp. milk. Bake at 350° about 20 minutes. While buns are still warm, glaze tops with egg white beaten with 1/2 cup sugar.

Mrs. Mary Belanger

100% WHOLE WHEAT ROLLS

1/2 cup milk, scalded	1 cake compressed yeast
2 tbsp. oil	1 egg, beaten
1 tbsp. honey	3 cups whole wheat flour
1 tsp. salt	2 tbsp. fresh wheat germ
1/2 cup warm water	

Make a mixture of scalded milk, oil, honey and salt. Pour warm water into this mixture. Add crumbled yeast, egg, whole wheat flour and wheat germ. Mix well and let rise in warm place until bulk is doubled. Form into small rolls and place in oiled muffin pan. Bake at 400° for 20 minutes.

WHOLE WHEAT BUNS

1/3 cup packed brown sugar	1 tsp. sugar
3 tsp. salt	1 env. active dry yeast
1/3 cup shortening, melted	2 cups whole wheat flour
1 cup milk, scalded	2 cups flour
1/2 cup lukewarm water	Melted shortening

Stir brown sugar, salt and shortening into milk. Cool. Place lukewarm water in bowl, stir in sugar and sprinkle yeast over. Let stand 10 minutes. Stir well and stir into the lukewarm milk mixture. Combine flours and stir half into yeast mixture. Beat until smooth. Stir in remaining flour mixture. Turn onto lightly floured board. Knead until smooth and elastic. Place in greased bowl and brush top with shortening. Cover. Let rise in warm place about 1 hour until double in bulk. Punch down, turn onto board, shape into buns and place in pans. Bake at 400° for 15 to 20 minutes.

BAKEDAY SURPRISES

When the bread dough is ready for the pans, pinch off some pieces, form into small balls and put in a deep baking pan. Let rise until fairly high and pour the following sauce over them:

1 cup sour cream
1 tsp. soda

1 cup brown sugar
1 tsp. cinnamon

Mix the cream with the soda, sugar and cinnamon. Pour it over the rolls and bake at 325° for 30 to 40 minutes. Watch very carefully for they burn easily. Serve with cream.

Jeanette Gordon

BUTTER HORNS

1 env. active dry yeast
1/4 cup warm milk
3 cups flour
1 cup sugar
1 cup butter

3 egg yolks
1 cup milk
1/2 tsp. salt
1 cup walnuts

Soak yeast in the warm milk. Rub flour, sugar and butter together. Beat egg yolks well. Add milk and salt and beat again. Mix all together and knead well. Set in a cool place, just under freezing, for 6 to 8 hours or overnight. Divide into five parts. Roll each into a circle to thickness of pie crust on sugared board. Do not use flour. Spread with finely-crushed walnuts. Cut in triangles. Roll up wide end first. Let rise 31/2 hours. Bake at 400° for 20 minutes.

Mrs. William Fuhr
Mrs. Olive McKibbon

COCONUT PINEAPPLE COFFEE CAKE

3 tbsp. butter **or** margarine
2 tbsp. brown sugar
1/3 cup crushed pineapple
1/3 cup milk
1/3 cup sugar
3/4 tsp. salt
1/4 cup shortening

1/2 cup lukewarm water
1 tsp. sugar
1 env. active dry yeast
1 egg, well beaten
1/2 tsp. vanilla
2 cups flour
1/2 cup shredded coconut

Melt the butter in a 9 x 9-inch pan and sprinkle with the brown sugar. Drain the pineapple and add. Scald the milk and stir in 1/3 cup sugar, salt and shortening. Cool to lukewarm. Meanwhile, combine lukewarm water and 1 tsp. sugar and sprinkle yeast over. Let stand 10 minutes. Stir well. Stir in the lukewarm milk mixture. Add the egg and vanilla and stir in the flour, blending well. Add coconut. Turn into prepared pan and spread evenly. Cover with damp cloth. Let rise in warm place about 1 hour until double in bulk. Bake at 350° for 35 minutes. Turn out of pan immediately. Serve warm.

DANISH COFFEE CAKE

1 tsp. sugar	1 cup butter
1/2 cup lukewarm water	1/4 cup sugar
1 env. active dry yeast	1/2 tsp. salt
2 cups flour	2 eggs, well beaten

Add 1 tsp. sugar to lukewarm water. Add yeast and let mixture stand for 10 minutes. Combine flour, butter, sugar and salt as for pie crust. Add eggs to yeast. Pour liquid mixture into flour mixture. Mix to a soft smooth dough. Divide into two parts. Roll each portion into an 18 x 10-inch rectangular shape.

1/2 cup soft butter	1/2 tsp. vanilla
1/2 cup sugar	1/2 cup flaked almonds
1 tsp. flour	

Combine all ingredients. Spread on each dough rectangle. Fold outside edges of each rectangle towards middle, leaving a 2-inch gap in center. Fold up ends and pinch well. Place rectangles on well-greased cookie sheet. Cover and let rise until double in bulk. Bake until golden brown at 375° for 20 to 30 minutes.

Elizabeth Pedersen

WELSH CURRANT CAKES

3 cups flour	1 cup shortening **or** butter
1 1/2 tsp. baking powder	1 cup currants **or** raisins
1/2 tsp. soda	2 eggs, slightly beaten
1 cup white sugar	5 tbsp. milk
1 tsp. nutmeg	

Sift dry ingredients together. Cut in shortening. Add currants. Add egg and milk. Mix only to blend. Chill. Divide dough into three parts. Roll to 1/4-inch thickness and cut as for biscuits. Heat ungreased electric pan or griddle to 350°. Cook until puffed and shiny on top and bottom is nicely browned. Turn and cool on rack.

Mrs. James Lovell

If in doubt about freshness of eggs stored on refrigerator shelf, test them by placing in a pan of cold water. An egg which floats is unfit for use. One that stands on end is going stale and should be discarded. The egg that lies at an angle is semi-fresh and the one lying on the bottom of the pan is like new.

To tint cocount, add food coloring to 1 tbsp. water until you get color desired. Put coconut in jar, add colored water, cap jar and shake. Dry on paper towel.

ORANGE CRESCENT DOUGH

1 env. active dry yeast	2 tbsp. butter, melted
1/4 cup warm water	3/4 cup sugar
1/4 cup sugar	3/4 cup coconut
1 tsp. salt	2 tbsp. grated orange rind
2 eggs, well beaten	3/4 cup sugar
1/2 cup sour cream	1/2 cup sour cream
6 tbsp. butter	2 tbsp. orange juice
23/4 - 3 cups flour	1/4 cup butter

Soften yeast in the warm water in large bowl. Beat in 1/4 cup sugar, salt, eggs, sour cream and butter and stir in part of the flour. Continue beating until all flour is used. You cannot over-beat this dough! Cover and let rise in warm place about 2 hours until double in bulk. Knead dough on floured board, cut into two equal parts. Roll each half into a 12-inch circle and brush with butter. Sprinkle with the filling made of the 3/4 cup sugar, coconut and grated orange rind. Spread evenly over dough and cut each circle into 12 wedges. Roll each wedge starting at the wide edge. Place rolls point-side down in three rows in a well-buttered 12 x 9-inch pan. Cover and let rise in warm place about 1 hour until double in bulk. Bake at 350° for 25 to 40 minutes until golden. Meanwhile, mix 3/4 cup sugar, 1/2 cup sour cream, orange juice and 1/4 cup butter. Boil for 3 minutes, stirring frequently. Pour over hot crescents. Sprinkle with more coconut and broil 3 to 5 minutes or until coconut is toasted.

Janet Hagstrom

SOUR CREAM TWISTS

1 cup sour cream	1/2 cup lukewarm water
3 tbsp. shortening	1 tsp. sugar
3 tbsp. sugar	3 cups flour
1/8 tsp. soda	2 tbsp. butter
1 tsp. salt	1/3 cup brown sugar
1 egg	1 tsp. cinnamon
1 env. active dry yeast	

Boil the sour cream, shortening, 3 tbsp. sugar, soda and salt. Let cool. Add egg. Dissolve the yeast in warm water and 1 tsp. sugar. Add to cooled sour cream mixture. Work in flour and mix well. Let stand 5 minutes. Roll out dough in strips about 24 x 6 inches. Spread with a topping of the butter, brown sugar and cinnamon. Place on half of dough covering 24 x 3 inches. Fold remaining half over this and press edges together. Cut into 1 x 3-inch strips. Twist and place on greased pan. Let rise. Bake at 375° for about 10 to 15 minutes. Ice while warm or sprinkle with nuts if desired.

Mrs. June Edwards
Mrs. Helen Kuhn

ROHALKY

2 tsp. sugar	1 tsp. salt
1/2 cup lukewarm water	1/2 lb. shortening **or** butter
2 env. active dry yeast	1/2 cup lukewarm milk
4 cups flour	4 eggs, well beaten
1/2 cup sugar	Jam, jelly **or** marmalade

Combine 2 tsp. sugar, lukewarm water and sprinkle with yeast. Let stand about 10 minutes. Sift flour, 1/2 cup sugar and salt. Blend in shortening until crumbly. Make well in center, pour in milk, eggs and yeast. Mix well by spoon and knead by hand. Let stand 4 hours in warm place. Divide dough into 3 portions. Roll out one-third at a time. Cut into desired sized squares. Put in small amount of jam in center or each. Fold the two opposite corners to overlap (about 1/2 inch at center). Dip in beaten egg whites and sprinkle with sugar. Let rise again. Bake at 350° until light brown.

Mrs. Anne Bzwoy

HONEY BUN RING

3/4 cup milk	1 egg, well beaten
1/3 cup sugar	1 tsp. grated lemon rind
1 tsp. salt	4 cups flour
1/4 cup shortening	1/2 cup brown sugar
1/2 cup warm water	1/2 cup liquid honey
1 tsp. sugar	3/4 cup walnuts, cut fine
1 env. active dry yeast	Melted butter

Scald the milk and add 1/3 cup sugar, salt and shortening. Cool. Combine warm water, 1 tsp. sugar and yeast. Let stand about 10 minutes. Stir well. Add cooled milk mixture, egg and lemon rind. Stir in 2 cups flour and beat until smooth, then add about 2 more cups flour and knead well. Place in greased bowl. Cover. Let rise until double in bulk in warm place. Punch down. Roll out into a 9 x 12-inch rectangle. Combine the brown sugar and honey. Spread over dough and sprinkle with chopped walnuts. Beginning at long side, loosely roll up like jelly roll. Lift carefully into 81/2 inch tube pan and join ends of dough to form a ring. Brush with melted butter. Cover. Let rise until double in bulk. Bake at 375° for 45 to 50 minutes. Brush top with honey and sprinkle with more nuts.

Carrie Hansen

To heat flour for bread baking, measure into large bowl and microwave on High for 3 to 4 minutes until warm.

Always allow yeast breads to rise in warm place, free from drafts.

BISCUITS

BASIC BAKING POWDER BISCUIT RECIPE

2 cups flour
4 tsp. baking powder
1/2 tsp. salt

4 tbsp. shortening, chilled
2/3 - 3/4 cup milk **or** water

Sift measured dry ingredients together twice. Cut shortening finely into dry ingredients. Add liquid slowly, stirring only until soft dough forms a ball. Turn dough onto lightly-floured board and toss until sparingly coated with flour. Knead lightly for a few minutes. Pat or roll out 1/2 to 3/4-inch thick. Cut into desired shapes. Place on pan. Bake at 450° for 12 to 15 minutes. Cook until light golden brown. Yield: 12 medium biscuits. VARIATIONS: Cheese Biscuits: Add 1/2 cup grated cheese to sifted flour mixture in the basic recipe. Orange Biscuits: Dip sugar cubes into orange juice and press into top of each biscuit. Sweet Biscuits: Substitute 3 eggs, 4 tbsp. sugar, 1/4 cup oil and 1 tsp. almond flavoring for shortening and milk or water. Bake at 400° for 10 minutes. Whole Wheat Biscuits: Substitute whole wheat flour for white flour and increase shortening to 1/4 cup. Bake at 400° for 12 to 15 minutes.

MAKE-AHEAD BISCUIT MIX

10 cups flour
6 tbsp. baking powder
1 tbsp. salt

1 1/2 cups butter, margarine **or**
   shortening

Combine half the flour with baking powder and salt. Cut in butter until particles are fine. Add remaining flour and mix until well. Place in container with tight lid. Refrigerate or freeze for later use. Yield: 13 cups. Keeps 4 to 5 weeks in the refrigerator and several months in the freezer.

Fern Tolenon
Miss Joyce Lewis

JIM DANDY BREAKFAST CAKE

1/4 cup graham cracker **or**
   cookie crumbs, divided
1 cup *Make-Ahead Biscuit Mix*
1/4 cup sugar

2 tbsp. butter **or** margarine,
   melted
1/3 cup milk
1 egg, beaten
Jam **or** marmalade

Butter 9-inch pie plate. Place a buttered glass, open-end up, in center. Sprinkle with1 tbsp. crumbs. Combine *Make-Ahead Biscuit Mix*, sugar, melted butter, milk and egg. Stir only until dry ingredients are moistened. Drop by spoonfuls around edge of plate. Add remaining crumbs. Drop 1/2 tsp. jam in center of each spoonful of batter. Microwave on High 2 1/2 to 4 1/2 minutes, rotating after 1 or 2 minutes. Yield: 1 9-inch coffee cake.

CINNAMON RING

2 cups *Make-Ahead Biscuit Mix*
2/3 cup milk
1/2 cup sugar
1/4 cup graham cracker crumbs
2 tsp. cinnamon

1/4 cup finely chopped nuts
or flaked or shredded coconut
1/4 cup butter **or** margarine
Vanilla icing

In mixing bowl, combine *Make-Ahead Biscuit Mix* and milk just until dough forms. If sticky, add 1 - 2 tbsp. mix. Knead on floured surface 10 times. Roll out or pat to 1/4 to 1/2 inch thickness. Cut into 2-inch rounds with floured cutter. Combine sugar, crumbs, cinnamon and nuts. Coat rounds with melted butter and sugar mixture. Stand rounds in 1-qt. ring mold or arrange around edge of pie dish or large plate, overlapping rounds. Microwave on High 4 to 7 minutes, or until top springs back when touched in several places, rotating a half turn after 2 to 3 minutes. Cool 2 minutes, loosen and turn out onto serving plate. Frost with vanilla icing while warm.

BASIC BISCUIT MIX

1 cup *Make-Ahead Biscuit Mix*
1/4 - 1/3 cup milk

2 tbsp. butter **or** margarine
1/3 cup dry bread crumbs

Combine *Make-Ahead Biscuit Mix* and milk in mixing bowl. Stir only until dough clings together. If sticky, add 1 or 2 tbsp. mix. Knead dough on floured surface about 10 times for lightness, flakiness and height. Roll or pat out to 1/2-inch thickness. Cut into biscuits. Melt butter and brush on. Sprinkle with crumbs. Place close together in a ring around edge of large pie plate or baking sheet. Microwave on High 2 to 4 minutes or until dry and puffy, rotating a half turn every minute. Remove to wire rack immediately. Serve warm. Yield: 9 biscuits. VARIATION: Add 1 tsp. herbs, poppy or caraway seed, or use half grated parmesan cheese.

Fern Tolenon

RHUBARB AND STRAWBERRY ROLY-POLY

2 cups water
1 cup sugar
Basic Biscuit Mix
2 cups rhubarb, 1/2-inch slices

1 cup sliced strawberries
1/3 cup sugar
1/2 tsp. cinnamon
Butter

Make a syrup of water and 1 cup sugar dissolved over heat in a 9 x 13-inch pan. Prepare *Basic Biscuit Mix* and roll out to 10 x 12-inch rectangle. Spread evenly with rhubarb and strawberries. Sprinkle with 1/3 cup sugar and cinnamon. Dot with butter. Roll up lengthwise and slice into 12 slices 1-inch thick. Place slice in syrup in pan. Bake 20 to 25 minutes at 375°.

OLD TIME DUMPLINGS

3 tbsp. shortening
2 tbsp. baking powder
1 1/2 tbsp. sugar
3 1/2 cups flour

1 tbsp. salt
2 cups milk, slightly warmed
Parsley flakes, if desired

Cut shortening into dry ingredients. Add milk and parsley flakes. Stir until blended. Drop by spoonfuls into broth or gravy that is boiling rapidly. Cover tightly. Cook for 14 minutes without lifting lid. Serve immediately.

Mrs. Donna-Faye Brown

NO-KNEAD YEAST DOUGHNUTS

1 env. active dry yeast
1/2 cup lukewarm water
1 1/2 tsp. sugar
4 cups scalded milk
3/4 cup oil

3/4 cup sugar
1/2 tsp. salt
4 eggs, beaten
6 cups flour

Dissolve yeast in lukewarm water and 1 1/2 tsp. sugar. Let stand 10 minutes. Scald milk. Add oil and 3/4 cup sugar. Cool. Add salt to eggs and add to milk mixture. Add to yeast mixture. Sift flour into large bowl. Add liquid mixture and mix. Continue adding flour until dough is stiff. Let rise once. Punch down dough and roll out to about 1/2-inch thick. Cut with doughnut cutter. Let doughnuts rise on a floured surface. Fry in oil at 360°. Drain and cool. Roll in sugar.

RAISED DOUGHNUTS

1 tsp. sugar
1/2 cup lukewarm water
1 env. fast rising yeast
1 1/2 cups sugar
1 cup butter

1 cup flour
1 tsp. vanilla **or** 1/2 tsp. nutmeg
3 cups boiling water
6 eggs
1 tsp. salt

Dissolve 1 tsp. sugar in lukewarm water. Sprinkle yeast over water. Let stand 10 minutes. Blend 1 1/2 cups sugar, butter, flour and vanilla in heavy saucepan . Add boiling water and stir well, until mixture reaches boiling point. Cool until lukewarm. Beat eggs until light and add to flour mixture. Add salt and yeast mixture. Add 9 to 10 cups flour. Mix until very thick. Knead dough, adding remaining flour. Let rise. Punch down and let rise again. Roll out 1/2-inch thick and cut with doughnut cutter. Let cut doughnuts rise again before frying in deep fat or oil at 375°. Fry doughnuts on both sides, turning only once. Drain on paper towelling. Roll in sugar or glaze. NOTE: Doughnuts freeze very nicely. When ready to use, take out of freezer and place a few doughnuts in a heavy brown paper bag in 300° oven for a few minutes. Tie end of bag. Watch closely so bag does not burn.

GREATGRANDMOTHER CALDWELL'S DOUGHNUTS

2 eggs, well beaten
2 cups buttermilk
1/2 tsp. nutmeg
4 tbsp. sour cream
11/2 cups sugar

Pinch of salt
4 tbsp. melted butter
2 tsp. soda
Flour to make soft dough

Mix ingredients together. Cut out and fry in hot oil or grease.

Mrs. M. Rains

DOUGHNUTS

1 cup sugar, 1 cup milk
2 eggs beaten - fine as silk
Salt and nutmeg, lemon will do
Of baking powder - teaspoons two.
Lightly stir 21/2 cups flour in,
Roll on pie-board - not too thin.
Cut in diamonds, twists or rings,
Drop in with care the doughy things,
Into fat that briskly swells,
Evenly the spongy cells.
Watch with care the time for turning -
Fry them brown - just short of burning!
Roll in sugar, serve when cool.
Price - a quarter for this rule.

Mrs. R.J. Page

SPUDNUTS & GLAZE

1 env. active dry yeast
3/4 cup lukewarm water
1 cup warm milk
1/2 tsp. salt
1 egg, well beaten
1/2 cup hot mashed potatoes

2 tbsp. shortening
1/2 cup sugar
1/2 tsp. vanilla
4 cups flour
11/2 cups milk
11/2 cups sugar

Dissolve yeast in lukewarm water. Scald 1 cup milk and cool. Add salt, egg, potatoes, shortening, 1/2 cup sugar and vanilla. Add yeast and mix in flour. Let rise about 1 hour, punch down and let rise again. Roll out thinner than other doughnuts and cut. Let rise slightly. To make the glaze, combine 11/2 cups milk and 11/2 cups sugar and boil. Turn heat down and simmer. Fry doughnuts and dip immediately into glaze. The glaze will thicken as doughnuts are dipped. If glaze gets too thick, add a little milk.

Mrs. Elsie Voyys

To make sour milk, add 1 tbsp. vinegar or lemon juice to 1 cup sweet milk.

MUFFINS & LOAVES

PLAIN MUFFINS

2 cups flour	1 egg
4 tsp. baking powder	1 cup milk
1/2 tsp. salt	4 tbsp. melted shortening
4 tbsp. sugar	1/2 tsp. vanilla (optional)

Sift measured dry ingredients together twice. Break egg into a mixing bowl and beat slightly. Stir in milk and shortening. Sift dry ingredients into wet mixture, stirring just until dry ingredients are moistened. The batter will be lumpy. Spoon into greased tins, 2/3 full. Bake at 400° for 20 to 25 minutes. Yield: 12 medium muffins. VARIATIONS: Orange muffins: Substitute 1/2 cup orange juice for 1/2 cup milk. Add 1 tsp. grated orange rind. Fruit or nut muffins: Add 1/2 cup raisins, dates, currants or nuts to the dry ingredients. Cheese muffins: Use only 2 tbsp. sugar, add 1 cup grated cheese to dry ingredients and use 2 tbsp. shortening.

APPLE MUFFINS (Old Style)

13/4 cups flour	3/4 cup apples,
3/4 tsp. salt	peeled and chopped
4 tsp. baking powder	1 egg, beaten
1/4 cup sugar	1 cup milk
1/4 tsp. nutmeg	1/3 cup melted shortening
1 tsp. lemon rind	

Combine dry ingredients. Add lemon rind, apples, egg, milk and shortening. Mix thoroughly. Bake at 350° for 25 minutes.

Edith Edwards
Mrs. E. Schon

BRAN MUFFINS

1 cup flour	1 egg, well beaten
1 tsp. baking powder	1/4 cup cooking oil
1 cup bran	1/2 cup molasses
1/2 tsp. salt	1/2 cup honey
1/4 tsp. baking soda	1/2 cup milk

Sift flour and add baking powder, bran, salt and baking soda. Mix all other ingredients but milk and add to flour mixture. Add milk and mix. Bake at 350° for 15 to 20 minutes.

Mildred Campbell

RAISIN BRAN MUFFINS

2 cups boiling water
2 cups bran
3 cups sugar
1 cup shortening
4 eggs
3 tbsp. soda

1 tbsp. salt
5 cups flour
4 cups buttermilk **or** sour milk
4 cups bran flakes
1 cup raisins

Add 2 cups boiling water to the bran and let stand for 15 minutes. Add remaining ingredients and mix thoroughly. Leave in a covered bowl overnight. Bake in the morning at 350° for 25 minutes.

Mrs. William Lesher

MICROWAVE BRAN MUFFINS

2 cups water
4 cups all-bran cereal
1/2 cup butter
1/2 cup vegetable oil
2 cups sugar
4 eggs

4 cups buttermilk
2 cups bran
5 cups flour
4 tsp. soda
1 tsp. salt

Microwave water until boiling and pour over all-bran. Mix in butter and oil and let stand 5 minutes. Add sugar and eggs, mixing well. Stir in buttermilk. Mix bran, flour, soda and salt together and combine with sugar misture. Cover tightly and store up to 6 weeks in the refrigerator. Microwave 6 muffins for 21/2 to 4 minutes.

Georgina Taylor

REFRIGERATOR BRAN MUFFINS

3/8 cup shortening
1 cup sugar
2 eggs
11/2 cups bran
21/2 cups flour
1 tsp. salt

1 tbsp. baking powder
11/2 tsp. soda
2 tbsp. hot water
1/2 cup raisins
11/2 cups buttermilk **or**
    sour milk

Beat shortening and sugar together until creamy. Add eggs and beat again. Add bran, flour, salt and baking powder. Dissolve soda in hot water and add. Mix well and add raisins and milk. Refrigerate for 24 hours. Bake at 375° for 15 to 20 minutes. Mixture may be kept in refrigerator for two weeks. Use as required.

Mrs. Marion Alberts

When baking muffins, fill tins about two-thirds full. Leave muffins in tins for a few minutes after removing from oven. To reheat muffins, wrap loosely in foil and heat at 425° for 5 to 10 minutes.

BUTTERMILK BRAN MUFFINS

1 cup flour	1 egg
1/2 tsp. soda	1 1/2 cups bran
2 tsp. baking powder	1 cup buttermilk **or** sour milk
1/2 tsp. salt	1 tbsp. butter **or** margarine
1/2 cup brown sugar	melted

Sift dry ingredients together twice. Break egg into a mixing bowl and beat slightly. Combine bran and milk and add. Stir in melted butter. Sift dry ingredients into wet mixture, stirring just until dry ingredients are moistened. The batter will be lumpy. Spoon into greased tins, 2/3 full. Bake at 425° for 20 to 25 minutes.

LOW CALORIE BRAN MUFFINS

1 cup flour	1 tbsp. salad oil
1/4 tsp. salt	2 tbsp. each molasses
4 tsp. baking powder	2 tbsp. brown sugar
1/2 cup natural bran	3/4 cup skim milk
1 egg, well beaten	

Sift flour, salt and baking powder into bowl. Add bran. Combine remaining ingredients and pour all at once into the dry mixture. Stir lightly until flour mixture is dampened. Spoon into 10 or 12 oiled muffin cups. Bake at 400° for 15 to 20 minutes. NOTE: Half teaspoon non-calorie sweetener may be used in place of brown sugar. 77 calories per muffin.

BRANANA MUFFINS

Milk	1/2 cup health bran **or**
Mashed ripe bananas	wheat germ
3 tbsp. oil	2 tsp. baking powder
2 tbsp. liquid honey	1 tsp. soda
1 egg, well beaten	1 cup flour
1 cup all-bran cereal	1/2 cup brown sugar
	3/4 cup raisins **or** dates

Add enough milk to bananas to make 1 cup. Add oil and honey to egg, mixing well. Add banana mixture and mix again. Stir in brans and mix. Let soak for at least 5 minutes. Sift baking powder and soda with flour. Stir brown sugar into liquid mixture. Add fruit and the dry ingredients. Mix only until flour disappears. Put in greased or lined muffin tins and bake at 400° for 25 minutes. Yield: 12 large muffins.

Mrs. Fred Vincent

Any of the following can be added to muffins individually or as a combination: sliced bananas, cut-up pineapple, dates, nuts, figs, raisins, or orange rind.

ENGLISH MUFFINS

2 tbsp. sugar	1 tsp. sugar
1 tsp. salt	1 env. active dry yeast
1/4 cup shortening	4 - 6 cups flour
1 cup milk, scalded	Oil **or** melted shortening
1 cup warm water	Cornmeal

Stir 2 tbsp. sugar, salt and 1/4 cup shortening into milk. Heat until lukewarm. Pour warm water into bowl. Sprinkle with 1 tsp. of sugar and yeast. Stir until dissolved and stir in lukewarm milk. Slowly add 3 cups flour and stir with wooden spoon until smooth. Stir in enough additional flour to make stiff dough. Turn out on lightly-floured board, knead 10 minutes or until smooth and elastic. Put dough in warm greased bowl and brush top with oil. Cover with clean cloth and let rise1 hour in warm place until double in bulk. Punch dough down and divide in half. On board heavily sprinkled with cornmeal, roll out each half to 1/4-inch thick. Cut into 3-inch rounds, cover and let rise 30 minutes. Place round, cornmeal side down on lightly-greased medium hot griddle and cook for 15 minutes or until bottom is light brown. Yield: 24 muffins.

OAT MUFFINS

1 cup rolled oats	1/2 tsp. salt
1 cup sour milk	1 cup packed brown sugar
1 cup whole wheat flour	1/2 cup raisins
1 tsp. baking powder	1 egg, beaten
1/2 tsp. soda	1/4 cup melted butter

Combine oats and sour milk. Combine flour, baking powder, soda and salt. Stir well. Add brown sugar and raisins and stir. Add egg and butter to oat mixture. Mix well. Add oat mixture to dry ingredients. Stir until ingredients are moistened. Fill well-greased muffin cups. Bake at 400° for 20 to 25 minutes. Remove from tray and cool on wire rack.

Judy Pimm

BANANA MUFFINS

2 cups flour	1 tsp. soda
1/2 tsp. salt	2 eggs, separated
1 tsp. baking powder	1/2 cup shortening
1 tsp. lemon flavoring	1 1/2 cup sugar
1 tsp. vanilla	1 cup mashed bananas
1/2 cup buttermilk	

Sift flour, salt and baking powder together. Stir flavorings into buttermilk and add soda. Beat egg whites. Cream shortening and sugar. Add egg yolks. Add dry ingredients alternately with buttermilk. Add bananas. Fold in egg whites. Fill muffin tins and bake at 370° for 20 minutes. Ice with lemon icing if desired.

Dorothy Kuehn

RAISIN MUFFINS

1 1/2 cups raisins
1 1/2 cups water
1/2 cup butter
2/3 cup brown sugar
1 egg, beaten

1 1/2 cups flour
1 tsp. baking powder
1 tsp. baking soda
Pinch of salt
1 tsp. vanilla

Cook raisins in water about 20 minutes until plump. Drain and reserve 1/2 cup liquid. Cream butter and add sugar and egg. Beat. Stir in sifted dry ingredients and add vanilla. Use greased and floured muffin tins or paper baking cups. Fill 3/4 full. Bake at 350° for about 20 minutes. Ice when cool (optional).

Mrs. Betty Ohman

HEALTH MUFFINS

1 egg
1 cup milk
1/4 cup cooking oil
2 tsp. wheat germ
1 3/4 cups flour

1/4 cup sugar
3 tsp. baking powder
1 tsp. salt
2 tbsp. soy flour
2 tbsp. non-fat dry milk

Beat egg, milk and oil together thoroughly with a fork. Stir in wheat germ. Sift flour, sugar, baking powder, salt, soy flour and dry milk together into liquid ingredients. Stir just to blend. Spoon into greased muffin tins, filling 2/3 full. Bake at 400° about 25 minutes. Yield:10 large muffins.

CARROT MUFFINS

1/2 cup chopped raisins
1 1/2 cups flour
1 tsp. baking soda
1 tsp. baking powder
1 tsp. cinnamon
1 tsp. vanilla

3/4 cup cooking oil
1 cup sugar
1 cup grated carrots
Pinch of salt
2 eggs, well beaten

Cover raisins with hot water, let cool, drain, chop and coat with flour. Mix all ingredients together, adding the eggs last. Bake in muffin tins which are lined with paper baking cups. Bake at 375° for 15 to 20 minutes.

Mrs. Pat Felstad

HUSH PUPPIES

1 1/2 cups cornmeal
1/2 cup flour
2 tsp. baking powder
1 tbsp. sugar

1/2 tsp salt
1 chopped onion
1 egg, well beaten
3/4 cup milk

Combine dry ingredients and onion. Make a well in the center and add egg and milk. Stir just until mixed. Do not over stir. Bake in muffin tins at 375° for 20 minutes.

ZUCCHINI CARROT MUFFINS

1 1/2 cups milk
1 1/2 cups rolled oats
1 egg
1/2 cup melted butter
1 cup whole wheat flour
1 cup flour
1/2 cup packed brown sugar

3 1/2 tsp. baking powder
1 tsp. salt
1 tsp. cinnamon
1/2 tsp. nutmeg
1 cup cooked carrots, mashed
1 cup zucchini

Pour milk over oats and let stand 5 minutes. Add egg and butter and mix well. Combine flours, sugar, baking powder, salt and spices into a large bowl. Stir oat mixture into dry ingredients and mix until just moistened. Fold in carrots and zucchini. Spoon into paper cups and fill to top. Bake at 400° for 20 minutes. Yield: 12 muffins.

BLUEBERRY POPPINS

2 cups flour
1 tsp. salt
2 tsp. baking powder
1 cup white sugar
1 cup milk
1/4 cup melted butter
2 eggs

1 1/2 cups blueberries
1/2 cup flour
1/4 tsp. salt
1/4 cup butter
1/4 tsp. cinnamon
3/4 cup brown sugar

Mix 2 cups flour, 1 tsp. salt, baking powder and white sugar together and stir in milk, butter, eggs and blueberries. Fill muffin tins 2/3 full with mixture. Combine remaining ingredients and spread on top of each poppin. Bake at 375° for 20 minutes.

Mrs. F. Giacchetta

NACHYNKA (Cornmeal Casserole)

1 small onion
3 tbsp. butter **or** oil
1 cup cornmeal
1 tsp. salt
1 tsp. sugar

1/4 tsp. pepper
1/4 tsp. cinnamon (optional)
3 1/2 cups scalded milk
1/2 cup light cream
2 - 3 eggs, well beaten

Cook onion in butter until tender, but not brown. Add cornmeal, salt, sugar, pepper and cinnamon, combining thoroughly. Add scalded milk and mix well. Cook until thickened. Remove from stove, add cream and blend. Then fold in eggs. Bake in buttered 2-qt. casserole for 1 hour at 350°. VARIATIONS: Put pieces of chicken on top of cornmeal casserole or use as stuffing for roast chicken.

Mrs. Mary Osadczuk

Honey has a tendency to absorb moisture and will keep foods fresher longer.

NUTRITIOUS BREAKFAST PUFFS

1 yeast cake
1/4 cup lukewarm water
1 cup milk
1 tsp. salt
2 tbsp. brown sugar
1/2 cup golden oil
2 eggs, well beaten

3 cups whole wheat flour, sifted
2 tbsp. wheat germ
2 tbsp. soy flour
1/2 cup brown sugar
1/2 tsp. cinnamon
1/4 cup chopped nuts

Break yeast cake into lukewarm water. Scald milk and add salt, 2 tbsp. sugar and oil. Let cool to lukewarm. Add the yeast mixture. Stir in eggs, flour, wheat germ and soy flour. Mix well. Let rise for 1 1/2 to 2 hours. Drop by spoonful into oiled muffin pans, filling cups half full. Make a mixture of 1/2 cup brown sugar, cinnamon and chopped nuts. Sprinkle on tops of muffins. Let rise again until double in bulk. Bake at 375° for 25 minutes.

LOAFS

CARROT BREAD

1/2 cup cooking oil
1 cup sugar
2 eggs, beaten
1 cup shredded carrot
1 1/2 cups flour

1 tsp. soda
1 tsp. baking powder
1/4 tsp. salt
1 tsp. cinnamon
1/2 cup milk

Preheat oven to 350°. Mix oil and sugar. Add eggs and stir in carrot. Sift together the dry ingredients. Add dry ingredients alternately with milk. Bake in well-greased 9 x 5 x 3-inch loaf pan for 55 minutes.

Margaret R. Burpee
Mrs. Cliff Deyell

GRANDMA'S CARROT LOAF

1 1/4 cups sugar
1 1/4 cups water
1 cup raisins
1 tbsp. butter
2 carrots, finely grated
1 tsp. cinnamon
1 tsp. cloves

1 tsp. nutmeg
1 cup chopped walnuts
2 1/2 cups flour
1/2 tsp. salt
1 tsp. soda
2 tsp. baking powder

Simmer the sugar, water, raisins, butter, carrots, cinnamon, cloves and nutmeg in a saucepan for 5 minutes. Cover and let stand for 12 hours. Add remaining ingredients, mixing well. Bake in greased loaf tins at 350° for 2 hours. Cool, wrap and store in cool place. Serve warm or cold.

Doris Felstad

CHRISTMAS CARROT LOAF

1 1/2 cups chopped cherries
1 1/2 cups glazed fruit
1 1/2 cups currants
6-oz. can frozen concentrated
   orange juice
3 cups grated carrots
3 cups sugar
7 eggs

1 1/4 cups cooking oil
2 tsp. baking soda soaked in
   1 tsp. water
1/2 tsp. salt
2 tsp. baking powder
1 tsp. vanilla
5 cups flour

Mix cherries, glazed fruit and currants. Add frozen orange juice and leave to soak overnight. Add carrots. Meanwhile, mix the sugar and eggs and beat until very fluffy. Add the oil, soda, salt, baking powder, vanilla and flour. Mix well and add to the fruit mixture. The batter will be very stiff. Spoon into loaf pan lined with oiled paper and bake at 350° for 1 1/2 hours.

Mrs. Annie Dart

BANANA BREAD

4 tbsp. butter
1 cup brown sugar
1 egg, beaten
1 1/2 cups flour
1/2 tsp. salt

1 tsp. baking powder
1 tsp. baking soda
3 ripe bananas, mashed
1/2 cup chopped walnuts

Cream butter and brown sugar. Add egg and beat until mixture is light and fluffy. Combine dry ingredients. Add alternately with banana. Fold in nuts. Pour into greased and floured loaf pan. Bake at 325° for 60 to 70 minutes.

Elsie Jossy

BANANA BRAN BREAD

1 cup sugar
1/4 cup shortening
1 egg
1 1/2 cups flour
2 tbsp. baking powder
1/2 tsp. salt

1/2 tsp. nutmeg
1 cup bran flakes cereal
1 tbsp. orange rind
1 1/2 cups mashed banana
1/2 tsp. soda
2 tbsp. water

Cream sugar and shortening. Add egg and beat until fluffy. Combine flour, baking powder, salt, nutmeg, bran cereal and rind. Add alternately with banana. Mix soda and water. Add and pour immediately into greased 9 x 5 x 3-inch loaf pan. Bake at 350° for 60 minutes.

To toast nuts in the microwave, spread 1/2 cups nuts in pie plate. Cook on High for 6 to 8 minutes, stirring occasionally until golden brown.

BANANANUT LOAF

2¹/4 cups flour
2 tsp. baking powder
1/4 tsp. salt
3/4 tsp. baking soda
1¹/2 cups sugar
3/4 cup shortening

1/2 cup brown sugar
6 tbsp. buttermilk
1¹/2 cups mashed banana
3 eggs
1¹/2 tsp. vanilla
3/4 cup walnuts

Combine the flour, baking powder, salt, baking soda and sugar in a bowl. Add the shortening, sugar, buttermilk and bananas and mix for 2 minutes. Add the eggs and vanilla and beat for 1 minute. Fold in the walnuts and pour into a loaf pan. Bake at 375° for 30 minutes.

Shirley W. Steward

ZUCCHINI LOAF

2 cups flour
3/4 tsp. salt
1/2 tsp. baking powder
3/4 tsp. baking soda
1¹/2 tsp. cinnamon
1/2 tsp. nutmeg

1 cup sugar
2 eggs
1/2 cup vegetable oil
1¹/2 tsp. vanilla
1/2 cup walnuts
1¹/2 shredded zucchini

Combine flour, salt, baking powder, baking soda, cinnamon, nutmeg and sugar. Blend eggs, oil, vanilla and walnuts together and add to flour mixture. Add zucchini. Bake in greased loaf pan at 350° for 75 minutes.

HONEY DATE LOAF

2 tbsp. butter
1/4 cup liquid honey
1 egg
2 tsp. lemon juice
1¹/2 cups flour
1/8 tsp. soda

1/4 tsp. salt
1 tsp. baking powder
1/2 cup sour milk
1 cup chopped dates
1/2 cup chopped walnuts

Cream butter and gradually add honey. Beat well. Add egg and lemon juice. Sift dry ingredients and add alternately with sour milk. Add dates and nuts. Pour into greased 9 x 4-inch loaf pan and bake at 350° for about 50 minutes.

Mrs. H. Begin

To substitute honey for sugar in your favorite recipe, reduce liquid by 1/4 cup for each cup of honey used in place of 1 cup sugar. For best results, use 1/2 sugar and 1/2 honey in your recipes. Cakes and loaves made with honey retain moisture longer than those made with sugar. They also freeze much better. Bread made with honey has a much finer flavor, texture, color and aroma.

HONEY PRUNE BREAD

1 cup cooked prunes
1 egg
1/2 cup liquid honey
2 tbsp. salad oil
1 cup buttermilk
1 tsp. salt

11/2 cups whole wheat flour
3/4 tsp. soda
1/2 tsp. cinnamon
11/2 cups flour
21/2 tsp. baking powder

Cut up the prunes. Combine the egg, honey, salad oil and buttermilk. Add prunes. Mix dry ingredients well and add. Stir well and pour into 13 x 41/2 x 21/2-inch pan. Bake at 350° for 1 hour.

HONEY APRICOT NUT LOAF

1/2 cup dried apricots, cut
1 cup water
1/2 cup mayonnaise
1/2 cup honey
1/4 cup walnuts
1 tsp. lemon rind

1/4 cup sugar
1/2 tsp. salt
2 cups flour
1 tsp. soda
1/4 tsp. cinnamon
1/4 tsp. nutmeg

Simmer apricots in water for 10 minutes. Drain, reserving liquid. Beat mayonnaise and honey until fluffy. Add apricots, nuts and lemon rind. Sift dry ingredients together and add to creamed mixture. Add apricot liquid. Stir until well blended. Pour into 9 x 5 x 4-inch loaf pan lined with wax paper. Bake at 350° for 1 hour. Stays fresh and moist when wrapped in foil and stored in cool place.

Mrs. Florence Freeman

PINEAPPLE DATE & NUT BREAD

81/2-oz. can crushed
    pineapple, undrained
8-oz. pitted dates,
    coarsely chopped
1/4 cup butter **or** margarine
21/4 cups flour
2 tsp. baking powder

1 tsp. baking soda
1/2 tsp. salt
1 egg
1/4 cup sugar
1 cup walnuts **or** pecans,
    finely chopped

Preheat oven to 350°. Grease a 9 x 5 x 3-inch loaf pan. Add water to crushed pineapple to measure 11/2 cups. Bring just to boiling. Pour over dates and butter in a medium bowl, stirring to melt butter. Let cool to room temperature. Sift flour with baking powder, soda and salt on sheet of waxed paper and set aside. Beat egg and sugar until well combined in large bowl. Stir in date mixture. Add flour mixture and beat until smooth. Fold in nuts and mix well. Turn batter into prepared pan and bake 55 to 60 minutes or until toothpick comes out clean. Run knife around sides of pan to loosen. Turn out onto wire rack. Let cool. Wrap and let stand overnight before slicing.

Mrs. Lyle Alwood

FOUR FRUIT BREAD

3/4 cup dried apricots, cut up
1 cup flour
1/2 cup brown sugar
2 tbsp. baking powder
1 cup whole wheat flour
1 tsp. salt
1/2 cup chopped dates

1 cup seedless raisins
1/2 cup chopped nuts
1 tbsp. orange rind
1 egg
1 cup orange juice
1/4 cup salad oil

Soak apricots in cold water for 1 hour. Sift dry ingredients together. Prepare fruits, nuts and orange rind. Beat egg together with orange juice and salad oil. Add apricots and fruit mixture to the dry ingredients, stirring well. Bake at 350° for 1 hour.

NUT AND DATE LOAF

1/2 cup brown sugar
1 cup chopped nuts
1/2 lb. dates
2 cups whole wheat flour
1 tsp. salt

4 tsp. baking powder
1 cup white flour
1 egg
2 cups milk
2 tbsp. shortening, melted

Combine sugar, nuts, dates, whole wheat flour and salt. Sift baking powder and white flour and add. Add egg, milk and shortening. Bake at 350° for 1 hour.

CHERRY LOAF

1 small jar maraschino cherries
Milk
1 egg
1/2 cup butter
1 cup brown sugar

2 cups flour
2 tsp. baking powder
1/2 tsp. salt
1 cup nuts

Make 1 cup of liquid by adding cherry juice and milk. Combine egg, butter and liquid. Combine sugar, flour, baking powder, salt and nuts and add. Add chopped cherries and mix. Pour into greased loaf pan and bake at 350° for 1 hour.

RAISIN LOAF

4 eggs
2 cups sugar
1 cup butter
3 cups flour
1/2 tsp. salt

2 tsp. baking powder
1/2 cup milk
1 tsp. vanilla
1 cup raisins

Beat eggs, add sugar and butter and mix well. Combine dry ingredients and add alternately with milk. Add vanilla and raisins and pour into pan. Bake at 350° for 1 hour.

Hilda Elke

TROPICAL FRUIT BREAD

2/3 cup sugar
1/3 cup shortening
2 eggs
1 cup mashed bananas
1/4 cup sour milk
1 1/4 cups flour

1 tsp. baking powder
1/2 tsp. salt
1/2 tsp. soda
1 cup whole bran
3/4 cup chopped apricots
1/2 cup chopped walnuts

Line 9 x 5 x 3-inch loaf pan. Cream sugar and shortening. Mix in eggs thoroughly. Combine bananas and milk. Sift dry ingredients and blend. Add alternately with banana mixture. Stir in bran, apricots and walnuts. Pour in pan. Bake at 350° for 60 to 70 minutes.

Helen Couper

CRANBERRY BREAD

1 cup seedless raisins
1/4 cup shortening
1/2 cup sugar
1 tsp. salt
1 1/2 tsp. baking powder
1 tsp. soda

2 cups flour
15-oz. can whole
   cranberry sauce
1 tbsp. orange rind
1/4 cup orange juice

Cover raisins with boiling water, let stand 5 minutes and drain. Cream shortening and sugar. Combine dry ingredients and add. Add cranberry sauce, rind, orange juice and raisins. Pour into 9 x 5 x 2-inch pan and bake at 350° for 70 minutes.

DATE NUT LOAF

1 cup boiling water
1 cup chopped dates
1 tsp. soda
2 tbsp. butter
1/2 cup sugar
1 egg

1 tsp. vanilla
2 cups flour
2 tsp. baking powder
Pinch of salt
1/2 cup chopped walnuts

Pour boiling water over dates and soda. Let stand until cool. Blend butter with sugar. Add egg, vanilla, flour, baking powder, salt and walnuts to this mixture. Add the date mixture and mix well. Pour into loaf pan and bake at 350° for 65 minutes.

Miss Ila Ewing

Brazil nuts may be sliced very easily if you soak the shelled nut in boiling water for a few minutes or freeze for a few hours.

Photo: Aly Heins

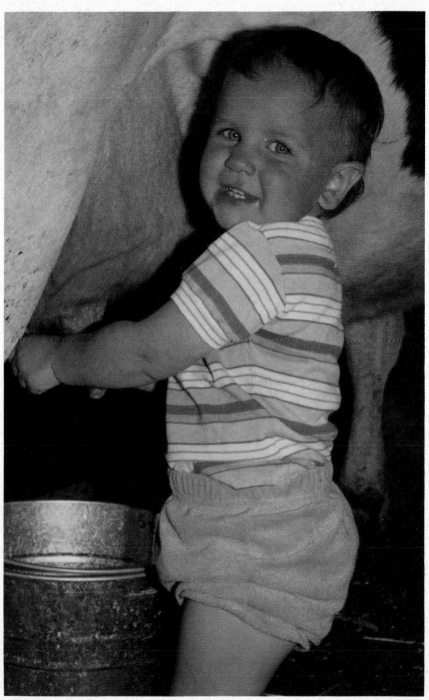

Photo: Loretta Harasiuk

Photo: Selma Alleman

Photo: Debbie Dennis

Photo: Steve Major

Photo: H. Thompson

Photo: Dimphy Bonusic

Photo: Diane Green

Photo: Ian Macdonald

Photo: Lauri Duncan

Photo: Mary S. Howe

Photo: H. Thompson

Photo: Linda Hartley

Photo: Gary Mykitiuk

Photo: Peggy Oracheski

Photo: Linda Kraay

Photo: Diane Green

Photo: Oliver Dechant

Photo: Lori Gauthier

Photo: B. Blake

Photo: Lorene Stulberg

Photo: Max Wiese

Photo: Norm Hellum

LEMON LOAF

2 eggs	1/4 tsp. salt
6 tbsp. shortening	1/2 cup milk
1 cup sugar	Juice and rind of 1 lemon
1 1/2 cups flour	1/3 cup icing sugar
1 1/2 tsp. baking powder	

Beat eggs well, add shortening and beat again. Add sugar to creamed mixture and beat well. Sift together dry ingredients and add alternately with milk. Add grated rind of lemon. Place batter in a loaf pan and bake at 350° for 1 hour. Remove cake from oven. Stir lemon juice and icing sugar together and pour over hot loaf. Remove from pan when slightly cooled.

Mrs. R.C. Healing

PUMPKIN LOAF

2 eggs, beaten	3/4 tsp. salt
1 1/2 cups sugar	1/2 tsp. cloves
1 cup pumpkin	1/2 tsp. cinnamon
1/2 cup oil	1 2/3 cups flour
1/4 cup water	1 cup raisins (optional)
1/4 tsp. baking powder	1 cup walnuts (optional)
1 tsp. soda	

Beat eggs, add sugar and mix well. Add pumpkin, oil and water. Add dry ingredients and mix. Add raisins and nuts. Bake in loaf tins at 350° for 1 hour or in a 9 x 12-inch cake pan at 375° for 35 minutes.

Mrs. Bertha Webber

SELF-ICED DATE LOAF

1 1/2 cups boiling water	1/2 cup cake flour
1/2 cup raisins	1 tsp. salt
3/4 cup chopped dates	1 tsp. vanilla
1 tsp. soda	5 tbsp. butter
1 cup white sugar	1/2 cup brown sugar
1/2 cup shortening	2 tbsp. milk
2 eggs	1/2 cup finely-chopped nuts
1 cup flour	

Boil water and raisins for 5 minutes. Add dates and soda. Let cool. Cream white sugar and shortening. Add eggs. Beat well. Add flours, salt and vanilla to boiled fruit. Put in well-greased pan and bake at 350° for 45 minutes. When cake is done, make icing by combining the butter, brown sugar, milk and nuts. Spread over loaf. Return to oven until topping is light brown and bubbling.

Mrs. E. Tomalty

PIES & PASTRY

AUNT SAL'S HOT WATER PASTRY

1 lb. lard	1/2 tsp. baking powder
1 tsp. salt	6 cups flour
1 cup boiling water	

Beat lard, salt and boiling water to a cream. Set in pan of cold water to chill. Then add baking powder and flour. Knead well, wrap in wax paper and store in a cold place until ready to use.

Mrs. H.C. Driver

PLAIN PASTRY

1 1/2 cups flour	1/2 cup pastry lard
1/2 tsp. salt	4 - 5 tbsp. water

Sift dry ingredients, add lard and blend together with a pastry blender until it is crumbly. Sprinkle iced water over floured mixture and blend. Roll on lightly-floured board. Roll dough outwards from center. Keep in circular form. Yield: 1 double crust pie.

COCONUT PASTRY

2 cups sweetened shredded **or** flaked coconut	1/4 cup melted butter **or** margarine

Toss coconut and butter together with a fork. Press into bottom and sides of a pie pan. Bake at 300° for about 25 minutes or until coconut is golden. Chill. Use as a baked pastry shell.

EXCELLENT PIE PASTRY

1 lb. pastry lard	4 tsp. brown sugar
5 cups flour	1 egg, slightly beaten
1 tsp. baking powder	1 tbsp. vinegar
2 tsp. salt	Water

Sift dry ingredients. Cut in lard. Add vinegar and water to egg to make 1 cup liquid. Pour over dry ingredients and mix well. Chill well before rolling.

Mrs. E. Tomalty

Wrap fruit cakes and fruit pies first in plastic film or waxed paper and then cover with aluminum foil. The combination of acid in the fruit and high moisture content causes foil to pit.

HAZEL STEVENETT PIE CRUST

51/2 cups flour   2 tsp. salt
1 lb. lard

Blend ingredients together to a fine crumb stage with a pastry blender. Place in a jar. When pie crust is required, combine mixture and cold water to form crust. Keeps well.

Hazel Stevenett

CHEESE PASTRY

1/4 cup cream cheese   1/2 tsp. salt
1/4 cup butter   1 cup flour

Cream cheese, butter and salt together. Blend in flour and wrap in wax paper to chill overnight. Remove from refrigerator. Ten minutes later, roll to a thickness of 1/4 inch. Cut into tiny cookies or fingers. Bake until golden brown at 475°. Serve with soup, salads or dips.

APPLE PIE

Pastry for 2-crust pie   1/2 tsp. cinnamon
3 cups tart apples, sliced   1/8 tsp. salt
1 tbsp. flour   1 tbsp. butter
1 cup sugar

Roll out pastry and fit into pie plate. Combine ingredients and fill. Dot with butter and cover with remaining pastry. Bake at 450° for 15 minutes, then reduce heat to 350° for 35 to 45 minutes.

Mrs. Sam Simpson

CHEESE APPLE PIE

5 cups sliced apples   4 slices process cheddar
3 tbsp. melted butter   cheese
1/2 cup sugar   1/2 cup flour
1 tbsp. cornstarch   1/4 cup brown sugar
1/4 tsp. cinnamon   1/4 tsp. cinnamon
9-inch unbaked pie shell   1/4 cup butter

Coat apples with butter. Mix sugar, cornstarch and cinnamon. Sprinkle 2 tbsp. of mixture into pie shell and stir remainder into apples. Arrange apples in pie shell and cover with slices of halved process cheese. Combine flour, brown sugar and cinnamon. Cut in butter until mixture resembles coarse bread crumbs. Sprinkle over apples. Bake at 450° for 15 minutes. Reduce heat to 350° and continue baking about 30 minutes until apples are tender. Yield: 6 servings.

To toast coconut in microwave, spread in glass pie plate. Cook on High until golden brown, stirring frequently.

APPLE-PLUM PIE

Pastry for 2-crust pie
2 tbsp. tapioca **or** flour
1/8 tsp. salt
1/2 tsp. cinnamon
1 cup sugar

1 cups apples, sliced
12 blue plums, stoned and cut
in half
1 tbsp. butter

Line pie plate with pastry. Combine dry ingredients. Save 1/2 cup to cover top. Mix sugar with apples. Place in pie plate, cover with plums and sprinkle with remaining sugar. Dot with butter. Cover with pastry. Bake at 400° for 15 minutes, then reduce heat to 350° for 35 to 40 minutes.

GENERAL MCARTHUR APPLE PIE

Pastry for 2-crust pie
8 green apples, peeled
1 cup pineapple juice
1/2 cup brown sugar
1/2 cup butter

1/2 cup white sugar
Cinnamon
2 tbsp. cornstarch
Small amount water

Slice the apples thickly and drop into boiling mixture of pineapple juice and brown sugar. Drain in colander, reserving juice, and put fruit gently into pie crust. Dot with butter and sprinkle lightly with white sugar and cinnamon, or if desired red cinnamon candy drops. Thicken juice with cornstarch mixed with a little water. Cook until thick and pour over fruit. Cover with lattice top pastry. Bake at 450° for 5 minutes, then reduce heat to 350° for 15 to 20 minutes.

Mrs. Dorothy Elias

DANISH APPLE PIE

5 tbsp. butter **or** margarine
1 1/4 cups fine wafer crumbs
1 tbsp. sugar
7 apples

3/4 cup sugar
2 tbsp. flour
1 tsp. cinnamon
Pinch of salt

Combine butter, crumbs and sugar and press into 9-inch glass pie plate, reserving 2 tbsp. crumb mixture for top of pie. Microwave on High for 1 1/2 to 2 minutes. Peel, core and slice apples and combine with remaining ingredients. Fill crumb crust, and top with remaining crumb mixture. Microwave on High for 12 to 14 minutes.

Doris Barker

Sprinkle a mixture of a few grains of citric acid and sugar on pure saskatoon pie to tenderize the berries. Another way to have tender saskatoon pie is to put a thin layer of fresh raspberries (for acidity) in between two layers of saskatoons.

SOUR CREAM APPLE PIE

Pastry for single-crust pie
2 tbsp. flour
1/8 tsp. salt
3/4 cup sugar
1 egg, unbeaten
1 cup dairy sour cream
1 tsp. vanilla

1/4 tsp. nutmeg
2 cups diced apples
1/3 cup sugar
1/3 cup flour
1 tsp. cinnamon
1/4 cup butter

Line pie plate with pastry. Sift together 2 tbsp. flour, salt and 3/4 cup sugar into a bowl. Add egg, sour cream, vanilla and nutmeg. Beat to a smooth, thin batter. Blend in apples and pour into pastry shell. Bake at 400° for 15 minutes, then reduce heat to 350° and bake for 30 minutes. Mix 1/3 cup sugar, 1/3 cup flour, cinnamon and butter and sprinkle over pie. Brown at 400° for 10 minutes.

RED CHERRY PIE

2/3 cup sugar
3 tbsp. cornstarch
1/4 tsp. salt
14-oz. can pitted red cherries

1 tbsp. butter
1/2 tsp. almond flavor
Few drops red food coloring

Mix sugar, cornstarch and salt. Add some cold cherry juice to form smooth paste. Heat remainder of can of cherries in saucepan. Add a little hot mixture to cold paste. Mix, then add to hot mixture gradually, stirring all the time until relatively clear and thickened. Remove from heat immediately. Stir in butter, flavoring and coloring. Pour into unbaked 9-inch pie crust. Cover with enough pastry for top crust, or make lattice top. Bake at 425° for 25 to 30 minutes.

GRAHAM CHERRY PIE

3 tbsp. powdered sugar
12 graham wafers, rolled fine
4 tbsp. butter, softened
1 cup boiling water

6-oz. pkg. cherry jello
3/4 cup cherry juice
31/3 cups cherries, strained

Add sugar to wafers and work in butter. Press mixture into buttered glass pie plate and chill. Mix water and jelly powder and stir until dissolved. Add juice, cherries and chill. When almost set, pour jelly into crust and allow to set. Cover with whipped cream and serve.

Mrs. B. Leviciki

When a recipe calls for fruits and nuts to be soaked 12 to 24 hours with a quantity of rum or brandy, use the microwave. Use the same quantity of fruits, nuts and rum or brandy. Mix in a large bowl. Microwave 5 minutes, covered with waxed paper.

MERINGUE

3 egg whites   1/3 cup sugar
Pinch of salt   1 tsp. vanilla
1/4 tsp. cream of tartar

Beat egg whites and pinch of salt in small bowl until foamy. Add cream of tartar. Continue beating until moist peaks are formed. Gradually beat in sugar and vanilla. Continue to beat until meringue is stiff and sugar is well blended. Pile on top of filling and bake at 325° for 20 minutes or until golden brown.

FLUFFY MERINGUE TOPPING

2 egg whites   1 tbsp. cornstarch
1 tbsp. cold water   1/2 tsp. baking powder
2 tbsp. sugar

Beat egg whites with cold water until they hold their shape. Mix sugar, cornstarch and baking powder. Add this to egg whites and beat until well blended. Bake at 375 to 400° for 15 minutes. NOTE: This meringue will not stick to your knife when you cut it.

NEVER FAIL MERINGUE TOPPING

2 egg whites   Pinch of salt
1 tbsp. water   2 tbsp. sugar
1/4 tsp. baking powder

Beat egg whites with water until stiff. Add baking powder, salt and sugar. Beat until soft peaks are formed. Spread on pie and brown lightly in moderate oven.

WHIPPED TOPPING

1/2 cup powdered skim milk   2 tbsp. lemon juice
1/2 cup ice water   1/4 cup sugar

Place bowl and beaters in refrigerator until cold. Beat powdered milk and ice water until soft peaks form. Add lemon juice. Beat until firm. Add sugar. Yield: 2 1/2 cups topping. This can be used instead of whipped cream.

LEMON BUTTER

7/8 cup sugar   1/4 cup butter
Rind and juice of 2 lemons 2 eggs

Combine sugar, rind, juice and butter. Heat until sugar is dissolved. Cool. Return to heat and add eggs. Stir until thick. Do not boil.

Mrs. E. Pearson

Be sure to bring meringue out to edge of the crust. This will prevent the meringue from shrinking when baked.

LEMON PIE FILLING

13/4 cups water
1 cup sugar
Pinch of salt
Grated rinds of 2 lemons
2 tbsp. cornstarch
1/3 cup water

3 eggs yolks
Juice of 2 lemons
1 tbsp. butter
9-inch pie shell
Meringue

Bring 13/4 cups water, sugar, salt and rind to a boil. Thicken with cornstarch mixed with 1/3 cup water. Add egg yolks which have been beaten with lemon juice. Allow to cook 2 minutes longer. Remove from heat and add butter. Pour into baked 9-inch pie shell and cool. Pile meringue on top of filling, bringing it out to the edge of the crust. Swirl to make meringue stand in peaks. Place pie in 325° oven for about 20 minutes or until golden brown. This lemon pie filling doubled will make 3 medium-sized pies.

Hazel Stevenett

HONEY LEMON PIE

5 tbsp. cornstarch
3/4 cup honey
1/2 tsp. salt
1/2 cup cold water

1 cup boiling water
Juice and rind of 1 lemon
2 egg yolks, well beaten
1 tbsp. butter

Mix together cornstarch, honey, salt and cold water. Add boiling water and cook in double boiler until starch flavor is gone. Remove from heat. Add lemon and egg yolks diluted with a small amount of hot mixture. Return to heat for a few minutes, add butter and pour into baked pie shell and cover with meringue.

JEAN'S PUMPKIN PIE

9-inch pie crust
2 tbsp. butter **or** margarine,
  melted
11/2 cups canned pumpkin
3/4 tsp. ginger
1/2 tsp. nutmeg

3/4 tsp. cinnamon
2 eggs
2 tbsp. flour
3/4 cup brown sugar
1/2 tsp. salt
11/2 cups milk

Line 9-inch pie plate with pastry. Make high standing rim and flute. Chill in freezer section while preparing filling. Combine butter, pumpkin and spices. Beat eggs until light and add. Combine flour, sugar and salt. Add along with milk. Pour into pie shell. Bake at 450° for 15 minutes. Reduce heat to 350° and bake 30 to 40 minutes until knife blade inserted in center comes out clean.

Mrs. Jean Leskow

For flakey pastry, substitute 7-up or club soda for water.

PUMPKIN PIE

2/3 cup brown sugar
1 tbsp. cornstarch
1/8 tsp. cinnamon
1/8 tsp. cloves
1/8 tsp. nutmeg
1/2 tsp. salt

1 1/2 cups cooked pumpkin
2 eggs, slightly beaten
1 cup milk
1 cup cream
1 baked pie shell

Mix sugar, cornstarch and spices. Add to pumpkin, eggs, milk and cream and cook until thick. Pour into pie crust and pile high with sweetened whipped cream. Dust with cinnamon.

Mrs. A. Mack

CRUSTLESS PUMPKIN PIE

3/4 cup honey
1/2 tsp. ginger
1/2 tsp. cinnamon
1/2 tsp. nutmeg

1/2 tsp. salt
1 3/4 cups pumpkin
3 eggs, beaten slightly
1 cup evaporated milk

Add honey, spices, salt and pumpkin to eggs. Mix well and add undiluted evaporated milk. Butter or oil deep 9-inch pie pan. Pour pumpkin custard into pan. Bake at 325° for one hour, or until knife blade comes out clean. Cool thoroughly before cutting. Serve in pie-shaped wedges and top with honey-sweetened whipped cream, if desired.

SPECIAL PUMPKIN PIE

Pastry for-1 crust pie
3 eggs
1/4 cup preserved ginger, cut fine
1 cup thick sour cream
Syrup from ginger

1/2 tsp. cinnamon
1/4 tsp. salt
1/4 tsp. each mace and cloves
1/4 cup cognac
1 cup cooked pumpkin

Line pie plate with pastry. Pierce with fork and bake at 425° for 5 minutes. Combine ingredients. Fill pastry with mixture. Reduce heat to 375° and bake 35 to 40 minutes.

MICROWAVE PUMPKIN PIE

16-oz. can pumpkin
3/4 cup brown sugar, firmly packed
1/2 tsp. cinnamon
1/4 tsp. ground cloves
1/4 tsp. ginger

1/4 tsp. allspice
1/8 tsp. nutmeg
2 eggs
1 cup evaporated milk
9-inch baked pie shell

Mix pumpkin, sugar and spices in a large mixing bowl. Beat eggs and milk together. Stir into pumpkin mixture. Pour filling into pie shell. Microwave on Level 6 for 18 to 20 minutes, or until filling is set and knife inserted near center comes out clean.

Francis Seatter

PUMPKIN CHIFFON PIE

2 egg yolks	1 tsp. cinnamon
1/2 cup yellow sugar	1/2 tsp. nutmeg
1 cup cooked pumpkin	1 env.unflavored gelatin
1/2 cup milk	1/4 cup cold water
1/2 tsp. salt	2 egg whites, beaten stiff
1/2 tsp. ginger	1/2 cup white sugar

Beat egg yolks and 1/2 cup yellow sugar until thick. Add pumpkin, milk, salt and spices. Cook in top of double boiler until thick. Remove from heat. Soften gelatin in cold water. Stir into hot mixture. Beat egg whites until stiff and add 1/2 cup white sugar gradually, beating until very stiff. Fold meringue into pumpkin mixture. Pour into cooled baked shell and chill. Serve with whipped cream, if desired.

Mrs. Iris Humble

PUMPKIN CHEESE PIE

2 tbsp. butter	3 eggs
1 cup fine graham crumbs	11/2 tbsp. flour
1/4 cup brown sugar	1 tsp. cinnamon
8 oz. cream cheese	1/2 tsp. nutmeg
1 cup canned pumpkin	1 tsp. vanilla
3/4 cup brown sugar	Pecan halves (optional)

Place butter in 9-inch glass pie plate and microwave on High for 30 to 60 seconds until melted. Add graham crackers and sugar and mix. Press mixture firmly against bottom and side of pie plate. Microwave on Medium High (70%) 2 to 4 minutes, turning plate once or twice. Cool. Place cream cheese in medium bowl. Microwave on Medium (50%) 1 to 2 minutes until softened. Add remaining ingredients. Beat at medium speed of electric mixer until smooth and well blended. Microwave on Medium-High (70%) 6 to 8 minutes until hot and thickened, stirring every 2 minutes. Pour into crust. Reduce power to Medium. Microwave 10 to 15 minutes until filling is firm to the touch. Center may appear soft - set. Garnish with pecan halves if desired. Refrigerate until set.

Louise Van Camp

CARROT PIE

21/4 cups pureed carrots	1 tsp. salt
1 tsp. melted butter	1 tsp. cinnamon
1 tsp. ginger	1 tbsp. molasses
2/3 cup sugar	2 eggs, well beaten
11/2 cups evaporated milk	Unbaked pie shell

Mix ingredients and pour into unbaked pie shell. Bake at 400° for about 45 minutes until done.

RHUBARB PIE

3 tbsp. quick-cooking tapioca	4 cups cut rhubarb
1 1/2 cups sugar	Pastry for 2 crust 9-inch pie
1/4 tsp. salt	1 tbsp. butter

Combine tapioca, sugar, salt and rhubarb. Line pie pan with pastry. Fill pie shell with rhubarb mixture and dot with butter. Make a lattice top with pastry. Flute rim. Bake at 425° for 45 minutes or until fruit is well cooked. VARIATION: Add 1 tsp. grated orange rind to rhubarb mixture.

RHUBARB PIE DELUXE

2 cups cut rhubarb	1 cup sugar
2 tbsp. flour, mixed with sugar	1 tbsp. butter
2 egg yolks, well beaten	Meringue

Mix ingredients together. Cook slowly until jelly-like and stir to prevent burning. Pour into baked pie shell. Cover with meringue and brown in oven.

Mrs. N. Robinson
Mrs. Rose-Marie Grusie

RAISIN PIE

1 cup raisins	1 1/2 cups water
1/2 cup brown sugar	2 tbsp. flour
1/2 cup white sugar	1/4 tsp. salt
1 tsp. cider vinegar	1 egg, beaten
1 tbsp. butter **or** margarine	Pastry for 2-crust pie

Mix raisins, sugars, vinegar, butter and water. Bring to boil in saucepan. Add flour and salt. Mix with raisins to thicken. Remove from heat. Add egg. Pour into unbaked pie shell. Cover with top crust. Bake at 350° for 35 to 40 minutes until browned.

Mrs. Frances A. Chambers

HONEY RAISIN PIE

1 1/2 cups raisins	1/2 tsp. salt
1 cup water	3/4 cup honey
3/4 cup cold raisin juice	2 tbsp. butter
4 tbsp. lemon juice	9-inch pie shell
4 tbsp. cornstarch	Beaten egg and sugar

Cook raisins in water until done. Combine raisin juice, lemon juice, cornstarch, salt, honey and butter. Mix well and add to hot raisin mixture. Cook, stirring until thick. Pour into 9-inch pie shell and cover top with beaten egg and sugar for glaze. Bake at 400° about 45 minutes or until done. Serve with ice cream.

RAISIN CRUMB PIE

1 cup brown sugar	1 cup cookie crumbs
1/8 tsp. salt	1 tsp. cinnamon
3 eggs, beaten	1/4 tsp. ginger
1/2 cup water	1/3 cup flour
3/4 cup raisins	1/4 tsp. nutmeg
Unbaked pie shell	1/3 cup butter

Combine sugar, salt, eggs and water. Pour over raisins in the pie shell. Combine remaining ingredients and mix as pie crust. Sprinkle over raisin mixture. Bake at 325° for 25 to 30 minutes, or until done.

RAISIN SOUR CREAM PIE

2 cups raisins	1/3 cup sugar
1 cup water	1/4 tsp. nutmeg
2 cups sour cream	1/2 tsp. cinnamon
3 egg yolks	Baked pie shell
1 tbsp. flour	Meringue

Simmer raisins in water. Mix sour cream, egg yolks, flour, sugar, nutmeg and cinnamon and add to raisins. Cook slowly. When thick, pour in baked pie shell. Use egg whites for meringue.

Mrs. Guy Kirk

CRANBERRY AND RAISIN PIE

1 cup cranberries	1/2 tsp. salt
1 cup raisins	1 tsp. vanilla
1 cup sugar	Pastry for 2-crust pie
1 tbsp. flour	

Cover cranberries and raisins with water. Cook 20 minutes. Combine sugar, flour, salt and vanilla and add to cooked fruits. Return to heat and cook until thick, stirring constantly. Pour into unbaked pie shell. Cover with lattice top or solid crust. Bake at 350° for 35 to 40 minutes until browned.

Mary Lea

EASY MINCEMEAT

1/2 lb. suet, ground	1 cup molasses, fruit juice **or**
1 lb. raisins	apple cider
1/4 lb. mixed peel	3 lbs. apples, chopped
6 tsp. pastry spices	1/2 lb. currants
1 1/2 cups brown sugar	2 tsp. salt

Combine and put in sealers. This will keep without cooking.

Sofia Efrom

HOMEMADE MINCEMEAT

10 lbs. green tomatoes
10 lbs. chopped apples
1 cup mixed fruit
1 cup suet
2 tbsp. molasses
1 lb. seedless raisins
1 lb. currants

1 tsp. allspice
1 tsp. cinnamon
1 tsp. cloves
1 tsp. nutmeg
1/2 cup vinegar
4 cups brown sugar
2 cups white sugar

Put tomatoes through chopper and drain. Cover with cold water, boil for 30 minutes and drain. Repeat four times. Drain. Combine with remaining ingredients. Cook until thick, bottle and seal.

Mrs. Don (Miranne) Antal

RASPBERRY PIE

2/3 cups sugar
Dash of salt
21/2 tbsp. cornstarch

1 cup water
1 baked pie shell
Fresh raspberries

Mix sugar, salt and starch. Add water and cook to thicken. Fill pie shell with fresh raspberries and pour cooled sauce over the berries. Top with whipped topping.

Margaret Allan

PEAR PIE

10-inch unbaked crust
4 medium pears, peeled
1/4 cup flour
1/4 cup sugar

1/2 cup cream
1/2 cup milk
1 tsp. cinnamon

Line pie plate with crust. Core and quarter pears and cover bottom crust. Mix flour and sugar together and sprinkle over pears. Mix cream and milk together and pour over mixture. Sprinkle with cinnamon. Bake at 400° for approximately 25 minutes. Apples may be used instead of pears.

Marjorie Schmidt

APRICOT CHIFFON PIE

1 tsp. butter **or** margarine
11/3 cups flaked coconut
1 env. unflavored gelatin
11/2 cups apricot nectar

3 tsp. artificial sweetener
1 tsp. lemon juice
Dash of salt
2 egg whites

Mix butter and coconut and press into pie plate on bottom and sides of pie. Bake at 325° for 10 minutes. Cool. Soften gelatin in 1/2 cup cold nectar. Heat remaining cup of nectar just to boiling. Add gelatin and stir to dissolve. Add artificial sweetener, lemon juice and salt. Turn into mixing bowl. Chill until partially set. Add egg whites. Beat until soft peaks form. Pile into crust. Chill until firm. One serving: 130 calories.

BONNY BLUEBERRY PIE

1/4 cup flour
Pastry for 2-crust pie
1 1/4 cups sugar
1/8 tsp. salt
2 tbsp. cornstarch

1 tsp. grated lemon rind
1/4 tsp. nutmeg
4 cups blueberries
1 tbsp. lemon juice
1 tbsp. butter

Line 9-inch pie plate with half the pastry. Combine the flour, sugar, salt, cornstarch, nutmeg and lemon rind. Add the blueberries. Blend thoroughly. Turn into pie crust and dot with butter. Place top crust over filling and seal. Bake at 450° for 10 minutes. Reduce heat to 350° and bake for 35 minutes.

Lillian Hogg

BOSTON CREAM PIE

1 1/2 cups milk
1/2 cup sugar
1/4 tsp. salt
2 egg yolks
2 tbsp. cornstarch

2 tbsp. cold milk
1 tsp. vanilla
Apricots
Sponge cake **or** butter cake
Whipped cream

Combine 1 1/2 cups milk and sugar in top of double boiler and heat to boiling point. Combine salt, egg yolks and cornstarch moistened in 2 tbsp. milk. Mix well. Add to hot milk, stir and cook until thick and creamy. Remove from heat and add vanilla. Cool. Add sugar to taste to apricots and cook well. Mash to a pulp. Strawberries, raspberries, peaches or any other soft fruit may be substituted. Split one sponge cake with a sharp knife. Fill center with custard and top with fruit. Place other half of cake on top and garnish with whipped cream. Whipped egg whites may be used instead of cream but place cake in oven a few minutes to brown. Yield: 8 servings.

Mrs. Rose Charles

BUTTERSCOTCH CHIFFON PIE

1 tbsp. gelatin
1/4 cup cold water
3 eggs, separated
1 cup brown sugar, firmly packed
1 cup scalded milk

2 tbsp. butter
1/4 tsp. salt
1 tsp. vanilla
1/4 cup granulated sugar
9-inch baked pie shell

Soak gelatin in cold water for 5 minutes. Beat yolks gradually, beating in brown sugar and then milk. Add butter and salt. Cook in double boiler, stirring until custard-like. Stir in gelatin. Cool. Add vanilla. Beat egg whites until foamy. Gradually add granulated sugar and continue beating until stiff. When gelatin mixture is partly set, fold in stiffly-beaten egg whites. Turn into 9-inch baked pie shell. Chill.

Janetta Northcott

CHOCOLATE-LIME SWIRL PIE

25 - 30 chocolate wafers
3 tbsp. melted butter
3-oz. pkg. lime jello
1/4 cup sugar
3/4 cup boiling water

10 drops green food coloring
1 tsp. grated lemon rind
4 tbsp. lemon juice
1 cup undiluted evaporated
  milk **or** light cream

Crush all but 12 wafers. Mix crumbs with butter and spread on bottom of 9-inch pie plate, saving 1/4 cup for topping. Line sides with 12 whole wafers. Dissolve jello powder and sugar in boiling water. Add food coloring, lemon rind and 2 tbsp. juice. Chill until slightly thickened. Chill evaporated milk in refrigerator tray 15 to 20 minutes until soft ice crystals form around edges of tray. Whip about 1 minute until stiff. Add remaining lemon juice. Whip about 2 minutes until very stiff. Fold in jelly mixture. Spoon over cookie crumbs. Swirl remaining crumbs over top. Chill about 1 to 2 hours until firm.

Mrs. Chrystel Smyth

HONEY CHEESE PIE

9-inch pie shell
1 cup cream cheese
3 eggs
1/2 cup liquid honey
1/2 cup light cream

1/2 cup milk
1/4 tsp. salt
1 tsp. grated lemon rind
1 tbsp. lemon juice

Bake a 9-inch pie shell for 10 minutes at 425°. Cream the cheese, beat eggs, honey, cream, milk, salt and lemon rind. Add egg mixture to cheese gradually and beat until smooth. Add lemon juice. Pour mixture into partly baked pie shell and bake at 350° about 35 to 40 minutes until filling is firm. Chill. Before serving, top with glazed fruit.

SOUR CREAM PIE

3 eggs, separated
1 cup sugar
1/2 tsp. salt
1 tsp. cinnamon
1 tsp. nutmeg
1 tsp. cloves

1 cup sour cream
1 cup chopped raisins
  or currants
2 tbsp. vinegar
Pastry for single-crust pie
Meringue

Beat egg yolks in bowl, add sugar, salt and spices and beat again. Add sour cream, raisins and vinegar. Mix and pour into crust. Bake at 450° for 15 minutes, then reduce heat to 350° and bake for 45 minutes. Top with meringue.

Mrs. J.E. Brockelsby

Freeze pastry scraps. When you have collected enough, you have a free crust.

FRENCH CREAM PIE

12 graham wafers, rolled fine
2 cups icing sugar
1/2 cup butter
2 egg whites, beaten

1/2 cup walnuts, chopped fine
1/2 cup cherries, chopped fine
1 1/2 cups cream whipped

Place half the wafer crumbs in pie plate. Press on bottom and sides. Mix icing sugar with butter. Add to egg whites. Mix well. Fold walnuts and cherries into whipped cream. Spread butter mixture on crumb base and top with whipped cream mixture. Cover with rest of crumbs. Chill in refrigerator for 24 hours.

Mrs. Jeanne Auger

PINEAPPLE CHIFFON PIE

1 env. gelatin
1/4 cup cold water
3 eggs, separated
3/4 cup sugar
3/4 cups crushed pineapple

1 tsp. grated lemon rind
3 tbsp. lemon juice
1/4 tsp. salt
1/2 cup heavy cream, whipped
Baked pie shell

Add gelatin to cold water and set aside. In double boiler combine egg yolks, 1/4 cup sugar, pineapple, lemon peel and juice. Cook over hot water, stirring constantly until smooth and beginning to thicken. Add softened gelatin and stir until dissolved. Remove from heat. Add salt to egg whites and beat stiff. Gradually beat in the remaining 1/2 cup sugar. Fold in hot pineapple mixture. Heap into baked pie shell or wafer-crumb crust and chill about 3 hours or until set. Spread with whipped cream and decorate each serving with a spoonful of drained or crushed pineapple. Yield: 6 servings. This can be made the day before using.

PINEAPPLE CREAM PIE

1/2 cup brown sugar
1/4 cup melted butter
1/2 tsp. cinnamon
14 graham wafers, crushed
5 tbsp. flour
2/3 cup sugar
1/3 tsp. salt
1/3 cup cold milk

2/3 cup hot milk
2 egg yolks, slightly beaten
1 tbsp. butter
1/2 cup pineapple juice
2 tsp. lemon juice
1/2 cup crushed pineapple
2 egg whites, beaten stiff
2 - 3 tbsp. sugar

Combine brown sugar, melted butter and cinnamon with wafers and line pie plate. Mix flour, 2/3 cup sugar and salt with cold milk. Stir gradually into hot milk and bring to boiling point, stirring constantly. Pour hot mixture over egg yolks. Cook 2 minutes. Add butter, pineapple and lemon juice, and pineapple. Pour into pie plate. Chill for half an hour. Beat egg whites, gradually adding 3 tbsp. sugar until stiff, but not dry. Pile meringue on top and brown in oven.

Mrs. Gladys Baden

CREAM PIE

2/3 cup sugar
1/4 tsp. salt
1/3 cup flour **or**
   1/4 cup cornstarch
2 cups scalded milk
2 egg yolks, slightly beaten

2 tbsp. butter
1/2 tsp. vanilla
Baked pastry shell
2 egg whites
4 tbsp. sugar
Dash of salt

Mix sugar, salt and flour in top of double boiler. Add milk gradually, stirring constantly until mixture comes to a boil and thickens. Remove from heat. Add small amount to egg yolks. Stir into hot mixture. Cook one minute longer. Add butter and vanilla. Cool slightly. Pour into baked pastry shell. Make meringue with egg whites, sugar and salt. Bake at 350° for 12 to 15 minutes or until golden. VARIATIONS: For banana, slice 2 bananas in shell and add filling. For butterscotch, substitute 1 cup brown sugar for white sugar, increase butter to 3 tbsp. and add 1/2 tsp. butterscotch flavoring with vanilla. For chocolate, increase sugar to 1 cup. Add 2 squares of melted unsweetened chocolate to scalded milk.

MARSHMALLOW-GRAHAM WAFER PIE

20 graham wafers
5 tbsp. butter
1/2 lb. marshmallows
1/2 cup milk

1/2 pint whipping cream,
  whipped
1/2 cup fruit **or** chocolate chips

Roll wafers into crumbs and add butter. Place half the mixture in pie plate. Press on bottom and sides. Melt marshmallows in milk and cool. Fold in whipped cream, add fruit and pour into pie plate lined with crumbs. Top with remaining crumbs and chill.

Evelyn Ebl

ANGEL PIE

4 egg whites
1/4 tsp. cream of tartar
3/4 cup sugar
4 egg yolks
1/2 cup sugar
1/8 tsp. salt

1 tsp. grated orange rind
1 tsp. grated lemon rind
1 tbsp. lemon juice
2 tbsp. orange juice
1 cup cream
2 tbsp. powdered sugar

Beat egg whites until frothy and add cream of tartar. Beat until stiff but not dry. Gradually add sugar and beat until stiff. Spread in 9-inch ungreased pie plate. Do not spread too close to the edge of plate. Bake at 300° for 1 hour. Cool. Combine egg yolks, sugar, salt, orange and lemon rind and lemon and orange juice in double boiler and cook until thick. Cool. Whip cream and add powdered sugar. Spread half the cream over the cooled meringue crust. Add filling and spread the remaining whipped cream over the top. Chill 12 to 24 hours.

Mrs. Doreen Solbert

STRAWBERRY PIE GLAZE

3 cups sugar
2 tbsp. cornstarch
1 cup water

3 tbsp. strawberry **or**
raspberry jello

Boil sugar, cornstarch and water together for 3 minutes, while stirring. Add jello. Let cool and put over fresh strawberries in baked pie crust.

Barbara Vergenello

STRAWBERRY PARFAIT PIE

3-oz. pkg. strawberry jello
1 cup boiling water
11/2 cups cold water
1 quart vanilla ice cream

1 cup sliced fresh strawberries
or 1 pkg. frozen strawberries
1 baked pie shell **or** graham
wafer crust

Dissolve jello in boiling water. Add the cold water. Cut the ice cream into 6 pieces and add. Stir until ice cream melts. Refrigerate 30 minutes until it holds shape. Add strawberries. Pour into prepared crust and let set. Top with whipped cream. NOTE: If using frozen strawberries, thaw and drain before using.

Ellen Berg

PEACH RASPBERRY PIE

1/4 cup butter
2 tbsp. sugar
1 cup chocolate
   graham wafer crumbs
4 tbsp. toasted almonds
2 drops almond extract

30 large marshmallows
1/2 cup raspberry cocktail
1/4 cup water
1 cup whipping cream, whipped
2 cups diced fresh peaches

Place butter in 9-inch glass pie plate. Microwave on High for 30 to 40 seconds or until melted. Stir in sugar, crumbs, almonds and extract. Pat crumbs evenly over bottom and sides of pie plate. Microwave on High for 21/2 minutes. Cool. Place marshmallows, raspberry cocktail and water in 21/2-qt. casserole. Microwave on High for 3 to 4 minutes or until marshmallows are melted, stirring twice. Stir mixture until smooth. Place in refrigerator and chill until mixture begins to thicken. Fold in whipped cream and peaches. Pour into pie shell. Chill for 2 to 3 hours or until firm. Decorate with swirls of whipped cream and chocolate curls.

Mary Parsons

To prevent sticking when making a cream pie filling, put milk in pan, add required sugar and bring to the boiling point without stirring. Mix cornstarch in cold water and stir in quickly. Flavoring added after the filling cools retains slightly more flavor.

COCONUT CREAM PIE

2 cups graham crumbs
1/2 cup melted butter
1 1/2 cup flour
2/3 cup sugar
1/4 tsp. salt
2 1/2 cups scalded milk

3/4 cup coconut
3 egg yolks, well beaten
2 tbsp. butter
1 tsp. vanilla
3 egg whites
6 tbsp. sugar

Mix crumbs with butter and press on bottom and sides of glass pie plate. Microwave on Medium-High for 2 minutes. Cool. Mix flour, sugar and salt. Gradually add milk. Microwave on High until mixture thickens. Stir every minute. Add coconut and beat. Add egg yolks, stirring constantly. Microwave on High for 2 minutes, stirring twice. Add butter and vanilla. Cool slightly and pour into prepared crust. Make meringue with egg whites and 6 tbsp. sugar. Spread on pie, sprinkle with flaked coconut and brown at 350° for 12 minutes.

Mary Stott

RECEPTION DAINTIES

2 cups flour
1/4 tsp. salt
1 tsp. baking powder
1 cup butter **or** hard lard
2 tbsp. sugar
1 egg, beaten

1 tsp. vanilla
1/4 cup milk
2 lemons, grated rind and juice
1 cup sugar
4 egg yolks
1/2 cup butter

Mix first 5 ingredients together like pastry. Add egg, vanilla and milk. Either roll or press into small muffin tins and bake. Mix remaining ingredients together and cook in a double boiler until thick, stirring constantly. Put cold filling into slightly warm baked pastry shells. Put whipped cream on just before serving.

ORANGE-CREAM TARTS

1 1/2 cups sugar
2 tbsp. flour
1/4 cup cornstarch
1/2 tsp. salt
1 1/2 cups boiling water
3 egg yolks

6 tbsp. orange juice
Grated rind of 2 oranges
1/2 cup whipping cream
15 baked tart shells, cooled
Whipped cream (optional)

Mix sugar, flour, cornstarch and salt in saucepan. Add boiling water gradually, stirring constantly. Set over moderate heat and cook, stirring until mixture comes to a boil and is thick and clear. Beat egg yolks and orange juice with a fork. Add half of hot mixture to the egg yolk mixture, stirring constantly. Pour back into saucepan, add orange rind and bring just to a boil. Cover and cool until serving time. Whip cream just before serving, fold into orange mixture and fill tart shells. Top with a dab of whipped cream if desired.

BUTTER TARTS

1/4 cup butter	1 cup raisins **or** currants
1 cup brown sugar	1/2 cup walnuts, chopped
1 egg, beaten	Pastry for tarts

Cream butter and sugar. Add egg, raisins and nuts. Line muffin tins with rich pastry. Put one tsp. of filling in each tart and bake at 400° for 8 minutes. Reduce heat to 350° and bake 5 minutes until filling is firm.

HONEY BUTTER TARTS

3 eggs, well beaten	1/2 tsp. cinnamon
1 tbsp. butter	1 cup raisins
1 cup brown sugar	1/2 cup currants
1/4 cup honey	1/2 cup walnuts
1/2 tsp. nutmeg	Unbaked tart shells

Beat the eggs, butter, brown sugar, honey and spices until frothy. Add raisins, currants and walnuts and mix well. Pour 1 tbsp. of mixture into each tart shell and bake at 375° until done. Mixture may also be all poured into unbaked pie shell and baked at 375° until done. Cut into small wedges and serve.

COCONUT TARTS

6 eggs, beaten	1 1/2 cups shredded coconut
1/2 cup rum **or** fruit juice	Pastry dough for 24 tarts
3/4 cup firmly-packed brown sugar	Rum-flavored whipped cream
1/4 tsp. nutmeg	Toasted coconut
1/4 tsp. cinnamon	

Preheat oven to 375°. Line 2 dozen tart tins with pastry. Combine eggs, rum, brown sugar, nutmeg, cinnamon and coconut. Fill each tart two-thirds full. Bake at 350° for 20 to 25 minutes, or until set. Serve garnished with whipped cream and coconut.

SOUR CREAM TARTS

1 cup butter	Peach jam
1 1/2 cups flour	2 tsp. granulated sugar
1/2 cup sour cream	Water

Cut butter into flour as for pastry. Add sour cream and mix in gently with a fork. Shape into two balls and store in refrigerator overnight or at least 8 hours. Roll out as thinly as possible. Cut into 2-inch rounds or diamond shapes. Cut a small hole in the center of half of the rounds and place these on top of the plain rounds. Fill each hole with 1/2 tsp. peach jam. Brush tops with sugar mixed with a few drops of water. Bake at 350° for 20 to 25 minutes. Add only a few drops of water to sugar in order to get glazed appearance, otherwise sugar soaks into pastry.

Ada Osing

CAKES & FROSTINGS

CHOCOLATE CAKE

2 egg whites
1/2 cup sugar
13/4 cups cake flour
1 cup sugar
3/4 tsp. baking soda
3/4 tsp. salt

1/3 cup salad oil
1 cup sweet milk **or** buttermilk
2 egg yolks
2 sq. unsweetened chocolate,
    melted and slightly cooled
1 tsp. vanilla

Beat egg whites until frothy. Gradually add 1/2 cup sugar and continue beating until very stiff. Measure and sift cake flour, 1 cup sugar, baking soda and salt into a bowl. Add salad oil and 1/2 cup sweet milk. Beat for one minute at medium speed on electric mixer. Scrape sides and bottom of bowl frequently. Add remaining sweet milk, egg yolks, chocolate and vanilla. Beat for 1 minute. Gently fold meringue into batter until mixture is blended. Pour into two greased 8-inch square pans. Bake at 350° for 30 to 35 minutes. NOTE: 5 tbsp. of cocoa may be used in place of the chocolate squares. Sift the cocoa in with the flour.

Anna Vail

MARY'S CHOCOLATE CAKE

21/4 cups flour
3/4 cup cocoa
1 tsp. salt
17/8 cup sugar
13/4 tsp. soda
1 cup butter **or** shortening

1 cup buttermilk **or** sour milk
3 eggs
1/2 cup buttermilk **or** sour milk
1 tsp. vanilla
1 tsp. lemon (optional)

Combine flour, cocoa, salt, sugar and soda. Knead in butter, like pastry. Add 1 cup buttermilk and beat for 2 minutes. Add eggs, 1/2 cup buttermilk, vanilla and lemon. Beat 2 minutes. Bake at 350° for 30 to 40 minutes.

Mary Spornitz

EGG SUBSTITUTE: 1 egg may be omitted from cakes and cookies calling for more than 2 eggs. Use 1/2 tsp. extra baking powder and 2 tbsp. extra milk. In custard mixtures and in rich fillings for cakes and pies, 2 tbsp. of flour may be substituted for 1 egg.

UNBAKED CHOCOLATE CAKE

1/2 cup melted butter
1 cup sugar
1/2 cup cocoa
1 egg, beaten

1 tsp. vanilla
20 single graham wafers, crushed
3/4 cup walnuts, chopped

Mix butter, sugar, cocoa and egg in saucepan and bring to boil. Simmer 1 minute. Add vanilla, wafers and walnuts. Mix well and press down in cake pan. Cover with thin layer of icing. Cut in squares and serve.

Mrs. Lee Potter

CHOCOLATE CHIP LOAF

2 cups flour
21/2 tsp. baking powder
1 tsp. salt
2/3 cup shortening
1 cup sugar

3 eggs, unbeaten
2/3 cup milk
11/2 tsp. vanilla
1/2 cup chopped nuts
6 oz. chocolate chips

Sift flour, baking powder and salt. Cream shortening and sugar. Add eggs one at a time, beating well after each addition. Add vanilla. Continue beating until fluffy. Add flour alternately with milk. Stir in nuts and chips. Bake in a 9 x 13-inch pan at 350° for 60 to 70 minutes.

Mrs. K.D. Galloway

CHOCOLATE FLECK CAKE

2 eggs, separated
1 cup sugar
1/2 cup butter
1 tsp. vanilla
1 cup milk

2 cups cake flour
3 tsp. baking powder
Pinch of salt
2 sq. semi-sweet chocolate, shredded

Beat egg whites stiff. Gradually add 1/2 cup sugar and beat to meringue. Set aside. Cream butter and remaining sugar until very light. Add vanilla to milk. Sift dry ingredients together. Add milk alternately with flour mixture. Gently fold in meringue and chocolate. Bake in a 9 x 13-inch pan at 350° for 45 minutes.

Johanna Cossins

CHOCOLATE MIX CAKE

2 cups milk, scalded
1 pkg. non-instant chocolate pudding

1 chocolate cake mix
1/2 cup chocolate chips
1/2 cup chopped walnuts

Let milk cool slightly. Add pudding powder. Cook until slightly thickened. Add cake mix. Spread in a 9 x 13-inch loaf pan. Sprinkle batter with chocolate chips and walnuts. This forms a glaze on top of cake when cooked. Bake at 350° for 35 to 40 minutes.

Mrs. Mary Briault

CHOCOLATE SAUERKRAUT CAKE

21/4 cups flour
1 tsp. soda
1/2 cup cocoa
1 tsp. baking powder
1/4 tsp. salt
2/3 cup shortening

11/2 cups sugar
11/4 tsp. vanilla
3 eggs
1 cup water
1/2 cup drained, chopped
  sauerkraut

Sift flour, soda, cocoa, baking powder and salt together. Cream shortening with sugar until light and fluffy. Blend in vanilla. Add eggs one at a time, beating after each addition. Add water and sauerkraut and mix thoroughly. Pour into well-greased 13 x 9-inch pan. Bake at 375° for 35 minutes. Cool in pan. Spread with desired frosting.

Sofia Efrom
Irene Bennett

SWEET CHOCOLATE CAKE

4 sq. sweet chocolate
1/2 cup boiling water
1 cup butter **or** shortening
2 cups sugar
4 egg yolks, unbeaten
1 tsp. vanilla

1/2 tsp. salt
1 tsp. baking soda
21/2 cups cake flour
1 cup buttermilk
4 egg whites, beaten stiff

Combine chocolate and boiling water in saucepan. Place over low heat and stir until chocolate melts and thickens slightly. Cream butter and sugar until light and fluffy. Add egg yolks, one at a time, beating after each. Add chocolate mixture and vanilla, mixing well. Sift together salt, soda and flour. Add alternately with buttermilk to chocolate mixture, beating well after each addition. Beat until batter is smooth. Fold in egg whites. This will make three 8-inch layer cakes. Bake at 350° for 30 to 40 minutes.

1 cup sugar
1 cup evaporated milk
3 egg yolks, beaten slightly
1/2 cup butter

1/3 cup coconut
1 cup chopped nuts
1 tsp. vanilla

Put sugar, milk, egg yolks and butter in a saucepan. Cook about 12 minutes until thick. Remove pan from heat and add coconut, chopped nuts and vanilla. Let cool and beat. Put between layers and on top of cake.

BAKING POWDER SUBSTITUTE: 1 tsp. cream of tartar mixed with 1/2 tsp. baking soda is equal to 1 tsp. baking powder.

DARK CHOCOLATE CAKE

1/2 cup butter
11/2 cups sugar
2 eggs, well beaten
2 cups cake flour
2 tsp. baking powder

3/4 tsp. soda
1 cup sour milk **or** sweet milk
1/2 cup cocoa
1/2 cup hot water

Cream butter and sugar. Add the eggs. Sift the flour before measuring and sift once more with the baking powder and soda. Add to the butter mixture alternately with the sour milk. Dissolve the cocoa in the hot water and add to the batter. Bake at 350° for about 45 minutes.

Mrs. Mary Gordon
Mary Stimson

GRANDMA'S CHOCOLATE CAKE

1/2 cup butter
11/4 cups sugar
2 eggs, well beaten
13/4 cups flour
1/2 tsp. salt

1 tsp. soda
1 cup sweet milk
1 tsp. vanilla
1/2 cup cocoa, dissolved
   in a little hot water

Mix butter and sugar. Add eggs. Sift dry ingredients and add alternately with milk. Add vanilla and cocoa. Bake at 375° for 45 minutes.

Mrs. Margaret Erickson

MAYONNAISE CHOCOLATE CAKE

3 cups flour
11/2 cups sugar
1/3 cup cocoa
21/4 tsp. baking powder

11/2 tsp. soda
11/2 cups mayonnaise
11/2 cups water
11/2 tsp. vanilla

Sift flour, sugar, cocoa, baking powder and soda together. Stir in mayonnaise. Gradually stir in water and vanilla until smooth and well blended. Bake in two layer pans or large pan at 350° about 30 minutes.

QUICK CHOCOLATE CAKE

3/4 cup melted butter **or** margarine
2 eggs
6 tbsp. cocoa
1 tsp. baking soda
1 tsp. vanilla

1 cup cold water
11/2 cups brown sugar
2 cups flour
1/2 tsp. salt

Mix all ingredients in a bowl and beat for several minutes. Put in pan and bake at 375° for 35 minutes.

Mrs. Ida Schonberner
Mrs. S. Neuman

TEXAS CHOCOLATE CAKE

1 tsp. soda
1 cup sliced dates
1 cup boiling water
1 cup margarine
1 cup sugar
2 eggs

13/4 cups flour
3 tsp. cocoa
1 tsp. salt
1 tsp. vanilla
6 oz. chocolate chips

Sprinkle soda over dates, add boiling water, bring to a boil and boil 1 to 2 minutes. Cool. Cream margarine and sugar; add eggs one at a time, beating well after each addition. Sift dry ingredients and add alternately with date mixture to butter mixture. Add vanilla. Pour into 8-inch square pan. Cover top with chocolate chips. Bake at 350° for 45 minutes.

Mrs. Adrian DeGroot

EASY RED DEVIL'S FOOD CAKE

1 1/2 cups cake flour
3/4 tsp. soda
1 1/4 cups sugar
3/4 tsp. salt
2/3 cup water

1/2 cup butter **or** shortening
2 sq. unsweetened chocolate
2 eggs
1 tsp. vanilla

Add sifted dry ingredients and water to softened butter. Beat 2 minutes. Melt chocolate and add along with eggs and vanilla. Beat 1 minute longer. Scrape bowl often. Turn batter into 9 x 9 x 2-inch greased pan, lined with paper. Bake at 350° for 45 minutes.

Mrs. Sally Smart

MICROWAVE DEVIL'S FOOD CAKE

2 cups flour
1/4 tsp. soda
1/4 tsp. salt
1/2 cup shortening **or** margarine
2 cups sugar

1/2 cup cocoa
3 eggs, well beaten
1 tsp. vanilla
1 cup water
1/2 cup buttermilk **or** sour milk

Grease a 2-qt. casserole. Sift flour, soda and salt into a large bowl. Cream shortening, sugar, cocoa, eggs and vanilla together in a bowl. Microwave water on High about 2 1/2 minutes until it boils. Stir water and buttermilk into creamed mixture, mixing well. Add dry ingredients and beat until smooth. Pour into prepared casserole. Microwave on Medium for 8 minutes. Turn and microwave on Medium an additional 5 minutes and then on High approximately 4 minutes.

Florence Keyser

For thickening, 1 tbsp. flour equals 1/2 tbsp. cornstarch.

WACKY COCOA CAKE

3 cups flour
2 cups sugar
6 tbsp. cocoa
2 tsp. soda
2 tsp. baking powder

2 tbsp. vinegar
2 tsp. vanilla
3 tbsp. oil
2 cups lukewarm water

Sift dry ingredients together in an ungreased 9 x 13 x 2-inch pan. Level mixture off and make three holes. In one hole, put the vinegar; in another put the vanilla and in the third put the oil. Pour water over the entire mixture and stir until flour disappears and is well mixed. Bake at 350° for about 45 minutes.

WHITE CAKE

3 cups flour
51/2 tsp. baking powder
1/2 tsp. salt
11/2 cups sugar

3/4 cup shortening
5 eggs
11/4 cups milk
1 tsp. vanilla

Sift dry ingredients together and blend in shortening. Add eggs, milk and vanilla. Beat for five minutes. Bake in 13 x 9 inch-pan at 350° for 50 to 55 minutes.

Mrs. Elmer Lewin

MARBLE CAKE

4 tbsp. sugar
1/4 cup boiling water
21/2 sq. unsweetened chocolate,
   melted
1/4 tsp. soda
3 tsp. baking powder
1/2 tsp. salt

3/4 cup butter
2 cups sugar
3 cups cake flour
1 cup milk
1 tsp. vanilla
6 egg whites

Add 4 tbsp. sugar and boiling water to melted chocolate. Stir until blended. Add soda and stir until thickened. Cool. Sift flour once, measure and add baking powder and salt. Sift three times. Cream butter and add 2 cups sugar gradually, creaming until mixture is light and fluffy. Add flour alternately with milk, a small amount at a time, beating after each addition until smooth. Add vanilla. Beat whites until they hold up in moist peaks. Stir quickly into batter. Divide batter. To one half, add the chocolate mixture. Place by tablespoon into greased layer pans, alternating the dark and light mixtures. Cut through the batter with a knife. Bake at 350° for 35 minutes or until done. Spread with boiled icing.

3 tbsp. cocoa plus 1 tbsp. shortening equals 1 sq. of unsweetened chocolate.

CHOCOLATE UPSIDE-DOWN CAKE

1 1/4 cups flour	2 tbsp. cocoa
3/4 cups sugar	2 tbsp. butter
2 tsp. baking powder	1/2 cup milk
1/4 tsp. salt	1 tsp. vanilla

Sift flour, sugar, baking powder, salt and cocoa. Melt butter and mix with milk and vanilla. Stir into the dry mixture. Pour into a greased glass layer cake dish.

2 tbsp. cocoa	1/2 cup white sugar
1/2 cup brown sugar	1 1/4 cups boiling water

Mix together cocoa and sugars and spread over top of cake. Pour the boiling water over all and bake at 300 to 350° for 1 hour. Serve warm or cool with whipped cream.

Mrs. V. Vestrum

RHUBARB UPSIDE-DOWN CAKE

1 tbsp. flour	1 cup flour
1/3 cup brown sugar	1/4 tsp. nutmeg
1 tsp. cinnamon	4 crushed, shredded wheat
2 cups rhubarb, chopped	biscuits
1/2 cup corn syrup	1/2 cup white sugar
1/2 cup shortening	2 eggs
3/4 cup milk	3 tsp. baking powder
3/4 tsp. orange rind	1 tsp. salt

Mix flour, sugar and cinnamon. Pour flour mixture and corn syrup over rhubarb. Make a batter of remaining ingredients and pour over mixture. Place in a 9 x 13-inch pan. Bake at 350° for 1 hour.

Helen Harris

BURNT SUGAR CAKE

1/2 cup sugar	1 cup sugar
1/2 cup water	2 egg yolks
2 1/2 cups cake flour	1 tsp. vanilla
1/4 tsp. salt	1 cup milk
2 1/2 tsp. baking powder	3 tbsp. burnt sugar syrup
1/2 cup shortening	2 egg whites, stiffly beaten

Cook 1/2 cup sugar in skillet until dark brown, stirring constantly. Add 1/2 cup water and boil slowly until sugar is dissolved. Sift flour, add salt and baking powder and resift. Cream shortening and 1 cup sugar, blending in egg yolks and vanilla. Add milk and sugar syrup alternately with sifted flour. Fold batter into egg whites. Bake in two 9-inch layer cake tins at 350° for 40 to 50 minutes. Ice with confectioner's sugar mixed with burnt sugar syrup and cream to a spreading consistency.

Mrs. J.A. Aitcheson

PEANUT BUTTER CAKE

2 cups flour	1/3 cup peanut butter
1 1/3 cups granulated sugar	1/2 cup butter **or** shortening
3 tbsp. baking powder	1 cup milk
1/2 tsp. salt	2 eggs

Sift dry ingredients into a mixing bowl. Add peanut butter, butter and 2/3 cup milk. Beat well with electric beater. Add remaining milk and eggs, one at a time and beat well. Bake in a greased square pan at 350° for 30 to 40 minutes. Cool and ice with a butter icing to which peanut butter has been added.

Mildred Latam

BLITZ TORTE

1/2 cup butter	1 tsp. baking powder
3 egg yolks	1 tsp. vanilla
1 cup flour	4 egg whites
1/2 tsp. salt	1 cup sugar
1/2 cup sugar	Coconut
5 tbsp. milk	

Mix all but last three ingredients and spread in two layer pans. Batter will be stiff. Beat egg whites until stiff, gradually adding 1 cup sugar. Spread meringue on unbaked layers and sprinkle with coconut. Bake at 325° for 30 to 35 minutes. Cool.

3/4 cup milk	1/2 cup sugar
1 tsp. cornstarch	1 egg yolk
Pinch of salt	

Combine ingredients in saucepan and cook until thickened. Spread between layers.

Mrs. D. (Iona) Horton

PRIZE GINGERBREAD

1/2 cup butter **or** shortening	2/3 cups boiling water
1 cup brown sugar	1 tsp. soda
1/2 cup molasses	2 cups flour
1/2 tsp. salt	1 tsp. baking powder
1/2 tsp. nutmeg	1/2 tsp. ginger
1/2 tsp. cinnamon	2 eggs, well beaten

Cream butter and sugar. Add molasses, salt, nutmeg and cinnamon. Pour boiling water over baking soda and add to first mixture. Add flour which has been sifted with baking powder and ginger, and the eggs. Beat well. Bake in a 9 x 13-inch pan at 325 to 350° for 40 minutes.

Mrs. George Platt

DAFFODIL CAKE

6 egg whites
1/2 tsp. cream of tartar
1/2 cup flour
1/8 tsp. salt

1/2 tsp. baking powder
2/3 cup sugar
1/2 tsp. vanilla **or** lemon

Beat egg whites until stiff and add cream of tartar. Sift flour, salt and baking powder three times and combine with sugar and vanilla. Fold in. Put mixture in bottom of angel food tin.

6 egg yolks
2 tbsp. hot water
1/8 tsp. salt
1/2 cup flour

1/2 cup sugar
1 tsp. baking powder
1/2 tsp. vanilla **or** lemon

Beat egg yolks with hot water and salt until light and cream colored. Add flour, sugar and baking powder sifted together three times and vanilla. Place on top of white mixture and bake at 375° for about 35 minutes.

Mrs. Conrad Johnson
Mrs. M. Latham

KOEK (DUTCH CAKE)

31/2 cups flour
2 tsp. baking soda
1/2 tsp. cinnamon
Small amount of cloves
1 cup citron peel

21/2 cups sugar
1/2 tsp. nutmeg
3/4 tsp. ginger
3 cups boiling milk

Mix all dry ingredients and add boiling milk. Bake in a 9 x 13-inch pan at 350° for 45 minutes.

Margo DeJong

LAZY DORIE CAKE

1 cup brown sugar
1 cup flour
1 tsp. baking powder
Pinch of salt

1 tsp. vanilla
2 eggs, beaten
1/2 cup milk
3 tbsp. butter **or** margarine

Add sugar, flour, baking powder, salt and vanilla to eggs. Boil milk and butter together and add to first mixture. Bake in moderate oven for 25 minutes.

8 tbsp. brown sugar
3 tbsp. butter

4 tbsp. milk
1 cup coconut

Boil sugar, butter and milk together. Add coconut and spoon on top of hot cake. Heat in oven until brown.

Mrs. Doreen Sexty

LEMON CRUMBLE CAKE

3/4 cup shortening
1/2 cup sugar
1 cup coconut
1/4 tsp. salt

3/4 cups flour
13/4 cup cracker crumbs
1 tsp. baking powder

Mix ingredients and put half in an 8-inch square pan.

1 cup sugar
2 tbsp. flour
1 cup water
1 egg beaten

1/8 tsp. salt
1 tsp. lemon rind
2 tbsp. lemon juice

Blend all ingredients except rind and juice. Cook well. Add rind and juice. Pour over crumbs in pan and cover with remaining crumbs. Bake at 375° for 30 to 40 minutes.

MAPLE CAKE

1/2 cup butter
1/2 cup brown sugar
1/2 cup maple syrup
2 eggs, well beaten
2 cups flour

1/4 tsp. baking soda
21/2 tsp. baking powder
1/4 tsp. salt
1/2 cup milk

Cream butter well, add brown sugar and mix well. Beat in the maple syrup, then the eggs. Mix and sift dry ingredients and add alternately with the milk. Beat until smooth. Bake in an 8-inch square pan or a buttered angel food pan at 350° for 40 to 50 minutes.

2 tbsp. soft butter
1 cup brown sugar

1 tbsp. maple syrup

Combine ingredients and ice cake.

Rose Ducie

MOIST CHOCOLATE OATMEAL CAKE

1 cup boiling water
1/2 cup oatmeal
1/2 cup shortening
11/3 cups brown sugar
3 eggs
1 tsp. vanilla

1 cup flour
1 tsp. baking powder
1/2 tsp. salt
6 tbsp. cocoa
1 tsp. soda, dissolved
   in hot water

Pour boiling water over the oatmeal and let cool. Cream together shortening, sugar, eggs and vanilla. Sift in dry ingredients. Add oatmeal mixture and soda. Beat well. Pour into 8-inch greased square pan. Bake at 350° for about 25 minutes.

Mrs. Dora Hollman

OATMEAL WONDER CAKE

1 1/4 cups boiling water	1 1/2 cup flour
3/4 cup rolled oats	1 tsp. soda
1/2 cup margarine	1/2 tsp. baking powder
1 cup white sugar	1/2 tsp. salt
1 cup brown sugar	1 tsp. cinnamon
1 tsp. vanilla	1/2 tsp. nutmeg
3 eggs	1 cup raisins (optional)

Mix boiling water and oatmeal and let stand 20 minutes. Cream margarine, sugars, vanilla and eggs. Add dry ingredients, oatmeal mixture and raisins. Mix well. Bake in a 9 x 13-inch pan at 375° for 50 to 55 minutes. Ice with *Broiled Coconut Frosting*.

ROLLED OAT CAKE

1 cup boiling water	1 tsp. soda, dissolved in
1 cup rolled oats	a little hot water
1/2 cup butter	2 eggs
2 cups brown sugar	1 cup raisins, cut fine
1 cup flour	

Pour boiling water over oats and let stand 10 minutes. Add butter and let stand 10 minutes more. Add remaining ingredients. Bake at 350° for 40 minutes.

Mrs. Don (Viola) MacPhee

GUMDROP CAKE

1 cup shortening	2 cups raisins, boiled in 1/2 cup
1 cup sugar	water for 5 min., then cool
2 eggs	1 lb. gumdrops, cut and floured
1 cup unsweetened applesauce	2 cups flour
1 tsp. soda, dissolved in	2 cups mixed peel (optional)
2 tbsp. hot water	

Mix in order given. Bake in 9 x 13-inch pan at 350° for 30 to 40 minutes .

Mrs. Irene Benson

BUTTER SUBSTITUTES: 1 cup shortening plus 1/2 tsp. salt equals 1 cup butter. Lard is 100 percent fat and when it is substituted for butter, the amount should be decreased. 7/8 cup lard plus 2 tbsp. liquid and 1/2 tsp. salt equals 1 cup butter.

To freeze whip cream, beat until stiff and fold in 2 to 4 tbsp. sugar per cup of liquid cream used. Drop by spoonful onto a foil-covered cookie sheet or use a pastry bag and make rosettes. Freeze until firm. Transfer frozen dabs into a freezer bag and return to freezer. These handy toppings thaw at room temperature in 10 to 15 minutes.

WIND CAKE

4 egg yolks	1/2 cup cornstarch
3/4 cup water	1/2 tsp. salt
1 1/4 cups sugar	Lemon extract
1 cup flour	4 egg whites

Put egg yolks in deep bowl and beat for 5 minutes. Add water gradually while beating. Add sugar and beat for another 5 minutes. Sift flour, cornstarch and salt together three times. Gradually add to the egg yolk mixture. Add lemon extract. Beat egg whites until stiff and gradually fold into batter. Bake in a tube pan at 400° for 1 hour.

Mrs. Elsie Hasse

HONEY BUN CAKE

3/4 cup sugar	3 tbsp. honey
2 eggs	4 cups flour
1/2 cup soft shortening	1/2 tsp. soda
4 tbsp. milk	1 tsp. baking powder

Mix sugar, eggs, shortening, milk and honey. Sift flour, soda, baking powder and salt together and add. Form a ball and divide into four parts. Roll out on floured 11 x 16-inch cookie sheet. Bake each layer separately at 400° for about 6 to 8 minutes or until golden brown.

6 tbsp. cream of wheat	1 cup butter
2 cups milk	3/4 to 1 cup sugar

Cook cream of wheat in milk until thick. Cool. Cream butter and sugar, beating until light and creamy. Add cooled cream of wheat mixture and beat well together well. Fill between the 4 layers. Ice top of cake with chocolate icing to which a little instant coffee has been added. This cake should be made the day before slicing.

CUP CAKES

1/2 cup butter	4 tsp. baking powder
1 cup sugar	1/2 cup milk
8 egg yolks	1 tsp. flavoring
1 3/4 cups cake flour	

Cream butter and sugar. Beat egg yolks until light and add to butter and sugar. Sift flour and baking powder several times. Add flour and milk alternately to butter, sugar and eggs. Add flavoring. Place in muffin tins. Bake at 375° for 20 minutes. This recipe enables you to use the egg yolks left over from an angel food cake.

Mrs. Eileen Trigg

Lightly butter your measuring cup before measuring honey, molasses or syrup to prevent sticking.

HEAVENLY ANGEL CAKE

12 fresh egg whites	11/2 cups sifted sugar
3/4 tsp. salt	1 tsp. vanilla
11/2 tsp. cream of tartar	1 cup flour

With egg whites at room temperature, add salt and beat until frothy. Add cream of tartar and beat until the bubbles are small and white but shiny. Fold half the sugar into the beaten egg whites a tablespoon at a time to dissolve sugar thoroughly. Add vanilla. Sift flour and remaining sugar four times and fold gently into the meringue about a half-cup at a time with a motion that brings the mass up from the bottom, over the top near the surface and down the opposite side. Handle gently. Fill 10-inch ungreased tube cake tin and bake at 375° for 30 to 35 minutes. Invert on rack to cool.

Mrs. Elsa Higley
Merilda Spearn

VARIATIONS OF HEAVENLY ANGEL FOOD CAKE

BUTTERSCOTCH: Substitute 1 cup packed brown sugar, sifted, for granulated sugar. Add 1 tsp. butterscotch flavoring.

CHERRY: Fold 1/2 cup chopped, drained maraschino cherries into the batter. Add 1/2 tsp. almond flavoring.

CHOCOLATE: Reduce flour to 3/4 cup and sift 1/4 cup cocoa with the dry ingredients.

CHOCOLATE RIPPLE: Grate 1 oz. unsweetened chocolate. Pour 1/4 of batter into tube pan and sprinkle with 1/3 of grated chocolate. Continue in this manner, finishing with the batter on top **or** fold the grated chocolate into batter.

MAPLE WALNUT: Reduce vanilla to 1/2 tsp. and add 1/2 tsp. maple extract. Add 1/4 cup finely chopped walnuts with last addition of flour.

PEPPERMINT: Add 1/2 tsp. peppermint extract and a few drops of green food coloring.

FILLED ANGEL FOOD CAKE

1 angel food cake, baked	1 cup whipping cream
2 env. unflavored gelatin	1/2 cup almonds, slivered
2 cups sweet pineapple juice	and toasted
11/2 cups apricot jam	1/2 tsp. almond extract

Hollow out cake leaving about 3/4 inch thick walls and bottom. Chill. Soften gelatin in juice. Let soak about 5 minutes, then heat, stirring constantly until gelatin is dissolved. Stir in apricot jam and chill until it begins to set. Beat whip cream until frothy and fold into gelatin mixture. Fold in almonds and the flavoring. Use to fill hollowed-out cake and frost sides and top of cake.

CHOCOLATE ANGEL FOOD CAKE

3/4 cup cake flour
4 tbsp. cocoa
1 1/4 cups sugar
1 1/4 cups egg whites

1 tsp. salt
1 tsp. cream of tartar
1 tsp. vanilla
1/4 cup flour

Sift flour once, measure, add cocoa and 1/4 cup sugar and sift together four times. Beat egg whites and salt. Add cream of tartar and continue beating until eggs are stiff enough to hold up in peaks, but not dry. Add remaining sugar, 2 tbsp. at a time, beating after each addition until sugar is just blended. Fold in vanilla. Sift flour over mixture, fold in lightly and repeat until all is used. Turn into ungreased 9-inch tube pan. Cut gently through batter with knife to remove air bubbles. Bake at 325° about 50 minutes. Remove from oven and invert pan one hour or until cool. Can be served plain, with butter icing, or with seven minute frosting. Frosted cake may be decorated with melted chocolate.

Mrs. P.E. Mahoney
Mrs. Nellie Sigurdson

FRUITED ANGEL FOOD CAKE

1 angel food cake, baked
1 cup whipping cream
3 tbsp. sugar
1/2 tsp. vanilla
2 cups miniature marshmallows

1/4 cup maraschino cherries, cut small
1/4 cup crushed pineapple
1/2 cup chopped walnuts
1/2 pint whipping cream

Hollow out angel cake, leaving 3/4-inch thick walls and bottom. Whip 1 cup cream, gradually adding sugar and vanilla. Fold in marshmallows, cherries, pineapple and walnuts. Fill cake and chill several hours. When ready to serve, frost with 1/2 pint whipped cream.

STRAWBERRY ANGEL LOAF

3-oz. pkg. strawberry jello
1 cup hot water
1/3 cup sugar
2 cups whipped cream

2 cups crushed, sweet strawberries
1 angel cake, baked

Dissolve jelly powder in hot water. Chill until partially set. Fold sugar into whipped cream, fold in strawberries and then fold this mixture into gelatin. Chill until thick. Cut cake cross-wise into three layers. Fill layers and frost cake with strawberry mixture. Chill about 1 1/2 hours until firm. Garnish with fresh berries.

CORNSTARCH SUBSTITUTE: 2 tbsp. flour equals 1 tbsp. cornstarch.

ANGEL FOOD ORANGE CREAM

Juice of 2 oranges	6 egg yolks
Rind of 1 orange	1 cup whipping cream
1 cup sugar	

Combine and beat juice, rind sugar and yolks. Cook in a double boiler until clear. Cool. Add to whipped cream. Serve over angel food slices.

Mrs. W. Schlecker

MILLIONAIRE CAKE

5 eggs, separated	1 pkg. gelatin
3/4 cup sugar	1/4 cup cold water
3/4 cup lemon juice	1/2 cup sugar
Rind of 1 lemon	1 angel food cake, baked

Combine egg yolks beaten with 3/4 cup sugar, lemon juice and rind in top of double boiler. Cook until mixture coats a spoon. Soften gelatin in cold water and add to above mixture. Cool slightly. Beat egg whites, gradually adding 1/2 cup sugar. Add custard and blend. Break angel food cake into bits in a large bowl. Add custard and mix lightly. Pour into greased tube pan and press lightly. Set in refrigerator overnight. Serve covered with whipped cream.

Mrs. Arline Woyen

BURNT SUGAR CHIFFON CAKE

3/4 cup sugar	5 egg yolks, unbeaten
1 cup boiling water	6 tbsp. water
21/4 cups cake flour	1 tsp. vanilla
3 tsp. baking powder	6 tbsp. burnt sugar syrup
11/4 cups sugar	1 cup egg whites
1 tsp. salt	1/2 tsp. cream of tartar
1/2 cup oil	

To make syrup, melt 3/4 cup sugar in a heavy skillet over low heat until clear and medium brown. Add boiling water. Stir over low heat until lumps dissolve. Sift dry ingredients together. Make a well. Add oil, egg yolks, 6 tbsp. water, vanilla and burnt sugar syrup. Beat until smooth. Combine egg whites and cream of tartar. Beat until they form very stiff peaks. Fold egg yolk batter into egg white mixture. Bake in tube pan at 325° for 55 minutes, then at 350° for 10 to 15 minutes. Invert pan until cake is cool. VARIATION: Orange Chiffon Cake: Substitute 2 tbsp. grated orange rind and juice of two oranges for water, vanilla and burnt sugar syrup.

Mrs. N. H. Hall

CHIFFON CAKE

2 1/4 cups cake flour
1 1/2 cups sugar
3 tsp. baking powder
1 tsp. salt
1/2 cup oil

7 egg yolks, unbeaten
3/4 cup water
12 egg whites
1/2 tsp. cream of tartar
1 tsp. vanilla

Sift cake flour, sugar, baking powder and salt together four times. Make a well and add, in order, the oil, egg yolks and water. Mix well. In a second bowl, beat the egg whites until foamy. Add cream of tartar and vanilla. Beat until very stiff and shiny. Fold egg yolk mixture into beaten egg whites, very slowly until blended. Do not stir. Add flavoring, folding gently. Immediately, pour into ungreased 10 x 4-inch tube pan. Bake at 350° for 65 to 70 minutes or until top of cake springs back when lightly touched. Invert and cool. VARIATIONS: 1/2 cup poppy seeds sprinkled on top and folded in; any other flavoring such as orange, almond, strawberry or maple walnut. Ice with favorite icing.

Mary Wojcicki
Mrs. Charles Osbaldeston

CHOCOLATE CHIFFON CAKE

3/4 cup boiling water
1/2 cup cocoa
1 3/4 cups flour
1 3/4 cups sugar
3 tsp. baking powder
1 tsp. salt

1/2 cup salad oil
7 eggs, separated
1 tsp. vanilla
1/4 tsp. red food coloring
1/2 tsp. cream of tartar

Add boiling water to cocoa and cool. Sift flour, sugar, baking powder and salt. Make a well in center of flour mixture and add salad oil, egg yolks, cocoa mixture, vanilla and food coloring. Combine and beat until smooth. Sprinkle cream of tartar over egg whites and beat until very stiff. Gradually fold egg yolk mixture into the egg white mixture. Turn into ungreased 10-inch deep tube pan and bake at 300° for 80 minutes. Immediately invert pan and cool.

2 oz. unsweetened chocolate
1/4 cup milk
1 unbeaten egg **or** 2 egg yolks

2 tbsp. butter
1/2 tsp. vanilla
1 cup icing sugar

Melt chocolate and combine all ingredients. Beat for 5 minutes and spread thickly on cake.

SWEET MILK SUBSTITUTE: When using sour milk as a substitute, allow 1/2 tsp. baking soda for each cup of sour milk and reduce baking powder to 1 tsp. for each cup of flour. In mixtures containing eggs, reduce an additional 1/2 tsp. baking powder for each egg.

SPICY CHIFFON CAKE

2 cups flour
1 1/2 cups sugar
3 tsp. baking powder
1 tsp. salt
1 tsp. cinnamon
1/2 tsp. nutmeg
1/2 tsp. allspice

1/2 tsp. cloves
1/2 cup salad oil
3/4 cups cold water
7 egg yolks
1 cup egg whites
1/2 tsp. cream of tartar

Measure flour, sugar, baking powder, salt and spices into a bowl. Sift. Make a well and add, in order, the salad oil, water and egg yolks. Beat until smooth. Measure egg whites and cream of tartar into a large bowl. Whip until whites form very stiff peaks. Pour egg mixture gently over egg whites. Fold gently with rubber scraper until blended. Pour into ungreased tube pan. Bake at 350° for 1 hour. Immediately invert pan. Leave for 1 hour before removing.

Paula Jasman

MAPLE WALNUT CHIFFON CAKE

2 cups flour
3 tsp. baking powder
1 tsp. salt
1 1/2 cups sugar
1/2 cup salad oil
5 egg yolks

3/4 cup water
1 tsp. vanilla
1/4 tsp. maple flavoring
1 cup finely-chopped walnuts
1 cup egg whites
1/2 tsp. cream of tartar

Sift dry ingredients and make a well in the center. Add the salad oil, egg yolks, water, vanilla and maple. Stir to mix and beat until smooth. Stir in walnuts. Measure egg whites into a large bowl, sprinkle with cream of tartar and beat until very stiff. Add batter to egg whites, one-quarter at a time, folding in gently. Bake in tube pan at 350° for 1 hour.

Mrs. Janice Felzien

POPPY SEED CHIFFON

1/2 cup poppy seeds
3/4 cup cold water
2 cups flour
3 tsp. baking powder
1 1/2 cups sugar
1 tsp. salt

1/2 cup cooking oil
2 tsp. vanilla
7 egg yolks, unbeaten
1 cup egg whites
1/2 tsp. cream of tartar

Soak poppy seeds in cold water. Sift dry ingredients into large bowl. Make a well and add oil, vanilla, egg yolks, poppy seeds and water. Beat until very smooth. Mix egg whites and cream of tartar together and beat until they form very stiff peaks. Gently fold into egg yolk batter. Bake in ungreased 10-inch tube pan at 350° for 65 to 70 minutes. Invert pan when cake is done and let cool. Ice with vanilla butter frosting.

Florence Keyser

MILDRED'S SPONGE CAKE

5 eggs, separated
3 tbsp. cold water
11/2 cups granulated sugar
1/2 cup boiling water
1 tsp. vanilla
1 tsp. almond flavoring

11/2 cups flour
1/4 tsp. salt
1/2 tsp. baking powder
1/4 tsp. salt
1/2 tsp. cream of tartar

Beat egg yolks with cold water until thick. Gradually add sugar and beat for another minute. Slowly add boiling water. Continue beating for 2 minutes. Add flavorings. Sift flour with 1/4 tsp. salt and baking powder. Beat into first mixture a small amount at a time, beating well after each addition. Beat egg whites with 1/4 tsp. salt until frothy. Add cream of tartar and beat until peaks form, but not dry. Fold carefully into batter until blended. Bake in a tube pan at 325° for 1 hour. Cake should shrink a little when done. Invert and cool for 1 hour before removing from pan.

Mildred Pollock

JELLY-ROLL SPONGE CAKE

4 egg yolks
3 tbsp. cold water
1 cup sugar
11/2 tbsp. cornstarch
7/8 cups flour

11/4 tsp. baking powder
1/4 tsp. salt
4 egg whites
1 tsp. vanilla **or** lemon

Beat egg yolks and water until thick and lemon colored. Gradually add sugar and beat for two minutes. Sift together cornstarch, flour, baking powder and salt. Beat into egg mixture. Beat the egg whites with vanilla until very stiff. Fold into egg yolk mixture. Bake in an 8 x 12-inch pan or two layer pans at 350° for 30 minutes. NOTE: For Jelly Roll, make 11/2 times recipe and bake in 11 x 16-inch jelly roll pan.

LIGHT SPONGE CAKE

7 eggs, separated
1 cup sugar
21/4 cups cake flour
3 tsp. baking powder
1/2 tsp. salt

3/4 cups water
1/2 cup cooking oil
1 tsp. vanilla **or** lemon
1/2 tsp. cream of tartar
1/2 cup sugar

Beat egg yolks well and gradually add 1 cup sugar. Beat very well. Sift dry ingredients into egg yolks, add liquids and beat. Beat egg whites until they form soft peaks. Add cream of tartar and 1/2 cup sugar gradually. Beat again until soft peaks form. Folk into egg yolk mixture. Bake in a greased 13 x 9-inch pan, lightly dusted with flour. Bake at 350° for 40 to 50 minutes. Cake should shrink away from sides of pan when done. Ice cake to retain freshness.

ANGEL SPONGE CAKE

1 2/3 cups cake flour
1 tsp. baking powder
1/2 tsp. salt
10 - 12 egg yolks

1/2 cup hot water
1 cup sugar
Flavoring

Sift flour once, measure, add baking powder and salt and sift again. Beat egg yolks until slightly thickened, add hot water gradually and beat until very light. Add sugar and flavoring to egg yolk and beat again. Add flour one-quarter at a time, folding to blend. Bake in ungreased tube pan at 350° for 40 minutes. Invert pan and cool.

Mrs. John Evjen

CHOCOLATE SPONGE CAKE

4 eggs, separated
1 cup granulated sugar
1/4 cup hot water
1 tsp. vanilla

2/3 cup flour
1/3 cup cocoa
1/3 tsp. baking powder
1/2 tsp. salt

Beat yolks until thick. Beat in 1/2 cup sugar. Add hot water and vanilla. Beat whites until firm and add remaining sugar. Fold into yolk mixture. Sift flour, cocoa and baking powder together. Fold into mixture. Bake in tube pan at 325° for 40 minutes.

Mrs. V. McLaughlin

EGG YOLK SPONGE CAKE

11 egg yolks
1 whole egg
1 3/4 cup sugar
1/2 cup water
1 tbsp. strained orange juice

1 tbsp. grated orange rind
1/2 tsp. lemon extract
2 cups flour
2 tsp. baking powder
1/2 tsp. salt

Beat egg yolks and egg thoroughly. Add sugar and beat well. Add water, juice, rind and extract and beat. Sift flour, baking powder and salt. Fold in slowly. Divide batter into two tube pans. Bake at 350° for 40 minutes.

SPICE SPONGE CAKE

14 egg yolks
1 cup sugar
1/2 cup flour
1/2 tsp. salt
2 tsp. baking powder

1/2 tsp. cloves
1 tsp. cinnamon
1/2 cup walnuts, chopped fine
1 tsp. almond extract
3 egg whites, beaten stiff

Beat the egg yolks with a rotary beater. Slowly add the sugar and beat the mixture 15 minutes. Sift the flour, salt, baking powder and spices together. Fold into beaten yolks. Add nuts and flavoring and fold in egg whites. Pour into tube pan. Bake at 325° for 50 to 55 minutes.

Mrs. Eva Said

SPICE CAKE

1/2 cup butter	1/2 tsp. allspice
1 cup brown sugar, firmly packed	1 tsp. cinnamon
2 eggs	3/4 tsp. cloves
11/2 cups flour	1/8 tsp. salt
3 tsp. baking powder	3/4 cup sweet milk
1/2 tsp. nutmeg	11/2 tsp. vanilla

Cream butter and sugar and add eggs. Sift flour, baking powder, spices and salt. Add dry ingredients to first mixture alternately with milk. Add vanilla. Bake in 9-inch pan at 350° for 45 minutes.

Mrs. A. Payne

APPLESAUCE SPICE CAKE

21/2 cups flour	1 cup margarine
2 tsp. baking powder	2 eggs
1 tsp. soda	11/2 tsp. vanilla
3/4 tsp. salt	14-oz. can sweetened
11/4 tsp. cinnamon	applesauce
3/4 tsp. allspice	1/2 cup chopped walnuts
3/4 tsp. nutmeg	2 cups dark raisins
11/2 cups sugar	

Sift flour, baking powder, soda, salt and spices together. Cream sugar and margarine together. Beat in eggs and vanilla. Add dry ingredients to creamed mixture alternately with applesauce. Add nuts and raisins. Pour into two 8-inch square pans or one large pan 16 x 18 inches. Bake at 350° for 50 to 55 minutes. When cool, frost with Brown Sugar Icing.

Bernice Saunders

CHOCOLATE SPICE CAKE

2 cups flour	1 cup chopped nuts
7/8 cup sugar	2 tbsp. unsweetened
1 tsp. baking soda	chocolate, finely grated
1 tsp. baking powder	1 cup raisins
1 tsp. salt	1/2 cup melted butter
1 tsp. cinnamon	11/2 cups cooked applesauce
1 tsp. nutmeg	

Mix dry ingredients and spices. Add nuts, chocolate and raisins. Mix butter with applesauce. Add to dry ingredients. Bake in loaf pan at 375 ° for 45 minutes.

MILK SUBSTITUTES: 1/2 cup evaporated milk and 1/2 cup water equals 1 cup milk. 1/4 cup dried skim milk and 1 cup water and 2 tsp. butter or melted fat equals 1 cup milk. 1 cup skim milk plus 2 tsp. melted fat or salad oil equals 1 cup milk.

MOLASSES SPICE CAKE

1/2 cup shortening
1 cup sugar
2 eggs
1/3 cup molasses
1/2 tsp. salt
21/3 cup cake flour **or**
  2 cups all-purpose flour

1/4 tsp. soda
1 tsp. cinnamon
1/2 tsp. nutmeg
1/4 tsp. cloves
2 tsp. baking powder
2/3 cups milk

Cream shortening and sugar. Add eggs and beat well. Add molasses and mix. Sift dry ingredients together and add alternately with milk. Bake in 9 x 13-inch pan at 350° for 35 minutes. Ice and sprinkle with nuts.

SOUR CREAM SPICE CAKE

2 eggs
11/2 cups brown sugar
1 cup thick sour cream
2 cups flour
1/4 tsp. salt
1 tsp. soda

1/2 tsp. allspice
1/2 tsp. cinnamon
1/2 tsp. cloves
1/2 tsp. nutmeg
1/2 cup sweet milk
1 tsp. lemon juice

Beat eggs. Add sugar gradually, beating after each addition. Add sour cream, beating well. Add sifted dry ingredients alternately with milk. Add spices and lemon juice. Bake at 350° for 35 minutes.

JELLY ROLL

11/2 cups flour
1/2 tsp. salt
2 tsp. baking powder
6 egg yolks

1 cup sugar
1/2 cup boiling water
1 tsp. vanilla

Combine flour, salt and baking powder. Beat egg yolks until thick. Continue beating until fluffy, adding sugar gradually. Add boiling water and beat until fluffy. Add vanilla to flour mixture. Pour into greased jelly roll pan. Bake at 350° for 25 minutes. Immediately turn out cake onto wax paper sprinkled with icing sugar. Trim off edges. Roll immediately without filling. Let cool, unroll, spread with jam or jelly and roll up again.

NEVER-FAIL JELLY ROLL

1/2 cup milk
1 tbsp. butter
1/8 tsp. salt
3 eggs

1 cup sugar
1 cup cake flour
11/2 tsp. baking powder
1 tsp. vanilla

Boil milk, butter and salt. Beat eggs and add sugar gradually, beating until thick. Sift flour and baking powder and add along with hot milk. Bake at 350° for 25 minutes. Spread with jelly. Roll immediately in damp cloth.

Mrs. Don Nelson

CHOCOLATE JELLY ROLL

3/4 tsp. baking powder
4 eggs, beaten until very light
3/4 cup sugar
1/8 tsp. salt

1/2 tsp. vanilla
1/2 cup cake flour
1/4 cup cocoa
Icing sugar

Sprinkle baking powder on top of eggs. Add sugar, salt and vanilla gradually. Beat until very light. Sift cake flour and cocoa together. Add to first mixture and blend. Put in 15 x 10-inch jelly roll pan lined with wax paper. Bake at 375° for 10 to 12 minutes. Immediately invert the cake onto a sheet of wax paper thickly sprinkled with icing sugar and roll up.

STRAWBERRY SHORTCAKE

2 cups flour
3 tsp. baking powder
1/4 tsp. salt
2 tbsp. butter

4 oz. cream cheese
Milk
1 egg, slightly beaten

Sift dry ingredients together. Cut in butter and cream cheese and blend with fork until fine. Add enough milk to the egg to make 3/4 cup liquid. Dough will be soft. Knead for 30 seconds to prevent lumps. Roll gently to 3/4-inch thickness. Cut into circles with a floured cutter. Arrange close together on a cookie sheet for soft-sided biscuits, or far apart for crispy ones. Bake at 450° for 12 to 15 minutes. VARIATION: Batter may be poured into an 8-inch square pan and baked for 20 minutes. Serve biscuits cut in half with strawberries and whipped cream.

CHEESECAKE

3 tbsp. margarine
1 cup graham crumbs

1/4 cup brown sugar

Place margarine in 9-inch pie plate. Microwave on High 30 to 60 seconds until melted. Add graham crumbs and sugar. Press mixture firmly against bottom and side of pie plate. Microwave on Medium High (70%) 2 to 4 minutes until hot, turning twice during cooking. Cool .

8 oz. cream cheese,
   softened
1/2 cup sugar
2 eggs, separated
1 tbsp. lemon juice

1 tsp. grated lemon peel
1/2 cup dairy sour cream
1 tbsp. sugar
1/2 tsp. vanilla

Beat cream cheese and sugar until light and fluffy. Beat in egg yolks, lemon juice and peel until smooth. Beat egg whites until stiff peaks form. Fold beaten egg whites into cream cheese mixture. Spread evenly in prepared crust. Microwave at medium (50%) 10 to 15 minutes until center is set. Refrigerate several hours before serving. Mix sour cream, sugar and vanilla. Carefully spread over cheesecake before serving.

Louise Van Camp

CHEESE CAKE

1/3 cup butter	6 tbsp. sugar
1 cup flour	1 egg

Mix ingredients and put in the bottom of a 9 x 12-inch pan and bake at 350° for 10 minutes.

2/3 cup cottage cheese	1 tsp. lemon juice
1 tsp. salt	2 tbsp. cornstarch in
3/4 cup sweet cream	1/4 cup milk
3/4 cup sugar	2 eggs, separated

Beat all ingredients together except egg whites. Add stiffly beaten egg whites. Put on top of partly-baked crust, sprinkle with cinnamon and bake an additional 20 minutes.

Hilda Elke

LEMON CHEESE CAKE

3-oz. pkg. lemon jello	8 oz.cream cheese
1 cup hot water	1 cup sugar
22 crushed graham wafers	2 tsp. vanilla
1/4 cup butter	1/4 tsp. lemon extract
1/3 cups sugar	1 can evaporated milk

Cook jello and water until syrupy. Make a crust of the wafers, butter and 1/3 cup sugar. Press into a 9 x 13-inch cake pan, saving a few crumbs for topping. Cream the cream cheese with 1 cup sugar, vanilla and lemon extract. Whip milk that has been chilled overnight in the refrigerator. Add jello and cream cheese mixture and blend well. Pour on crumbs and chill in refrigerator as desired. VARIATION: Substitute 1 pkg. Dream Whip for evaporated milk.

Mrs. Robina Nichols
Audrey Zilli

RHUBARB CAKE

2 cups flour	1 1/2 cups sugar
1/2 cup butter	1/2 cup flour
1 egg	1/2 cup melted butter
1 tsp. baking powder	2 eggs, beaten
1/4 tsp. salt	4 cups chopped red rhubarb

Mix 2 cups flour, butter, 1 egg, baking powder and salt together with a fork. Reserve 1 cup for topping. Flatten remaining amount into 9 x 13-inch pan. Combine 1 1/2 cups sugar, 1/2 cup flour, butter, 2 eggs and rhubarb. Pour into pan. Cover with left over crust mixture and sprinkle with sugar and cinnamon. Bake at 350° for 40 to 50 minutes.

Agnes Galloway
Mary Wright

STRAWBERRY DREAM LAYER CAKE

1/2 carton frozen strawberries
1 pkg. cake mix
3-oz. pkg. strawberry jello
2 tbsp. flour

4 eggs
1/2 cup water
3/4 cup cooking oil

Thaw strawberries. Mix cake mix, jello, flour, eggs and water together. Beat 2 minutes at medium speed. Add berries, including juice and mix for 1 minute. Add oil and beat 1 minute more. Bake in two layers at 350° for 30 to 40 minutes.

1/2 cup butter
1/2 tsp. vanilla

3 cups icing sugar
1/2 box strawberries

Combine ingredients. Strawberries may be crushed or left whole. Fill and frost cake.

Mrs. Mary E. Hoke

SASKATOON CAKE

1 cup butter
1 cup sugar
5 eggs
1 cup sweet milk
1 tsp. soda

1 tbsp. hot water
1 quart saskatoons
3 cups flour
1 tsp. cinnamon
1 tsp. nutmeg

Combine butter, sugar and eggs. Beat well. Add milk. Dissolve soda in hot water and add. Dredge saskatoons in part of the flour. Add spices to remaining flour and add to egg-butter mixture. Add berries. Pour into 9 x 13-inch greased pan. Bake at 350° for 30 to 35 minutes.

Mrs. Bertha Orr

APPLE SAUCE CAKE

1/2 cup shortening **or**
   1/3 cup cooking oil
1 cup sugar **or** 3/4 cup honey
1 cup warm apple sauce
1 cup raisins

1 tsp. baking powder
1 tsp. soda
1 tsp. cinnamon
1/2 tsp. nutmeg
13/4 cup flour

Combine ingredients. Bake in greased loaf pan at 350° for 45 minutes.

Mrs. Fern Fevang

APRICOT CAKE

11/2 cups margarine
1 cup sugar
1/3 cup apricot puree
3 tsp. baking powder
Dash of salt

3 eggs
2 cups flour
1/2 cup milk
1 tsp. almond extract

Combine ingredients and bake in bundt pan at 325° for 30 minutes.

Doris Barker

ORANGE KISS ME CAKE

Pulp and rind of 1 orange
1 cup seedless raisins
1/3 cup walnuts
2 cups flour
1 tsp. soda
1 cup sugar
1 tsp. salt

1/2 cup shortening
1 cup milk
2 eggs, unbeaten
Juice from 1 large orange
1/3 cup sugar
1 tsp. cinnamon
1/4 cup walnuts

Grind pulp and rind of orange with raisins and 1/3 cup walnuts. Set aside. Sift flour, soda, sugar and salt together. Add shortening, 3/4 cup of the milk and beat for 11/2 minutes. Add eggs and remaining milk and beat 11/2 minutes. Fold orange raisin mixture into batter and turn into greased square pan. Bake at 350° for 40 to 50 minutes. Drizzle orange juice over warm cake. Combine 1/3 cup sugar, cinnamon and 1/4 cup walnuts and sprinkle over cake.

Theresa Maykut

ORANGE CAKE

1/2 cup shortening **or** butter
1 cup sugar
2 eggs, beaten
2 cups flour
1/2 tsp. baking powder
1/2 tsp. soda

1/2 tsp. salt
1 cup sour milk
Rind of 1 orange
1 cup raisins
Juice of 1 orange
1/2 cup sugar

Cream shortening and 1 cup sugar. Add eggs and beat until smooth. Combine flour, baking powder, soda and salt with milk and gradually add to mixture. Grate rind and add. Mix well. Bake at 350° for 50 minutes. Pour orange juice over 1/2 cup sugar. Let stand until cake is baked and pour over cake while hot.

Elisabeth Rottier

APPLE CAKE

1 cup sugar
4 eggs, well beaten
1 cup cooking oil
4 tbsp. cold water
2 cups flour
1/2 tsp. salt

3 tsp. baking powder
5 apples, peeled and shredded
1 tsp. cinnamon
1/2 cup sugar
Walnuts (optional)

Add 1 cup of the sugar to eggs and beat. Add cooking oil and beat 2 minutes. Add cold water and beat. Combine flour, salt and baking powder. Mix. Put half batter in 9 x 13-inch pan. Arrange apples on top. Combine cinnamon and sugar and sprinkle half over apples. Cover with remaining batter. Sprinkle a little more sugar and cinnamon on top. Bake at 350° for 1 hour .

Mrs. Lucy Redlak

Please Take Note

RE: _____

_____

_____

_____

_____

_____

_____

_____

_____

_____

_____

_____

_____

_____

CO-OP PRESS LIMITED
7929 CORONET ROAD
EDMONTON, ALBERTA
T6E 4N7
(403) 465-5408

"A Complete Printing Service"

PINEAPPLE SANDWICH CAKE

4 tbsp. melted butter
1 cup sugar
1 egg, beaten
2 1/2 cups flour
3 tsp. baking powder
Pinch of salt

1/4 tsp. ground cloves
1 cup milk
1 tsp. vanilla
10-oz. can pineapple
    chunks, drained

Cream butter and 1/2 cup sugar. Beat in egg. Sift dry ingredients together, except for cloves. Add alternately with milk. Add vanilla. Spread half of batter into buttered 9-inch square pan. Cover batter with pineapple. Mix remaining sugar with cloves and sprinkle over pineapple. Spread remaining batter over this. Bake at 350° for 40 minutes.

Mrs. Olga Koroluk

PRUNE CAKE

1/2 cup butter
1 cup sugar
3 eggs
5 tbsp. sour cream
1 1/2 cups flour
1 tsp. baking powder

1 tsp. soda
1/2 tsp. allspice
1/2 tsp. nutmeg
1/3 cup prune juice
1 cup pitted prunes, cooked

Cream butter and sugar. Add eggs and beat well. Add sour cream. Sift dry ingredients and add along with prune juice. Cut prunes into small pieces and add. Bake in two layers at 350° for 30 minutes. Use lemon filling between layers and ice with Cream Cheese Icing.

Mrs. Lorraine Heppler

PINEAPPLE CARROT CAKE

8-oz. can crushed pineapple
2 cups flour
2 tsp. baking powder
1 1/2 tsp. baking soda
1 tsp. salt
1 tsp. cinnamon
2 cups sugar
1 cup salad oil

2 eggs, well beaten
2 carrots, finely grated
1/2 cup nuts
1 cup fine coconut
1/2 cup milk
8 oz. cream cheese
2 1/2 cups icing sugar
1 tsp. vanilla

Drain pineapple. Sift flour, baking powder, baking soda, salt and cinnamon together. Add sugar and salad oil. Mix in eggs. Blend in carrots, nuts, coconut and pineapple. Bake in 9 x 13-inch pan at 350° for 40 to 60 minutes. Blend milk, cheese, icing sugar and vanilla together and spread on cooled cake.

Gertrude Foster

CARROT CAKE

2 cups sugar	3 cups finely-grated carrots
2 cups flour	2 tsp. vanilla
2 tsp. baking soda	8 oz. cream cheese
2 tsp. cinnamon	1/2 cup margarine
Pinch of salt	2 cups icing sugar
1 1/4 cup vegetable oil	1 tsp. orange juice
4 eggs	1 tsp. vanilla

Mix sugar, flour, baking soda, cinnamon and salt together. Blend in oil and add eggs, carrots and 2 tsp. vanilla. Blend well and bake in 13 x 9-inch pan at 350° for 45 to 50 minutes. Blend cream cheese and margarine together. Gradually add icing sugar. Add 1 tsp. vanilla and orange juice. Use to ice cooled cake.

Carol Stott

BOILED FRUIT CAKE

1 cup raisins	1/2 tsp. soda
1 cup water	1/2 tsp. salt
1 cup sugar	1/2 tsp. cloves
1/2 cup shortening	1/2 tsp. allspice
1 egg, beaten	1/2 tsp. cinnamon
1 1/2 cups flour	1/4 tsp. nutmeg
1 tsp. baking powder	

Simmer raisins and water a few minutes. Remove from heat and add sugar and shortening. Cool. Add egg. Sift flour, baking powder, soda, salt and spices. Add to raisins until mixed. Bake in 9-inch square pan at 350° for 45 minutes. VARIATION: Other dried fruits such as currants or apricots may be substituted for raisins.

B. Chesterman
Mrs. Lawrence Monner

BOILED RAISIN CAKE

2 cups raisins	1/2 tsp. salt
Water	1/2 tsp. nutmeg
2 tbsp. shortening	1 tsp. soda
2 eggs	1/2 tsp. cloves
1 cup sugar	1 tsp. cinnamon
2 cups flour	1 cup thick sour cream

Cover raisins with water and bring to a boil. Simmer a few minutes and cool. Combine shortening, eggs and sugar. Add cooled raisins. Sift dry ingredients together. Add alternately with sour cream. Bake in long loaf pan at 350° for 45 minutes.

Mrs. C.A. Ketchum

WALDORF CAKE

1 cup sugar	1 1/3 tsp. soda
1 cup oil	1 1/3 tsp. baking powder
3 eggs	1 1/3 tsp. cinnamon
1 1/3 cup flour	2 cups finely-grated raw carrot
1/2 tsp. salt	1/2 cup finely chopped nuts

Combine sugar and oil and beat in eggs, one at a time. Sift dry ingredients and add. Beat well and fold in carrots and nuts. Bake at 300° for 1 hour in two 8-inch layer pans or one 9 x 12-inch pan.

8 oz. cream cheese	2 1/2 cups icing sugar
4 tbsp. butter	2 tsp. vanilla

Soften cheese and butter and beat. Add sugar and vanilla. Beat until light and fluffy. Spread on cooled cake.

Mrs. Leslie Hide
Mrs. M. Griffin

ANNIE'S FRUIT CAKE

3 cups flour	1 tsp. baking powder
1 1/2 cups cherries	1 1/2 cups sugar
2 cups nuts	1 cup oil
1 cup glazed fruit	15-oz can crushed
3 cups white raisins	pineapple, undrained
2 tsp. salt	4 eggs, beaten

Mix 1 cup flour with cherries, nuts, fruit and raisins. Set aside. Mix 2 cups flour, salt, baking powder and sugar. Add oil, pineapple and eggs and mix. Add fruit mixture. Bake at 275° for 2 1/2 to 3 hours.

Mrs. Annie Dart

FRUIT CAKE

6 cups assorted raisins	2 tsp. cinnamon
2 cups dried apricots	1/2 tsp. baking soda
1/2 cup water	1 1/2 tsp. nutmeg
1 cup butter **or** margarine	1/2 tsp. cloves
1 1/2 cups brown sugar	1 tsp. salt
6 eggs	1 pkg. large assorted fruit
3 tbsp. molasses	1 pkg. assorted large peel
1/2 cup apricot jam	2 cups walnuts
3 cups flour	

Wash raisins and apricots and steam with 1/2 cup water for 15 to 20 minutes or until dry. Beat butter and sugar. Add eggs one at a time. Blend in molasses and jam. Sift dry ingredients and add them. Add fruit and nuts. Bake in 3 loaf tins at 275° for 3 hours along with a shallow pan of water.

Marion Beebe

AUSTRALIAN WHITE FRUIT CAKE

1 1/2 cups citron peel, sliced finely
3 cups glaze cherries, halved,
   1/2 red and 1/2 green
4 cups white bleached sultanas
Glazed pineapple rings,
   4 green, 4 red and 2 yellow
4 cups flour
1 tsp. salt
1 tsp. baking powder
2 cups butter
2 cups sugar
12 eggs
Juice and grated rind of 1 lemon
1/2 lb. almonds, sliced

Prepare cake pans and set aside. This recipe just fits three square wedding cake tins. Prepare fruit and set aside. Measure sifted flour and sift again with salt and baking powder. Cream butter and sugar and beat in six whole eggs, one at a time. Add the grated lemon juice and rind. Separate yolks and whites of remaining eggs and beat separately. Add beaten yolks to butter mixture, then flour, fruit and nuts and last of all the stiffly beaten egg whites. Bake at 275° for 2 to 3 hours. Remember that the cakes in the smaller tins will bake in a shorter time. Let cakes cool in tins. Wrap well to keep moist and and leave to ripen.

Mrs. J. L. Branum

HONEY BLONDE FRUIT CAKE

1 cup dried prunes
1 cup dried apricots
1 1/2 cups seedless raisins
1 1/2 cups golden seedless raisins
2 1/2 cups diced candied
   mixed peel
1 cup candied cherries, halved
2 cups diced candied pineapple
1 1/4 cup shortening
1 1/4 cups honey
6 eggs
2 1/2 cups flour
1 1/4 tsp. salt
1 tsp. baking powder
1 tsp. cinnamon
1/2 tsp. cloves
1 cup blanched almonds
1 cup walnuts

Line pans with greased foil, or two layers of greased brown paper and one of greased wax paper. Cover prunes and apricots with boiling water. Let stand 5 minutes. Rinse and drain raisins. Cut prunes from pits and chop finely. Slice apricots. Combine all fruits. Blend shortening, honey and add eggs one at a time beating well after each addition. Blend in sifted dry ingredients. Add fruits. Sliver almonds and coarsely chop the walnuts and add. Yield: 7 1/2-lb. of cake. Use one 10-inch tube pan or one 8-inch tube pan and two to three small loaf tins. Fill prepared pans to within 1/2 inch of top. Bake at 250° with shallow pan of hot water on floor of oven. Bake 5 hours in tube pans and about 2 hours in loaf pans.

Lottie Breitkreitz

1 lemon will give you 3 tbsp. lemon juice and 1 1/2 tsp. grated lemon rind. 3 medium oranges will give you 1 cup of orange juice and 1 orange will give you 2 tsp. grated orange rind.

ELSIE'S FRUIT CAKE

2 cups butter
2 cups packed yellow sugar
7 egg yolks, well beaten
4 cups flour
1 tsp. salt
2 tsp. baking powder
2 tsp. mace
2 tsp. cinnamon

51/2 cups seedless raisins
51/2 cups currants
11/2 cups cherries
5 cups dates
41/2 cups walnuts
Rind and juice of 1 orange
2 tbsp. pineapple juice
7 egg whites

Cream butter and sugar. Add egg yolks. Sift flour, salt, baking powder and spices together. Mix 1 cup of flour mixture with fruits and nuts. Set aside. Grate rind and add to butter mixture along with juices. Beat until light and fluffy. Add fruit to creamed mixture. Mix well. Beat egg whites until stiff but not dry. Fold into cake batter. Bake at 275° for 3 to 4 hours.

FAVORITE FRUIT CAKE

51/2 cups currants
11/2 cups glazed red and
   green cherries
1 cup almonds,
   blanched and chopped
51/2 cups raisins
1/2 cups candied peel
4 cups flour

2 cups shortening **or** margarine
2 tsp. vanilla
1/2 tsp. almond extract
21/4 cups packed brown sugar
7 eggs
1/2 tsp. salt
1 tsp. soda
1 cup milk

Mix fruit and nuts with 1/2 cup flour. Cream shortening and add flavorings. Add sugar gradually and cream well. Add eggs one at a time, beating well after each addition. Sift remaining flour, salt and soda together and add to creamed mixture alternately with milk. Add fruit and nuts, mixing very well. Put into lined pans. Bake at 275° for 3 to 31/2 hours or until done.

Florence Keyser

PINEAPPLE WHITE FRUIT CAKE

1 cup coconut
1 cup candied cherries, halved
21/4 cups sultana raisins
11/2 cups walnuts
3/4 cup soft butter
1 cup sugar
3 eggs

20-oz. can crushed pineapple
1 tsp. vanilla
1 tsp. almond extract
3 cups flour
2 tsp. baking powder
1 tsp. salt

Line 10-inch tube pan with wax paper. Combine coconut, cherries, raisins and nuts. Cream butter and gradually add sugar. Beat well after each addition. Add eggs. Beat until light and fluffy. Stir in pineapple and flavorings. Sift flour, baking powder and salt over fruit. Mix and add to cake ingredients. Bake at 300° for 13/4 hours.

Mrs. Shirley Boyce

UNBAKED BRAZIL NUT CAKE

3 cups brazil nuts
4 1/2 cups crushed graham wafers
1 1/2 cups seedless raisins
1 1/2 cups cherries
1 1/4 cups dates, cut up
1 cup diced candied fruit
1 lb. marshmallows
3/4 cup orange juice

1 tbsp. grated orange rind
1/2 tsp. allspice
1/2 tsp. ginger
1/4 tsp. cinnamon
1/4 tsp. nutmeg
1/4 tsp. cloves
1 tsp. vanilla

Line two loaf pans with double thickness of wax paper, extending paper over rim 3 inches. Place whole nuts in large mixing bowl, add graham wafer crumbs and fruit. Cut marshmallows into double boiler, add orange juice, rind and spices. Heat until marshmallows are melted, stirring constantly. Add to fruit mixture. Add vanilla and mix well. Press down in pans. Fold wax paper over cake. Store in refrigerator for several weeks.

Mrs. Fred Wasyleski

BANANA NUT CAKE

1/2 cup butter
1 cup sugar
2 eggs, well beaten
1 tsp. soda
4 tbsp. boiling water

1 cup mashed bananas
2 cups flour
1/4 tsp salt
2 tsp. baking powder
1 cup chopped walnuts

Cream butter. Add sugar and eggs and beat well. Dissolve soda in boiling water and add to bananas. Sift flour, salt and baking powder together and add alternately with bananas. Add chopped walnuts. Bake in two layer cake pans at 375° for 25 minutes or a square cake pan at 350° for 35 to 40 minutes.

Mrs. Sam Alberts

DATE CAKE

1 cup dates, chopped
1 tsp. soda
1/2 cup boiling water
3/4 cup butter
1 cup sugar
2 eggs
1 2/3 cups flour

1 tsp. baking powder
1/2 tsp. salt
1/2 cup brown sugar
1/2 cup chopped walnuts
1/2 cup chocolate chips
2 tsp. flour

Mix dates, soda, and boiling water and let stand. Cream butter and sugar. Add eggs and beat together. Add date mixture and mix well, then add 1 2/3 cups flour, baking powder and salt. Pour into 9 x 12-inch pan. Combine brown sugar, walnuts, chocolate chips and 2 tsp. flour and sprinkle over cake. Bake at 375° for 30 minutes.

Mrs. Alice Murray

OAT DATE CAKE

1 cup flour	1/4 cup shortening
1/2 tsp. salt	1 cup rolled oats
1 tsp. soda	1 cup boiling water
1 tsp. cinnamon	2 eggs, slightly beaten
1/2 tsp. cloves	1/2 cup chopped dates
2 cups brown sugar	1/2 cup chopped walnuts
1/4 cup butter	

Sift dry ingredients together. Combine sugar, butter, shortening, oats and boiling water. Let stand 20 minutes. Add eggs. Add dry ingredients, dates and nuts. Turn into greased 9 x 13-inch pan and sprinkle with 1/4 cup chopped walnuts. Bake at 350° for 45 minutes.

Mrs. Joan Beck

APPLE & DATE COFFEE CAKE

1/2 cup butter	1 cup dates, cut up
1 cup sugar	Pinch of salt
2 eggs	2/3 cup milk
1 tsp. vanilla	1 apple, diced
2 cups flour	1/4 cup sugar
4 tsp. baking powder	1/2 tsp. cinnamon

Cream butter and sugar. Add eggs and vanilla and beat well. Sift dry ingredients together and add alternately with milk. Mix in apple. Sprinkle 1/4 cup sugar and cinnamon on top. Bake at 350° in 9 x 13-inch pan for 30 to 40 minutes.

Mrs. Violet Kaun

PRIZE COFFEE CAKE

2/3 cup sugar	2 tsp. baking powder
2 tbsp. butter **or** shortening	1 1/4 cups flour
1 egg, beaten	1 tsp. vanilla
1/2 tsp. salt	3/4 cup milk

Grease and flour 8-inch square pan. Blend sugar and butter together. Stir in egg. Mix salt, baking powder and flour together. Add vanilla to milk. Add to batter alternately with dry ingredients. Spread a little of batter in pan, sprinkle with half of topping. Cover with remaining batter and sprinkle with remaining topping. Bake at 350° for 25 to 30 minutes. Cool 10 to 15 minutes before serving.

1 tsp. cinnamon	1/4 cup brown sugar
1 cup chopped nuts	1/4 cup white sugar

Combine ingredients and use as topping for cake.

Helen Couper

When your recipe calls for 1 cup mashed bananas, you will need 3 small bananas.

DATE-FILLED COFFEE CAKE

1 cup dates, cut up
1/4 cup brown sugar
1/2 cup water, approximately
6 tbsp. oil
1/2 cup sugar
2 cups flour
4 tsp. baking powder

1 egg, beaten
2/3 - 1 cup milk
1 tbsp. cinnamon
2 tbsp. flour
3 tbsp. butter
5 tbsp. sugar

Cook dates, brown sugar and enough water to make mixture of a spreading consistency. Cream oil and 1/2 cup sugar until fluffy. Sift 2 cups flour and baking powder together. Mix the beaten egg and milk. Add to flour mixture alternately with the oil and sugar. Spread half of the batter in a 9-inch square pan. Spread the filling and remainder of batter on top. Sprinkle with cinnamon, 2 tbsp. flour, butter and 5 tbsp. sugar. Bake at 350° for 25 to 30 minutes.

Mrs. M.S. Reed

A MAN'S CAKE

1/2 cup shortening
1 cup sugar
2 eggs, separated
21/4 cups flour
2 tsp. baking powder

1/2 tsp. salt
1 cup strong, cold coffee
1 tsp. vanilla
3/4 cup walnuts

Blend shortening, sugar and egg yolks. Add sifted dry ingredients and coffee alternately. Stir in nuts and flavoring. Beat egg whites and add. Bake in a tube pan at 350° for 1 hour.

1/2 cup strong coffee
1 cup brown sugar
1/2 cup white sugar

1/4 tsp. salt
2 egg whites, beaten

Cook coffee, sugars and salt until it spins a thread. Pour 1/3 of this syrup over egg whites. Cook remaining syrup to 238° and add to icing. Beat to spreading consistency.

Mrs. Ruth Graham

POUND CAKE

1 cup margarine
2 cups sugar
5 eggs, slightly beaten
2 cups flour

1/2 tsp. salt
1 tsp. vanilla
1/2 tsp. lemon flavoring **or** juice
1/2 tsp. almond flavoring

Cream margarine and sugar well. Add eggs alternately with flour. Add salt and flavorings, beating well. Bake in well-greased and floured tube pan or loaf pan at 300° for 1 hour.

Mrs. Jean Leskow

CHERRY POUND CAKE

1/2 cup butter	11/4 cups flour
1/2 cup sugar	1 tsp. baking powder
2 eggs, well beaten	1/4 tsp. salt
1/2 tsp. vanilla flavoring	1/4 cup almonds, slivered
1/2 tsp. almond flavoring	3/4 cup cherries
1/2 tsp. lemon flavoring	2 tsp. lemon juice
2 tbsp. milk	

Cream butter and beat until fluffy. Add sugar and continue beating until creamy. Add eggs, flavorings and milk. Sift flour, baking powder and salt and add. Add almonds, cherries, and lemon juice. Pour into a greased 9 x 5-inch loaf pan. Bake at 325° for 1 hour.

Mrs. Helen James

HONEY POUND CAKE

3/4 cup shortening	11/2 cups seedless raisins
3/4 cup honey	1 tsp. orange extract
3 eggs, well beaten	1/2 tsp. salt
21/2 cups flour	21/2 tsp. baking powder

Cream shortening and honey. Add eggs. Add half the flour, raisins and flavoring. Blend remaining flour, salt and baking powder and add. Bake at 325° for about 2 hours.

Mrs. Wm. Maxfield

HERMIT CAKE

1 cup butter	1/2 tsp. baking soda
11/2 cups brown sugar	3/4 cups milk
3 eggs	1 lb. chopped dates
21/2 cups flour	1/2 lb. chopped walnuts
1 tsp. cream of tartar	

Mix butter and brown sugar, add eggs and beat. Add flour, cream of tartar and baking soda alternately with the milk. Fold in dates and nuts. Mix and pour into a greased 7 x 11-inch pan. Bake at 350° for about 45 minutes. When cool, ice with a brown sugar icing and sprinkle with nuts.

Mrs. Muriel Shadlock

FROSTINGS

CHOCOLATE ICING

1 cup sugar	1/4 cup milk
1/4 cup cocoa	1/4 cup butter

Combine ingredients and cook 1 minute. Cool a little and then beat.

Mrs. Boyd Cooker

CHOCOLATE FROSTING

2 sq. unsweetened chocolate
1/2 cup granulated sugar
1/4 cup water
4 egg yolks

1/2 cup butter **or** margarine
1 tsp. vanilla
2 cups icing sugar

Combine chocolate, granulated sugar and water in saucepan. Cook over low heat, stirring constantly until chocolate melts and mixture is smooth. Add egg yolks, beating thoroughly. Cool. Cream butter and vanilla and blend in icing sugar gradually, creaming well. Add chocolate mixture and beat until smooth. Fills and frosts a two-layer cake.

ANNABEL'S CHOCOLATE ICING

2 sq. unsweetened chocolate
2 tbsp. butter
2 cups icing sugar

1 egg, unbeaten
1/2 tsp. vanilla

Melt chocolate and butter in pan. Add 1 cup of the sugar and egg. Mix well. Add remaining sugar and vanilla and beat until smooth. Spread on cake.

Mrs. Annabel Parslow

ECONOMY ICING

3 tbsp. cocoa
3 tbsp. icing sugar

3 tbsp. flour
Cream

Mix together dry ingredients and stir in sufficient cream to make a smooth icing the right consistency for frosting cake. A little vanilla or maple may be added if desired. This is sufficient for a large cake or a layer cake. VARIATION: Cold, strong coffee may be used instead of cream.

Mrs. D.W. Baker

FRENCH MOCHA ICING

2 cups icing sugar
1/4 cup butter **or** margarine
1 tbsp. cocoa

3 tbsp. hot, strong coffee
1/2 tsp. vanilla

Combine and beat ingredients well and spread on cake.

PRALINE ICING

5 tbsp. brown sugar
2 tbsp. butter

3 tbsp. cream
Coconut

Combine sugar, butter and cream and boil 3 minutes. Pour over hot cake. Sprinkle with coconut and place in oven again for a few minutes.

Mrs. Edith Shantz

ONE, TWO, THREE, FOUR ICING

1 tbsp. water
2 tbsp. butter
3 tbsp. cream

4 tbsp. brown sugar
Icing sugar
1/2 tsp. vanilla

Combine water, butter, cream and brown sugar and boil for 2 1/2 minutes. Thicken with icing sugar and add vanilla flavoring.

Mrs. W.L. Barker

SELF-ICING TOPPING FOR CAKES

2 egg whites
1/2 cup brown sugar

Chopped nuts
Coconut

Beat egg whites until stiff but not dry. Gradually beat in sugar and beat until glossy. Spread over hot cake. Sprinkle with nuts and coconut and return to oven at 375° for 10 to 15 minutes.

WHITE SNOW-DRIFT FROSTING

1/2 cup corn syrup
1/2 cup sugar
2 tbsp. water

2 egg whites
1/2 tsp. vanilla

Boil corn syrup, sugar and water in saucepan just to soft ball stage. Beat egg whites until they form soft peaks, gradually add heated syrup, beating continuously until mixture stands in stiff peaks. Add vanilla and beat thoroughly.

Anna Vail

FLUFFY ICING

1 1/2 cups sugar
1/3 cup water
1/8 tsp. salt

1/4 tsp. cream of tartar
2 egg whites
1/2 tsp. maple flavoring

Combine sugar, water and salt and boil for 3 minutes. Add cream of tartar to egg whites. Beating constantly, pour syrup over egg whites. Continue beating for 5 minutes or until right consistency to spread. Beat in flavoring.

Mrs. Henry Houseman

CHIFFON FROSTING

1 1/2 cups brown sugar
1/2 cup water

2 egg whites, stiffly beaten
1/2 tsp. vanilla

Combine sugar and water and boil until thread stage. Pour into egg whites. Add flavoring. Spread on cake when cool.

Mrs. Eva G. Said

BUTTER DECORATING ICING

1 cup butter　　　　　　　　3 or 4 egg whites
2 cups icing sugar　　　　　　Flavoring

Cream butter and add icing sugar. Beat egg whites until stiff and add butter mixture. Beat well. Add enough icing sugar to make icing very stiff to hold shape. Use to decorate cake with decorating tube. NOTE: This icing will not set hard like ornamental icing.

BUTTER ICING

1/3 cup soft butter　　　　　　1 1/2 tsp. flavoring
3 cups icing sugar　　　　　　3 tbsp. cream

Blend butter and icing sugar. Add flavoring and enough cream to make mixture of spreading consistency.

Mrs. Carol O. Keirle

BANANA BUTTER FROSTING

1/2 cup mashed, ripe bananas　　1/4 cup butter
1/2 tsp. lemon juice　　　　　　3 1/2 cups icing sugar

Mix bananas with lemon juice. Cream the butter and add the sifted icing sugar alternately with the banana mixture. Beat the frosting until light and fluffy, then spread between layers of banana cake, and cover the sides and top.

Mrs. E.F. Schmidt

LEMON BUTTER FROSTING

7/8 cup sugar　　　　　　　　1/4 cup butter
2 lemons　　　　　　　　　　2 eggs

Combine sugar , rind and juice of lemons and butter in saucepan. Heat until melted and cool. Beat the eggs. When sugar is cool, return to stove. Add eggs. Stir until thick. Do not boil.

Mrs. E. Pearson

CINNAMON BUTTER ICING

1/4 cup butter **or** margarine　　2 cups icing sugar
1/2 tsp. ground cinnamon　　　Hot cream
Pinch of salt　　　　　　　　1/2 tsp. vanilla

Cream the butter and mix in cinnamon and salt. Gradually blend in icing sugar alternately with about 2 tbsp. hot cream to make an icing of spreading consistency. Mix in vanilla.

Gertrude O. Chambers

DOUBLE BOILER FROSTING

2 egg whites	1/2 cup honey
1/4 tsp. salt	1/2 tsp. vanilla
1 tbsp. water **or** fruit juice	

Combine egg whites, salt and water in top of double boiler and beat until egg whites hold their shape. Continue beating while adding honey in fine stream. Cook over boiling water about 5 minutes, beating constantly until mixture forms peaks when beater is raised. Remove from heat. Add vanilla and beat about 2 minutes until frosting is of spreading consistency. This will frost top and sides of two 9-inch layers.

SEVEN MINUTE ICING

2 egg whites	2 tbsp. corn syrup
Pinch of salt	1/4 tsp. cream of tartar
1 1/4 cups sugar	1 tsp. vanilla
5 tbsp. water	1 tsp. almond

Combine egg whites, salt, sugar, water, syrup and cream of tartar in top of double boiler. Beat over hot water until frosting will stand in peaks. Add flavorings. Pile on top of cake and spread on sides. VARIATION: Chocolate chips may be added. Stir enough to marble mixture.

Mildred Pollock

ORANGE SEVEN-MINUTE FROSTING

1 1/2 cups brown sugar	2 egg whites
2 tsp. corn syrup	1/3 cup water
Pinch of salt	2 tsp. grated orange rind

Combine first 5 ingredients in the top of a double boiler. Place over boiling water and beat about 7 minutes until mixture holds its shape. Fold in orange rind. Fills and frosts one 9-inch layer cake.

Mrs. Arthur D. Brown

JELLO SEVEN-MINUTE FROSTING

3 1/2 tbsp. jello, any flavor	2 egg whites, unbeaten
1/2 cup hot water	Dash of salt
1 1/4 cups sugar	

Dissolve jello in water in top of double boiler. Add sugar, egg whites and salt. Beat mixture for about 1 minute with rotary or electric beater until well mixed. Place over rapidly boiling water and beat about 7 minutes or until frosting will stand up in peaks. Immediately transfer frosting to another bowl and beat about 1 minute, or until thick enough to spread. Frosts one angel food cake. NOTE: This frosting takes the color and flavor from jello that is used.

Mrs. Mary Stimson

BROILED FROSTING

1/2 cup oil
1 cup brown sugar, firmly packed
6 tbsp. light cream

1 tsp. vanilla
1 1/2 cups shredded coconut

Combine the ingredients. Spread on warm cake in pan. Place under broiler (medium heat) about 2 minutes until mixture bubbles and browns. Sufficient frosting for two 8-inch layers.

BROILED COCONUT FROSTING

1/4 cup butter **or** margarine, melted
1/2 cup packed brown sugar
2 tbsp. milk

1/4 cup chopped walnuts
3/4 cup shredded **or** flaked coconut

Combine all ingredients. Spread evenly over cake. Broil 3 to 5 minutes until frosting becomes bubbly. Cake may be served warm or cold.

EASY FUDGE ICING

1/4 cup butter
1/2 cup packed brown sugar

2 tbsp. milk
1 cup icing sugar

Boil butter and sugar until melted and brown. Add milk and bring back to a boil. Cool to lukewarm and beat in icing sugar.

NEVER FAIL CARAMEL FROSTING

1 1/2 cups brown sugar
3/4 cup cream

2 tsp. butter
1/2 tsp. vanilla

Add sugar, cream and butter in a heavy saucepan. Stir until dissolved. Boil over low heat until at the soft ball stage. Cool slightly. Add vanilla and beat until creamy. Frost cake immediately.

CREAMY CARAMEL ICING

2 cups sugar
1 cup cream
1/4 cup corn syrup

1/2 tsp. vanilla
1/2 tsp. almond flavoring

Combine sugar, cream and syrup and boil until a very soft ball forms when a little is dropped into cold water. Cool for 30 minutes. Add flavorings and beat until texture changes. If frosting is too thick, hot water may be added to thin the frosting to spreading consistency. VARIATION: If chocolate is desired, add cocoa to taste and stir it into sugar.

Mildred Pollock

CARAMEL ICING

1/4 cup butter   2 tbsp. milk
1/2 cup brown sugar   3/4 cup icing sugar

Melt butter and brown sugar and cook 2 minutes, stirring. Add milk and stir until mixture boils. Remove from heat, cool and add icing sugar.

Miss Elsie Hallum

ALMOND-COFFEE TORTE FILLING

3 tbsp. butter   1 tsp. instant coffee
1/2 cup fine sugar   1 tbsp. hot water
1/4 cup chopped almonds Cream **or** canned milk

Cream butter and sugar. Add almonds. Dissolve coffee in hot water and add. Add enough cream to give a spreading consistency.

ALMOND ICING

1 large, baked potato   4 tsp. rosewater
Icing sugar   1 lb. almonds

While the potato is hot, mash and work in icing sugar and rosewater until spreading consistency. Blanch and dry almonds, but do not harden. Put through fine food grinder. Mix with potato and sugar until smooth. This will not harden.

Mrs. A. Johnson

ALMOND PASTE FOR CAKE

3 cups sugar   3 cups almonds
11/2 cups hot water   2 egg yolks
2 tsp. cream of tartar Few drops almond extract

Bring sugar, water and cream of tartar to a boil and continue boiling about 12 minutes until it makes a soft ball in cold water. Grind or finely chop almonds and pour mixture slowly over them. Stir well. Add yolks and extract. Stir until stiff enough to spread.

Mrs. W. Southern

CREAMY CHEESE FROSTING

1/4 cup margarine **or** butter 1 tsp. vanilla
4 oz. cream cheese   1/4 cup chopped walnuts
2 cups icing sugar

Cream margarine and cheese together. Add icing sugar and beat until light and fluffy. Add vanilla. Sprinkle the nuts over the iced cake. VARIATION: Omit vanilla and add 1 tsp. orange or lemon juice.

LEMON CHEESE TOPPING

1/2 cup butter
2 cups sugar
Juice of 3 lemons

Rind of 2 lemons, grated
6 eggs, well beaten

Melt butter and sugar in top of double boiler. Add lemon juice, rind and eggs. Cook until thick. Yield: 1 quart.

Mrs. E. Whitfield

CURRANT JELLY ICING

1/2 cup currant jelly
1 egg white

1/8 tsp. salt

Place ingredients in saucepan over low heat. Beat with double egg beater or electric beater until icing stands in peaks. Use on sponge cake, white or banana cake.

Miss E. Lothian

SUGARLESS ICING

1 egg white

3/4 cup corn syrup

Combine egg white and corn syrup in top of double boiler. Cook over rapidly boiling water for 7 minutes, beating continuously with egg beater. Remove from heat and beat until mixture stands in peaks.

Mrs. N. Branchflower

FABULOUS FROSTING

1/2 cup milk
21/2 tbsp. flour
1/2 cup sugar

1/2 cup butter
1/2 tsp. vanilla

Combine milk and flour and cook over medium heat until thick. Cool. Meanwhile, cream butter and sugar. Add vanilla and cooked flour mixture. Beat well. NOTE: This never hardens and freezes well.

Minnie Blair

TANGY CRUNCH CAKE TOPPING

4 tbsp. butter
1/2 cup brown sugar

2 tbsp. lemon juice
1 cup chopped nuts

Combine butter, sugar and lemon juice and bring to a boil. Add nuts. Pour over warm white or ginger bread cake. Place in a slow broiler until nuts are slightly toasted.

COOKIES

ALL-HONEY COOKIES

1 cup butter
1 cup honey
3 3/4 cups flour

4 3/4 tsp. baking powder
1 tsp. cinnamon
1/4 tsp. soda

Melt butter and honey. Cool. Sift dry ingredients and add. Blend well. Roll thin, cut and bake at 350° for 12 minutes.

HONEY PEANUT COOKIES

1 cup honey
1 cup butter
1 cup peanut butter
1/2 cup brown sugar
2 eggs

1 tsp. vanilla
2 cups flour
1 tsp. soda
1 tsp. salt
1 tsp. baking powder

Cream honey, butter, peanut butter and sugar. Add eggs and vanilla and beat well. Add dry ingredients. Drop by spoonfuls onto greased cookie sheet. Bake at 350° for 12 to 15 minutes.

Mrs. Jill Hill

OATMEAL HONEY DROP COOKIES

1 cup honey
2 eggs
1 cup sour cream
2 cups flour
1/2 tsp. salt
1/2 tsp. nutmeg

1/2 tsp. cloves
1/2 tsp. cinnamon
1 tsp. soda
2 cups oatmeal
1 cup raisins
1/2 cup chopped nuts

Combine ingredients and drop by spoonful onto cookie sheet or muffin tins. Bake at 350° for 12 to 15 minutes. Freezes well.

Mrs. Elsie McCue

CHEESE PINWHEELS

2 cups flour
4 tsp. baking powder
1/2 tsp. salt

4 tbsp. shortening
1 cup grated cheddar cheese
3/4 cup milk

Sift flour, baking powder and salt together. Cut in shortening. Add grated cheese and mix well. Add milk slowly and mix into a soft dough. Roll out on lightly-floured board. Spread with well-blended mixture of grated cheddar cheese and cream to make a smooth paste. Roll, cut into 1-inch slices and bake pinwheels at 400° for 15 to 20 minutes.

MONSTER COOKIES

1 dozen eggs
41/2 cups brown sugar
4 cups white sugar
1 tbsp. vanilla
4 cups margarine
6 cups peanut butter

1 cup flour
8 tsp. baking soda
18 cups rolled oats
22/3 cups chocolate chips
22/3 cups M & M's **or** smarties

Mix all ingredients together well. Roll into balls and flatten a little on cookie sheet. Bake at 350° for 12 minutes. Yield: 22 dozen.

Miriam Galloway

CRUNCHIE COOKIES

1/2 cup soft shortening
1/2 cup granulated sugar
1/2 cup honey
1 egg
1 1/2 cups flour
1 tsp. salt
1/2 tsp. baking soda

1 tsp. cinnamon
1/4 cup milk
1/2 cup raisins
1/2 cup chopped walnuts
4 crumbled, shredded
   wheat biscuits

Blend shortening, sugar, honey and egg together. Sift dry ingredients together and add alternately with milk to creamed mixture. Stir in raisins, walnuts and biscuits. Drop onto greased cookie sheet and bake at 375° for 12 to 15 minutes.

MYRTLE'S GINGER SNAPS

2 tsp. soda
2 cups molasses **or**
  1 cup molasses and
  1 cup coffee
1 cup sugar

1 cup lard **or** shortening
1/2 tsp. salt
2 tbsp. ginger
5 cups flour

Dissolve soda in a little hot water. Combine and add remaining ingredients. Roll out and cut. Bake at 400° for 10 to 12 minutes.

Myrtle Monner

DAISY'S GINGER SNAPS

1 cup butter **or** shortening
1 cup sugar
1 cup molasses **or** 1/2 cup
  syrup and 1/2 cup molasses

3 cups flour
1 tsp. baking soda
1 tbsp. ginger

Cream butter and add sugar and molasses. Sift together dry ingredients. Add to creamed mixture. Mix well. Roll into balls. Do not flatten. Place on cookie sheet. Bake at 350° about 12 minutes. The amount of ginger must be followed closely.

Mrs. Daisy Jensen

GINGER SNAPS LIKE YOU BUY

1 cup molasses **or** 1/2 cup	1 tsp. ginger
syrup and 1/2 cup molasses	1/2 tsp. salt
1 cup sugar	1/2 cup boiling water
1 cup shortening	Flour to stiffen
1 tsp. soda	

Combine ingredients and leave for 1 hour or more. Pinch off bits of dough and roll into balls. Place 1 inch apart on cookie sheet. Bake at 350° for 12 to 15 minutes.

Mrs. Holland

GINGER SNAPS

11/3 cups oil	1 tsp. salt
3 cups sugar	6 tsp. baking soda
6 eggs	2 tsp. cinnamon
3/4 cup molasses	2 tsp. ginger
6 cups flour	

Beat oil, sugar, eggs and molasses until light and fluffy. Add sifted, mixed dry ingredients. Mix well. Bake at 375° for 12 to 15 minutes.

FAT GINGER COOKIES

1 cup sugar	31/2 cups flour (soft dough)
1 cup shortening	11/2 tsp. ginger
3/4 cup sour milk	1 tsp. cinnamon
3 - 4 eggs	1/2 tsp. cloves
1 cup cooking molasses	1/2 tsp. allspice
3 tsp. soda	1/2 tsp. salt

Mix ingredients together. Chill. Roll and cut quickly or form into a roll in wax paper and freeze and slice. Bake at 350° until done. These are soft cake-like cookies. Sprinkle with sugar or ice with lemon glaze.

Mrs. Lawrence Monner

GINGER SPARKLES

3/4 cup shortening	2 tsp. baking soda
1 cup brown sugar	1/4 tsp. salt
1/4 cup molasses	1 tsp. ginger
1 egg	1 tsp. cinnamon
2 cups flour	1/2 tsp. cloves

Cream together shortening, brown sugar, molasses and egg until light and fluffy. Measure flour, soda, salt and spices and mix thoroughly. Stir in creamed mixture. Shape into small balls. Roll in granulated sugar and place on greased baking sheet. Bake at 375° for 8 to 10 minutes.

Janetta Northcott
Carol Stott

LEMON DELIGHT

1 pkg. lemon cake mix
1/2 cup oil

2 eggs
1 tsp. grated lemon peel

Combine all ingredients and mix well. Drop by teaspoon onto ungreased cookie sheet. Bake at 350° for 10 to 12 minutes until golden brown. Cool on cookie sheet for 1 minute and then remove from pan. VARIATION: Peanut Butter Delight: Substitute 1 cup peanut butter and 2 tbsp. water for grated lemon peel.

PINEAPPLE WHOLE WHEAT COOKIES

1 cup flour
1/2 tsp. soda
1/2 tsp. baking powder
1/2 tsp. salt
1 cup whole wheat flour
1/2 cup shredded coconut
1/2 cup crushed cornflakes

1/4 cup butter
1/4 cup shortening
1 cup yellow sugar
1 tsp. almond flavor
1 egg, well beaten
2/3 cup crushed pineapple

Sift white flour, soda, baking powder and salt, then add wholewheat flour, coconut and crushed cornflakes. Blend butter, shortening, sugar and flavoring together thoroughly. Add egg and beat well. Alternately add dry ingredients and drained pineapple. Drop by spoonful onto greased cookie sheet and bake at 375° for 12 minutes. Yield: 6 dozen.

ALMOND COOKIES

1/2 cup butter **or** margarine
2 hard-boiled egg yolks
1/4 cup sugar

1 cup flour
1/2 tsp. almond extract
24 blanched almonds

Cream butter. Add egg yolks that have been pushed through a sieve. Add sugar and beat until fluffy. Sift in flour, blend and add almond extract. Chill. Roll in balls and place on greased cookie sheet 1-inch apart. Press an almond into each cookie. Bake at 400° for 10 minutes.

R.E. Adams

ALMOND CHRISTMAS BALLS

1 cup butter
1/4 cup icing sugar
2 cups flour
1/2 tsp. salt

1 cup ground almonds
1 tsp. almond flavoring
18 - 20 cherries, cut in halves

Cream butter and sugar . Add flour, salt, almonds and flavoring. Form 1 tsp. of dough into a ball around a cherry half. Bake at 325° for 35 minutes. Roll in icing sugar while warm.

Miss Elas Maurer

BACHELORS BUTTONS

1 cup butter **or** margarine	1/4 tsp. salt
1 cup brown sugar	1 cup chopped walnuts
1 egg	1 cup coconut
21/3 cups flour	Sugar
1 tsp. soda	

Cream butter and sugar. Beat in egg. Sift flour, soda and salt. Add along with walnuts and coconut. Combine well. Roll into balls. Dip in sugar and bake at 375° for 10 to 12 minutes on greased cookie sheet until brown.

Mrs. Norma Van

BANANA OATMEAL COOKIES

11/2 cups flour	1 cup sugar
1/2 tsp. soda	1 egg, beaten
1/2 tsp. salt	1 cup mashed bananas
3/4 tsp. cinnamon	13/4 rolled oats
1/4 tsp. nutmeg	1/2 cup chopped nuts
3/4 cup shortening	1/4 cup raisins

Sift flour, soda, salt and spices together. Cream shortening. Gradually add sugar and cream until fluffy. Add egg and beat well. Add bananas, rolled oats, nuts and raisins. Beat well. Add flour mixture and mix thoroughly. Drop by teaspoonful onto ungreased cookie sheet 11/2 inches apart. Bake at 400° for 12 to 15 minutes. Yield: 6 dozen.

Isa Oldfield

BILLY GOATS

11/2 cups brown sugar	1 tsp. soda
3/4 cup shortening	21/2 cups rolled oats
1 tsp. vanilla	21/2 cups walnuts
3 eggs	2 cups flour

Blend in order given. Spread 1/4-inch thick on cookie sheet. Bake at 350° to 375° until browned. Cut into bars. Sprinkle with icing sugar.

Mrs. Lars Hagenson

BUTTER BUDS

1 cup butter	1 tsp. baking powder
1 cup brown sugar	1/4 tsp. salt
2 eggs	2 tsp. vanilla
2 - 21/2 cups flour	

Cream butter. Add sugar gradually. Beat eggs until thick and add. Sift flour, baking powder and salt. Combine mixtures. Add flavoring and more flour if necessary. Press through a pastry bag or roll into round balls and press down slightly with a fork. Bake at 350° for 10 to 12 minutes.

Philippine Albus

BROWN-EYED SUSANS

1 cup margarine,
   butter **or** shortening
3 tbsp. sugar

1 tsp. almond extract
2 cups flour
1/2 tsp. salt

Cream margarine. Add sugar, almond extract, flour and salt. Roll level tbsp. of this mixture into balls. Place on greased cookie sheet and flatten slightly. Bake at 400° for 10 to 12 minutes.

1 cup sifted icing sugar
2 tbsp. cocoa
2 tbsp. hot water

1/2 tsp. vanilla
Almond halves

Combine sugar and cocoa. Add the water and vanilla. Put 1/2 tsp. of frosting on each cookie, with a half almond in center. Yield: 3 dozen cookies.

CHERRY WINKS

21/4 cups flour
1 tsp. baking powder
1/2 tsp. salt
1/2 tsp. baking soda
3/4 cup butter **or** margarine
1 cup sugar
2 eggs

2 tbsp. milk
1 tsp. vanilla
1 cup pitted chopped dates
1 cup chopped nuts
1/3 cup cut-up maraschino
   cherries
Crushed cornflakes

Sift together flour, baking powder, salt and soda. Beat butter until creamy, add sugar gradually and beat until light and fluffy. Add eggs one at a time. Stir in milk and vanilla. Add flour mixture, dates, nuts and cherries. Mix well. Roll into balls and roll in cornflakes. Top each with one-quarter of a maraschino cherry. Bake at 375° for 12 minutes.

CHEWY OATMEAL FRUIT COOKIES

1 cup brown sugar
1 cup white sugar
1 cup shortening
2 large eggs
1 tsp. vanilla
1 cup flour
1/2 tsp. salt

1 tsp. soda
4 cups rolled oats
1 cup raisins
1 cup pitted dates
1 cup chopped pecans
1 cup coconut

Cream sugars and shortening together. Add the eggs and vanilla. Sift together the flour, salt and soda. Add to the creamed mixture, blending well. Add the rolled oats and mix well. Grind the raisins, dates, pecans and coconut and add to batter. Drop by teaspoonful onto greased cookie sheets. Bake at 325 to 350° for 10 to 12 minutes. NOTE: Grinding the raisins, dates, pecans and coconut enhances the flavor.

Mrs. August Vion

COCONUT DATE MACAROONS

3 egg whites
1 tbsp. cornstarch
1 cup icing sugar

1 cup coconut, sweetened
1 cup dates, chopped

Beat eggs whites until foamy. Combine cornstarch and sugar. Add gradually to the egg whites, beating after each addition until well-blended. Continue beating until mixture will stand in peaks. Fold in coconut and dates. Drop by teaspoonful onto greased heavy paper or cookie sheet. Bake at 325° for 20 minutes.

COCONUT MACAROONS

3 egg whites
3/4 tsp. cream of tartar
1 cup sugar

1 tbsp. cornstarch
1 tbsp. vanilla
2 cups coconut

Place egg whites, cream of tartar and sugar in double boiler and beat over heat with egg beater until quite stiff. Remove from heat and add the cornstarch, vanilla and coconut. Drop by spoonful onto cookie sheet. Decorate with small pieces of green and red maraschino cherries and bake at 325° for 15 to 20 minutes until slightly brown.

Mrs. Roy Lambright

CHEESE COOKIES

1 cup butter
4 oz. cream cheese
4 tbsp. sugar
1/4 tsp. salt

2 cups flour
1 egg, beaten
Chopped walnuts

Cream butter and cheese. Sift sugar, salt and flour together. Divide dough and form 1-inch rolls. Place in refrigerator overnight. Cut in thin slices. Brush with egg mixed with a little milk. Sprinkle with nuts. Bake at 350° for 10 minutes on ungreased cookie sheet.

Mrs. F. Redmond

CHOCOLATE COOKIES

1 cup butter **or** margarine
1 1/2 cups sugar
2 eggs
2 tsp. vanilla
2/3 cups cocoa

2 cups flour
1/2 tsp. salt
3/4 tsp. baking soda
1 - 2 cups raisins

Cream the butter, sugar, eggs and vanilla together. Sift dry ingredients and add. Fold in raisins. Drop by teaspoonful onto oiled baking sheet. Bake at 350° for 8 to 10 minutes. Yield: 4 dozen.

Miriam Galloway

CHOCOLATE COOKIES (Unbaked)

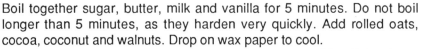

2 cups sugar
1/2 cup butter **or** shortening
  plus 1/2 tsp. salt
1/2 cup milk
1 tsp. vanilla

3 cups rolled oats
1/2 cup cocoa
1 cup coconut
1/2 cup walnuts (optional)

Boil together sugar, butter, milk and vanilla for 5 minutes. Do not boil longer than 5 minutes, as they harden very quickly. Add rolled oats, cocoa, coconut and walnuts. Drop on wax paper to cool.

Mrs. Peter Josey
Mrs. Edna Stewart
Mrs. C. Bettenson

CHOCOLATE CHIP MACAROONS

2/3 cup condensed milk
6 oz. semi-sweet
  chocolate chips

2 cups shredded coconut
1 tsp. vanilla extract
3/4 tsp. almond extract

Mix together milk, chocolate chips, coconut and flavorings. Drop by tablespoonful about 1-inch apart onto a well-greased baking sheet. Bake at 350° about 8 to 10 minutes or until delicately browned around the edges.

CHOCOLATE DROP SUGAR COOKIES

11/2 cups sugar
2 eggs, beaten
1 cup melted butter, creamed
6 tbsp. sugar
6 tbsp. cocoa
6 tbsp. hot water

1 tsp. vanilla
21/2 cups flour
1 tsp. baking powder
1/2 tsp. salt
2 cups cornflakes
1 cup chopped nuts

Add 11/2 cups sugar and eggs to butter gradually. Dissolve 6 tbsp. sugar and cocoa in hot water and add to creamed mixture. Add vanilla and mix well. Sift the flour, baking powder and salt together and add along with cornflakes and chopped nuts. Drop by teaspoonful onto greased cookie sheet. Bake at 350° for 10 minutes or until browned.

Mrs. Audrey Thompson

CHOCOLATE PEANUT CLUSTERS

8 oz. semi-sweet chocolate chips
2/3 cup sweetened
  condensed milk

1/2 cup peanuts
1/2 cup golden raisins

Melt chocolate over low heat, remove and add milk. Mix. Add peanuts and raisins. Drop by teaspoonful onto wax paper or buttered baking sheet. Chill several hours.

Emily Saide

CHOCO-SCOTCH CLUSTERS

6 oz. semi-sweet chocolate chips
6 oz. butterscotch
  flavored chips
2 tbsp. peanut butter
4 cups rice krispies

Melt chips and peanut butter together in heavy saucepan over low heat, stirring constantly until well blended. Remove from heat. Add rice krispies and stir until well-coated. Drop by tablespoonful onto wax paper or buttered baking sheets. Let stand in cool place until firm.

Mrs. Pat Felstad

CORNFLAKE CHOCOLATE COOKIES

2 cups sugar
1/2 cup milk
1/2 cup margarine
1/8 tsp. salt
6 tbsp. cocoa
3 cups crushed cornflakes
1 cup coconut

Combine sugar, milk and margarine and stir until dissolved. Bring to boil. Remove from stove and stir in salt, cocoa, cornflakes and coconut. Mix well. Drop by spoonful onto wax paper. Cool. Keep in refrigerator.

Mrs. Jean Jacques

CHOW MEIN COOKIES

1 cup butterscotch chips
1 cup chocolate chips
2 cups chow mein noodles
1 cup salted peanuts

Melt chips in double boiler and stir in the noodles and peanuts. Drop by teaspoonful onto wax paper and chill.

Mrs. Freda Wolff

CHRISTMAS FRUIT DROPS

1 cup almonds, blanched
1 cup brazil nuts
1 lb. dates
1 cup candied red **or**
  green cherries
4 rings candied pineapple
21/2 cups flour
1 tsp. baking soda
1 tsp. salt
1 tsp. cinnamon
1 cup butter
11/2 cups sugar
2 eggs, beaten
1 tsp. vanilla

Skin almonds and chop coarsely. Spread thinly on cookie sheet and toast at 225° until golden. Chop brazil nuts and dates. Cut cherries in quarters and slice pineapple in slivers. Sift flour with soda, salt and cinnamon. Cream butter. Gradually add sugar. Add eggs and vanilla and mix in flour about one-quarter at a time. Stir in fruit and nuts. Drop by teaspoonful onto ungreased pan. Bake at 400° for 10 minutes. Yield: 12 dozen.

Mrs. Pearl Young

DAD'S COOKIES

1 cup brown sugar	1 1/2 cups rolled oats
1 cup white sugar	3/4 cup coconut (optional)
1 cup butter **or** half	1 1/2 cups flour
shortening and half butter	1 tsp. baking powder
1 egg	1 tsp. baking soda
1 tsp. vanilla	

Combine sugars, butter, egg and vanilla. Add oats and coconut. Sift flour, baking powder and soda and add. Blend thoroughly. Form dough into walnut-sized balls. Space on greased cookie sheet. Press down with fork. Bake in moderate oven about 15 minutes until golden brown. VARIATION: Substitute 1 cup Spanish nuts for coconut.

Mrs. Donna Faye Brown
Mrs. Neil Randal

DOUBLE CHOCOLATE RAISIN DROPS

1 cup shortening	2 1/2 cups flour
1 1/2 cups packed brown sugar	1 tsp. salt
3 tbsp. cocoa	2 tsp. baking powder
3 eggs	1/2 tsp. soda
1/2 cup buttermilk **or** milk	1 1/2 cups dark seedless raisins
1 tsp. vanilla	1 cup chocolate chips

Beat shortening and sugar together thoroughly. Stir in cocoa, beat in eggs, add buttermilk and vanilla. Sift flour, salt, baking powder, baking soda together and add to mixture. Add raisins and chocolate chips. Drop by teaspoonful onto greased cookie sheet. Bake at 375° for 12 to 15 minutes.

Mrs. Anne Smook

FIG NEWTONS

1 cup shortening	1 tsp. cream of tartar
1 cup brown sugar	1 tsp. vanilla
2 eggs	3/4 tsp. soda dissolved in
3 cups flour	1 tbsp. hot water
1 tsp. salt	

Beat shortening with brown sugar until light and fluffy. Add eggs and beat well. Sift flour, salt and cream of tartar together. Add half of this to the egg batter. Add vanilla and soda dissolved in hot water, then remaining flour mixture. Place in refrigerator to chill.

3 cups chopped figs	1 tbsp. butter
2/3 cups brown sugar	1 tbsp. lemon juice
2/3 cup water	

Cook ingredients in double boiler, then cool. Roll out dough 1/8 inch thick and cut into squares or circles. Place a little filling on cookie then place another cookie on top and press around edge.

FOREST RANGERS

1 cup white sugar	2 cups coconut
1 cup brown sugar	2 cups flour
1 cup shortening	1 tsp. salt
2 eggs, beaten	4 tsp. baking powder
1 tsp. vanilla	1 tsp. baking soda
2 cups rolled oats	

Combine sugars, shortening, egg and vanilla. Add oats and coconut. Sift flour, salt, baking powder and soda and add. Blend thoroughly. Form into balls and place on greased cookie sheet. Press down with fork. Bake at 350° for 15 minutes.

Mrs. Irene Bensen

HOPSCOTCH CRUNCHIES

6 oz. butterscotch chips	3 oz. chow mein noodles
1/2 cup peanut butter	1 cup miniature marshmallows

Melt butterscotch chips and peanut butter over hot, not boiling, water. Remove from heat. Stir in chow mein noodles and marshmallows. Drop by teaspoon onto wax sheet. Chill until set. Yield: 30.

Esther Richards

INVENTOR'S COOKIES

1 cup shortening	2 cups flour
1 1/2 cups sugar	4 tsp. baking powder
2 eggs	Liquid added to egg, to make
1 tsp. salt	a firm dough
2 cups oatmeal	

To this basic dough recipe, add one of the following:
1. 1 cup raisins, 1 tsp. cinnamon, 1/2 tsp. nutmeg (use brown sugar)
2. 3/4 cup flaked coconut, 1/2 tsp. almond flavoring (use white sugar)
3. 1 cup raisins, 1 tsp. instant coffee, 1/2 tsp. vanilla (use brown sugar)
4. 3/4 cup "Fruit Cake" fruit, lemon flavoring (use white sugar)
5. 1 cup dates, chopped very fine, 1/2 tsp. vanilla (use brown sugar)
Bake at 350° for 12 to 15 minutes.

Mrs. K. Maxfield

JAM COOKIES

1 cup shortening	2 1/2 cups flour
1 cup brown sugar	1 tsp. soda
1 cup white sugar	1 tsp. salt
2 eggs	Jam

Cream shortening and sugars. Add eggs and beat well. Add dry ingredients. Drop by spoonful onto greased cookie sheet. Press thumb in center of each and add a little jam. Bake at 350° for 12 to 15 minutes.

JAM-JAMS

1 cup brown sugar	1 tsp. vanilla
1 cup shortening	2 tsp. soda
2 eggs, well beaten	3 - 4 cups flour
6 tbsp. corn syrup	1/4 tsp. salt

Cream sugar and shortening. Add eggs, syrup and vanilla. Sift soda, flour and salt and add. Roll out, cut and bake at 350° for 12 to15 minutes. Spread jam or date filling between two cookies.

Mrs. Romona Koch

JELLY FINGERS

1 cup soft butter **or** margarine	1/4 tsp. salt
3/4 cup brown sugar	1 cup rolled oats
1 egg	1/2 cup walnuts, chopped
2 cups flour	Jam

Cream butter. Add sugar, beating well. Add egg. Sift flour, salt and add to butter mixture. Blend in oats. Chill dough. Shape dough into ovals about 11/2 inches long and roll in walnuts. Place on ungreased cookie sheet. Indent along each center with finger. Bake at 350° for about 10 minutes. Cool slightly and fill with jam.

LACY BUTTER COOKIES

3 tbsp. flour	1 cup butter, softened almost
21/4 cups brown sugar	to melting stage
1/2 tsp. salt	1 egg, slightly beaten
21/4 cups rolled oats	1 tsp. vanilla

Mix dry ingredients together, then stir in butter. Blend in egg and vanilla. Mix well. Drop by small teaspoonful onto cookie sheet. Place far apart, six to a sheet. Bake at 375° for about 7 minutes or until light brown. Cool slightly before removing from pan.

Mrs. Nora Holmbert

MARSHMALLOW ROLLS

4 squares semi-sweet chocolate	1 cup icing sugar
2 tbsp. butter	1 cup chopped walnuts
1 tsp. vanilla	41/2 cups miniature
1 egg, well beaten	marshmallows

Melt chocolate and butter over hot water. Add vanilla to egg, mix with melted chocolate and cook for 2 to 3 minutes. Cream in sugar, add remaining ingredients and mix well. Refrigerate for 5 to 10 minutes. Divide mixture in half and form into two rolls. Sprinkle coconut on waxed paper and roll mixture in it. Chill for several hours. Slice and serve.

Sharon Hallman
Mrs. Jeanette Seely

MILK CHOCOLATE CHIP OATMEAL COOKIES

1 cup soft shortening	1 tsp. baking soda
3/4 cup firmly-packed brown sugar	1/4 cup boiling water
1/4 cup granulated sugar	2 cups rolled oats
1 tsp. vanilla	1/2 cup chopped nuts
1 1/2 cups flour	1 cup milk chocolate chips
1/2 tsp. salt	

Beat shortening, sugars and vanilla until fluffy. Add flour and salt. Mix well. Dissolve baking soda in boiling water and blend into mixture. Stir in rolled oats, nuts and chocolate chips. Drop from teaspoon onto ungreased cookie sheets, 2 inches apart. Flatten with fork dipped in cold water. Bake at 350° for 10 to 12 minutes. Yield: 7 dozen cookies. VARIATION: Use coconut or raisins instead of nuts.

Hazel Rupertus

JUMBO RAISIN COOKIES

1 cup water	4 cups flour
2 cups raisins	1 tsp. baking powder
1 cup shortening	1 tsp. baking soda
2 cups sugar	1 1/2 tsp. salt
3 eggs	1 1/2 tsp. cinnamon
1 tsp. vanilla	1/4 tsp. nutmeg
1 cup chopped nuts	1/4 tsp. allspice

Add water to raisins and boil 5 minutes. Cool. Cream shortening and add sugar. Add eggs and beat well. Add vanilla and cooled raisin mixture. Add nuts. Sift together flour, baking powder, baking soda, salt, cinnamon, nutmeg and allspice. Add to raisin mixture and blend well. Drop by teaspoon onto greased cookie sheet. Bake at 375° for 12 to 15 minutes.

Mrs. Harold Doel
Gladys White

INDIVIDUAL SHORTBREADS

1 cup butter	2 cups flour
2/3 cups brown sugar **or**	Chopped candied cherries **or**
1/2 cup berry sugar	nuts, if desired

Cream butter until very soft. Gradually blend in the sugar and beat until light and fluffy. Add sifted flour to the mixture, working it in well. Turn the dough onto a lightly-floured board and knead in additional flour until cracks appear on the surface of the dough. Roll the dough until 1/3-inch thick. Using a floured knife, cut dough into oblongs about 1 x 1 1/2 inches or use fancy cutters. Prick the top with a fork and decorate with nut or cherries. Bake at 325° for 20 minutes.

Mrs. W.C. Taylor

WHIPPED SHORTBREAD

2 cups soft butter
1 cups icing sugar

1/2 cup cornstarch
3 cups flour

Whip ingredients together with electric beater until it looks like stiff whipped cream. Drop by teaspoonful onto a cookie sheet. Bake at 325° for 20 minutes.

Mrs. G. Templeton

MY MOTHER'S SHORTBREAD

2 cups butter
1 cup berry sugar

1 tsp. vanilla
3 1/2 cups flour

Cream butter until very light. Add sugar and flavoring. Gradually add flour. Knead well. Divide the dough into three parts. Roll out to fit a pie plate. Pinch the edges and prick through with a fork all over. Bake until golden brown at 275° to 300°. Cut in pie-shaped wedges with a sharp knife immediately on removing from oven.

Elizabeth Pedersen

SCOTCH SHORTBREAD

2 1/2 cups flour
1/3 cups sugar, half brown
   and half white

1/2 tsp. salt
1 cup butter

Mix ingredients like pastry and press smoothly into a glass 9 x 13-inch pan. Prick with fork, bake at 350° for 35 to 40 minutes or until golden brown. Cut while hot.

Mrs. Adelaide G. Adie

ALMOND SHORTBREAD WEDGES

1/3 cup butter
1/4 cup sugar
1/2 tsp. almond extract

1 1/2 cups flour
2 tsp. sugar
Pinch of nutmeg

Microwave butter 10 to 15 seconds until softened. Blend in 1/4 cup sugar and almond extract. Mix in flour until crumbly and evenly mixed. Place a paper towel in an 8-inch round pan or pie plate, pressing into bottom and allowing edges to extend. Place crumb mixture in pan, press firmly and evenly in pan. Press edges with tines of a fork. Microwave uncovered for 2 minutes, turn half-way, microwave 1 to 2 minutes longer until shortbread has a dry, flaky appearance. Do not overcook as shortbread will harden on cooling. Cut into 16 wedges. Combine 2 tsp. sugar and nutmeg and sprinkle over shortbread. Lift from pan using edges of paper towel. Cool slightly. Remove from paper.

Elizabeth Durie

CHOCOLATE SHORTBREAD COOKIES

1 cup butter	1/2 tsp. baking powder
1 cup brown sugar	2 tbsp. instant coffee
2 cups flour	16 oz. chocolate chips
1/4 tsp. salt	

Cream butter until light, add brown sugar and cream thoroughly. Add flour and salt and mix well. Add baking powder, instant coffee and chocolate chips and mix well. Bake at 300° for 25 minutes in 10 x 15-inch pan. Slice when slightly cool.

Mrs. Dorothy James

QUICK SHORTBREAD

1/2 cup butter	Pinch of salt
1/2 cup icing sugar	1/2 tsp. vanilla extract
2 cups flour	1/2 tsp. almond extract

Cream butter and add sugar. Add flour, salt and flavorings. Mix with electric beater. Drop onto cookie sheet. Top with a cherry or walnut. Bake at 225° to 250° for 20 to 30 minutes.

Esther Richards

WALNUT CRESCENTS

6 egg yolks	6 egg whites
1 cup cream	2 cups icing sugar
1 cup butter	2 cups finely-chopped walnuts
4 cups flour	

Beat egg yolks and add cream and butter. Work in flour. Mix well. Roll into small balls and put in refrigerator overnight. Next day, beat egg whites and add icing sugar and walnuts. Roll out each ball and fill crescents with mixture. Roll up and shape into a crescent. Bake at 325° for 20 to 25 minutes.

NELLIE'S FILLED COOKIES

1 cup brown sugar	3 cups flour
1/2 cup butter **or** shortening	1 tsp. soda
1/2 cup sour milk	1 tbsp. molasses

Mix in order given and roll out. Cut in squares or rounds. Bake at 350° for 12 to 15 minutes. When done, these can be filled with dates or figs cooked with 1 tbsp. of sugar to about 1 lb. of fruit.

Mrs. Melvin Morris

The secret of a fine grained, flaky shortbread is thorough kneading.

NOTHINGS

3 eggs
2 tbsp. heavy cream
1/4 cup sugar
3 cups flour, approximately
1 1/2 tbsp. melted shortening

1 tbsp. brandy flavoring
1/2 tsp. salt
1/2 tsp. ground cardamon seed
   (optional)

Beat eggs thoroughly with cream and sugar. Add 2 cups of flour, shortening, flavoring, salt and cardamon seeds. Mix well. Stir in enough flour to make a stiff dough. Wrap in wax paper, refrigerate for 1 hour or longer. Heat 2 inches fat or oil. On lightly floured surface, roll half of dough until paper thin. Cut into 3-inch diamonds. Cut a slit and pull ends through. Fry in oil to a delicate brown. Cool. Dust with powdered sugar.

ANGEL WINGS

6 egg yolks
1 tsp. sugar
1 tsp. salt

1 cup flour
1/2 tsp. vanilla
1 tbsp. rum flavoring

Beat egg yolks, sugar and salt until fluffy. Add remaining ingredients and blend well. Let mixture sit in covered bowl for 2 hours. Then roll to 1/8-inch thick. Cut in triangles, slit and fold. Fry in hot fat (375°) for 1/2 minute or until light brown.

Mrs. F. Geachetta

NUT COOKIES

1 cup butter
1 1/2 cups brown sugar
2 eggs
1 cup raisins
1/2 cup chopped walnuts
2 cups flour

1 tsp. cinnamon
1/2 tsp. cloves
1/2 tsp. nutmeg
1 tsp. salt
1/3 cup hot water to which
   2 tsp. soda is added

Cream butter and brown sugar. Add eggs and mix well. Add remaining ingredients and mix well. Drop by teaspoonful onto cookie sheet. Bake at 350° for 10 to 12 minutes until golden brown.

Mrs. A.E. Kett

OATMEAL CRISPIES

1 cup shortening
1 cup white sugar
1 cup brown sugar
2 eggs, beaten
1 tsp. vanilla
1 1/2 cups flour

1 tsp. salt
1 tsp. soda
3 cups rolled oats
1 cup currants **or** raisins
1/2 cup chopped walnuts

Combine ingredients. Form in a roll and chill. Slice and bake at 375° for 10 to 15 minutes until brown.

Mrs. Dick Northcott

PRECIOUS MOMENTS

1/2 pint whipping cream
26 large marshmallows
12 single graham wafers,
   finely crushed

1/2 cup crushed walnuts
1/2 cup fine coconut

Fold marshmallows carefully into whipped cream. Put in refrigerator overnight. In morning, combine wafers, walnuts and coconut. Lift out marshmallows one at a time and roll in coating mix.

Helene Busk

ORANGE ALMOND CRISP

1 cup shortening
1/2 cup brown sugar
1/2 cup white sugar
1 egg, beaten
23/4 cups flour

1/2 tsp. soda
2 tbsp. orange juice
1 tbsp. grated orange rind
1/2 cup chopped almonds

Cream shortening and sugars and add egg. Sift flour and soda together and add alternately with orange juice. Add orange rind and nuts. Blend well. Shape into 2 smooth rolls. Roll in wax paper and chill for several hours or overnight. Slice very thin and place on greased cookie sheet. Bake at 370° for 8 to 10 minutes or until lightly brown.

Mrs. Hazel Howie

RANGER COOKIES

1/2 cup margarine
1/2 cup brown sugar
1/2 cup white sugar
1 egg, beaten
1/2 tsp. vanilla
1 cup flour

1/2 tsp. baking powder
1/2 tsp. soda
1/4 tsp. salt
1 cup rice krispies
1/2 cup coconut
1 cup rolled oats

Mix ingredients together. Drop by teaspoonful onto cookie sheet. Flatten with fork. Bake at 350° for 10 minutes.

POP NEWMAN'S COOKIES

11/2 cups flour
1 cup brown sugar
1 tsp. baking powder
11/2 cups rolled oats
1 cup white sugar

1 tsp. soda
1/2 tsp. salt
1 cup vegetable shortening
2 eggs, beaten

Blend dry ingredients. Work in softened shortening as for shortbread. Add eggs and mix. Drop by teaspoon on greased cookie sheet or chill and roll into balls to produce an even shape. Bake at 375° for 10 to 12 minutes until brown. NOTE: Do not substitute butter for shortening.

Margaret Paul

ORIENTAL TREASURES

1 2/3 cups flour
1 1/2 tsp. baking powder
1/2 tsp. soda
1/2 cup packed yellow sugar
1/2 cup white sugar
1/2 cup shortening

1 egg
1 tbsp. soya sauce
1/2 tsp. almond flavoring
1/2 cup slivered almonds
1 tsp. granulated sugar
1/2 tsp. soya sauce

Sift together flour, baking powder and soda. Cream the sugars and shortening together. Add to flour mixture and add egg, soya sauce and flavoring. Mix thoroughly, shape into small balls and dip in a mixture of almonds, white sugar and soya sauce. Bake on ungreased cookie sheet about 2 inches apart. Bake at 350 to 375° for 12 to 15 minutes.

Mrs. Emogene Guest

OLIEBOLLEN OR DEEP FRIED FRUIT BALLS

1 env. active dry yeast
3 tbsp. sugar
1/2 cup lukewarm milk, scalded
2 eggs, well beaten
1 1/2 cups lukewarm milk

1/2 tsp. vanilla
1 tsp. salt
4 cups flour
2 cups seedless raisins
3 apples, peeled and diced

Soak together yeast, sugar and the 1/2 cup lukewarm milk for 10 minutes. Mix this with eggs, 1 1/2 cups milk, vanilla and salt. Beat in flour gradually. Add raisins and apples. Cover bowl and let rise 1 1/2 hours. Drop by heaping teaspoonful into hot cooking oil. Turn if necessary. Some balls will turn by themselves when cooking. Remove from oil with a straining spoon. Sprinkle with icing sugar while still hot. Serve hot or cold. Yield: 5 dozen.

Mrs. M. Engler

PEANUT CHEWS

1 cup corn syrup
1/2 cup sugar
1 tsp. vanilla
1 cup peanut butter
2 cups rice krispies

2 cups cornflakes
1 cup peanuts, chopped
3 sq. unsweetened chocolate
1 tbsp. butter

Mix corn syrup, sugar, vanilla and peanut butter over low heat until dissolved. Remove from heat. Add rice krispies, cornflakes and peanuts. Mix all together and press in pan. Melt 3 squares of semi-sweet chocolate and 1 tbsp. butter and spread on top.

Dorothy Kuehn
Mrs. Lucelle DeKeyser

RAISIN COOKIES

1 1/2 cups seedless raisins	1/4 cup packed brown sugar
1/4 cup apple juice	2 tbsp. soft butter
2/3 cup flour	1 egg
1 tsp. baking soda	2 cups pecans **or** walnuts
3/4 tsp. cinnamon	4 oz. candied cherries,
1/4 tsp. cloves	quartered

Soak raisins in apple juice for 1 hour. Drain. Sift flour, soda and spices. Cream sugar, butter and egg until fluffy. Add dry ingredients, mixing well. Stir in drained raisins, nuts and cherries. Drop by teaspoonful onto cookie sheets. Bake at 325° for about 12 minutes. When cool, store in airtight container. Yield: 4 dozen cookies.

Mrs. Lois Dunford

SURPRISE RAISIN DROPS

1 cup soft butter **or**	1 tsp. salt
1/2 shortening and butter	1 cup raisins
2 cups packed brown sugar	1/2 cup water
3 eggs	1/2 cup white sugar
1 tsp. vanilla	1 tbsp. cornstarch
3 cups flour	1 tbsp. lemon juice
1 tsp. soda	1 tbsp. butter

Cream butter, brown sugar and eggs. Add vanilla. Sift flour, soda and salt. Blend into mixture. For the filling, cook raisins in water and add white sugar and cornstarch. Remove from heat and add lemon juice and butter. Drop cookies on cookie sheet. Put a small amount of filling on and top with more batter. Bake at 350° for 12 to 15 minutes.

Mrs. Katherine Towers

RAISIN DROPS

1 cup butter	2 cups flour
1 1/4 cups brown sugar	Pinch of salt
2 eggs	2 tsp. baking powder
1 tsp. vanilla	1/2 cup walnuts
1/4 tsp. almond extract	1 cup raisins

Mix in order given. Drop on greased cookie sheet and bake at 375° for 12 to 15 minutes.

Opened packages of prunes, raisins, dates, figs, grated coconut and ground coffee will maintain freshness when frozen. Marshmallows don't dry out and are less sticky to use. Potato chips remain crisp.

LENTIL PUREE

4 cup lentils   10 cups water

Wash lentils, add water and bring to boil. Reduce heat and simmer about 45 to 50 minutes until very tender. Drain and puree, using stock to blend with lentils if needed. Freeze in 1 cup quantities.

OATMEAL LENTIL CHIP COOKIES

1 cup margarine	1 1/2 cups flour
1 cup brown sugar	1 cups rolled oats
1/2 cup *Lentil Puree*	1 tsp. baking soda
1 tsp. vanilla	1 tsp. salt
2 eggs, beaten	2 cups chocolate chips

Cream margarine, sugar and puree. Stir in vanilla and eggs. Combine dry ingredients and stir in. Add chocolate chips. Drop from spoon onto greased cookie sheet. Bake at 375° for 12 to 14 minutes.

LENTIL SPICE COOKIES

1/2 cup margarine	1/4 tsp. nutmeg
1 cup sugar	1/4 tsp. ginger
2 eggs	1 cup raisins
1 cup *Lentil Puree*	1 cup chopped nuts
2 cups flour	1/2 cup icing sugar
1 tsp. salt	1/2 tbsp. lemon juice
2 tsp. baking powder	1/2 tsp. lemon rind
1 tsp. cinnamon	

Cream margarine, add sugar and beat well. Add eggs and the puree. Combine dry ingredients, add, and fold in raisins and nuts. Bake at 350° for 15 minutes. Combine icing sugar, lemon juice and rind and drizzle over baked cookies.

REFRIGERATOR FRUIT AND NUTS COOKIES

1 cup brown sugar	3 tbsp. hot water
1 cup white sugar	1 cup chopped dates
1 cup shortening	1 cup chopped nuts **or** walnuts
3 eggs, well beaten	3 cups flour
1 tsp. vanilla	1 tsp. salt
1 tsp. soda	

Cream sugar and shortening together. Add the eggs, vanilla and soda mixed with hot water. Stir well. Add dates and nuts. Sift flour and salt together, add and knead until blended. Form into rolls. Chill for several hours, slice thinly and bake at 400° for 10 to 15 minutes.

Alice Laurin

RICE KRISPIE BALLS

1/2 can sweetened condensed milk	1 1/2 large toffee bars
1/2 cup butter	1 lb. large marshmallows
	Bowl of rice krispies

Melt milk, butter and toffee together in a double boiler. Stir until thick. When thick, using a fork, dip a large marshmallow into the mixture. Then roll in rice krispies. Will keep indefinitely in refrigerator or freezer.

Isabell Turnbull

SESAME CRISPS

1 cup margarine	1/2 tsp. baking soda
1 cup sugar	1/2 tsp. salt
1 egg yolk	1 cup cornflake crumbs
1 tsp. vanilla	1/4 cup sesame seeds
2 cups flour	

Cream margarine and sugar. Add egg yolk and vanilla and beat well. Combine cornflake crumbs and seeds and add, reserving 1/4 cup. Roll cookies in remaining crumbs and seeds. Bake at 275° until brown.

Mrs. Betty Norris

SKILLET COOKIES

2 tbsp. butter	2 eggs
1 cup finely-cut dates	1 tsp. vanilla
1 cup sugar	3 cups puffed rice
1/8 tsp. salt	3/4 cup walnut pieces

Melt butter. Add dates, sugar, salt and eggs. Cook over low heat, stirring constantly until mixture is quite thick. Remove from heat, add vanilla and cool slightly. Stir in rice and nuts. Sprinkle 2 sheets of waxed paper with icing sugar or toasted coconut. Make mixture into 2 rolls 2 inches in diameter. Place a roll on each sheet, wrap and chill well before slicing.

SPANISH PEANUT COOKIES

1 cup white sugar	2 tsp. baking powder
1 cup brown sugar	1/2 tsp. soda
1 cup margarine	2 cups Spanish peanuts
2 eggs, beaten	1 cup oatmeal
2 tsp. vanilla	2 cups cornflakes
2 cups flour	

Cream sugar and margarine. Add eggs and vanilla and beat well. Combine remaining ingredients and gradually add to first mixture. Mix well. Drop by teaspoonful onto greased cookie sheet. Bake at 350° about 12 to 15 minutes. Yield: 6 dozen cookies.

Ella Barnes

SPREAD AND CUT COOKIES

1/2 cup shortening
1/2 cup brown sugar
1/2 cup white sugar
2 eggs
1 tbsp. molasses
1/2 cup prepared mincemeat
1 cup flour

1 tsp. cinnamon
1 tsp. baking powder
1/4 tsp. soda
1 tsp. salt
1 cup rolled oats
1 cup chopped walnuts

Cream shortening and sugars. Add eggs and molasses and mix well. Blend in mincemeat. Add sifted dry ingredients, oatmeal and walnuts. Mix well. Bake in 9 x 12-inch pan at 350° until done. Cut while still warm.

Margaret Armstrong

SPICY ORANGE DIAMONDS

2/3 cup shortening
11/2 cups brown sugar
2 eggs
2 tbsp. grated orange rind
3 tbsp. orange juice
2 cups flour
1 tsp. soda

1/2 tsp. salt
1 tsp. cinnamon
1/2 tsp. nutmeg
1/2 tsp. cloves
1 cup seedless raisins
1 cup chopped walnuts

Cream shortening, sugar and eggs. Stir in orange rind and juice. Sift together flour, soda, salt and spices. Add to creamed mixture and mix well. Stir in raisins and walnuts. Spread in greased 9 x 12-inch pan. Bake at 350° for 30 minutes. Cool and cut in diamonds.

Margaret Armstrong

SPICE DROP COOKIES

11/2 cups sugar
1/2 cup lard **or** shortening
2 eggs
1/2 cup milk
3 cups flour
11/2 tsp. baking powder
1/8 tsp. salt
1/4 tsp. soda

1 tsp. cloves
2 tsp. cinnamon
1 tsp. allspice
1 cup raisins
1 cups nuts, optional
1 tsp. vanilla
Mixed fruit can be used also

Blend all ingredients thoroughly and drop with teaspoon on greased cookie sheet. Bake at 375° to 400° for 10 to 20 minutes.

Mrs. Rhoda Fossen

S'MORES

Place a piece of flat chocolate bar the size of a graham cracker on a graham cracker and top with a large marshmallow. Place under broiler until slightly toasted. Excellent dessert for unexpected company.

SOUR CREAM CHOCOLATE COOKIES

1/2 cup butter
1 cup brown sugar
1 egg, beaten
1 cup walnuts
2 sq. unsweetened chocolate,
   melted

2 cups flour
1/2 tsp. salt
1/2 tsp. baking soda
2 tsp. baking powder
1/2 tsp. cinnamon
1 cup sour cream

Mix ingredients in order given. Drop by teaspoonful onto cookie sheet. Bake at 375° for 15 minutes.

Mrs. R.C. Healing

SUGAR COOKIES

1 cup butter
1 cup sugar
2 eggs
1 tsp. lemon flavoring

1/4 cup milk
3 cups flour
2 tsp. cream of tartar
1 tsp. baking soda

Cream butter and sugar. Beat in eggs one at a time. Beat in flavoring and milk. Sift dry ingredients together and stir into mixture. Chill for a few hours. Roll into balls and place on buttered cookie sheet. Press the balls flat with the bottom of a glass that has been buttered and dipped in sugar. Bake at 350° for 10 to 12 minutes.

Mrs. Earle Murray

VALENTINE COOKIES

2 cups flour
1/2 tsp. salt
2 tsp. baking powder
1/2 tsp. ground mace
1 cup sugar

1 cup shortening
1 egg
1 tsp. grated orange rind
2 tbsp. orange juice

Sift flour, salt, baking powder and mace together. Cream sugar and shortening. Beat in egg. Add orange rind and juice. Gradually add flour mixture. Chill dough overnight. Divide into 4 parts. Roll each 1/8-inch thick on lightly-floured board. Cut with heart-shaped cutter and place on baking sheets. Bake at 375° for 8 to 10 minutes. Cool on rack. Decorate.

Mrs. George Friesen

CHEESE MOONS OR TURNOVERS

1/2 cup grated cheese **or**
   processed cheese spread
1/2 cup butter

1 cup flour
1 tbsp. milk **or** water
Crabapple jelly

Mix all ingredients but jelly like a pastry, roll out and cut into circles. Put jelly on and fold over. Pinch or press edges. Bake at 375° for 8 to 10 minutes.

Miss Elsa Maurer

CHOCOLATE DOTTED PEPPERMINT MERINGUES

2 egg whites	1/2 tsp. peppermint extract
1/8 tsp. salt	3/4 cup sugar
1/8 tsp. cream of tartar	6 oz. sweet chocolate chips

Beat egg whites, salt, cream of tartar and flavoring until soft peaks form. Add sugar gradually, beating until stiff peaks form. Set aside about 2 dozen chips and fold in remainder. Cover cookie sheet with plain brown paper. Drop mixture by teaspoonful onto paper and top each one with chocolate chip. Bake at 300° for 25 minutes or until done. Remove from paper while slightly warm.

Mrs. Beamish

CHOCOLATE CHEW

1 pkg. chocolate cake mix	1/3 cup water
1 cup chopped nuts	2 tbsp. oil
1 tsp. cinnamon	1 egg

Mix ingredients and drop by teaspoonful onto greased cookie sheet. Bake at 350° for 10 to 12 minutes.

PEANUT OAT CRISPS

1/2 cup flour	1/2 cup peanut butter
1 tsp. baking soda	2/3 cup brown sugar
1/2 tsp. salt	1/3 cup creamed honey
1/2 cup whole wheat flour	1 egg
1 cup rolled oats	1 tsp. vanilla
1/2 cup butter **or** margarine	Jam **or** jelly

Sift flour, soda and salt together. Stir in whole wheat flour and rolled oats. Set aside. Blend butter and peanut butter. Beat in sugar gradually and add the honey. Add egg and vanilla and blend well. Combine dry ingredients and mix well. Drop by small spoonful onto greased cookie sheet. Flatten with fork dipped in sugar. Make a hollow in center of each cookie. Bake at 350° for 5 minutes, then remove and place a little jam in the depression of each cookie. Bake another 5 minutes. Yield: 5 dozen. NOTE: For a different flavor, roll into a ball and roll in banana-flavored quick-mix drink powder. Flatten with fork and bake 8 to 10 minutes.

When making cookies with oatmeal, mix the shortening and oatmeal together first, then add other dry ingredients. A crisper cookie will result.

DESSERTS

FUDGE PUDDING WITH SAUCE

1 cup flour	1/2 cup milk
2 tsp. baking powder	2 tbsp. vegetable shortening
1/4 tsp. salt	1 cup walnuts, chopped
3/4 cup white sugar	2 cups hot water
2 tbsp. cocoa	1 cup packed brown sugar
2 tbsp. instant coffee	1 pint whipped cream

Mix flour, baking powder, salt and white sugar. Combine cocoa and coffee and add half to mixture. Add milk, shortening and walnuts. Spread in greased 8 x 8 x 2-inch cake pan or large casserole. Mix hot water, brown sugar and remaining coco-coffee mixture in bowl. Pour over cake pudding. Bake at 350° for about 45 minutes. Serve warm or cold with whipped cream. Yield: 8 to 12 servings.

Mrs. C.G. Winter

LEMON PUDDING BAKE

1 tbsp. butter	2 egg yolks
1 cup sugar	1 cup milk
2 tbsp. flour	2 egg whites, stiffly beaten
Juice and rind of 1 lemon	

Cream butter and sugar. Add flour, lemon juice and rind. Add egg yolks beaten with milk and mix well. Fold in egg whites and pour this mixture into greased mold. Place mold in a pan of water and bake at 325° for 30 to 45 minutes until meringue is lightly browned.

Mrs. Florence Fletcher

LEMON SNOW PUDDING

1 tbsp. gelatin	1/4 cup grated lemon rind
1/4 cup cold water	1/4 cup lemon juice
1/2 cup sugar	2 egg whites, stiffly beaten
3/4 cup hot water	

Soak gelatin in cold water for 10 minutes. Dissolve sugar in hot water and add lemon rind. Boil for 2 to 3 minutes. Pour hot liquid over softened gelatin. Stir well to dissolve gelatin. Add lemon juice. Chill until partly set. Beat until foamy, add egg whites and continue beating until mixture begins to thicken. Pour into molds rinsed with cold water, or pile lightly in serving dishes. Serve with custard sauce.

BAKED LEMON PUDDING

3 eggs, separated
1/4 tsp. salt
1 tbsp. non-caloric liquid
   sweetener

5 tbsp. flour
1/3 cup lemon juice
11/2 cups skim milk
2 tbsp. melted butter

Combine egg whites, salt and sweetener. Beat until moist firm peaks form. Combine yolks with remaining ingredients. Beat until smooth. Gradually fold egg yolk mixture into whites. Pour into greased 11/2-qt. casserole. Set in pan of hot water and bake at 350° for 40 to 50 minutes. Let casserole cool in pan of water to keep pudding from shrinking. Yield: 6 servings. 110 calories per serving.

ANNAPOLIS VALLEY APPLE PUDDING

6 medium apples, sliced
3 tbsp. sugar
1/4 cup soft shortening
3/4 cup sugar
1 egg, well beaten
11/2 cups flour

3 tsp. baking powder
1/2 tsp. salt
3/4 cup milk
1 tbsp. sugar
1 tsp. cinnamon

Grease a 10 x 6 x 2-inch baking dish. Arrange apples in bottom of baking dish. Sprinkle with 3 tbsp. sugar. Cream shortening until fluffy. Gradually add 3/4 cup sugar, mixing until creamy. Add egg and beat well. Sift flour, baking powder and salt and add alternately with milk, folding in lightly after each addition. Pour over apples and sprinkle with combined 1 tbsp. sugar and cinnamon. Bake at 350° for 40 to 50 minutes. Serve warm, with cream.

E. Alwood

SELF-SAUCING PUMPKIN PUDDING

1/2 cup butter
11/3 cup brown sugar
1 egg
2/3 cup cooked mashed pumpkin
1 cup flour
2 tsp. baking powder
1/2 tsp. cinnamon

1/8 tsp. cloves
1/2 tsp. salt
1/4 tsp. nutmeg
1/2 cup raisins (optional)
1 tbsp. butter **or** margarine
12/3 cups boiling water
1/2 cup orange juice

Cream butter. Add 1/3 cup sugar and beat in egg. Add the pumpkin. Stir the dry ingredients together and add to pumpkin mixture. Spread in buttered casserole. Add raisins, making sure there is enough room for sauce. Sprinkle with remaining sugar and dot with butter. Mix boiling water and orange juice and pour over top. Bake at 350° for 1 hour.

Jean Leskow

RHUBARB PUDDING

1/2 cup brown sugar
4 cups diced rhubarb
3/4 cup white sugar
1 egg, well beaten
1/2 cup white sugar
2 tbsp. cooking oil

1/4 cup milk
1 cup flour
1 tsp. baking powder
1/4 tsp. salt
1/2 tsp. vanilla

Grease baking dish. Cover the bottom with the brown sugar. Add rhubarb and sprinkle 3/4 cup white sugar over rhubarb. Combine egg, 1/2 cup sugar, cooking oil, milk, flour, baking powder and salt. Mix well and add vanilla. Pour this mixture over rhubarb. Bake at 375° until done. Serve with whipped cream.

INDIAN PUDDING

6 cups milk
1/2 cup yellow cornmeal
3/4 cup molasses
6 tbsp. sugar

3/4 tsp. salt
11/2 tsp. ginger
Fresh cream, whipped cream
or ice cream

Scald 4 cups milk in top of double boiler. Mix cornmeal with 1/2 cup milk and slowly stir into scalded milk. Cook uncovered, stirring occasionally for about 20 minutes. Add molasses, sugar, salt and ginger, mixing well. Pour into buttered shallow 11/2-qt. baking dish and bake at 325° for 1 hour. Stir in remaining milk and bake about 11/2 hours longer. Serve warm with the fresh cream.

CUSTARD PUDDING

2 tbsp. sugar
1 tsp. flour
1/8 tsp. salt

2 egg yolks, slightly beaten
11/2 cups milk
1/2 tsp. vanilla

Mix sugar, flour and salt. Add egg yolks to milk and add to sugar mixture. Cook over hot water, stirring constantly, until mixture coats a spoon. Add vanilla. Yield: 4 servings.

SUETLESS STEAMED PUDDING

1 cup sugar
2 eggs
1/4 cup butter
1 cup buttermilk
2 cups flour
1 tsp. soda

1/2 tsp. baking powder
1 tsp. cinnamon
1/2 cup molasses
1 cup raisins
1/4 cup dates
1/2 cup nuts

Combine ingredients and steam for 3 hours.

Mrs. Jack McLay

SWEETHEART PUDDING

1 cup flour	1 cup raisins
4 tsp. baking powder	1/2 cup chopped walnuts
1/4 tsp. salt	2 cups water
1/2 cup milk	2 tbsp. butter
2 cups brown sugar	

Sift flour, baking powder and salt into 1 1/2-qt. casserole. Stir in milk. Combine and add 1 cup brown sugar, raisins and nuts and spread in casserole. Boil remaining brown sugar and water for 10 minutes. Add butter. Pour over batter, but do not stir. Bake at 350° for 40 minutes. Yield: 6 to 8 servings. Serve plain or with cream.

Connie Hastings
Mrs. P. Lamoureux
Mrs. Rita Doucet

TAPIOCA BUTTERSCOTCH PUDDING
(Old fashioned)

2 egg whites	2 1/4 cups milk
4 tbsp. brown sugar	3 tbsp. tapioca
1/4 cup butter	1/8 tsp. salt
1/3 cup packed brown sugar	1/2 tsp. vanilla
2 egg yolks	1/3 cup pecans, cut lengthwise

Beat egg whites until foamy. Add 4 tbsp. brown sugar, 1 tbsp. at a time and continue beating until mixture stands in soft peaks. Set aside. Melt butter in saucepan. Add 1/3 cup brown sugar and cook until dissolved. Mix egg yolks with small amount of milk in saucepan. Add tapioca, salt and remaining milk. Cook, stirring over medium heat until it comes to a boil. Remove from heat. Add brown sugar mixture and vanilla. Pour into 1-qt. casserole. Pile meringue lightly on top of tapioca mixture. Sprinkle with pecans. Bake at 375° for 15 minutes or until golden brown. Yield: 6 servings.

Pelican Unifarm Local

To soften dried fruit, sprinkle water over fruit, cover and microwave 1 to 2 minutes.

For a quick microwaved pudding, select your favorite 4-serving size pudding and pie filling mix. In a 4-cup glass measure, pour in milk as directed on package. Stir in pudding mix until dissolved. Microwave uncovered for 5 minutes or until mixture starts to boil, stirring twice during last 2 minutes. Pour into a dish and cool.

WASHINGTON PUDDING

1 cup brown sugar	2 cups hot water
2 tbsp. butter	1/4 tsp. salt

Combine ingredients in a large, heavy saucepan with a tight cover.

1/2 cup sugar	2 tbsp. butter
1/2 cup milk	2 tbsp. cocoa
1 cup flour	1 tsp. cinnamon
1/2 cup dates **or** 1 cup raisins	2 tsp. baking powder

Mix ingredients together and make a batter. Drop by spoonful into the hot brown sugar sauce. Cook for 35 minutes. Serve hot or cold.

Bernice Thompson

"GRAND PERES"

1 1/2 cups flour	2 eggs, well beaten
3 tsp. baking powder	1/3 cup milk
1/2 tsp. salt	2 cups maple syrup

Measure dry ingredients, mixing well. Add eggs and milk. Do not overmix. Drop by teaspoonful into hot boiling syrup and cook until done. Add more syrup if desired.

VEGETABLE FRUIT PUDDING

1 cup flour	1 cup raisins
1/4 tsp. nutmeg	1/2 cup chopped walnuts
1/4 tsp. salt	1 cup finely-grated potatoes
1/4 tsp. allspice	1 cup finely-grated carrots
1 tsp. cinnamon	2 tbsp. lemon rind
2 tbsp. baking powder	1 tsp. lemon juice
1 1/2 cups sugar	2 tbsp. melted butter

Sift dry ingredients together. Add remaining ingredients. Mix well. Pour into well-greased mold and steam for 2 1/2 hours.

CARROT PUDDING

1 cup shortening	2 tsp. baking powder
1 cup brown sugar	1 tsp. salt
2 eggs	1 tsp. cinnamon
2 cups cooked carrots	1 tsp. nutmeg
1 cup raisins	1 tsp. soda dissolved in
1 cup currants	2 tsp. water
2 1/2 cups flour	

Blend shortening, sugar and eggs. Put carrots through dicer and add. Mix. Add raisins and currants. Mix well. Sift flour, baking powder and spices and add to mixture, stirring thoroughly. Add dissolved soda. Bake at 350° to 375° for 2 hours or steam in sealers for 3 hours. Keeps well.

Mrs. Dorothy Cameron

STEAMED CARROT PUDDING

1 cup flour	1 cup grated raw carrots
1 cup rolled oats	1 cup grated raw potatoes
1 cup brown sugar	1 cup chopped raisins
1/2 tsp. cinnamon	1/2 cup mixed candied fruit
1/2 tsp. allspice	1/4 cup candied orange peel
1/2 tsp. nutmeg	(optional)
1/2 tsp. ginger	3/4 cup nuts, chopped
1/2 tsp. salt	1/2 cup melted margarine
1 tsp. soda	1/2 cup fruit juice, if required

Combine first 9 ingredients thoroughly. Combine raisins, candied fruit and nuts with grated vegetables. Add the margarine and fruit juice. Fold in dry ingredients. Transfer batter to an 8-cup glass or china tube mold or a deep straight-sided souffle casserole with a small tumbler placed in the center. Cover with wax paper. Microwave at full power for 9 to 10 minutes or until a cake tester comes out clean when inserted in the center. Pudding dish should be turned twice during the baking period after about 3 and 6 minutes of baking. Allow pudding to stand about 20 minutes before unmolding. To simplify unmolding, oil mold and line with plastic wrap. Serve with the following nutmeg sauce.

1/4 cup brown sugar	1 cup hot water
1 tbsp. cornstarch	1 tsp. vanilla **or** 2 tbsp. rum
1/2 tsp. nutmeg	**or** brandy
1/4 cup melted margarine	

Combine sugar, cornstarch and nutmeg in a 4-cup measure. Stir in butter. Add water. Microwave uncovered 2 to 3 minutes or until thickened. Stir. Add flavoring. Serve warm.

Elizabeth Durie

FAMILY PLUM PUDDING

1 cup currants	1/8 tsp. ginger
3/4 cup chopped figs	1/4 tsp. cloves
1/3 cup chopped orange peel	1 cup dry bread crumbs
1/3 cup chopped citron	1 cup hot milk
1 1/4 cups seeded raisins	1/2 cup sugar
3/4 cup flour	4 eggs, separated
1 1/2 tsp. salt	2 cups chopped suet
1 tsp. nutmeg	1/2 cup apple juice
1/4 tsp. cinnamon	

Prepare fruits. Combine flour, salt and spices. Sift twice. Add fruit. Soak bread crumbs in hot milk for 10 minutes. Add sugar to egg yolks and beat until well blended. Add suet to soaked crumbs. Stir in flour mixture along with apple juice. Fold in stiffly beaten egg whites. Grease a 2-qt. mold, fill 3/4 with pudding. Cover with aluminum foil and tie down. Steam for 4 hours. Yield: 14 servings.

PLUM PUDDING

2 cups bread crumbs
1/2 cup milk
1 1/4 cups brown sugar
1/2 tsp. salt
6 eggs, well beaten
1 cup flour
1 tsp. baking powder
1/2 tsp. cinnamon
1/2 tsp. cloves

1/2 tsp. allspice
2 1/2 cups suet
1 cup mixed fruit
1 cup glaze cherries
6 cups raisins
1 grated carrot
1 whole lemon
1/4 cup fruit juice

Soak crumbs in milk. Add sugar, salt and eggs. Sift dry ingredients, add suet and combine with crumb mixture. Add fruit, carrot, lemon and juice. Pack into 4 well-greased 1-lb. pudding molds. Cover tightly and steam for 4 hours. To reheat for serving, steam for 2 hours.

Clare Johnston

UPSIDE-DOWN DATE PUDDING

1 cup pitted dates, cut up
1 cup boiling water
2 cups packed brown sugar
3 tbsp. butter **or** margarine
1/2 cup white sugar
1 egg

1 1/2 cups flour
1 tsp. baking soda
1/2 tsp. baking powder
1/2 tsp. salt
1 cup chopped nuts
1 1/2 cups boiling water

Combine dates with boiling water until soft. Cool. In bowl beat 1/2 cup brown sugar, 1 tbsp. butter, granulated sugar and egg. Sift flour, baking soda, baking powder and salt together. Stir into sugar mixture alternately with the date and water mixture. Add chopped nuts. Pour into 2-qt. baking dish. Mix the remaining brown sugar, remaining butter and 1 1/2 cups boiling water and pour over batter. Bake at 375° for 40 minutes. Serve warm and cut in squares with sauce spooned over top. Yield: 8 servings.

STEAMED DATE PUDDING

2/3 cup soft bread crumbs
2/3 cup sugar
2/3 cup milk
1 egg, beaten
2/3 cup suet **or**
    1/2 cup butter

2/3 cup flour
2 tsp. baking powder
1/4 tsp. salt
2/3 cup chopped dates
1 tsp. vanilla

Mix ingredients in order given and steam 3 hours. Very good served with lemon or vanilla sauce or thin cream.

Mrs. W.J. Edmunds

POOR MAN'S PUDDING

1 cup flour
1/2 tsp. soda
1/2 tsp. cinnamon
1/2 tsp. ginger
1/2 tsp. allspice
1/2 tsp. salt
1/4 cup molasses
1/2 cup sweet milk
1/2 cup raisins

Sift flour, soda, cinnamon, ginger, allspice and salt together. Add molasses, milk and raisins. Steam for 3 hours. Serve warm with cream.

OLD FASHIONED RICE PUDDING

1/2 cup uncooked rice
1/2 cup sugar
1/2 tsp. salt
1/2 tsp. nutmeg
3/4 cup washed raisins
3 eggs, well beaten
8 cups milk
1 tsp. butter
Cream (optional)

Mix rice, sugar, salt, nutmeg, raisins and eggs in a buttered shallow 2 1/2-qt. baking dish. Add milk. Drop bits of butter over milk. Bake at 325°, for 2 hours, stirring occasionally during first hour. Allow crust to form on pudding. Serve warm or cold with cream if desired. Yield: 8 servings. NOTE: To reduce baking time, cook rice 10 to 15 minutes in milk in top of double boiler before baking.

QUICK RICE PUDDING

3 cups milk
1/2 cup instant rice
3-oz. pkg. vanilla pudding
    and pie mix
3 tbsp. raisins
1/4 tsp. cinnamon

In 2-qt. bowl, combine all ingredients. Microwave covered on Medium for 11 to 12 minutes until pudding is thickened, stirring 3 times. Chill before serving. Variations: Use 1 tbsp. orange liqueur and 1/4 cup chopped candied fruit instead of raisins and cinnamon.

Florence Trautman

RICE AND PINEAPPLE PUDDING

1/3 cup rice
3/4 tsp. salt
2 tbsp. sugar
1/2 cup pineapple syrup
2 cups milk
1 cup crushed pineapple
1 cup heavy cream, whipped

Cook rice, salt, sugar and syrup. Slowly add milk. Cook uncovered over low heat, stirring occasionally with a fork for 30 minutes or until rice is tender and mixture is thick like a pudding. Remove from heat and cool. When cold, add drained pineapple and whipped cream.

Mrs. Bill Driscoll

CHERRY BREAD PUDDING

21/2 cups day-old bread crumbs
1 cup tart pitted cherries
2 cups milk
1/2 cup sugar
1/4 tsp. salt
2 egg yolks, slightly beaten

1 tsp. vanilla
2 egg whites
1/4 tsp. cream of tartar
Dash of salt
1/4 cup sugar

Combine bread crumbs and well-drained cherries. Mix milk, 1/2 cup sugar, 1/4 tsp. salt, egg yolks and vanilla and stir into bread crumb mixture. Pour into 10 x 6 x 2-inch baking dish. Bake at 350° for 35 to 40 minutes. Cool. Beat egg whites with cream of tartar and dash of salt until stiff peaks form. Gradually beat in 1/4 cup sugar. Spread over pudding. Bake at 350° for 10 to 25 minutes or until brown.

Mrs. Gordon Cannard

CHOCOLATE BREAD PUDDING

11/4 cups crushed bread crumbs
2 tbsp. butter **or** margarine
1/2 cup sugar
1 tbsp. unsweetened chocolate, melted
1/4 tsp. salt
2 cups scalded milk

2 eggs
1 tsp. vanilla
1/2 cup raisins
1/2 cup flaked coconut
3 tbsp. jam **or** jelly
12 marshmallows

Combine crumbs, butter, sugar, chocolate and salt in bowl. Cover with milk. Stir and set aside to cool. Beat eggs and vanilla until fluffy. Add to bread mixture. Stir in raisins and coconut. Pour into buttered shallow 11/2-qt. baking dish. Bake at 350° for 45 minutes. Remove from oven. Spread with thin layer of jam or jelly. Arrange marshmallows on top. Return to oven for 10 to 15 minutes until marshmallows are melted. Serve warm. Yield: 6 servings.

CHRISTMAS PUDDING

1 lb. shredded suet
2 tsp. salt
3 cups flour
1/4 cup molasses
Juice and rind of 2 lemons
23/4 cups sultana raisins
1/3 cup chopped almonds
11/2 tsp. nutmeg
1 tsp. almond flavoring
11/4 cups water

2 cups sugar
6 eggs
11/4 cups bread crumbs
1/2 tsp. soda
21/2 cups currants
21/2 cups mixed peel
1 cup glazed cherries
1 tsp. mixed spices
1 tsp. vanilla

Combine ingredients and let stand overnight to ripen. Steam for 2 hours before serving.

Mrs. Bertha Webber

MARY'S CHRISTMAS PUDDING

1 1/4 cups flour	1/4 tsp. cinnamon
1/4 tsp. nutmeg	1/4 tsp. mace
1/4 tsp. cloves	1/2 tsp. salt
2 1/2 cups bread crumbs	3/4 cup shredded suet
1 1/2 cups brown sugar	1 cup sultana raisins
3/4 cup seeded raisins	1 cup seedless raisins
1 cup currants	1 1/2 cups mixed peel
3/4 cup almonds	1 cup glaze cherries, halved
1/2 cup strained honey	4 eggs, well beaten
1/2 cup fruit juice, wine **or** brandy	1/2 - 2/3 cup milk

The amount of milk added depends upon the staleness of crumbs. Mix ingredients in order given. Fill jars 2/3 full and steam for 5 hours. Leave lids very loose. To reheat for serving, steam for 2 hours.

1 tbsp. flour	2 tbsp. butter
1 1/2 cups brown sugar	1 tsp. vanilla
1 1/2 cups boiling water	

Mix flour and sugar thoroughly. Add to boiling water. When thick, add butter and vanilla. Serve over pudding.

Mrs. Mary Gordon

EGG CUSTARD

1 cup milk	1/2 cup honey **or** 1/3 cup sugar
4 eggs	Nutmeg
1 tsp. salt	

Beat slightly to blend milk, eggs, salt and honey. Pour into custard baking dishes. Sprinkle tops with nutmeg. Bake at 325° until blade of knife comes out clean when inserted in custard center.

GRAHAM CUSTARD DESSERT

4 cups graham wafer crumbs	1 cup sugar
2 cups brown sugar	4 cups milk
1/2 tsp. nutmeg	4 egg yolks
3/4 cup melted butter	1 tsp. vanilla
6 tbsp. cornstarch	4 egg whites

Mix crumbs with brown sugar, nutmeg and melted butter to moisten crumbs. Save about 3 tbsp. of this crumb mixture to sprinkle on top of meringue. Press crumbs into a 9 x 9-inch pan or pie plate. Dissolve cornstarch and sugar in 1/2 cup milk. Beat egg yolks and add. Add vanilla and combine with remaining milk in double boiler. Stir until thick. Pour on top of crumb mixture. Beat egg whites until stiff and pile of top of filling. Sprinkle with remainding crumb mixture. Bake at 350° for 30 to 35 minutes until brown.

Mrs. Marlene Erickson

MICROWAVE BAKED CUSTARD

13/4 cup milk   1/4 tsp. salt
1/4 cup sugar   1/2 tsp. vanilla
3 eggs   Nutmeg **or** cinnamon

Combine all ingredients except nutmeg in 4-cup measure. Beat well with rotary beater. Pour into 6-oz glass custard cups. Sprinkle with nutmeg or cinnamon. Microwave on Defrost for 15 to 16 minutes or until knife inserted in center comes out clean. Let stand 5 minutes before serving. Cups should be rotated every 5 minutes for even cooking. VARIATION: If diet is sugar restricted, substitute 11/2 tsp. non-calorie sweetener for sugar. Nutrasweet will break down during cooking.

Mildred Hitesman

PUMPKIN CUSTARD

2 cups canned pumpkin   1 tsp. ginger
1 cup brown sugar   1 tsp. nutmeg
1 tbsp. flour   2 tbsp. butter **or** margarine
1/8 tsp. salt   11/2 cups milk
1 tsp. cinnamon   4 eggs, slightly beaten

Mix pumpkin, brown sugar, flour and salt. Add spices, butter and milk. Cook and stir 5 minutes. Cool slightly and pour over eggs. Pour into well-buttered 11/2-qt. casserole. Place in pan of hot water in oven and bake at 350° for 1 hour or until custard is set.

1 cup cream   1/4 cup confectioners sugar
1/4 cup chopped preserved ginger 1 tsp. vanilla

Whip cream. Mix ginger, sugar and vanilla into whipped cream and serve over custard. Yield: 6 servings.

VELVET CUSTARD

1/2 cup sugar   3 eggs, well beaten
Pinch of salt   2 cups scalded milk
2 tsp. vanilla

Add sugar, salt and vanilla to eggs and beat. Add milk and mix slowly . Pour into pyrex dish. Set in pan of hot water and bake at 350° for 25 to 30 minutes until knife inserted in center comes out clean.

Mrs. Luella Callies

TRIFLE

1 stale cake, cut into squares   1 custard recipe
6-oz. pkg. jelly powder   Whipping cream
2 cups boiling water

Line serving dish with stale cake. Dissolve a package of any flavored jelly powder in 1 pint boiling water. Let cool. Pour over cake and allow to jell. Cover with a layer of thin custard. Top with whipped cream.

SWISS ALMOND APPLE TORTE

1 cup flour	Almonds
1/3 cup sugar	3/4 cup sour cream **or** yogurt
1/2 cup butter	1/2 cup sugar
4 apples **or** other fruit	2 eggs, beaten
2 tbsp. sugar	2 tbsp. flour
1 tsp. cinnamon	1 tsp. lemon rind

Combine 1 cup flour and 1/3 cup sugar in medium bowl. Cut in butter until crumbly. Press into bottom and sides of 10-inch spring form pan. Peel and slice the fruit and toss with sugar and cinnamon. Arrange over the crust. Sprinkle almonds over filling. Combine the cream, sugar, eggs, 2 tbsp. flour and lemon rind in medium bowl and mix well. Pour evenly over apples. Bake at 450° for 10 minutes. Reduce temperature to 400° and cook for 40 to 50 minutes until fruit is tender. Serve warm or cold.

Ineke Bottier

CHERRY MERINGUE TORTE

2 tbsp. cornstarch	1/8 cup pastry flour
1/4 tsp. cinnamon	1/2 tsp. salt
2 cups pitted sour red cherries	2 tsp. baking powder
2 tbsp. sugar	1 tsp. vanilla
1/8 tsp. nutmeg	1/2 cup milk
1/4 cup shortening	1 cup uncooked rolled oats
1/2 cup sugar	2 egg whites
2 egg yolks	2 tbsp. sugar

Mix cornstarch, cinnamon, cherries with juice, 2 tbsp. sugar and nutmeg together until well-blended. Pour into greased 9-inch square cake pan. Bake at 375° for 15 minutes. Blend shortening and 1/2 cup sugar and mix well. Add egg yolks one at a time, beating well after each addition. Sift flour, salt and baking powder together. Add vanilla to milk. Alternately add sifted ingredients and milk. Stir in oats. Spread batter over cherries in pan. Bake for 30 to 35 minutes. Turn cake upside down on ovenproof platter. Beat egg whites until they hold soft peaks and gradually beat in 2 tbsp. sugar. Spread over cherries and cake. Return to oven for about 10 minutes until lightly browned. Serve hot or cold.

MERINGUE TORTE

6 egg whites	2 cups sugar
11/2 lemon juice	

Beat egg whites with lemon juice until frothy. Add sugar gradually, 1 tbsp. at a time, beating continuously until very stiff and glossy. Spoon into 2 layered cake pans, oiled and lined with brown paper. Raise edge of meringue slightly with back of spoon to shape. Bake at 300° for 1 hour or until done. Turn oven off and leave meringue in oven for several hours. Fill with favorite filling, fruit cream, custard, ice cream, etc.

ORANGE SOUFFLE

1/4 cup butter	3 tbsp. frozen orange juice
1/4 cup flour	2 tbsp. orange marmalade
1/4 tsp. salt	1/4 cup fine cake crumbs,
2/3 cup milk	(optional)
3 egg yolks	3 egg whites
1/2 cup sugar	1/4 tsp. cream of tartar

Melt butter in saucepan over low heat and gradually stir in flour and salt. Add milk and cook, stirring constantly until mixture thickens. Remove from heat. Beat egg yolks until thick, add sugar, orange juice, marmalade and all but 2 tbsp. of the cake crumbs. Blend thoroughly. Add white sauce mixture and mix well. Beat egg whites until frothy, add cream of tartar and continue beating until stiff. Fold egg yolk mixture into egg whites. Pour into buttered 6-cup casserole. Sprinkle with remaining crumbs. Set in pan of hot water at least 1 inch deep and bake at 350° for 50 minutes or until silver knife inserted into center of pudding comes out clean. Serve immediately. Yield: 6 to 8 servings.

CHILLED ORANGE SOUFFLE

8 eggs, separated	2 6-oz. cans frozen
1 cup cold water	orange juice
2 env. gelatin	1 cup sugar
1/2 tsp. salt	1 cup cream, whipped

Beat egg yolks slightly. Add cold water, gelatin and salt. Dissolve in top of double boiler. Add orange juice and sugar. Cool. Fold in 1 cup whipped cream and stiffly beaten egg whites. Pour mixture into buttered mold and chill overnight.

PINEAPPLE MOUSSE

2 env. gelatin	2 tbsp. granulated sugar
1/4 cup cold water	2 eggs, separated
19-oz. can crushed pineapple	16-oz. can evaporated milk
Juice of 1 lemon	Maraschino cherries

Soften gelatin in 1/4 cup cold water. Drain pineapple, reserving liquid. Heat 1 cup pineapple juice and add softened gelatin. Stir until dissolved. Cool until half set. Add lemon juice and sugar to egg yolks and beat until thick and pale. Set aside. Beat cold evaporated milk until thick. Add lemon mixture and beat in slightly thickened gelatin. Fold in drained, crushed pineapple and stiffly-beaten egg whites. Pour into buttered 1-qt. mold. Chill until set. Unmold and decorate as desired. Use pineapple and maraschino cherries for decoration.

CHOCOLATE WHIP

1 env. gelatin
1/2 cup sugar
Dash of salt
4 tbsp. cocoa
1 1/4 cups water

2 egg yolks, beaten
1 tsp. vanilla
2 egg whites, beaten stiff
1 cup heavy cream, whipped

Combine gelatin, sugar, salt and cocoa in saucepan. Blend In 1/4 cup water. Add remaining water and egg yolks. Cook over medium heat about 3 minutes, stirring constantly. Remove from heat. Cool. Add vanilla. Chill until syrupy. Fold in egg whites and whipped cream. Pour into 1-qt. mold. Chill until firm. Unmold and trim with a frill of whipped cream or banana slices.

CRANBERRY WHIP OR PIE FILLING

3-oz. pkg. orange gelatin
2 cups thick cranberry sauce

1/2 cup evaporated milk
1 tsp. lemon juice

Dissolve gelatin in heated cranberry sauce. Chill until mixture starts to thicken. Chill the evaporated milk in refrigerator until ice crystals form and whip about 1 minute until soft peaks form. Add the lemon juice and beat until stiff. Fold into thickened gelatin. Chill. Yield: 6 servings.

COFFEE WHIP

1 env. gelatin
1/2 cup cold water
1 1/2 cups hot strong coffee
1/2 tsp. vanilla

1 tbsp. liquid non-calorie
  sweetener
Dash of salt

Soften gelatin in cold water. Dissolve in hot coffee. Add vanilla, sweetener and salt. Chill until syrupy. Beat thickened gelatin with rotary beater until it almost doubles in volume. Spoon into sherbet glasses. Chill until firm. Yield: 6 servings.

WHIPPED TOPPING

1/2 tsp. gelatin
3 tbsp. boiling water
1/3 cup cold water
1/2 cup skim milk powder

1/2 tsp. non-caloric liquid
  sweetener
1/2 tsp. flavoring

Dissolve gelatin in boiling water. Cool. Add cold water and skim milk powder. Beat until peaks form. Beat in sweetener and flavoring. This topping stays fluffy up to 2 hours in refrigerator. Stir before serving. Leftover topping may be covered and stored in refrigerator and whipped again before using. Yield: 2 cups. Allow 2 tbsp. per serving. 14 calories per serving. NOTE: 2 tbsp. sugar may be used in place of liquid sweetener. Calories per serving: 20.

RASPBERRY OR STRAWBERRY WHIP

1¼ cup fresh berries
1 cup icing sugar

1 egg white

Beat ingredients together about 10 minutes until stiff and fluffy. Serve over pieces of sponge or angel cake, or serve with custard sauce.

Mrs. Beamish

CRUNCHY TOPPING

1 cup margarine
1½ cups brown sugar
2 cups quick oat flakes **or**
  rolled oats
1 cup coconut

1 cup whole grape nuts
½ - 1 cup chopped walnuts
½ tsp. cinnamon
½ tsp. ground cardamom
  (optional)

Melt margarine in an 8 x 8-inch baking dish. Stir in sugar, oat flakes, coconut, grape nuts, walnuts, cinnamon and cardamom thoroughly. When well-mixed, cook covered for 5 minutes, stirring every minute. Cool and store. This will keep for 7 to 8 weeks in a covered plastic box. Use on puddings, ice cream, cakes, pies or cereal, or just munch away.

Readymade Local

RHUBARB CRISP

½ cup butter
1¼ cups sugar
2 eggs
½ tsp. nutmeg

½ tsp. vanilla
3 cups toasted bread cubes
4 cups cereal flakes
4 cups diced rhubarb

Blend butter and ½ cup sugar. Add eggs and beat well. Stir in nutmeg, flavoring, bread cubes and cereal. Pour half into buttered baking dish. Arrange rhubarb over this. Sprinkle remaining sugar over rhubarb and cover with remaining cereal mixture. Bake at 375° for 40 minutes or until rhubarb is tender. Serve warm with whipped cream. Yield: 10 servings.

Mrs. Jule Jolinette

APPLE CRISP FOR TWO

2 tbsp. rolled oats
2 tbsp. brown sugar
1 tbsp. flour
1 tbsp. chopped walnuts

Pinch of salt
Pinch of cinnamon
1 tbsp. butter **or** margarine
1 large apple

In small bowl, combine oats, sugar, flour, walnuts, salt and cinnamon. Cut in butter and blend until crumbly. Peel, core and chop apple and put into 2-cup casserole. Sprinkle oat mixture over fruit. Microwave uncovered on Medium 4½ to 5 minutes, turning after 2 minutes. Serve with ice cream, if desired. VARIATION: Substitute frozen or fresh blueberries, rhubarb or other fruit for the apple.

Elleline Ansell

APPLE-OATMEAL CRISP PUDDING

3 - 4 cooking apples
1/4 cup white sugar
1/2 cup flour
1 tsp. cinnamon

3/4 cup packed brown sugar
3/4 cup rolled oats
1/2 cup butter **or** margarine

Pare apples, thinly slice and arrange in buttered shallow baking dish. Coat with white sugar. Mix flour, cinnamon, brown sugar and oats in bowl. Stir and cut in butter until crumbly. Sprinkle over apples. Bake at 350° until crumbs are golden and apples are soft when pierced with fork.

CHERRY CRUNCH

1 cup rolled oats
1 cup brown sugar
1/2 cup flour

1/2 cup chopped walnuts
1/2 cup butter
1 can cherry pie filling

Combine rolled oats, sugar, flour and nuts. Cut in butter until mixture is crumbly. Save 1/2 cup for topping. Pat crumbs into bottom of square 8-inch greased pan. Spoon the pie filling onto the crumb mixture and sprinkle with remaining crumbs. Bake at 350° for about 40 minutes. Serve warm with cream.

Mrs. Lois Dunford

COCONUT CRUNCH

1 cup flour
1/4 cup brown sugar
1/2 cup margarine
1 cup coconut

1 1/2 cups stale bread crumbs
1 pkg. instant vanilla pudding
1 pkg. Dream Whip **or**
    1 cup whipped cream

Mix flour, sugar, margarine, coconut and bread crumbs until crumbly. Place in shallow pan and bake at 350° until brown, stirring as necessary. Reserve a small portion. Press remainder into a cake tin. Prepare pudding mix and spread over crumbs in pan. Prepare Dream Whip. Spread over mixture and sprinkle with remaining crumbs. Refrigerate.

Doris Felstad

BERRY CRUMBLE

3 cups raspberries, blueberries
    or saskatoons
1/2 - 2/3 cup packed brown sugar
1/2 cup whole wheat flour
2/3 cups rolled oats

1/3 cup margarine, softened
3/4 tsp. cinnamon (optional)
1/4 tsp. salt
Cream **or** ice cream (optional)

Spread raspberries in baking dish or round cake pan. Mix sugar, flour, oats, margarine, cinnamon and salt. Sprinkle on top of fruit. Microwave uncovered 7 to 10 minutes until fruit is hot and bubbly. Let stand 10 minutes. Serve warm with cream if desired. Yield: 4 to 6 servings.

Georgina Taylor

PINEAPPLE CHEESE DESSERT

1 1/3 cups crushed graham
   wafer crumbs
1/4 cup melted butter
2 tbsp. sugar
1 pkg. lemon pie filling
1/4 cup sugar

2 eggs, separated
1/2 cup pineapple syrup
1 1/2 cup water
1 cup pineapple, crushed
8 oz. cream cheese
1/4 cup sugar

Combine crumbs, butter and 2 tbsp. sugar. Reserve 1/4 cup for topping. Pat crumbs into bottom of 9 x 12-inch pan. Combine the pie filling, 1/4 cup of sugar, egg yolks and pineapple syrup. Add water and crushed pineapple. Cook until thick. Remove from heat. Add cream cheese and whip until well-blended. Beat egg whites, gradually adding 1/4 cup sugar until stiff. Fold meringue into lemon-cheese mixture, blending well. Pour filling over crumbs. Garnish with 1/4 cup remaining crumbs. Chill.

PINEAPPLE DELIGHT

2 1/4 cups graham wafer crumbs
1/2 cup melted butter
2 eggs
1 1/2 cups icing sugar

1/2 cup butter
1 cup cream
1 cup crushed pineapple,
   drained

Mix crumbs with melted butter. Keep half of crumbs for topping and put remainder in an 8 x 12-inch pan, pressing down firmly. Beat eggs, icing sugar and butter together and spread over crumbs. Whip cream and add drained pineapple. Spread over above mixture. Top with crumbs and place in refrigerator. Will keep for days and is a delicious dessert. Cut in small squares and serve. Keeps well. VARIATION: Substitute vanilla wafers for graham wafers.

Mrs. Leigh Williams

PINEAPPLE SNOW

20-oz. can crushed pineapple
1 env. gelatin
4 egg whites

1/2 cup sugar
1 1/4 cups whipping cream
Flavoring

Drain pineapple, reserving syrup. Sprinkle gelatin over 1/4 cup pineapple syrup, and let stand 5 minutes to soften. Dissolve over boiling water. Cool. Meanwhile, beat egg whites until stiff but not dry. Gradually beat in sugar and continue to beat until meringue forms stiff peaks. Whip cream until soft peaks are formed. Gradually beat in dissolved gelatin and flavoring. Fold in meringue and pineapple. Spoon into sherbet glasses. Chill until firm.

Mrs. August Vion

INDIVIDUAL UPSIDE-DOWN CAKES

5 1/2 tbsps. melted butter	1 egg
1 cup brown sugar	1 tsp. vanilla
1 cup drained crushed pineapple	1 1/3 cups pastry flour
8 maraschino cherries	1 1/2 tsp. baking powder
1/3 cup shortening	1/4 tsp. salt
1/2 cup granulated sugar	1/2 cup pineapple syrup

Place 2 tsp. butter in each of eight individual baking dishes. Sprinkle each with 2 tbsp. of brown sugar and pineapple. Press a cherry into middle of each dish. Blend shortening and white sugar. Add egg and vanilla and beat well. Sift dry ingredients and add alternately with pineapple syrup. Spread batter carefully over pineapple in dishes. Bake at 350° for about 35 minutes. Let stand 5 minutes. Loosen sides and turn out onto dessert dishes. Serve warm with cream.

BLUEBERRY DESSERT

32 single graham wafers, crushed	1 tsp. vanilla
1/2 cup melted butter	2 eggs
1 cup sugar	1 can blueberry pie filling
8 oz. cream cheese	Whipped cream **or** Dream Whip

Mix wafers, butter and 1/2 cup sugar together and press into a 9 x 13-inch pan. Beat the cream cheese, remaining sugar, vanilla and eggs and spread on top of wafer crust. Bake at 375° for 20 minutes and cool. Spread with the pie filling and top with whipped cream. Refrigerate. NOTE: When using Dream Whip, use 1 tbsp. vanilla, 1/2 cup sugar and a pinch of salt after it has been whipped.

Mrs. Geneva Helmig

RASPBERRY DESSERT

1/3 cup sugar	1 cup boiling water
1/3 cup melted butter	2 cups frozen raspberries
1 1/2 cups crushed graham	3 cups miniature marshmallows
wafer crumbs	1/2 cup milk
6-oz. pkg. raspberry jello	1 pint whipping cream

Mix sugar and butter with crumbs and spread on bottom of pan. Dissolve jello in boiling water and mix in the raspberries. Spread over crumb base and refrigerate. Melt the marshmallows in the milk in top of double boiler. Cool. Whip cream and fold in marshmallows. Spread on top of jellied mixture. Refrigerate.

Mollie Leonhudf

When referring to sugar in most recipes, it usually means granulated sugar. Berry, fruit or powdered sugar is very finely granulated and dissolves quickly. Use in meringues, whipping cream or drinks.

RASPBERRY SQUARES

2 cups graham wafer crumbs   1/2 cup brown sugar
1/2 cup melted butter

Combine and pack 3/4 of this mixture into 8-inch square pan and refrigerate.

1 pkg. frozen raspberries, thawed   1 cup whipping cream
2 tbsp. cornstarch   2/3 cup miniature marshmallows
1/2 cup sugar

Mix raspberries, cornstarch and sugar until starch dissolves. Cook in double boiler until thick. Chill. When raspberry mixture is well chilled, spread on top of graham crust in pan. Whip cream. Fold in marshmallows and spread on top of raspberry mixture. Sprinkle remaining crumbs on top and refrigerate.

Mrs. Rose Marie Grusie

RASPBERRY DELIGHT

8 double graham wafers, rolled   1 cup whipped cream
2 tbsp. brown sugar   3-oz. pkg. raspberry jello
2 tbsp. melted butter   1 1/2 cups hot water
1 pkg. marshmallows   3 cups raspberries
1 cup milk

Mix wafers, sugar and butter together. Put 3/4 of mixture in 9 x 12-inch pan. Melt marshmallows in milk and cool. Add whipped cream. Dissolve jello in hot water, add raspberries and cool until almost set. Put half marshmallow mixture in pan, then raspberry jello and remaining crumbs on top. Refrigerate until set.

Lottie Breitkreitz

RUBY-RED BAKED APPLES

8 baking apples   1/2 cup very ripe
1/2 cup sugar   mashed bananas
1 tsp. cinnamon   2 tbsp. water
1 can whole cranberry sauce   1/2 cup chopped walnuts

Wash and core apples. Place in a glass baking dish 2 inches deep. Combine sugar and cinnamon. Fill cavities with the sugar mix. Combine remaining ingredients. Pour over apples. Microwave on High for 7 to 9 minutes. Baste apples several times with the fruit sauce. Serve warm with ice cream.

Edna Dempsey

To make sweetened condensed milk, mix 1 1/4 cups powdered skim milk in 1/2 cup water. Microwave on High for 1 to 2 minutes. Add 3/8 cup sugar and 3/8 cup honey. Stir and cool.

CHERRY DELIGHT

50 crushed graham wafers
1/2 cup brown sugar
1/2 cup melted butter

1 pint whipping cream
1 pkg. colored marshmallows
1 can cherry pie filling

Mix wafers, sugar and butter together and press 2/3 of this onto bottom of pan. Pack well. Whip cream and mix with the marshmallows. Put half of this cream mixture onto the crumb mixture. Next spread with pie filling. Spread remainder of cream mixture over cherries and top with the remaining crumb mixture. Refrigerate overnight.

Miss Rita Ewing
Mrs. Brenda Flintoff

RHUBARB BLUSH

2 cups rhubarb, washed and cut
2 tbsp. water

2 tbsp. sugar
11/2 oz. raspberry jello

Put rhubarb into 11/2-qt. casserole with water. Cover. Microwave on High for 4 minutes, stirring once. Add sugar and jello. Stir well. Microwave 1 minute longer. Cover and cool. Yield: 4 servings.

Whitla - Seven Persons

QUICK CHAFING DISH FRUIT COMPOTE

15-oz. can peach halves
15-oz. can pear halves
16-oz. can figs
Cornstarch

8 maraschino cherries
Rum **or** brandy flavoring
2 tbsp. lime **or** lemon juice

Drain fruit and measure juice. For each cup of juice, use 2 tsp. cornstarch for thickening. Pour all but 1/2 cup of juice into top pan of chafing dish and heat. Mix cornstarch with reserved juice. Stir into juice and cook until clear. Add flavoring and lime juice to taste. Sweeten if necessary and add fruits. Reheat thoroughly and serve with cold rich custard sauce or whipped cream. Yield: 6 to 8 servings. 16 calories per serving.

APPLE RUM CHUTNEY

5 cups apples, pared, cored
  and chopped
1 lemon, seeded and chopped
1 cup brown sugar
1 cup granulated sugar
11/2 cups seedless raisins

2 tbsp. candied ginger
11/2 tsp. salt
1/2 tsp. dried red pepper
1 cup cider vinegar **or**
  Japanese vinegar
1/2 cup dark rum

Combine ingredients in a 4-qt. casserole. Cover and microwave for 10 minutes. Uncover and microwave for 25 minutes or until thick and syrupy. Let stand 15 minutes. Bottle and refrigerate. Yield: 4 to 5 cups. VARIATION: 2 cups pears may be substituted for 2 cups apples.

Joyce Templeton

PEACH TAPIOCA CREAM

1 cup sliced dietetic peaches
2 egg yolks, slightly beaten
3 cups skim milk
1/3 cup tapioca
2 1/4 tsp. non-caloric sweetener

1/8 tsp. salt
2 egg whites
1/4 tsp. almond flavor
1 1/2 tsp. vanilla

Drain peaches and chill. Put egg yolks into 1-qt. saucepan and gradually add the milk, stirring well. Add tapioca, sweetener and salt. Bring to boil and cook about 5 to 8 minutes over medium heat, stirring constantly. Do not overcook. Remove from heat. Beat egg whites until rounded peaks form. Add small amount of hot tapioca mixture gradually to egg whites, stirring constantly. Quickly blend in remaining tapioca mixture and the flavoring. Cool. Stir once after 15 or 20 minutes. Alternate layers of tapioca cream with peach halves into parfait glasses. Allow 3 halves per serving, begin and end with peach halves. Yield: 8 servings. 83 calories per serving.

APPLE CRANBERRY CASSEROLE

2 cups cranberries
3 cups sliced peeled apples
1 cup white sugar
1 tbsp. lemon juice
1/4 tsp. salt

1 cup brown sugar
1 cup rolled oats
1/2 cup flour
1/3 cup butter **or** margarine, soft

Combine cranberries, apples, white sugar, lemon juice and salt and turn into shallow 1 1/2-qt. baking dish. Combine brown sugar, rolled oats and flour. Cut in butter. Spoon over cranberry-apple mixture. Bake at 325° for 1 hour. Serve warm with ice cream if desired. Yield: 6 servings.

APPLE NUT DESSERT

1 cup sugar
3/4 cup flour
2 tsp. baking powder
1 tbsp. soft shortening
1/2 cup cream
1 tsp. vanilla

1/2 cup nuts, chopped
3 cups peeled, chopped apples
2 tbsp. brown sugar
1/3 cup flour
2 tbsp. soft butter

Mix the sugar, flour, baking powder and shortening. Press into 9-inch square pan. Mix the cream and vanilla. Add the nuts and apples and stir until well coated. Spread evenly over mixture in pan. Mix the brown sugar, flour and butter and sprinkle over apple mixture. Bake at 350° for 30 to 35 minutes or until done.

Mrs. Norman Bower

APPLE FLIP-FLAPS

3 sour apples, cored and peeled   1/4 tsp. salt
1 cup sugar   1 egg, well beaten
3/4 cup flour   1/4 cup milk
1 tsp. baking powder   1 tbsp. butter, melted

Chop the apples and mix with sugar. Sift flour, baking powder and salt. Beat egg and milk and stir into batter. Add the butter. Mix the apples with the batter until every piece is well coated. Fill greased muffin tin and bake at 400° for 20 to 30 minutes or until firm and brown on top. Serve with cream or fruit juice.

Mrs. I.W. Dunford

MOM'S APPLE ROLL

2 cups water   1 egg, well beaten
1 1/2 cups sugar   1/2 cup milk
2 cups flour   2 tbsp. cinnamon
4 tsp. baking powder   2 tbsp. sugar
1/2 tsp. salt   6 medium apples, sliced
3 tbsp. shortening

Prepare a syrup of water and sugar. Boil slowly for a few minutes and set aside. Sift flour, baking powder and salt. Mix in shortening and beaten egg. Add milk. Mix well together. Roll dough out to 1/2-inch thick. Spread with sliced apples. Sprinkle a bit of cinnamon and sugar over apples. Roll and cut into 2-inch thick slices. Place in 8 x 10-inch pan. Pour the hot syrup over this. Bake at 375° until apples are done. Delicious served hot or cold with whipped cream. Yield: 8 to 10 servings.

Mrs. Melvin E. Morris

SNOW MOUNDS

4 eggs, separated   1/2 cup sugar
1/4 cup sugar   1/4 tsp. vanilla
4 cups milk   1/4 tsp. almond extract

Beat egg whites until stiff. Add 1/4 cup sugar and continue to beat until glossy. Place milk in pan and bring to boil. With tablespoon, drop egg white mixture by spoonfuls into boiling milk, giving room to expand while cooking. When done on one side, turn gently with fork to finish cooking. Lift out gently and set in glass dish and finish cooking remainder in same way. When all egg white mounds are cooked, add the 1/2 cup sugar to the boiling milk and gradually add the egg yolks, stirring constantly until mixture thickens. Cool. Add vanilla and almond flavor. Slowly pour this into dish with snow mounds, being careful not to spill sauce over the snow-mounds.

SPANISH CREAM

1 env. gelatin	4 tbsp. sugar
2 cups milk	1 tsp. vanilla
2 eggs, separated	

Soak gelatin in milk and heat, stirring until dissolved. Add well-beaten egg yolks with 2 tbsp. sugar. Stir until it reaches boiling point. Remove from stove. Beat egg whites with 2 tbsp. sugar until stiff and add to mixture, stirring briskly until well mixed. Flavor and turn into mold. Serve with whipped cream or custard sauce.

Mrs. William Harry Wilkinson

GRAPE GELATIN

1 env. gelatin	2 tbsp. lemon juice
1/4 cup cold water	1 tsp. liquid non-caloric
3/4 cup hot water	sweetener
3/4 cup bottled grape juice	1/4 tsp. salt

Soften gelatin in cold water. Dissolve in hot water. Add grape and lemon juice, sweetener and salt. Chill until syrupy. Beat thickened gelatin with rotary beater until it almost doubles in volume. Spoon into 1-qt. mold. Chill until firm. Yield: 6 servings.

BROKEN GLASS DESSERT

21/4 cups graham wafer crumbs	1 env. gelatin
1/2 cup melted butter	1/4 cup cold water
1/4 cup brown sugar	1 cup pineapple juice, heated
3 3-oz. pkgs. jelly powder,	1 cup whipping cream
red, green and yellow	1/4 cup sugar
41/2 cups boiling water	1 tsp. vanilla

Mix crumbs, butter and brown sugar. Put in bottom of 13 x 9-inch pan. Dissolve each jelly powder in 11/2 cups boiling water and pour each one into oiled loaf pans. When well set, cut into 1/4 inch cubes. Dissolve gelatin in cold water and add to pineapple juice. Cool until thickened. Whip cream. Add sugar and vanilla gradually. Fold in pineapple mixture and jelly cubes. Pour on top of graham wafer crust. Set.

Mrs. Elwood Galloway

LIME RICE DESSERT

3-oz. pkg. lime jello	1 cup instant rice
3/4 cup hot water	1 pkg. Dream Whip
1/2 cup cold water	1 can crushed pineapple

Dissolve jello in hot water and add cold water. Chill until slightly thickened. Cook rice. Cool. Whip Dream Whip and fold rice, Dream Whip and undrained pineapple into jello. Chill until firm.

Elizabeth Pedersen

JELLO DESSERT

2 1/4 cups graham wafer crumbs
1/4 cup brown sugar
1/2 cup melted butter

6-oz. pkg. red jello
1 cup whipped cream
1 pkg. lemon chiffon pie mix

Mix crumbs, sugar and butter together. Reserve 1/2 cup for topping. Press crumb mixture into 9 x 15-inch pan. Bake at 350° for 10 minutes. Cool. Mix jello as directed on package. Set until almost firm. Pour on top of crumbs and chill in fridge. Spread whipped cream on the jello. Mix the lemon pie mix as directed on package and spread on the cream mixture. Sprinkle with remaining 1/2 cup crumb mixture. Chill.

BLANC MANGE

1 env. gelatin
1/4 cup cold skim milk
1 3/4 cup hot skim milk
3/4 tsp. liquid non-caloric
    sweetener

1 tsp. vanilla
1/4 tsp. salt
1/8 tsp. nutmeg

Soften gelatin in cold milk. Dissolve in hot milk. Add sweetener, vanilla, salt and nutmeg. Chill until syrupy. Beat thickened gelatin with rotary beater until almost double in volume. Pour into 1-qt. mold. Chill 2 hours or until firm. Yield: 6 servings.

LOW-CAL ICE CREAM

1 env. gelatin
1 tbsp. cold water
1/2 cup sugar
1/4 cup skim milk powder
1/8 tsp. salt

2 tsp. cornstarch
1 cup hot water
1 tsp. vanilla
1/2 cup skim milk powder
1/2 cup cold water

Soften gelatin in cold water. Combine sugar, 1/4 cup skim milk powder, salt and cornstarch. Slowly add hot water. Cook and stir until thick. Add gelatin and stir until dissolved. Add one of the variations, the vanilla and chill in freezing tray until firm. Whip 1/2 cup skim milk powder with 1/2 cup cold water until stiff. Put frozen mixture in bowl and beat or break up with a fork. Add whipped milk and freeze until firm. Yield: 6 to 8 servings.
VARIATIONS: 1/2 cup slivered browned almonds; 2 bananas mashed and pressed through sieve with 1 tbsp. lemon juice; 1/2 cup finely-chopped maraschino cherries, 1/2 cup chopped semi-sweet chocolate pieces; 3 tbsp. instant coffee; 1 cup sweetened strawberry, raspberry or peach pulp with 1 tbsp. lemon juice; 1/2 cup crushed pineapple, drained and 1/3 cup chopped maraschino cherries; 1/4 cup preserved ginger, finely chopped and 1 tbsp. ginger syrup.

ORANGE ICE CREAM DESSERT

1 env. gelatin	6-oz. can frozen orange juice
1/4 cup cold water	1 pint vanilla ice cream
6 cups marshmallows	Semi-sweet chocolate, grated

Grease 9 x 13-inch pan. Mix gelatin in cold water. Heat marshmallows in double boiler. Add softened gelatin and stir until marshmallows melt. Combine frozen juice and ice cream and add to marshmallow mixture. Stir until blended. Sprinkle with chocolate and freeze until firm.

Mollie Leonhardt

ICE BOX DESSERT

2 egg yolks	1/2 cup cold milk
1/3 cup sugar	2 egg whites, beaten
3/4 cup milk	1 cup whipped cream
1/4 tsp. salt	20 single graham wafers
1 tsp. vanilla	2 tsp. brown sugar
2 env. gelatin	6 tbsp. melted butter

Cook yolks, 1/3 cup sugar and milk in a double boiler until slightly thickened. Remove from heat. Add salt and vanilla. Meanwhile, dissolve gelatin in cold milk. Add to hot mixture. Cool in cold water until mixture thickens. Add egg whites and whipped cream. Roll out graham wafers. Add brown sugar and butter. Put part of this mixture in the bottom of a 9 x 9-inch pan. Spread the cold, thick custard mixture over the crumbs and top with crumbs. VARIATION: When custard is set well, use a can of prepared cherry pie filling on top.

Mrs. M. Babey

FROSTY STRAWBERRY DESSERT

1 cup flour	1/2 cup sugar
1/4 cup brown sugar	15-oz. pkg. frozen strawberries
1/2 cup chopped walnuts	2 tbsp. lemon juice
1/2 cup melted butter	1 cup whipping cream, whipped
2 egg whites	

Stir the flour, brown sugar, walnuts and melted butter. Mix well and place into shallow pan. Bake at 350° for about 20 minutes, stirring occasionally. When done, sprinkle 2/3 of the crumbs into 13 x 9 x 2-inch baking pan. Combine the egg whites, sugar, berries and lemon juice in bowl. Beat at high speed about 10 minutes until stiff peaks form. Fold in whipped cream and spoon over crumbs. Top with remaining crumbs. Freeze 6 hours or overnight. Cut into large squares. Top each with a whole berry.

Joyce McElroy

HAND FREEZER ICE CREAM

6 cups skimmed milk
6 eggs, well beaten
Pinch of salt

11/2 - 2 cups sugar
1 tsp. vanilla **or** to taste
11/2 cups heavy cream

Scald the milk. Beat eggs well with salt and sugar until creamy. Pour the hot milk into the egg mixture, stirring well. Cook in double boiler over hot water until custard coats a spoon. Chill overnight. Add the heavy cream and vanilla and freeze with hand freezer. NOTE: This will fill freezer 2/3 full but will whip up during freezing process until it is full.

11/2 cups brown sugar
4 tbsp. butter

2/3 cup corn syrup
3/4 cup fresh cream

Combine brown sugar, butter and corn syrup and cook until it threads from spoon. Remove from heat. Add salt. Let stand 15 minutes. Stir in the cream, chill and serve over ice cream.

Mrs. Margarite Godkin

VANILLA ICE CREAM

2 egg yolks
1/3 cups sugar
4 tbsp. corn syrup
1/4 tsp. salt

1 tsp. vanilla
2 cups light cream
2 egg whites

Beat egg yolks. Add sugar, corn syrup, salt and vanilla and beat well. Add cream and beat lightly. Freeze in refrigerator trays until firm. Transfer to a bowl, add egg whites and beat mixture until light and fluffy. Return to refrigerator trays and freeze until firm.

Mrs. W. J. Barlett

BAKED ALASKA

4 egg whites
1/8 tsp. cream of tartar
1/2 cup sugar

1 qt. ice cream
meringue

Beat egg whites and cream of tartar until stiff. Gradually beat in sugar and continue beating until stiff. Put several thicknesses of brown paper on cookie sheet. Set the ice cream, frozen hard, on the papers. Cover completely with meringue. When ready to serve, set in a 450° oven and brown lightly about 5 minutes. Yield: 6 to 8 servings. VARIATIONS: Baked Alaska on Sponge Cake: Put a 1/2 inch layer of sponge cake on the paper. Place ice cream on the cake, leaving a 1/2 inch rim of the cake all around. Cover with meringue. Baked Alaska Surprise: Before spreading ice cream with meringue, make a hollow in it and fill with crushed sweetened fruit. Frozen Meringue Pies: Fill baked pie shells or tart shells with ice cream. Cover with meringue. Sprinkle chopped toasted filberts or almonds on meringue before baking.

ALMOST DECADENT

CHERRY OAT CRUMBLE

20-oz. can cherry pie filling	1/2 cup flour
1/4 tsp. almond extract	1/2 cup rolled oats
3/4 tsp. cinnamon	3/4 cup brown sugar
3/4 tsp. nutmeg	1/4 tsp. salt
1/3 cup soft butter	Whipped cream **or** ice cream

Put pie filling in a baking dish. Stir in almond extract. Make crumbs of remaining ingredients, except whipped cream. Sprinkle over fruit. Bake at 375° for 25 minutes. Serve with whipped cream. Yield: 6 to 8 servings.

PUFFED WHEAT HONEY SQUARES

1/3 cup butter	2 tbsp. cocoa
1/2 cup honey	1 tsp. vanilla
1 cup brown sugar	8 cups puffed wheat

Melt butter and add honey, sugar, cocoa and vanilla. Cook until it bubbles. Remove from heat and add puffed wheat. Mix well. Pour into buttered 9 x 13-inch pan. Press down well and cut into squares.

AMBROSIA SQUARES

1 tsp. sugar	2 tsp. grated orange rind
1/2 cup lukewarm water	1 1/2 cups flour
1 env. fast-rising yeast	1/4 cup butter **or** margarine
2 eggs	3/4 cup fine shredded coconut
1 tsp. salt	1/2 tsp. vanilla
2 tbsp. sugar	1/4 cup cream
1/3 cup melted butter **or** margarine	1 cup pineapple marmalade

Stir 1 tsp. sugar into lukewarm water. Sprinkle with yeast. Let stand 10 minutes. Stir well. Beat eggs until light. Stir in salt, 2 tbsp. sugar, 1/3 cup butter, orange rind, dissolved yeast and one cup of the flour. Beat until smooth and elastic. Stir in additional flour to make a thick batter. Cover bowl with towel and let batter rise in warm place about 1 1/2 hours until doubled in bulk. Stir down batter and spread in a greased 10 x 15-inch jelly-roll pan. Let rise in warm place about 40 minutes until doubled in bulk. In the meantime, cream 1/4 cup butter. Blend in the coconut, vanilla and cream. Spread the marmalade over the risen batter and top with the coconut mixture. Bake at 350° for 30 to 35 minutes. Cool on a wire rack. Cut into strips lengthwise and cut each strip into 6 squares.

Mrs. George van Gyssel

ALMOND SQUARES

3/4 cup sugar
2 tsp. baking powder
2 egg yolks
13/4 cups flour

3/4 cup butter
11/2 tsp. almond flavoring
2 egg whites
3/4 cup icing sugar

Mix first 5 ingredients as for a pastry into a smooth ball. Press into 8-inch square pan. Bake at 400° until light brown. Beat egg whites until stiff. Add icing sugar gradually. Spread on cooked base and return to oven for about 10 minutes until meringue is browned.

Mrs. E. (Annebeth) Kievit

APPLE SQUARE

1/4 cup butter
1 cup sugar
1 egg, beaten
4 - 5 apples, peeled and grated
1 cup flour

1/2 tsp. nutmeg
1/4 tsp. salt
1/2 tsp. cinnamon
1 tsp. soda

Cream butter and sugar . Add egg and all but 1 cup apples. Sift flour and spices and add to butter mixture. Add soda to the 1 cup of apple and add to butter mixture. Bake in square pan at 350° for 25 minutes. Serve with whipped cream.

Mrs. A. Jerrom

BUTTERSCOTCH MARSHMALLOW BARS

1/4 cup butter
1 cup brown sugar
1 egg
1 tsp. vanilla
1 cup flour

1/4 tsp. salt
1 tsp. baking powder
1/2 cup chopped walnuts
20 marshmallows, cut in half

Cream butter, sugar, egg and vanilla. Add sifted dry ingredients. Add nuts and spread in greased 8-inch square pan. Bake about 30 minutes until golden brown. Place marshmallows on top of mixture and put back in oven for a few minutes.

1/4 cup butter
1 tbsp. flour
1/8 tsp. salt

1/4 cup milk
11/2 cups icing sugar
1/4 tsp. vanilla

Heat butter in saucepan until delicately browned. Remove from heat and blend in flour and salt. Add milk slowly. Return to moderate heat, stirring constantly. Bring to a boil and boil 1 minute. Mixture will separate. Remove from heat and stir in icing sugar and vanilla, stirring rapidly until thick enough to spread. Ice marshmallows bars while still warm.

Mrs. Martha O'Brien

BUTTER TART SQUARES

1 1/4 cup flour   1/4 cup brown sugar
1/2 cup butter

Mix ingredients and press in a 9-inch square pan. Bake at 350° for 15 minutes.

1/3 cup butter   1 cup brown sugar
2 tbsp. cream   1 egg, beaten
1 tsp. vanilla   1 tbsp. flour
1 cup raisins

Mix ingredients and spread over base. Return to oven and bake 20 to 30 minutes or until golden brown.

Mrs. Nora Holmberg

COCONUT ANGEL SQUARES

3/4 cup shortening   2 tbsp. flour
2 cups packed brown sugar   1/2 tsp. salt
2 cups flour   1/2 tsp. baking powder
2 eggs   1 cup walnuts, chopped
1 tsp. vanilla   1 1/2 cups coconut

Cream shortening and 1 cup brown sugar. Add 2 cups flour and pat in bottom of a well-greased 9 x 13-inch pan. Bake at 325° for 20 minutes. Do not brown. Beat eggs until light. Gradually add 1 cup brown sugar and vanilla. Add 2 tbsp. of flour, salt and baking powder. Fold in walnuts and coconut and spread on the baked crust. Bake 25 minutes. Cool.

2 1/2 cups icing sugar   1/2 - 1 tsp. grated lemon rind
2 tbsp. lemon juice   2 - 3 tbsp. orange juice

Combine ingredients. Cream may be added to make spreading consistency.

Mrs. Jeannette Crone

FRUITY BUTTERSCOTCH SQUARES

1/4 cup shortening   3/4 cup flour
1 cup brown sugar   Cherries
1 egg   Nuts

Cream shortening and add brown sugar gradually. Add egg and beat well. Add flour, fruit and nuts. Put in greased pan and bake at 350° for 20 minutes. Cool and ice.

1 cup brown sugar   3 tbsp. butter
4 tbsp. cream   1 tsp. vanilla
Pinch of salt

Boil sugar, cream, salt and butter together for 1 minute. Add vanilla. Beat with spoon until it reaches spreading consistency. Spread on squares.

Mrs. M. Parcles

BUTTERSCOTCH SQUARES

1/2 cup cooking oil	1/4 tsp. baking powder
1 cup brown sugar	1/4 tsp. salt
1 egg	1/2 cup chopped nuts
1 cup flour	1 tsp. vanilla

Mix oil, brown sugar and egg thoroughly. Sift flour, baking powder and salt together. Add gradually to first mixture. Add nuts and vanilla. Mixture will be stiff. Bake in greased 8-inch square pan at 350° for 20 minutes. Cut into 1-inch squares when cool.

Mrs. George van Gyssel

COFFEE SHEET SQUARES

2/3 cups hot coffee	12/3 cups flour
1 cup chopped dates	1 tsp. baking powder
2/3 cup butter	1/4 tsp. salt
1 cup brown sugar	1/2 tsp. cinnamon
1 tsp. vanilla	3/4 cup chopped nuts (optional)
2 eggs	

Pour coffee on dates and let stand. Cream butter, sugar and vanilla and add eggs, one at a time, beating thoroughly. Sift dry ingredients together and add to creamed mixture with dates and nuts. Bake in a 9 x 13-inch pan at 350° for 25 minutes. When cool, frost and cut in bars.

1 1/2 cups icing sugar	1 tsp. instant coffee
1/8 tsp. salt	2 tbsp. melted butter
2 tbsp. cream	1 tsp. vanilla

Combine ingredients and spread on bars.

Mrs. Kathleen Manning

PINEAPPLE SQUARES

1 cup graham cracker crumbs	1 cup flour
1 cup sugar	1 cup coconut
1 cup shortening	

Mix ingredients and blend until crumbly. Reserve 1 cup for topping. Pat remainder in pan.

2 cups crushed pineapple	2 egg yolks
1/2 cup sugar	2 egg whites
2 tbsp. flour	2 tbsp. sugar

To make the topping, combine pineapple, 1/2 cup sugar, flour and egg yolks. Cook until thick. Spread on base mixture. Beat egg whites until stiff, gradually adding 2 tbsp. sugar. Fold in 1 cup of crumbs. Spread over pineapple mixture. Bake at 350° for 30 to 35 minutes. Chill well.

Mrs. G. Hope

DAD'S COOKIE SQUARES

1 pkg. oatmeal cookies, crushed	1 egg
1/4 cup butter	1 1/2 cups icing sugar
3 sq. semi-sweet chocolate	1/2 cup walnuts, chopped
1/2 cup butter	1 tsp. vanilla

Combine cookies with 1/4 cup butter. Press half into an 8-inch square pan. Bake at 350° for 5 to 10 minutes. Mix the chocolate and 1/2 cup butter together. Add egg, icing sugar, walnuts and vanilla. Spread over crumb base and sprinkle with remaining crumbs. Refrigerate.

Mrs. Bert Friend

OATMEAL CHIP SQUARES

1 cup butter	6 oz. butterscotch chips
3/4 cups brown sugar	6 oz. chocolate chips
1 tsp. salt	1/2 cup shredded **or**
1 tsp. vanilla	flaked coconut
1 1/2 cups flour	1/2 cup chopped pecans
1 1/4 cups rolled oats	

Cream butter and gradually beat in sugar, salt and vanilla. Combine flour, rolled oats, butterscotch and chocolate chips, coconut and pecans. Stir into mixture. Press into 11 x 15-inch jelly roll pan. Bake at 375° for 22 to 25 minutes. Cool. Break into irregular pieces. Yield: 4 dozen pieces.

Mrs. K.D. Galloway

CHOCOLATE CHIP SQUARES

1 cup butter **or** margarine	6 oz. semi-sweet
1 cup brown sugar	chocolate chips
1 tsp. vanilla	1/2 cup chopped walnuts
2 cups flour	

Cream butter, sugar and vanilla. Add flour and mix well. Stir in chocolate chips and walnuts. Pour into ungreased 15 x 10 1/2 x 1-inch cookie sheet. Bake at 350° for 20 minutes. Cut into squares while hot.

Dorine Scott

EASY MALLOW SQUARES

Graham wafers	1 egg
1/2 cup margarine	1 tsp. vanilla
16 oz. butterscotch chips	3 cups white marshmallows
1 cup icing sugar	Coconut

Line 8-inch square pan with wafers. Melt margarine, add chips and melt. Remove from heat and add icing sugar, egg and vanilla. Mix together and add marshmallows. Spread over wafers and sprinkle with coconut. Allow to set until the wafers soften.

Carol Stott

PINK MARSHMALLOW SQUARES

3/4 cup butter
4 tbsp. brown sugar

1 1/2 cups flour

Cream butter and brown sugar together. Add flour and chill a few minutes. Press into a 9-inch square pan and bake at 325° for 20 minutes.

1 env. gelatin
3/4 cup cold water
3/4 cup sugar
Pinch of salt
3/4 cup icing sugar

3/4 tsp. baking powder
3/4 tsp. almond flavoring
3/4 tsp. vanilla
Coconut **or** finely-chopped
    walnuts

Soak gelatin in cold water. Add sugar and salt. Bring to a boil, stirring. Remove from heat, add icing sugar and let cool. Beat until foamy. Add baking powder, almond and vanilla flavoring. Beat until thick and stands in peaks. Tint with pink coloring if desired. Pour on lower layer and sprinkle immediately with coconut.

Mrs. Marilyn Henry

PUMPKIN SQUARES

1 cup margarine
1 cup white sugar
4 eggs
1 tsp. vanilla
2 cups flour
1 can of pumpkin

1 tsp. cinnamon
1/2 tsp. ginger
2/3 cup brown sugar
1 tsp. salt
1 cup milk
1/2 cup chopped nuts

Combine margarine, white sugar, 2 eggs, vanilla and flour and mix as a cake. Spread into a 9 x 13-inch pan. Combine pumpkin, cinnamon, ginger, brown sugar, salt, 2 eggs and milk and pour over the base. Bake at 400° for 10 minutes. Reduce heat to 300° and continue baking for 30 minutes or until set. Sprinkle the nuts over the top 10 minutes before the end of the baking time.

Mary Wright

RASPBERRY SQUARES

1 cup flour
1 tbsp. milk
1 egg

1/2 tsp. salt
1 tsp. baking powder
1/2 cup butter

Mix ingredients like a pie dough and roll to pan size 9 x 12 inches. Spread a thin layer of raspberry jam on top.

1 cup sugar
1/4 cup butter, melted
1 tsp. vanilla

1 1/2 cups coconut
1 egg, beaten

Mix ingredients well and spread over jam. Bake at 350° for 25 minutes. Cut in squares while warm.

Marie Lagler

RUM SQUARES

1/2 cup butter **or** margarine	2 eggs, beaten
1 cup sugar	3 1/2 cups flour
3 tbsp. liquid honey	1 tsp. baking soda
4 tbsp. sweet cream	

Cream butter and sugar. Add honey, sweet cream and eggs and mix. Add flour and baking soda. Divide into three equal parts. Roll dough to fit 10 x 15-inch pan. Bake each piece at 350° for 5 to 8 minutes.

2 cups milk	1 cup icing sugar
4 tbsp. cream of wheat, cooked and cooled	1 tbsp. rum **or** rum flavoring
	Few drops food coloring
1 cup butter	Chocolate icing

Combine milk and cream of wheat thoroughly. Beat in butter, icing sugar, rum and food coloring. Spread between layers. Ice with chocolate icing. Cut in triangles. These freeze well.

Marie Brecka

PLAINS' RUMMY CUBE

1 tsp. sugar	1 to 2 bottles rum
1 cup dried fruit	1 tbsp. brown sugar
2 large eggs	1 cup butter
1 tsp. soda	1 tsp. baking powder
1/2 pint lemon juice	1 cup nuts

Before starting, sample rum. If it is smooth, proceed. Select large mixing bowl and 4-cup measuring cup. Check rum again. To be sure rum is of "fine" quality, fill glass with rum and drink it. If rum tastes right, proceed. If not, repeat. With electric mixer, beat 1 cup of butter in a large and fluffy bowl. Add 1 seaspoon of thugar and beat again. Meanwhile, make suer rum is schtill allright. Try another cup. Open second bottle if neceshary. Add eggs, the fried druit and heat until bigh. If druit gets stuck in beaters, pry loose with screwdriber. Sample rum again, checking tonscisticity. Next sift 3 cups pepper or salt (really doesn't matter). Sift 1/2 pint lemon juice. Fold in chopped butter and melted nuts. Add 1 bablespoon of brown thugar or whatever color you can find. Grease oven. Turn cake pan to 350°. Pour mess into boven and ake. Check rum again and bo to ged.

B. B. Donahue
V. Harlton

FROSTED GRAPES: Dip bunch of grapes in lightly-beaten egg white to coat and sprinkle with sugar. Place on wax paper to dry.

LEMON SQUARES

1 cup flour
1/4 cup icing sugar
1/2 cup butter
Pinch of salt

2 eggs
3 - 4 tbsp. lemon juice
1 cup sugar

Mix flour, icing sugar, butter and salt and press into cake pan. Bake 20 minutes at 350°. Mix eggs, lemon juice and sugar and pour over crust when baked. Bake at 350° for 25 minutes. Sift icing sugar on top when done. Cool and cut into squares.

Mrs. Edith Hauck

UNBAKED SQUARES

1/2 cup butter
1/2 cup brown sugar
1 tbsp. cocoa
1 tbsp. instant coffee
1 egg, slightly beaten
1 tsp. vanilla

16 double graham wafers,
  roughly broken
4 sqs. semi-sweet chocolate
1 tbsp. oil
36 walnut halves **or** other nuts

Melt butter in saucepan. Mix together sugar, cocoa, coffee and egg and add to melted butter. Stir well and bring to a boil. Remove from heat, add vanilla and wafers and mix well. Place in greased pan, pressing down with spoon. Melt chocolate with oil, mix well and pour over mixture in cake pan. Decorate with walnut halves and cut into 36 squares.

Mrs. C.P. Winter

FRUIT COCKTAIL SQUARE

2 eggs
1 1/2 cups sugar
1 tsp. vanilla
2 cups fruit cocktail, drained
2 cups flour

1/2 tsp. salt
1 tsp. soda
1 1/3 cups flaked coconut
1/2 cup chopped walnuts

Beat eggs, sugar and vanilla until light. Add fruit cocktail. Mix dry ingredients and add to egg mixture, beating again. Pour into 15 x 10-inch well-greased pan. Sprinkle coconut and walnuts on top. Bake at 350° to 375° for 20 to 30 minutes until brown. VARIATION: Substitute 1/4 cup brown sugar for coconut.

1/2 cup butter **or** margarine
1/4 cup evaporated milk **or**
  thin cream

3/4 cup sugar
1/2 tsp. vanilla

Boil ingredients together gently for two minutes and pour over warm cake.

Mrs. Sophie Hough
Mrs. I. W. Dunford

RICE CRISPY SQUARES

1/4 cup butter **or** margarine	3 cups miniature marshmallow
40 large marshmallows **or**	5 - 6 cups rice krispies

Melt butter in saucepan. Add marshmallows and cook over low heat, stirring constantly, until mallows are melted and mixture is well blended. Remove from heat. Add rice krispies and stir until well coated. Press warm mixture into buttered 9 x 13-inch pan. Cut in squares when cool. NOTE: 2 cups marshmallow cream may be substituted for marshmallows. Add to melted butter and cook over low heat about 5 minutes, stirring constantly. Yield: 24 2-inch squares.

CHERRY CHEWS

1 cup flour	1/2 tsp. almond extract
1 cup rolled oats	2 tbsp. flour
1 cup brown sugar	1 tsp. baking powder
1 tsp. soda	1/2 tsp. salt
1/4 tsp. salt	1 cup coconut
1/2 cup butter	1 cup maraschino cherries
2 eggs	1/2 cup pecan halves
1 cup brown sugar	

Mix 1 cup flour, oats, 1 cup sugar, soda and 1/4 tsp. salt. Add butter and mix until crumbly. Press mixture into greased 13 x 9 1/2 x 2-inch pan. Bake at 350° for 10 minutes. Beat eggs and stir in 1 cup sugar and almond extract. Sift flour, baking powder and 1/2 tsp. salt and stir in. Add coconut and drained cherries and stir until blended. Pour over first mixture and spread evenly. Sprinkle with pecans. Bake for 25 minutes or until lightly browned. Cool and ice with Cherry Almond Icing below.

3 tbsp. soft butter	2 cups icing sugar
1/2 tsp. almond extract	2 tbsp. maraschino cherry juice

Blend all ingredients and spread on bars.

Mrs. Marion Henry

ALMOND OR BRAZIL NUT CRISP

Graham wafers	1/2 tsp. vanilla
3/4 cup butter	Brazil nuts, shaved **or**
3/4 cup brown sugar	slivered almonds
1 tbsp. water	

Line cookie sheet with graham wafers. Combine butter, sugar, water and vanilla and cook 4 minutes or until mixture bubbles. Pour over wafers, sprinkle with nuts and bake at 350° for 8 to 9 minutes. Cut each wafer in half while warm.

L. Grace Gore

CRUNCHY PEANUT MALLOW CANDY

8-oz. semi-sweet chocolate chips   2 cups miniature
1/2 cup crunchy peanut butter   marshmallows

Melt chocolate with peanut butter in double boiler over hot, but not boiling water. Stir until well-blended. Fold in marshmallows. Press into greased 8-inch square pan. Chill until firm. Cut in squares. VARIATION: Substitute 1/2 cup creamy peanut butter and 1/2 cup peanuts for crunchy peanut butter.

HELLO DOLLIES

1/4 cup margarine **or** butter   1 cup peppermint
1 cup crushed graham wafers   chocolate chips
1 cup coconut   1 can sweetened
1 cup walnuts   condensed milk

Melt margarine in a 9-inch square pan. Add graham wafers. Spread coconut, walnuts and chocolate chips over wafers. Pour condensed milk over this. Bake for 30 minutes at 325°. Loosen around edge with knife and refrigerate until needed.

Mrs. Don (Frances) Redmond
Mrs. Freda Wolff

NUT SMACKS

1/2 cup butter   1 cup flour
2 egg yolks   2 tsp. vanilla
1 tsp. baking powder   1/4 tsp. salt
1/2 cup brown sugar

Combine ingredients and pat down firmly in pan.

2 egg whites, beaten   1 tsp. vanilla
1 cup chopped nuts   1 cup brown sugar

Combine ingredients and cover base. Bake at 350° for 25 minutes.

Mrs. Edith Hauck

BUTTERSCOTCH DELIGHT

12 oz. butterscotch chips   1/2 cup peanut butter
1/3 cup butter **or** margarine   Pinch of salt
1 tsp. vanilla   1/2 pkg. miniature marshmallows
1/3 cup coconut

Melt and stir chips and margarine over low heat. Stir in remaining ingredients until well blended. Add marshmallows. Spread in an 8-inch square pan. Cool.

Mrs. G. Hope

PEANUT BUTTER JELLY KRISPS

1/3 cup butter **or** margarine
3/4 cup peanut butter
4 cups miniature marshmallows

5 cups rice krispies
1/2 cup raspberry **or** grape jelly

Melt butter and peanut butter over low heat. Add marshmallows, stirring until melted. Remove from heat. Stir in cereal and mix until well-coated. Press half into greased 9-inch square pan. Spread mixture with jelly and top with remaining cereal mixture. Chill and cut into squares.

NUT DREAM BARS

1/3 cup butter
1/3 cup brown sugar

1 cup rolled oats
1/3 cup flour

Cream butter and sugar. Add oats and flour. Mix well. Pat firmly in an 8-inch square pan. Bake at 350° for 10 minutes.

2/3 cup sweetened
condensed milk
1/2 tsp. vanilla

1 1/4 cups coconut
1/3 cup walnuts, chopped
1/4 sliced cherries (optional)

Combine ingredients and spread on top of first mixture. Return to oven and bake for 30 minutes. Cut into squares when cool.

Mrs. Marian Miller

CHOCOLATE CARAMEL BARS

1/2 cup plus 2 tbsp. butter
1/4 cup sugar

1 1/4 cups flour

Cream butter and sugar. Add flour and work together until crumbly. Press into 8-inch square pan and bake at 375° for 20 to 15 minutes.

1/2 cup butter
2 tbsp. corn syrup
1/2 cup brown sugar

1/2 can sweetened
condensed milk

Mix ingredients in saucepan. Bring to a boil . Reduce heat and boil 5 minutes, stirring constantly. Beat and pour over shortbread crust. When cool, pour 4 oz. of melted chocolate on top.

Mary Spornitz

OH HENRY BARS

1 egg
1/2 cup milk
1 cup white **or** brown sugar
1/3 cup butter
1 cup graham wafer crumbs

1/2 cup chopped walnuts
1 cup coconut
1/2 cup glazed cherries
Whole graham wafers

Combine egg, milk, sugar and butter and bring ingredients just to a boil. Add crumbs, walnuts, coconut and chopped cherries. Line pan with wafers. Pour filling over these and place another layer of wafers over filling. Ice with butter icing. Keep in refrigerator.

GERMAN LEBKUCHEN BARS

1 cup syrup	1 tbsp. cloves
1 cup honey	1 cup nut meats, chopped
3 cups sugar	1/2 cup almonds, chopped
1 cup butter	1/2 cup citron peel
2 tbsp. brandy	1 tbsp. baking soda
4 cups flour	1 cup water
1 tbsp. cinnamon	3 eggs, well beaten

Heat syrup, honey, sugar, butter and brandy and boil 5 minutes. Stir in 4 cups flour, spices, chopped nuts and peel. Cool. Dissolve soda in water and add. Add eggs and enough flour to make stiff dough. Let stand 4 days in covered kettle in cool place. Roll out and place on cookie sheets. Brush with milk and sprinkle with sugar. Bake at 350° for 5 to 10 minutes. Cut in squares or bars while hot.

CHEWY RAISIN BUTTERSCOTCH BARS

1/3 cup shortening, butter **or** margarine	1/2 tsp. baking powder
1 egg, beaten	1/2 tsp. vanilla
3/4 cup packed brown sugar	1 cup dark raisins, coarsely chopped
3/4 cup flour	1/2 cup semi-sweet chocolate
1/2 tsp. salt	chips **or** pieces

Melt shortening and cool slightly. Beat in egg and sugar. Sift flour, salt and baking powder and add. Stir in vanilla and raisins. Spread in 7 x 11-inch greased pan and sprinkle chocolate chips evenly over top. Bake at 350° about 35 minutes. Cut into bars while still warm. Yield: 18 bars.

Mrs. Romeo Belanger
Emily Saide

CHEWY APRICOT BARS

12 oz. dried apricots, slivered	1/4 tsp. baking powder
1/2 cup water	1/4 tsp. salt
1/4 cup sugar	3/4 cup brown sugar
1/4 cup lemon juice	1 1/4 cup rolled oats
3/4 cup flour	1/3 cup cold butter **or** margarine

Place apricots in 4-cup measure with water, sugar and lemon juice. Microwave on High for 5 minutes until it boils. Do not cover. Stir after 2 minutes. Measure remaining ingredients except butter into bowl. Blend with fork and cut in butter until crumbly. Press 2/3 into bottom of glass pie plate. Cover with apricot filling and sprinkle with remaining oat mixture. Place on inverted microwave safe cereal bowl. Microwave, uncovered on High for 4 1/2 to 5 minutes until firm. Rotate dish once during cooking. Cool. Yield: 20 squares or wedges.

Mildred Hitesman

FRUIT BARS

1 cup flour	1 egg, beaten
1 tsp. baking powder	1 tbsp. milk
1/3 cup butter	1/4 tsp. salt

Mix ingredients, roll out and put in a 8 x 12-inch pan. Spread with jam of your choice.

1/2 cup sugar	1 tsp. vanilla
1 egg, well beaten	2 cups coconut
1/4 cup butter, melted	

Mix ingredients and spread on top of first mixture. Bake at 350° for 25 minutes.

Mrs. Fred Djuve

JAM BARS

1/2 cup sugar	Grated rind of 1 lemon
1 1/4 cups pastry flour	1/3 cup shortening
1 tsp. baking powder	1 egg, well beaten
1/8 tsp. salt	1/2 cup strawberry jam

Mix and sift sugar, flour, baking powder and salt together. Add lemon rind. Cut in shortening with pastry blender or two knives until mixture resembles fine oatmeal. Add egg, blending thoroughly. Press 2/3 of mixture into a greased 7 x 12-inch pan and dot with the jam. Drop the remaining 1/3 of the mixture by spoonful onto the jam. Bake at 350° for 40 to 45 minutes or until lightly browned.

Edith Enright

NANAIMO BARS

1/2 cup butter	1 egg
1/4 cup sugar	2 cups graham wafer crumbs
5 tbsp. cocoa	1 cup coconut
1 tsp. vanilla	1/2 cup walnuts

Place butter, sugar, cocoa, vanilla and egg in a bowl. Set dish in boiling water and stir until butter is melted and mixture resembles thin custard. Combine wafer crumbs, coconut and nuts. Add to custard mixture and pack evenly in a well-buttered 9-inch square pan.

1/4 cup butter	2 cups icing sugar
2 tbsp. vanilla custard pudding	4 sqs. semi-sweet chocolate
3 tbsp. milk	1 tbsp. butter

Cream 1/4 cup butter and add custard powder combined with milk. Blend in icing sugar, spread over cookie base and cool 15 minutes. Melt the chocolate and 1 tbsp. butter and spread over custard icing. When set, cut into bars.

Mrs. L.F. Pharis
Mrs. Snider

SPICY ORANGE BARS

2/3 cup shortening	1/2 tsp. salt
1 1/2 cups brown sugar	1 tsp. cinnamon
2 eggs	1/2 tsp. nutmeg
2 tbsp. grated orange peel	1/4 tsp. cloves
3 tbsp. orange juice	1 cup seedless raisins,
2 cups flour	dark **or** light
1 tsp. soda	1 cup chopped walnuts

Cream together shortening, sugar and eggs. Stir in orange peel and juice. Sift together flour, soda, salt, and spices. Add to creamed mixture and mix well. Stir in raisins and nuts. Spread in greased 15 1/2 x 10 1/2 x 1-inch jelly roll pan. Bake at 350° for about 30 minutes or until done. Cut in bars. Sift confectioner's sugar over top if desired. Yield: 4 dozen.

Carole Laun

TROPICAL BARS

1 cup flour	1/4 cup butter
1/4 tsp. salt	1/4 cup brown sugar

Mix ingredients and press into 8 x 8-inch pan. Bake at 325° for 15 minutes.

1 egg, beaten	1/4 cup chopped cherries
1 cup brown sugar	1 tsp. rum flavor
1/2 cup crushed pineapple	1/2 cup flour
1 cup coconut	1 tsp. baking powder

Mix ingredients and put on top of first mixture. Bake for 30 to 35 minutes.

Esther Nelson

PEANUT BUTTER BARS

1/2 cup shortening	1 pkg. colored
1 cup peanut butter	miniature marshmallows
16 oz. chocolate chips	3/4 cups coconut, flaked fine
16 oz. butterscotch chips	1/2 cup unsalted peanuts
	Coconut

Melt shortening, peanut butter and chips together. Cool slightly and add marshmallow, coconut and chopped peanuts. Put in 11 x 16 inch-pan. Sprinkle with coconut.

Mrs. J.L. Saruga

To decorate a cake without using sweet frosting, lay a paper doilie over cake and dust with icing sugar. Gently remove doily.

CHOCOLATE SCOTCHEROOS

1 cup sugar
1 cup light corn syrup
1 cup peanut butter

6 cups rice krispies
6 oz. chocolate chips

Bring sugar and syrup to a boil. Remove from heat. Add peanut butter. Blend well and add rice krispies. Press into 9 x 13-inch pan. Ice with chocolate chips melted over hot water. Yield: 48 bars. VARIATION: Substitute honey and cornflakes for corn syrup and rice krispies.

LEMON SLICE

11/2 cups graham wafer crumbs
1/3 cup brown sugar
Pinch of salt

1/2 cup butter
1/2 tsp. baking powder

Mix ingredients together and put half in a pan.

1 can sweetened
   condensed milk

1 tsp. vanilla **or** almond
1/2 cup lemon juice

Mix ingredients together. Pour over crumbs in pan and top with remaining crumbs. Bake at 350° for 20 to 25 minutes.

M. Kenworthy

CHOCOLATE SLICE

3/4 cups raisins
1/2 cup butter
1 cup sugar
1 egg, well beaten

3 tsp. cocoa
12 graham wafers, crushed
1/2 cup chopped walnuts
Whole graham wafers

Boil raisins with a little water in a saucepan. Leave on heat and add butter, sugar, egg and cocoa. Cook for 1 minute. Remove from heat and add graham wafers and walnuts. Line 8-inch square pan with whole graham wafers. Pour mixture over top and ice with chocolate icing while filling is still warm.

Mrs. Violet Metzger

CHERRY MERINGUE SLICE

1/2 cup butter
1/4 cup brown sugar
1 cup flour
1 cup sliced maraschino cherries
2 egg whites

1/2 tsp. cream of tartar
1 cup brown sugar
Pinch of salt
1 tsp. vanilla

Work butter, 1/4 cup brown sugar and flour as for shortbread and press into 8-inch square pan. Cover with cherries and small amount of juice. Beat egg whites and cream of tartar until stiff. Add 1 cup brown sugar, salt and vanilla. Beat until stiff. Pour on top of cherries. Cook at 325° for 25 to 30 minutes until brown.

Mrs. Edna Kelly

CHERRY SLICE

1/2 cup butter   2 tbsp. sugar
11/2 cups flour   1/2 tsp. salt

Combine ingredients as for shortbread and pat in an 8-inch square pan. Bake at 350° for 10 minutes.

2 eggs, beaten   1/2 cup coconut
1 tsp. baking powder   1/2 cup chopped walnuts
2 tbsp. flour   1 cup glazed cherries
11/2 cups brown sugar

To make topping, beat eggs and fold in remaining ingredients. Spread over first mixture. Return to a 325° oven for 30 to 35 minutes. Frost with butter icing moistened with lemon juice. Top each square with a cherry.

Mrs. Margaret Johnston

TWILIGHT SLICE

1 cup butter   1/4 cup sugar
2 cups flour

Mix ingredients together and place in a 9 x 14-inch pan. Bake at 350° for 15 minutes. Cool.

20-oz. can crushed pineapple   1 drop red food coloring
3/4 cup sugar   3 tbsp. sugar
1/2 small bottle maraschino   1 tsp. cold water
   cherries, chopped   3 egg whites
3 tbsp. cornstarch   Coconut

Put pineapple, sugar and cherries in a saucepan. Mix cornstarch with enough water and food coloring until thin and add. Boil until thick. Cool and spread on top of crust. Add sugar and cold water to 3 egg whites and beat. Spread on top and sprinkle with coconut. Bake at 325° for 15 to 20 minutes until light brown.

Mrs. Ken Marle
Mrs. John Properzi

COCONUT SLICE

1/2 cup butter   1 cup shredded coconut, fine
11/2 cups icing sugar   1/2 cup drained
1 egg   maraschino cherries
Pinch of salt   1/2 cup chopped nuts
3/4 tsp. vanilla   Whole graham wafers

Cream butter and blend in icing sugar. Beat until light. Add egg and beat well. Add the salt, vanilla, coconut, cherries and nuts. Line a 9 x 13-inch pan with wafers. Pour filling over these and place another layer of wafers over filling and press down. Ice with your favorite icing.

Mrs. Grace Geissinger

MARSHMALLOW SLICE

1/2 cup melted butter
1 egg, well beaten
1/4 cup sugar
3 tsp. cocoa
1 tsp. vanilla

1 cup graham wafer crumbs
1/2 cup walnuts, chopped
1/2 pkg. colored miniature
   marshmallows

Cook butter, egg, sugar, cocoa and vanilla in double boiler for 1 minute. Mix wafers, walnuts and marshmallows. Add chocolate mixture to this. Pack in buttered pan, ice with a chocolate icing and refrigerate. Cut into squares.

Mrs. A.R. Brown

APRICOT SLICE

1 cup dried apricots, packed
1 cup flour
1/2 tsp. baking powder
1/4 tsp. salt
1/4 cup brown sugar
1/2 cup butter

2 eggs
1 cup brown sugar
1/2 cup flour
1/2 tsp. vanilla
1/2 cup chopped nuts

Cover apricots with cold water in small saucepan. Bring to a boil, reduce heat and boil gently for 10 minutes. Drain, lay on paper towel to cool and dry. Cut into small pieces. Lightly grease 8-inch square pan. Sift 1 cup flour, baking powder and salt into a bowl. Add 1/4 cup brown sugar and blend with a fork. Add butter and blend until mixture resembles shortbread. Press into prepared pan and bake 10 minutes. Beat eggs lightly with a fork, add 1 cup brown sugar, 1/2 cup flour, vanilla, nuts and apricots, blending well. Spread over base, return to oven and bake at 350° for 30 minutes or until set.

Mrs. Fred Wasyleski

CRISPY CRUNCH SLICE

1/2 cup brown sugar
1/2 cup corn syrup
2 cups cornflakes

1/2 cup peanut butter
1 cup rice krispies
1 tsp. vanilla

Melt sugar with corn syrup in double boiler. Do not boil. Add remaining ingredients and press into cake pan.

1 cup brown sugar
2 tbsp. butter

6 tbsp. cream
1 - 2 cups icing sugar

Mix sugar, butter and cream in double boiler and boil 3 minutes. Add icing sugar and stir well. Ice the slice.

Mrs. H. A. (Arlene) Ruste

BROWNIES

1/3 cup oil	1 tsp. vanilla
2 oz. unsweetened chocolate	3/4 cup sifted all-purpose flour
2 eggs	1/2 tsp. baking powder
3/4 cup sugar	1/2 tsp. salt
1/2 cup corn syrup	3/4 cup chopped walnuts

Cook oil and chocolate over low heat until mixture melts. Cool. Add eggs one at a time, blending after each addition. Beat in sugar, syrup and vanilla. Sift dry ingredients together and add. Beat until smooth. Add nuts and pour into greased pan. Bake at 350° for 40 minutes. Cool.

HAWAIIAN BROWNIES

3/4 cup butter	1/2 tsp. salt
11/2 cups sugar	1/2 tsp. cinnamon
3 eggs	14-oz. can crushed pineapple
1 tsp. vanilla	2 sqs. unsweetened
11/2 cups flour	chocolate, melted
1 tsp. baking powder	1/2 cup chopped nuts

Cream butter and sugar well. Add eggs and beat until light. Add vanilla, sifted flour, baking powder, salt and cinnamon. Remove 1 cup of dough and add well-drained pineapple. Mix well and set aside. To remaining mixture add chocolate and nuts. Spread 8 x 8-inch pan with enough chocolate mixture just to cover. Spread pineapple mixture over and add remaining chocolate mixture over this. Bake at 350° for 45 to 50 minutes. Ice with chocolate cream icing.

Johanna Cossins

ALMOND BROWNIES

1/2 cup butter	1/2 cup flour
1 cup sugar	1/2 cup walnuts
1/2 tsp. salt	2 tbsp. cocoa
2 tbsp. cocoa	1 tbsp. butter
2 eggs	1/4 tsp. almond flavoring
1/4 tsp. baking powder	Icing sugar

Combine first 8 ingredients and put in a square pan. Bake at 350° for 30 minutes. To make icing, combine the cocoa, 1 tbsp. butter, almond flavor and icing sugar as needed. Spread on cooled brownies.

Edna Meyer

When melting chocolate in a double boiler, set the pan over hot, not boiling, water. Stir constantly to keep it glossy. Make sure bowls and utensils are completely dry before using. Water makes chocolate seize up.

BROWNIE MIX BROWNIES

1 1/4 cups powdered milk	2 tsp. salt
4 cups flour	4 cups sugar
4 tsp. baking powder	1 1/4 cups cocoa

To make the Brownie Mix, sift the ingredients together. Store in cool place in tight container. Yield: 10 cups.

3 tbsp. water	1 1/2 tsp. vanilla
1/2 cup melted butter	2 1/2 cups *Brownie Mix*
2 eggs, beaten	1/2 cup chopped nuts

Combine liquids and stir into mix. Add nuts. Bake for 35 to 40 minutes at 350°.

Sharon Hollman

BUTTERSCOTCH BROWNIES

1/2 cup butter	2 tsp. baking powder
2 cups brown sugar	2 tsp. salt
6 oz. butterscotch chips	3 tsp. vanilla
2 eggs	3/4 cup walnuts
1 1/2 cup flour	1/2 cup dates (optional)

Melt butter. While warm, add sugar and chips and blend. Cool, add eggs and beat. Sift flour, baking powder and salt, and add to butter mixture. Add vanilla, walnuts and dates. Spread in pan and bake at 350° for 25 to 30 minutes. Cover with a thin icing.

Mrs. Lois Dunford

COCOA BROWNIES

3/4 cups flour	1/2 cup soft shortening
3/4 cup sugar	2 eggs
1/4 cup cocoa	1 tsp. vanilla
1/2 tsp. baking powder	1/2 cup chopped nuts
1/2 tsp. salt	

Sift flour, sugar, cocoa, baking powder and salt into bowl. Add shortening, eggs and vanilla. Beat for 2 minutes. Add nuts and mix well. Spread batter into greased 9 x 9 x 1 1/2-inch pan. Bake at 350° oven for 30 minutes.

Mrs. Betty Ohman

Plastic storage containers such as the ones used for cottage cheese or margarine are not recommended for microwave use. They break down when subjected to high temperatures.

GRAHAM WAFER BROWNIES

Whole graham wafers
1 egg
1 cup brown sugar
1/2 cup butter
1/3 cup milk
1/2 cup coconut

1 1/2 cups graham wafer crumbs
1/2 cup walnuts, chopped
1 cup icing sugar
1 tsp. softened butter
3 tsp. custard powder
1 - 3 tsp. milk

Line 7 x 11-inch foil pan with whole graham wafers. Bring egg, sugar, butter and milk to a boil. Cook 1 minute. Add coconut, crushed wafers and walnuts. Spread this filling over the whole wafers. Let cool. To make the icing, combine the icing sugar, butter, custard powder and milk. Spread on brownies. Keep brownies refrigerated.

Dorothy Bradley

FUDGEY BROWNIES

2 sq. unsweetened chocolate
1/2 cup butter
1 1/2 cups sugar
3 eggs

1 1/4 cups flour
1/8 tsp. salt
1 tsp. vanilla
1/2 cup chopped nuts

Place chocolate in medium mixing bowl. Microwave on High for 2 minutes or until almost melted. Add butter and microwave on High 1 to 2 minutes until butter is almost melted. Stir in sugar and beat in eggs. Stir in remaining ingredients. Spread batter in 2-qt. baking dish. Microwave for 7 minutes on Medium. Microwave for 3 to 4 minutes on High or until puffed and dry on top. Do not overcook. VARIATION: Place colored miniature marshmallows evenly on top of brownies and microwave for 2 minutes. Marshmallows will stick together. Cool well and frost with chocolate icing.

Carol Stott
Mary Wright

BLONDE BROWNIES

1 cup flour
1/2 tsp. baking powder
Dash of baking soda
1/2 tsp. salt
1/3 cup melted butter

1 cup brown sugar
1 egg, slightly beaten
1 tsp. vanilla
1/2 cup chopped nuts
1/2 cup chocolate chips

Combine flour, baking powder, soda and salt and blend well. Mix butter, sugar, egg and vanilla together. Add sifted dry ingredients. Add chopped nuts and chocolate chips. Batter will be stiff. Dip spoon in cold water and pat batter down in lightly-greased 10 x 10-inch pan. Bake at 350° for 20 to 25 minutes. Cool. Cut in squares. VARIATION: Use 1 cup fine coconut instead of chopped nuts.

Mrs. Lorraine Heppler

QUICK ONE-PAN BROWNIES

1/2 cup vegetable oil	3/4 cup flour
1/4 cup cocoa	1/2 tsp. baking powder
3/4 cup sugar	1/4 tsp. salt
2 eggs	3/4 cup chopped nuts
1 tsp. vanilla	

Measure oil and put in 8 x 8-inch pan. Stir in cocoa until well blended. Add sugar and mix until smooth. Add eggs and vanilla and beat until smooth. Mix in dry ingredients and beat until smooth. Stir in nuts and mix to blend. Smooth dough evenly on pan and bake at 350° for 25 to 30 minutes. Do not overcook. Can be iced with chocolate icing and decorated with nuts.

Irene Wagstaff

MATRIMONIAL CAKE

1/2 lb. dates	2 tbsp. brown **or** white sugar
1/2 cup cold water	2 tbsp. orange juice
Grated rind of 1/2 orange	1 tsp. lemon juice

Cook dates, water, orange rind and sugar in a small saucepan over moderate heat until thick and smooth. Remove from heat and add fruit juices. Mix well. Cool before spreading.

1 1/2 cups flour	1 cup butter
1/2 tsp. baking soda	1 cup brown sugar
1 tsp. baking powder	1 1/2 cups rolled oats
1/4 tsp. salt	

Sift flour, baking soda, baking powder and salt. Rub in butter with tips of fingers. Add sugar and rolled oats. Spread half in a greased 8 x 14-inch shallow pan. Press down. Spread evenly with cooled date filling and cover with remaining crumbs. Pat smooth. Bake at 325° for 30 to 35 minutes. Increase heat slightly towards end to brown.

Mrs. A.J. Patterson
Mrs. Ralph Goodman

WALNUT CAKE

2 tbsp. butter	1/3 cup coconut
2 eggs	5 tbsp. flour
1 cup brown sugar	1 cup walnuts
1/8 tsp. soda	1 tsp. vanilla

Preheat oven to 325°. Melt butter in 8-inch square pan in oven. Beat eggs and add remaining ingredients. Mix well and pour over butter. Do not stir. Bake at 325° for 20 minutes. Ice with almond icing.

Mrs. Helen Tymkow

ROCKY ROAD CAKE

6 oz. butterscotch chips	Whole graham wafers
1/2 cup margarine	2 cups colored
1 egg	miniature marshmallows
1 cup icing sugar	Coconut

Combine chips, margarine, egg and icing sugar in double boiler. Stir until melted and slightly thick. Set aside to cool. Line an 8-inch square pan with wafers. Pour mixture over wafers. Mix the marshmallows with the cooled filling and pour over wafers. Sprinkle with coconut. Refrigerate.

Mrs. Vera Lardner

COCONUT GRAHAM WAFER CAKE

1/2 cup butter **or** margarine	3 tbsp. flour
1 egg	1 tsp. baking powder
1 cup sugar	1 cup unsweetened coconut
1 tsp. vanilla	1/4 tsp. salt
2 cups graham wafer crumbs	

Cream butter, egg, sugar and vanilla. Add remaining ingredients. Place in greased and floured 8-inch square pan. Bake at 350° for 30 to 40 minutes. When cool, ice with brown sugar icing.

1 cup brown sugar	1 cup icing sugar, approximately
1/4 cup milk	1 tsp. vanilla
3 tbsp. margarine **or** butter	

Boil first 3 ingredients together 3 minutes. Beat until slightly cool and add enough icing sugar to make a smooth icing and vanilla.

Carsin E. Stukart

CREAM PUFFS OR ÉCLAIRS

1 cup boiling water	1 cup flour
1/2 cup butter	4 eggs
1/8 tsp. salt	

Place boiling water, butter and salt in a heavy saucepan and stir over heat. When mixture boils vigorously, add flour all at once, stirring briskly. Stir constantly until dough forms a soft ball and leaves sides of pan clean. Do not overcook. Remove from heat. Cool. Add eggs one at a time, beating with electric egg beater until mixture becomes stiff. Drop by tablespoon on ungreased muffin tin. Bake at 450° for 15 minutes, reduce heat to 350° for 25 minutes. When cold, cut side of shell and fill center with sweetened whipped cream or your favorite filling.

ECLAIR SHELLS: Follow above recipe but form dough into strips 1/4-inch thick. Bake 15 minutes at 450° and reduce heat to 350° for 10 minutes. When cold, ice top with a chocolate cream icing.

Mrs. E. Tomalty

MERINGUES

4 egg whites	1 cup instant dissolving
1/4 tsp. cream of tartar	(fruit powdered/berry) sugar
Pinch of salt	1/2 tsp. almond extract

Beat egg whites, cream of tartar and salt together until soft peaks form. Gradually add sugar, beating until stiff peaks form. Beat in almond extract. Draw 9-inch circle on foil-covered baking sheet. Spoon meringue in wreath shape inside circle. Bake at 275° for 1 1/2 hours or until meringue is slightly colored. Turn off oven and leave meringue in oven overnight. NOTE: Meringue can be prepared ahead and stored in airtight container for up to 1 week.

MARSHMALLOW ROLL

4 sqs. semi-sweet chocolate	1 pkg. colored
2 tbsp. butter	miniature marshmallows
1 cup icing sugar	1 tsp. vanilla
1 cup chopped walnuts	1 cup cherries or gumdrops
1 egg, well beaten	(optional)

Melt chocolate and butter in top of double boiler. Remove from heat. Add other ingredients. Mix well and place in refrigerator to set for 5 or 10 minutes. Sprinkle coconut on waxed paper and roll mixture in it. Divide mixture in half and form into two rolls. Chill for several hours. Slice when ready to eat.

Sharon Hallman
Mrs. Jeanette Seely

NUT ROLL

2 cups sugar	1 cup coconut
1 cup cream	1 cup walnuts
1/2 cup butter	1/2 cup almonds **or** brazil nuts
1 lb. chopped dates	

Combine sugar, cream and butter. Boil to soft ball stage. Remove from heat. Add dates and boil until mixture leaves the sides of the pan. Add coconut, walnuts and almonds. Beat until stiff. Shape into a long roll on a damp cloth. Refrigerate and slice.

Mrs. Gwen Golds

Melt marshmallows in the microwave and they will not burn.

To melt chocolate in the microwave, microwave on Medium for 2 minutes, stirring occasionally.

CANDY

AFTER DINNER MINTS

1 egg white	1 tsp. peppermint
Icing sugar	1 tsp. water

Beat the egg white stiff, add some icing sugar, peppermint and water. Add enough icing sugar to be able to roll in strips. Cut in 1/2-inch lengths and set to harden. Food coloring may be added to make mints the color desired.

Pansy Molen

HONEY CARAMEL CHEWS

1/4 cup butter	1/4 tsp. salt
1 cup undiluted evaporated milk	1 tsp. vanilla
1 1/2 cups sugar	1 cup chopped nuts
1/2 cup honey	

Heat butter and milk until butter is melted. Set aside. Mix sugar, honey and salt in heavy saucepan. Cook and stir over medium heat until sugar is dissolved and mixture comes to boil. Boil, stirring often to firm ball stage. Continue boiling, slowly adding hot milk and butter so that sugar mixture does not stop boiling. Cook and stir again until candy reaches firm ball stage. Remove from heat. Stir in vanilla and nuts. Pour into well-buttered pan. Cool. Cut into squares and wrap each in wax paper.

To make good candy, use the specified ingredients and follow the instructions "to the letter." One of the most important items is the candy thermometer. Always use a wooden spoon to stir candy mixture. Check your candy thermometer to see the degree that is registered when water boils rapidly. Water boils at 212° at sea level, e.g. if the rapidly boiling water registered 208° at your elevation and you are to cook a batch of candy up to 238°, you must subtract the 4° difference from 238° and you would cook the batch of candy at 234°. This test will also help to prevent overcooking or undercooking. Always read thermometer at eye level.
THREAD: 230°-234°. The syrup spins a 2-inch thread when dropped from a spoon.
SOFT BALL: 234°-240°. The syrup forms a soft ball when dropped into very cold water and flattens on removal.
FIRM BALL: 244°-248°. The syrup forms a firm ball when dropped into cold water and does not flatten on removal.
HARD BALL: 250°-265°. The syrup forms a ball which is hard, yet plastic when dropped into cold water.
HARD CRACK: 300°-310°. The syrup separates into threads which are hard and brittle when dropped into cold water.

HONEY CARAMEL

2 cups sugar
1/4 cup honey
1 cup sweet cream
1/4 cup butter

Blend all ingredients in saucepan. Place over low heat, mixing continuously until sugar is dissolved. Continue boiling at low temperature until firm ball stage is reached. Remove from heat. Cool slightly and beat until creamy. Pour into wax paper-lined greased pan. Cool and cut into squares.

CHOCOLATE CREAM CARAMELS

2 cups sugar
1/8 tsp. salt
1 cup corn syrup
3/4 cup shredded unsweetened
   chocolate
1/2 cup light cream
2 tbsp. butter
1/2 cup evaporated milk
1 tsp. vanilla
1/2 cup finely chopped nuts

Combine sugar, salt, syrup, chocolate and light cream. Boil to temperature of 230°. Add butter and stir. Add evaporated milk and boil slowly to a temperature of 244° or firm ball stage. Remove from heat. Add vanilla and nuts, if desired. Pour hot candy into oiled or buttered pan. When cooled to room temperature, cut and wrap individually in wax paper.

CREAM CARAMELS

2 cups sugar
1 cup butter
13/4 cups syrup
2 cups cream
1 tsp. vanilla

Mix sugar, butter, syrup and 1 cup of the cream in large saucepan. Bring to boil and while still boiling, add the remaining cream slowly. Continue boiling until mixture forms firm ball in cold water. Remove from stove, add vanilla and pour into pans to set. Cut and wrap in wax paper when cool. Coconut or nuts may be added if desired.

Mrs. G. L. Williams

ALMOND BRITTLE

1 1/4 cup sugar
2/3 cup butter
1/2 cup honey
1 lb. almonds **or** other nuts

Put sugar and butter in heavy fry pan. Heat until melted and brown. Add honey. Simmer slowly for 20 minutes. Stir in nuts and cook 10 minutes more. Drop candy by teaspoonful onto lined, oiled pan and allow to harden or spread on bottom of pan. Allow to harden and break into pieces to serve.

BROWN SUGAR CANDY

5 1/2 cups brown sugar
2 tbsp. syrup
1 can sweetened
   condensed milk

1 cup sweet milk
1/2 cup butter
1/8 tsp. baking powder

Combine ingredients and stir constantly while boiling. Boil until it reaches hard crack stage. Pour into pan to set.

Mrs. Wm. Hallum

BUTTER CRUNCH

2 cups blanched almonds
2 cups butter
2 cups sugar
1/4 cup water

1 tbsp. light corn syrup
12 oz. semi-sweet chocolate
   chips, melted

Chop blanched almonds fine and roast. Melt butter over low heat, add sugar and stir until dissolved. Add water and syrup and cook over low heat, stirring frequently, to brittle stage. Remove syrup from heat and immediately stir in 1 1/3 cup almonds. Pour layer 1/4 inch thick on greased trays. When cool, spread with thin coating of chocolate and almonds. When chocolate is firm, turn over and repeat. Break into pieces.

Lois Grant

FONDANT

2/3 cup sweetened
   condensed milk
1 tsp. salt

1/2 cup butter, creamed
5 1/2 cups icing sugar
1 tsp. vanilla

Add condensed milk and salt to butter and gradually add icing sugar and vanilla. Mix, pour onto baking board and knead with hands until smooth. You may divide and color and flavor each section as you wish. Make into small-sized shapes, let set overnight and dip in chocolate. NOTE: This may be made into Easter eggs by making yellow centers and covering with white portion. Make into egg shapes and dip in chocolate. Decorate with colored icing.

CHOCOLATE FUDGE

2 cups sugar
2 tbsp. corn syrup **or** honey
3/4 cup milk

4 tbsp. cocoa
1 tbsp. butter
1 tbsp. vanilla

Bring sugar, syrup and milk to rolling boil. Add cocoa. Continue cooking to soft ball stage. Let cool a minute, add butter and vanilla and beat until it creams. Pour into buttered dish. Cut into squares when cool.

Florence Rasmuson

FRENCH CHOCOLATE FUDGE

12 oz. chocolate chips
3 doz. large marshmallows
1/3 cup sweetened
   condensed milk

1 cup chopped, toasted
   almonds (optional)
1 tsp. vanilla

Combine chips, marshmallows and milk in double boiler. Cover until marshmallows begin to melt. Stir in almond and vanilla. Spread in 7-inch square pan and let cool at room temperature overnight.

Mrs. Verna Kett

DOUBLE-DECKER FUDGE

4 1/2 cups sugar
7-oz. jar marshmallow cream
1 1/3 cups evaporated milk
1/2 cup butter **or** margarine

Dash of salt
6 oz. semi-sweet
   chocolate pieces
6 oz. butterscotch pieces

Combine sugar, marshmallow cream, evaporated milk, butter and salt. Cook and stir over medium heat until mixture boils. Boil gently for 5 minutes, stirring frequently. Divide mixture in half. To one half, add chocolate pieces and stir until blended. Pour into buttered 13 x 9 x 2-inch pan. To remaining half, add butterscotch pieces, beating until smooth. Pour over chocolate layer. Cool. Cut in pieces.

Gladys Van Petten

BROWN SUGAR FUDGE

2 cups brown sugar
1 cup cream
1/2 tsp. salt

2 tbsp. butter
1/2 cup walnuts

Boil sugar, cream and salt until mixture forms soft ball stage. Remove from heat, cool slightly and beat until smooth and creamy. Add butter and walnuts. Pour into 8-inch square pan.

Mrs. Ralph Goodman

CHOCOLATE NUT FUDGE

1 cup white sugar
1/4 cup butter
1/4 cup syrup
1/2 tsp. vanilla
1 cup brown sugar

1/2 cup cream
2 sq. chocolate
1/2 cup flour
Walnuts

Combine all ingredients except flour and nuts and boil to soft ball stage. Remove from heat and stir in flour immediately. Beat until thick. Add walnuts and pour into pan to cool.

Ella Pederson

CREAM CHOCOLATE FUDGE

1 pint-sized jar marshmallow cream 1/4 cup margarine 1/4 tsp. salt 1/2 cup evaporated milk	11/2 cups sugar 11/2 cups chocolate chips 1 tsp. vanilla 3/4 cup walnuts, chopped

Combine first 5 ingredients and boil 5 minutes, stirring constantly. Add chocolate chips to mixture. Remove from stove and add vanilla and walnuts. Set in 9-inch square pan.

Mollie Leonhardt

HONEY FUDGE

4 cups sugar 1/2 cup butter	1 cup evaporated milk **or** cream 1/2 cup creamed honey

Combine ingredients in heavy pot. Cook on medium heat and bring to boil until soft ball stage. Let cool. Beat until it starts to thicken and pour into buttered pan. Mark into squares.

Mrs. Ken Gram

TWO MINUTE FUDGE

4 cups icing sugar 1/2 cup cocoa 1/4 tsp. salt 1/4 cup milk	1 tbsp. vanilla 1/2 cup butter 1 cup chopped nuts

Stir first 5 ingredients in 11/2-qt. casserole until partially blended. Put butter in center of dish. Microwave 2 minutes on High or until milk feels warm on underside of dish. Stir vigorously until smooth. Blend in nuts and pour into buttered 10 x 6 x 2-inch pan. Chill 1 hour in refrigerator. Yield: 34 squares.

Miriam Galloway

FIVE-MINUTE FUDGE (Never fail)

2/3 cup evaporated milk 12/3 cups sugar 1/4 tsp. salt 16 diced marshmallows	6 oz. chocolate chips 1 tsp. vanilla 1/2 cup chopped nuts

Mix milk, sugar and salt in saucepan over medium heat. Heat to boiling and cook 5 minutes, stirring constantly. Remove from heat. Add marshmallows, chocolate chips, vanilla and nuts. Stir 1 to 2 minutes until marshmallows melt. Pour into buttered 8-inch square pan. Cool. Cut into squares.

PANOCHA (Maple fudge)

2 1/2 cups brown sugar
1 tbsp. butter
1 tbsp. corn syrup
3/4 cups milk

Pinch of salt
1 tsp. Mapleine
1/2 cup chopped nuts

Mix sugar, butter, corn syrup, milk and salt in saucepan until sugar is dissolved. Cook to 236° or soft ball stage. Remove from heat. Allow mixture to cool. Add Mapleine. Beat until it begins to thicken. Add nuts and immediately pour out, spreading mixture in a well-buttered pan. When cool, cut candy into squares.

PEANUT BUTTER FUDGE

2 cups white **or** brown sugar
3/4 cup milk
1 tbsp. syrup

3 tbsp. peanut butter chunks
Few grains of salt
1 tsp. vanilla

Combine sugar, milk and syrup. Stir to dissolve sugar. Boil gently without stirring until soft ball stage. Remove from heat and let stand a few minutes. Add peanut butter, salt and vanilla and beat until it starts to hold shape. Pour quickly into buttered pan. Don't beat too long or it will be hard and crumbly when poured out. Cut into squares.

QUICK 'N EASY FUDGE

4 cup miniature **or** 32
   large marshmallows
2/3 cup evaporated milk
1/4 cup butter **or** margarine
1 1/2 cups sugar

1/4 tsp. salt
12 oz. semi-sweet
   chocolate chips
1 tsp. vanilla
1/2 cup chopped nuts (optional)

In a 3-qt. glass casserole or batter bowl, combine marshmallows, evaporated milk, butter, sugar and salt. Microwave on High 5 to 7 minutes until mixture comes to a boil, stirring occasionally. Microwave 1 minute longer. Beat in chocolate chips until melted. Stir in vanilla and nuts. Pour into a lightly-greased 8 x 8-inch glass pan. Cool until firm and cut into squares. Garnish each square with a pecan or walnut half.

Elizabeth Durie

QUICK CHOCOLATE FUDGE

1 pkg. chocolate pudding
   or pie filling
1/4 cup milk

2 tbsp. butter
1 1/2 cups icing sugar
1/4 cup nuts

Mix first three ingredients in saucepan. Bring to boil and boil 1 minute. Remove from heat. Blend in icing sugar and mix well. Add nuts. Put in 8-inch square pan and cut into squares.

Mrs. Peter Kellar

FRUIT JAM FUDGE

3 cups sugar
1/2 cup cream
1/3 cup water

1/2 cup jam
2 tbsp. butter

Mix sugar, cream and water in saucepan and boil slowly to temperature of 230°. Add jam and butter and boil to 236°. Remove from heat. Cool to 110°. Stir with wooden spoon until creamy. Mold into wax paper-lined pan. Cool and cut in squares.

GRAHAM WAFER CANDY

1 can sweetened
   condensed milk
3/4 - 1 cup sugar
2 oz. unsweetened chocolate

1/8 cup butter
2 - 21/2 cups rolled
   graham wafers

Place milk, sugar and chocolate in double boiler and bring to a boil. Add butter, thicken with graham wafers and place in greased pan. Cut when cool. VARIATION: 1 cup of nuts may be added. Yield: 1 pound of candy.

Mrs. M. James

JAUNTY SNOWMAN CENTERPIECE

9 cups puffed rice
1/4 cup butter
32 large marshmallows

Flaked **or** shredded coconut
Butter frosting

Heat puffed rice in shallow pan at 350° for 10 minutes. Pour into greased bowl. Melt butter and marshmallows over low heat and blend. Pour over puffed rice, stirring to evenly coat all kernels. With greased hands, shape into 3 balls for body. Shape some for arms. Immediately roll each piece in coconut for 'frosty' appearance. Assemble, using butter frosting to attach balls and toothpicks to attach arms. Use candies and cherries for finishing touches. Make top hat and frilly collar from paper.

MARSHMALLOWS

2 env. gelatin
4 tbsp. cold water
1/2 cup boiling water

11/2 cups sugar
1/2 tsp. vanilla

Warm small mixmaster bowl in hot water. Place bowl in pan of hot water to keep warm. Soak gelatin in cold water and dissolve in boiling water. When gelatin is completely dissolved, add sugar and flavoring. After sugar is dissolved, beat mixture with mixmaster until thick and foamy. When it looks like white boiled icing, quickly pour into wet mould or 8-inch square cake pan. When cold, cut into squares with slightly wet knife. Roll squares in fine cut coconut or crushed cornflakes, or a mixture of 1/2 cup icing sugar mixed with 1 tbsp. cornstarch.

Georgette Swenson

TOASTED COCONUT MARSHMALLOWS

1 pkg. flavored jello   1 cup sugar
3 tbsp. plain gelatin   2 1/2 cups water

Dissolve jello, gelatin and sugar in 1 cup boiling water. Add 1 1/2 cups water and heat gently to just under boiling point. Stir constantly. Cool to lukewarm. Beat with mixmaster at high speed until very light and frothy. Spread in pan lined with toasted fine coconut and cut with kitchen shears. Roll in more toasted coconut and serve.

CHOCOLATE CANDY

1/3 cup milk   3 tbsp. butter
1 pkg. chocolate   2 1/2 cups icing sugar
  pudding **or** pie filling   1/3 cup chopped nuts

Gradually blend milk with pudding mix in a medium bowl and mix until smooth. Add butter and stir well. Microwave uncovered on High for 1 minute. Stir and microwave 50 seconds on High. Mixture will start to foam or boil around edges. Do not overcook. Stir. Quickly blend in the icing sugar in 3 parts. Stir in nuts and pour into pan lined with wax paper. Chill 45 minutes.

Lorena Sime

HOME-MADE CHOCOLATES

10 cups icing sugar   2 tsp. vanilla
8 tbsp. butter   2 tbsp. corn syrup
1 can sweetened condensed   3/4 cake paraffin wax
  milk, less 2 tbsp.   8 sqs. unsweetened chocolate

Put icing sugar, butter, milk, vanilla and corn syrup in bowl and mix, kneading until it becomes smooth and solid. Divide into sections and add flavoring: strawberry, pineapple, almond, peppermint or coconut, according to taste. Place wax in top of double boiler, melt, add chocolate and melt. Dip centers one at a time into chocolate, remove with fork and place on wax paper. VARIATION: Nuts or cherries can be added to fondant.

Albertha Pederson

PEANUT BUTTER BALLS

3/4 cup peanut butter   1/2 cup glazed cherries
1 cup icing sugar   4 sq. semi-sweet chocolate
1 tbsp. melted butter   1/2 tsp. paraffin wax
1 cup nuts, chopped fine

Mix first 5 ingredients together and roll into balls. Melt chocolate and paraffin wax and dip each ball in this mixture. Put on tray in cool place.

Mrs. Celia De Groot

PEANUT BRITTLE

1 cup sugar
1 cup white corn syrup
2 cups shelled raw peanuts

1/2 tsp. salt
1 tsp. baking soda

Heat sugar in frying pan. Add syrup. Bring to boil. Add salt and peanuts. Stir constantly in figure 8 until syrup is light brown. Add soda, stir and immediately pour into buttered cookie pan. After the batch has been poured, let it cool enough to handle with hands. Flip the batch over, stretch out and make it thin enough so the nuts will show through.

PEANUT BRITTLE

1 cup sugar
1/2 cup corn syrup
3/4 cup roasted salted peanuts

1 tsp. butter
1/2 tsp. vanilla
1 tsp. baking soda

Microwave sugar and corn syrup in a 2-qt. measuring pitcher on High for 4 minutes. Stir once at 2 minutes. Stir in peanuts and microwave 3 to 5 minutes on High until light brown. Add butter and vanilla to syrup, stirring well. Microwave 1 to 2 minutes on High. This mixture is extremely hot. Add baking soda and stir until light and foamy. Immediately pour mixture onto greased cookie sheet. Let cool 1/2 hour. Break into small pieces and store in tight container.

Mary Wright
Vera Rude

PUFFED WHEAT CANDY

1 cup sugar
1 cup syrup **or** honey
1 cup butter **or** thick cream

3 tbsp. cocoa
12 cups puffed wheat

Boil first four ingredients until soft ball stage is reached. Pour over puffed wheat and mix well. Put in a well-buttered pan and press down. Cut into squares. VARIATION: Brown sugar may be substituted for white sugar and cocoa. Other cereals may be used instead of puffed wheat.

Mrs. Victor Mason

RUBY'S POPCORN BALLS

1 cup corn syrup
1/4 cup water
1 cup sugar
1 tsp. vinegar
2 tbsp. butter

2 tsp. vanilla
Red **or** green food coloring
1 tsp. baking powder
4 qts. popcorn

Combine first 4 ingredients and cook over medium heat, stirring constantly to hard ball stage. Remove from heat. Add butter, vanilla, food coloring and baking powder. Pour over popcorn. Yield: 15 balls.

Ruby Prior

POPCORN BALLS

1 cup sugar	1 tsp. salt
1/4 cup corn syrup	1 tsp. vanilla
1/4 cup water	8 cups popped corn
2 tbsp. butter	

Mix sugar, corn syrup, water and butter in saucepan until well blended. Place over low heat, stirring gently until mixture boils. Put in candy thermometer and continue boiling without stirring until 270° is reached or very hard ball almost to crack stage. Remove from heat. Add salt and vanilla. Pour the syrup over the popped corn, stirring rapidly with 2 forks to make certain all kernels are covered. Moisten the hands with cold water and press into desired shape. VARIATION: Crackerjack: Add 1/4 cup molasses at 240°. Cook syrup to 280°. Add 1/2 cup peanuts and stir only until well blended. Pour at once onto popcorn and mix quickly. When cool, break into clusters.

POPSICLES

3-oz. pkg. jello	2 cups boiling water
2/3 cup sugar	2 cups cold water
1 pkg. kool-aid	

Dissolve jello, sugar and flavoring in the boiling water. Add cold water. Stir, pour into popsicle holders and freeze for a day. NOTE: If using ready-sweetened kool-aid, do not use sugar.

Joyce Ewing

FUDGESICLES

1 pkg. butterscotch	2 1/2 cups milk
instant pudding	1/2 cup sugar

Mix ingredients well. Pour into paper cups and insert popsicle sticks in center. Freeze. VARIATION: Use chocolate instead of butterscotch.

Mrs. Adrian De Groot

HONEY PULL TAFFY

1 cup maple honey syrup	1 tbsp. vinegar
1 3/4 cup light corn syrup	1/4 tsp. soda
2 tbsp. butter	2 tsp. vanilla

Combine syrups, butter and vinegar in heavy saucepan. Bring to boil over medium heat. Stir well until blended. Continue cooking until hard ball stage is reached. Remove from heat. Add soda and vanilla. Beat quickly until it turns smooth and creamy. Pour into buttered plate. When cool enough to handle, butter hands and pull until satiny and light in color. Pull into long strips 3/4 inch wide. Cut strips into 1-inch pieces and wrap in wax paper. Yield: 1 1/2 lbs. hard taffy.

TAFFY

2 cups sugar	3/4 cup water
1 1/4 cups corn syrup	2 tbsp. butter
1 tsp. salt	

Mix sugar, corn syrup, salt and water until well-blended. Place over low heat until sugar has dissolved, stirring constantly with wooden spoon. Increase heat and continue to cook without stirring. Brush sides of pan with wet pastry brush to prevent crystallization. When syrup begins to boil, insert thermometer and cook to 252°. Remove from heat. Add butter and stir very gently. Pour mixture on oiled cookie sheet or slab and allow to cool. When cool enough to handle, add flavoring and color of your choice. With hands and fingers dipped in cornstarch to prevent sticking, start to pull taffy. Continue pulling until it becomes quite opaque and stretch it into long ropes about 3/4 inch in diameter. With shears, cut taffy into small pieces and wrap in cellophane or wax paper.

HONEY TAFFY

2 cups brown sugar	1 cup honey
1/2 cup water	1 1/2 cups molasses
1 tsp. vanilla	1/8 tsp. salt
3 tbsp. butter	

Combine and cook ingredients. Stir constantly until it cracks in cold water. Pour into buttered tins. Cool. Mark into squares before it hardens.

TOFFEE

2 cups brown sugar	1 can sweetened
1 cup butter	condensed milk
3/4 cup golden syrup	

Combine ingredients and bring to boil in heavy pot. Boil hard about 20 minutes, stirring constantly until toffee threads in cold water. Pour onto buttered baking sheet. Cool. Turn sheet upside down and break into pieces. Nuts may be added to pan before toffee is poured.

Mrs. Ruby Day

CREAM TOFFEE

2 cups brown sugar	1/2 can sweetened
1 cup white corn syrup	condensed milk
1 cup butter	

Mix all ingredients together and boil slowly, stirring constantly, until it forms a hard ball when tested in cold water, and leaves the pan when stirring. Remove from stove and beat until thick. Pour into buttered pan. When cool, mark into squares and break when cold.

P. Christopherson

CANDY APPLES

2 cups light brown sugar
1 tbsp. corn syrup
3/4 cups water
1/2 tsp. lemon extract

Red food coloring
8 apples and sticks
Ice water

Mix sugar, corn syrup and water in saucepan. Stir with wooden spoon until well-blended. Place over heat and continue stirring until all the sugar is dissolved. Cook until the temperature reaches 290°. Remove from heat. Add flavoring and food coloring. Submerge the skewered apple in candy mixture, withdraw apple and quickly place it in bowl of ice water. Leave in the water only the length of time it takes the candy coating to solidify. Drain and place the candy apple on a well-oiled pan.

WHITE DIVINITY

3 cups sugar
3/4 cup corn syrup
3/4 cup water
3 egg whites

1/4 tsp. salt
3/4 cup chopped pecans
or walnuts
1 tsp. vanilla

In a 2-qt. saucepan, combine sugar, corn syrup and water. Cook to temperature of 262°. While the syrup is cooking, pour the egg whites into a bowl and add salt. Beat egg whites until they cling to the bowl. Let candy mixture cool for a few minutes, and pour slowly over beaten egg whites, beating constantly. Be careful not to add hot syrup too rapidly as egg whites may cook. Continue to beat until candy falls in broken pieces from spoon. At this point the mixture will start to appear dull and retain its shape. Quickly fold in nuts and vanilla. Pour into a wax-lined pan. When cold and firm, cut into squares. Wrap in wax paper and store in airtight containers. VARIATIONS: Cherry Divinity: Prepare white divinity, add 1/2 cup or more of coarsely chopped candied cherries. Colored Divinity: Prepare white divinity. When syrup begins to boil, put in thermometer and add a few drops of color off your wet pastry brush to prevent crystallization. Sea Foam Divinity: Substitute 3 cups brown sugar for white sugar and corn syrup. Omit nuts.

3 oz. of melted chocolate is enough to decorate 40 small cookies or meringues.

To soften butter or cream cheese, microwave 1/2 cup at a time on Medium-Low for a few seconds.

ALMOND ROCHA

3/4 cup butter
1 cup sugar
1/4 tsp. salt

5 tbsp. water
8 oz. milk chocolate chips
1 1/2 cups almonds

Melt butter. Add sugar, salt and water. Cook until it reaches 300° or hard crack stage. Immediately pour onto buttered cookie sheet. Brush with melted chocolate and sprinkle sliced almonds over top. Break into pieces.

CRUNCHY CANDY

1 cup sugar
1 cup butter
1 tbsp. water

1 tbsp. corn syrup
3/4 cup chopped nuts
4 sq. semi-sweet chocolate

Bring sugar and butter to a boil. Add water and syrup and boil to a firm ball stage. Add nuts. Spread in greased pan. When fairly hard, spread each side with melted chocolate. Allow chocolate to set. Break up.

Audrey Hayworth

BRANDIED CHERRIES

Cherries with stems on
4 cups sugar

1 1/2 cups water
Brandy

Select perfect, tasty cherries with stems on and wash very carefully. Spread on towel to dry. Boil sugar and water until syrup is thick. Cool syrup slightly and measure it. Add 1 cup brandy to each cup syrup. Arrange cherries in sterilized jars very carefully and loosely with stems up. Fill with brandy syrup and seal. Store in cool place for about 3 months. Drain off syrup, saving it for pudding sauces. Remove cherries carefully and lay gently on absorbent paper to dry slightly. Dip each cherry in melted semi-sweet chocolate to coat evenly and form a seal. Place on lightly-oiled wax paper to harden. Store in a cool place.

CRYSTALIZED ROSE PETALS

Select fresh roses of a deep color. Wash and gently shake off excess water. Remove petals and gently pat dry on paper towel. Cut off white base from each petal as it has a bitter flavor. Brush both sides of petals with beaten egg white, using just enough to moisten, and sprinkle with fine granulated sugar. Place petals on wax paper in a tray and allow to dry in refrigerator. Fresh mint leaves may be prepared in the same way. Rose petals may be arranged to form roses with mint leaves to give a more natural effect.

CANNING
& PRESERVING

PICKLES & RELISH

BREAD AND BUTTER PICKLES

30 cucumbers
8 large white onions
2 sweet peppers
1/2 cup pickling salt
5 cups vinegar

5 cups sugar
2 tbsp. mustard seed
1 tsp. turmeric
1/2 tsp. cloves

Wash cucumbers and slice thinly. Chop onions and peppers. Combine with cucumbers and salt. Let stand for 3 hours. Drain. Combine vinegar, sugar and spices in large kettle. Bring to a boil. Add drained cucumbers. Heat thoroughly, but do not boil. Pack immediately in hot jars and seal.

MERTIN'S BREAD AND BUTTER PICKLES

4 qts. sliced fresh cucumbers
1 qt. sliced medium-sized onions
1 cup pickling salt
9 cups water
41/2 cups brown sugar

31/2 cups vinegar
11/2 cups water
1 tsp. turmeric
1 tbsp. celery seed

Put cucumbers and onions in brine made of the salt and 9 cups water. Soak overnight. Drain off the brine in the morning. Mix sugar, vinegar, 11/2 cups water, turmeric and celery seed together, add the drained onions and cucumbers. Cover and bring to a boil. Leave about 10 minutes and then put in sterilized jars and seal.

Mrs. Mertin G. Mehalcheon

PICKLES IN A BUCKET

Sliced cucumbers, washed
2 large onions
1 green pepper
4 cups sugar
2 cups vinegar

2 tbsp. pickling salt
1 tsp. turmeric
1 tsp. celery seed
1 tsp. mustard seed

Fill ice cream pail with cucumbers, onion and green pepper, mixing well. Combine remaining ingredients and pour over cucumber mixture. Cover and leave in refrigerator. The cucumbers are ready to eat in 3 days and will keep in the refrigerator indefinitely.

Eleanor Leskow

DILL PICKLES

Cucumbers	3 cups water
Dill	1 cup vinegar
Garlic clove (optional)	1/4 cup pickling salt

Wash cucumbers well. Place a head of dill and garlic clove in bottom of each hot sterilized jar. Pack cucumbers into jars. Bring water, vinegar and pickling salt to a boil and pour over cucumbers.

POLISH DILL PICKLES

Cucumbers	1 qt. vinegar
Dill	1 cup pickling salt
Garlic	1 cup sugar
3 qts. water	

Wash cucumbers well. Place a head of dill and garlic clove in bottom of each hot sterilized jar. Pack cucumbers into jars. Boil remaining ingredients together and pour over cucumbers. Yield: 12 quarts.

SWEET DILL PICKLES

1 cup sugar	Cucumbers, quartered
1 cup vinegar	Pickling spice
2 cups water	Garlic
2 tbsp. pickling salt	Dill
1 tbsp. turmeric	

Boil sugar, vinegar, water, salt and turmeric together and pour over cucumbers in jar. Add pickling spice, garlic and dill and seal. Set jars in hot water bath and boil until cucumbers change color to seal.

Christina Smith

GHERKINS

4 qts. cucumbers, 2 to 3" long	1/4 cup salt
4 qts. boiling water	1/4 cup mustard seed
1 cup table salt **or**	1/2 cup mixed pickling spices
11/2 cups coarse salt	71/4 cups sugar
8 cups vinegar	

Wash cucumbers well, drain and place in a crock. Cover with hot brine made with boiling water and salt. Cover and let stand overnight. Drain thoroughly, and place in clean dry crock. Prepare pickle mixture by combining vinegar, salt, spices and 1/4 cup sugar. Pour over cucumbers. Each morning for the next 14 days, add 1/2 cup sugar, stirring well to dissolve sugar. On last day, remove pickles from liquid and pack into sterilized jars. Strain pickle mixture to remove spices, heat liquid and pour over pickles. Seal jars.

SWEET & SOUR DILLS

1 qt. vinegar
2 cups water
4 cups sugar
1/2 cup pickling salt
2 qts. sliced cucumbers

1/2 qt. small, whole onions
1/2 qt. combined celery and
carrot slices
Cauliflower pieces (optional)
Dill weed (optional)

Bring vinegar, water, sugar and pickling salt to a boil. Pack vegetables and dill weed in jars, pour hot brine over and seal.

Mrs. J.L. Hodgins

ICE WATER PICKLES

3 qts. cucumber slices
1 qt. onion
3 green peppers
3 red peppers
1/2 cup salt, dissolved in water

1 qt. vinegar
6 cups sugar
2 tsp. mustard seed
2 tsp. turmeric
1 tsp. celery seed

Put cucumbers, onion, peppers and dissolved salt to soak overnight. Drain and rinse in the morning. Mix vinegar, sugar, mustard seed, turmeric and celery seed and bring to a boil. Add vegetables and simmer 5 minutes. Put in hot, sterilized jars and seal.

SALAD PICKLES

16 cups sliced, peeled cucumbers
4 cups thinly-sliced onions
4 cups broken-up cauliflower
1 green pepper, chopped
1/3 cup salt
4 trays ice cubes

5 cups sugar
3 cups cider vinegar
2 tbsp. mustard seed
1 1/2 tsp. celery seed
1/2 tsp. turmeric

Combine vegetables in large glass bowl and sprinkle with salt. Add ice cubes and mix through vegetables. Cover and let stand at room temperature for 3 hours. Drain well. Combine sugar, vinegar, mustard, celery seed and turmeric and bring to boil. Add vegetables and bring to boil. Put in hot, sterilized jars and seal.

Mrs. Mary Heppler

CUCUMBER RINGS

4 qts. sliced cucumbers
6 tsp. pickling salt
5 cups vinegar
1/2 tsp. curry powder

1 tbsp. celery seed
4 cups sugar
2 tbsp. mustard seed

Place slices in crock and sprinkle with salt. Let stand overnight. Drain slices and wash in clear, cold water. Bring remaining ingredients to a boil and add cucumber slices. Bring back to boiling point, but do not boil. Keep hot for 5 minutes. Pack into sterilized jars and seal.

NINE DAY SWEET PICKLE

2 gallons small cucumbers
9 cups cold water
1 cup pickling salt

4 cups vinegar
8 cups water
2 tsp. alum

Wash cucumbers. Soak for 3 days in brine made of the 9 cups water and pickling salt. On the fourth day, drain and put in fresh cold water to cover cucumbers, changing water every day for 3 days. On the seventh day, bring the vinegar, 8 cups water and alum to a boil. Cut cucumbers and add. Bring to boiling point again and remove from stove. Let pickles stand in solution until cold. Drain well.

20 cups sugar
8 cups vinegar

2 handfuls mixed pickling
    spice, tied in cheesecloth.

Boil ingredients for 2 minutes and pour over cucumbers. Let stand overnight. Drain and heat syrup. Pour over cucumbers. Do this for 2 days. On third day, fill jars, pour hot syrup over cucumbers and seal jars.

SWEET MIX PICKLE

1 qt. cucumbers
1 qt. onions
1 qt. cauliflowers

16 cups water
1 cup salt

Cut vegetables to uniform size. Make a brine by boiling the water and salt. Pour over vegetables. Let stand three days. Drain well. Rinse once with clear water.

6 cups vinegar
8 cups sugar
2 tbsp. pickling spice

2 tbsp. celery seed
2 tbsp. broken cinnamon

Tie seasonings in cheesecloth bag. Make a syrup by boiling the vinegar, sugar and spices. Pour syrup over pickles and let stand 24 hours. Drain. Bring the syrup to a boil and pour over pickles. Pack hot sterilized jars with vegetables.

SWEET MIXED PICKLES

1 cup pickling salt
2 qts. water
4 cucumbers, 6 inches long
1 qt. small onions
1 small cauliflower
3 tbsp. mixed whole spices

8 cups mild vinegar
2 cups sugar
1/2 tbsp. white mustard seed
1/2 tbsp. celery seed
1 hot red pepper, sliced
    (optional)

Use pickling salt and water for the brine. Wash cucumbers and cut into slices, peel onions and break cauliflower into chunks. Cover vegetables with the brine. Let stand overnight and drain. Tie mixed whole spices in a bag and boil with the vinegar, sugar, mustard and celery seed for five minutes. Remove spice bag. Add vegetables and red pepper. Pour into sterilized jars and seal. Yield: 3 quarts.

ALDRED'S MUSTARD PICKLES

1 qt. cucumbers	3 red peppers, chopped
1 doz. whole gherkins	1 cup salt
4 large onions, cut fine	1 qt. vinegar
1 lb. small, whole pickling onions	4 cups sugar
1 large cauliflower, broken up	1/2 tsp. celery seed
1 bunch celery, chopped	1/2 tsp. mustard seed

Cover vegetables with brine of salt and hot water. Leave overnight and drain. Heat the vinegar and sugar and add the drained vegetables, celery and mustard seed.

1 cup flour	1 cup vinegar
1 tbsp. turmeric	2 tsp. mustard

Mix ingredients into a paste and add to hot pickles. Simmer a few minutes, stirring constantly. Put in sterilized jars and seal.

Mrs. Wm. Aldred

MUSTARD PICKLES

1/2 cup salt	8 cups sugar
1 qt. large cucumbers, cut finely	4 tbsp. mustard seed
1 qt. whole pickling onions	8 cups vinegar
2 qts. chopped cauliflower	6 tbsp. celery seed
3 red peppers, chopped	2/3 cup flour
3 green peppers, chopped	8 tbsp. mustard
1 qt. finely cut onions	1 - 2 tbsp. turmeric
1 qt. midget dills	1 can pimentos

Sprinkle salt on cucumbers, onions, cauliflower, peppers, onions and dill. Let stand overnight. Drain in the morning. Boil sugar, mustard seed, vinegar and celery seed 10 minutes. Mix flour, mustard and turmeric with a little vinegar. Add to boiling ingredients and boil slowly a few minutes. Add chopped vegetables and boil until tender. Add pimentos just before sealing jars.

Mrs. B.P. Alberts

PICKLED COCKTAIL ONIONS

2 qts. silverskin onions	1 lemon, thinly sliced
1/2 cup pickling salt	1 tsp. allspice
2 cups vinegar	1 tsp. whole cloves
4 cups sugar	1 tbsp. stick cinnamon

Cover onions with boiling water. Let stand 5 minutes. Drain and cover with cold water. Peel. Wash thoroughly. Sprinkle with salt and cover with boiling water. Let stand overnight, drain and allow cold water to run through onions. Bring vinegar, 2 cups water, sugar, lemon and spices tied in bag to a boil. Remove lemon slices and spice bag and allow to cool slightly. Pour onions into sterilized jars, pour solution over and seal.

DILLED CARROTS

4 lbs. carrots, 4' long
Boiling water
2 tbsp. mixed pickling spice
2 tsp. dry dill seeds

4 cups vinegar
2 cups sugar
2 cloves garlic
4 fresh dill sprigs

Wash carrots and trim ends. Place in saucepan and cover with boiling water. Bring to boiling point and reduce heat to simmer. Cover pan and cook for 10 minutes. Drain and cool. Scrape off skins with vegetable parer. Wash and drain carrots again and place in large mixing bowl. Tie pickling spice and dill seeds in double thickness of cheesecloth and place in saucepan with vinegar and sugar. Bring to boiling point and stir until sugar is dissolved. Reduce heat and simmer 10 minutes. Discard spice bag. Pour syrup over carrots and cool. Cover and refrigerator overnight. Place carrots and syrup in preserving kettle and bring to boiling point. Boil uncovered for 3 minutes. Pack carrots into sterilized pint jars. Pare garlic and cut in each jar. Ladle hot syrup to within 1/2 inch of top of jar and add dill sprig. Seal at once. Yield: 4 pints.

Georgina Taylor

PICKLED BEETS

4cups vinegar
2 cups sugar
1 tbsp. cinnamon
1 tsp. allspice

1 tbsp. mustard seed
1 tsp. cloves
1 tsp. salt

Combine vinegar and sugar and stir. Add cinnamon, allspice, mustard seed, cloves and salt. Bring slowly to a boil. Pour over cooked beets in clean, hot jars. Seal. Yield: 4 quarts.

GREEN TOMATO PICKLES

8 lbs. tomatoes, peeled
1/2 cup salt
6 cups sugar
1 pint vinegar

1 pint water
Whole cloves
Cinnamon to taste

Cut tomatoes in half and let stand overnight. Sprinkle tomatoes with salt, cover with water and boil gently until tender. Try not to break tomatoes while boiling. Drain well. Make a syrup of sugar, vinegar, water and some whole cloves and cinnamon. Heat tomatoes thoroughly in this syrup. Put mixture in a crock and let stand for 2 days. Drain off syrup, boil it and return to tomatoes. Repeat this again in 2 days, then bottle and seal.

GREEN TOMATO PICKLES

24 medium-sized	2 tsp. celery seed
green tomatoes	2 tsp. dry mustard
3 medium onions	3 tbsp. pickling spice
4 tbsp. salt	2 tsp. mustard seed
5 thin slices of lemon	3 1/2 cups brown sugar
2 sweet red peppers	2 cups vinegar
1 green pepper	

Slice tomatoes and onions thinly. Place in crock in layers, sprinkling each layer with salt. Let stand overnight. In the morning, drain thoroughly, rinse in cold water and drain again. Slice lemon and peppers. Add to the tomato-onion mixture. Add celery seed and dry mustard. Tie pickling spice and mustard seed loosely in a cheesecloth bag. Add spice bag and sugar to vinegar. Bring to a boil. Add tomatoes, onions, lemon, pepper and celery seed. Cook for 1/2 hour or until thickened and the vegetables tender, stirring occasionally. Remove spice bag. Pack pickles into hot sterilized jars and seal at once. Yield: 6 pints.

Jessie Uruscheed

RED TOMATO PICKLES

4 large onions, sliced	1 cup sugar
6 apples, sliced	1 tbsp. salt
1 qt. ripe tomatoes, sliced	1/4 tsp. pepper
1 cup vinegar	

Simmer onions and apples until tender. Add tomatoes, vinegar, sugar, salt and pepper. Cook slowly a little longer until well blended. Put into sterilized jars and seal.

Mary Belanger

AUNT POLLY'S RIPE TOMATO PICKLES

2 qts. ripe tomatoes	1 tbsp. salt
1 cup chopped onion,	1 tsp. turmeric
celery **or** cucumber	2 tsp. dry mustard
2 cups vinegar	3 tbsp. flour
3 cups sugar	

Place tomatoes, vegetables and vinegar in saucepan. Cook until tender. Add sugar, salt, turmeric, dry mustard and flour. Simmer 10 to 15 minutes longer, then bottle and seal. This pickle can be used as a sweet and sour sauce for meat dishes.

Wash, rinse and sterilize jars by either boiling in water for 15 minutes or placing on a rack in a 225° oven for 10 minutes. Allow to cool slightly before using.

WINTER SALAD PICKLES

7 large cucumbers   1/2 cup salt
5 large onions

Put cucumbers and onions through grinder, mix and sprinkle with salt. Let stand overnight. Drain in the morning. Make the following dressing:

3 cups vinegar   1 cup water
1/2 tsp. powdered ginger   1/2 cup flour
3 cups sugar   3/4 tsp. turmeric
1 tbsp. celery seed   1 tbsp. mustard seed
1/8 tsp. red pepper

Boil ingredients until thick. Add onions and cucumbers and boil 10 minutes. Bottle and store. The color of these pickles changes to dull green after 2 or 3 weeks. Yield: 4 quarts.

Mrs. Harold Wight

YELLOW BEAN MUSTARD PICKLES

Wash 4 qts. of beans and cut into 1-inch pieces. Boil in salted water until tender. Drain well. Make a dressing of the following:

3 cups sugar   1/2 cup dry mustard
3 cups vinegar   1 tbsp. celery seed
1/2 cup flour   1 tbsp. turmeric

Combine ingredients and cook on low until thick, stirring constantly. Add beans and bring to a boil. Fill jars and seal.

SASKATOON PICKLES

3 cups sugar   1 tsp. cinnamon
1 tsp. cloves   1 cup cider vinegar
1/4 tsp. salt   5 lbs. saskatoon berries

Boil sugar, spices and vinegar for 10 minutes. Add berries and simmer gently for 10 minutes. Put in sterilized jars and seal. Very good with cold turkey, chicken or pork.

MARROW PICKLES

4 lb. marrow   1 tbsp. ground ginger
1/2 cup salt   1 cup sugar
4 cups vinegar   1/2 lb. onions, sliced
2 tbsp. turmeric   6 dry red peppers

Sprinkle marrow with salt. Let stand overnight. Drain. Boil vinegar, turmeric, ginger, sugar, onions and peppers for 10 minutes. Add marrow and boil slowly for 1/2 to 1 hour. Put in jars and seal.

J. M. Elliott

SWISS CHARD PICKLES

2 qts. Swiss chard stalk, cut up	6 cups sugar
2 bunches celery, chopped	Vinegar
2 lbs. onions, chopped	1 tbsp. mixed pickling spice
2 lb. apples, chopped	

Sprinkle chard stalks, celery and onions with salt and add water to cover. Let stand overnight. In morning, drain and add apples and sugar with vinegar and water (half and half) to cover. Put in pot with pickling spice in a bag, bring to a boil and simmer 1 hour. Then add the following:

1/2 cup flour	1 tbsp. curry powder
2 tbsp. mustard	1 1/2 tbsp. turmeric

Mix ingredients with cold water to form a paste and add to hot chard mixture. Allow to come to full boil, simmer a few minutes, pack in jars and seal.

SWEET PICKLED CHERRIES

4 - 4 1/2 lb. tart cherries	8 cups sugar
3 cups vinegar	

Wash and pit cherries. Cover with vinegar and let stand overnight. Drain liquid and mix cherries with sugar. Let stand for about 1 week, stirring them each day. Pack into sealers, seal and store in a cool, dark place.

SWEET PICKLED CRABAPPLES

6 lbs. crabapples	6 cups sugar
3 cups vinegar	1 tsp. whole cloves
3 cups water	3-inch stick of cinnamon

Wash crabapples. Trim blossom ends but leave stems. Prick each one several times with a needle. In a large pot, put vinegar, water, sugar and spices tied in a bag, and boil 5 minutes. Add crabapples and simmer gently until tender, but do not overcook. Pack into sterilized jars, cover with boiling syrup and seal.

CUCUMBER RELISH

2 qts. pared cucumbers	1 qt. vinegar
3 large onions	1 cup flour
12 large apples	3 tsp. mustard
1/2 cup salt	1 tsp. turmeric
7 cups brown sugar	2 tsp. celery seed

Put cucumbers, onions and apples through coarse food chopper and let stand in salt and water to cover overnight. Drain and add brown sugar and vinegar. Bring to a boil. Make a paste of flour, mustard, turmeric and celery seed and a little water. Add. Boil until thick. Pour into hot sterilized jars and seal at once.

Mrs. Anders H. Anderson

HOT DOG CUCUMBER RELISH

12 large cucumbers
1/2 cup salt
4 large onions, chopped finely
1 pint vinegar
21/2 cups sugar

1/2 cup flour
2 tsp. mustard
11/2 tsp. turmeric
1 tbsp. celery seed

Chop cucumbers in food chopper, sprinkle with salt, let stand 4 hours. Rinse and drain. Mix onions with cucumbers. Prepare remaining ingredients in large pot. Bring to a boil, add vegetables and cook at low heat for 20 minutes. Put in sterilized jars and seal.

Mrs. John Properzi

UNCOOKED TOMATO RELISH

7 lbs. ripe tomatoes
7 large onions
2 lbs. celery
1 cup pickling salt

2 red peppers, chopped
2 cups vinegar
6 cups sugar
3 oz. mustard seed

Put tomatoes, onions and celery through a food chopper. Mix with pickling salt and drain overnight. Add red peppers to pulp. Boil vinegar, sugar and mustard seed and add to pulp. Seal.

DUTCH RELISH

2 cups green tomatoes
2 cups peeled cucumbers
1 sweet red pepper
1 green pepper
1 large head celery with leaves
2 cups peeled onions
3 tbsp. salt

3 cups cider vinegar
4 tsp. dry mustard
11/4 tsp. turmeric
12/3 cups sugar
1/3 cup flour
1/2 cup cold water

Chop or grind tomatoes, cucumbers, peppers, celery and onions and combine in large aluminum or enamel kettle. Add salt, stirring well. Add just enough boiling water to cover mixture. Allow to stand 30 minutes. Spoon mixture into a cheese cloth bag, drain thoroughly and return to kettle. Add vinegar and bring to a boil. Meanwhile, combine mustard, turmeric, sugar and flour. Add cold water and blend to a smooth paste. Stir a few tablespoons of hot mixture into the mustard mixture, blending thoroughly. Stir into remaining hot mixture and mix well. Bring contents to a boil and boil 2 to 3 minutes. Pour into hot, sterilized jars and seal. Yield: 10 cups.

When making anything juicy, such as fresh cranberry relish, freeze first and then put through a food grinder while still frozen. End of mess.

HARVEST RELISH

1 large head cauliflower	6 large red peppers
1 medium red cabbage	8 large cucumbers
6 medium sized onions	1 small, whole bunch celery,
2 medium bunches broccoli	2 qts. cooked kernel corn

Wash vegetables and break or cut into fairly large pieces. Cover with a brine of 1 tbsp. salt to 1 pint of water. Strain.

1/2 cup flour	3 tsp. mustard
1/2 cup sugar	1 tsp. turmeric
1 tsp. paprika	Salt to taste
1 qt. vinegar	

Mix ingredients well and cook until thick. Add vegetables and boil for 5 minutes. Pack into jars and seal at once. Store in a cool, dark place.

THOUSAND ISLAND RELISH

8 large cucumbers	2 sweet red peppers
1 large cauliflower	1/2 cup pickling salt
12 large onions	5 cups water
2 sweet green peppers	

Put first five ingredients through a grinder. Cover with pickling salt and water. Let stand 1 hour or more and drain.

6 cups vinegar	1 tbsp. celery seed
2 cups water	1 cup flour
6 cups sugar	6 tbsp. dry mustard
1 tbsp. mustard seed	1 tbsp. turmeric

Mix ingredients. Pour over vegetables and cook about 1/2 hour. Put in sterilized jars and seal.

Elsie Vooys

MAC'S RELISH

8 green tomatoes	4 cups sugar
2 red peppers	2 tbsp. mustard
6 medium onions	1 cup flour
1 medium head of cabbage	1 tsp. turmeric
2 bunches of celery	2 tbsp. salt
Vinegar	

Put tomatoes, peppers and onions through food chopper. Chop cabbage and celery, add to tomato mixture and put in kettle with enough vinegar to nearly cover. Boil 15 minutes. Mix sugar, mustard, flour, turmeric and salt and add to above. Boil 10 minutes. Put in sterilized jars and seal. This is delicious for a winter salad or sandwich spread.

GOLDEN RELISH

4 cups carrots	2 pimentos
4 cups celery	2 cups sugar
2 green peppers	2 cups vinegar
4 tart apples	2 tbsp. salt
2 tbsp. celery seed	

Clean and chop all vegetables rather coarsely. Peel apples and chop. Put the vegetables and remaining ingredients in saucepan and cook gently until carrots and celery are almost tender. Pour into sterilized jars and seal while hot.

CORN RELISH

1/4 cup salt	3/4 qt. vinegar
6 green peppers, finely chopped	1 tbsp. celery seed
2 red peppers, finely chopped	1 tsp. turmeric
1 qt. ground onions	1 qt. sugar
1 qt. ground cucumbers	1 qt. kernel corn
1 qt. chopped tomatoes	

Sprinkle salt on peppers, onions and cucumbers. Place in colander and drain 2 hours. Combine tomatoes, vinegar, celery seed, turmeric and sugar. Add and boil 30 minutes. Add corn and boil 10 minutes more. Seal in hot sterilized jars.

RHUBARB RELISH

1 qt. rhubarb, chopped	1 tsp. allspice
1 chopped onion	1/2 tsp. cloves
1 pint vinegar	2 tsp. salt
51/2 cups brown sugar	1/2 tsp. pepper
1 tsp. cinnamon	

Combine ingredients and boil until thick. Seal in hot sterilized jars.

JAMS & JELLIES

APRICOT JAM

4 lbs. apricots, cut in halves	1 can pineapple, cut in cubes
Juice of 1 lemon	1 large orange, cut in 6 sections
8 cups sugar	and thinly sliced

Combine and let ingredients stand overnight. Boil quickly in the morning. Seal in hot sterilized jars.

Mrs. F.H. House

HEAVENLY JAM

4 large carrots	1 dozen peaches
5 whole lemons	1 dozen apples
5 whole oranges	10 cups water

Grate carrots and put lemon and orange through fine chopper. Skin and stone the peaches and then mash. Core and finely grate the apples. Combine with water and boil for 1 hour before measuring. To each cup pulp, add 1 cup sugar and boil again for 2 hours, stirring occasionally until it jells. Pour into hot sterilized jars and seal.

PEACH JAM

2 cups peeled peaches, chopped	Pectin
1 tbsp. lemon juice	2 3/4 cups sugar

Place peaches in 3-qt. casserole. Add lemon juice and pectin, stirring well. Microwave on High for 5 to 6 minutes until boiling. Stir and add sugar and return to microwave for 3 to 5 minutes to boiling again. Boil 1 minute and remove. Skim and stir for 5 minutes, then pour into sterilized jars. Yield: 2 to 3 small jars.

Martha O'Brien

PLUM JAM

31/2 plums, washed and pitted	4 cups sugar
1 tbsp. vinegar	2 tsp. ground cinnamon

Peel and quarter plums. In processor, finely chop plums, one-quarter at a time. Place in large pot. Add vinegar, sugar and cinnamon. Bring to boil and cook rapidly until clear and thick, about 20 minutes. Stir frequently to prevent sticking. Skim off any foam. Pour into sterilized jars and seal. Yield: 3 pints.

RASPBERRY JAM

6 cups raspberries, mashed	6 cups sugar

Boil raspberries for 2 minutes. Add sugar. Boil hard for 1 minute. Remove from heat and beat for 4 minutes. This thickens and has a wonderful flavor. You may strain to remove the seeds.

JAM: Precook fruit, except apricots, peaches and pear, in uncovered kettle. Add sugar and boil, stirring frequently. To test, remove kettle from heat. Place spoonful of jam on cold plate and chill. If it does not set, boil and test again. Pour into hot, sterilized jars to within 3/4 inch of top. Wipe rim with damp, clean cloth. Cool slightly. Cover with paraffin. Cool and cover with paraffin again, tilting the jar to cover the edge well. Cover with paper or metal lid.

RHUBARB JAM

5 cups diced rhubarb	6-oz. pkg. strawberry jello
5 cups sugar	1 cup drained pineapple
1 cup water	

Boil rhubarb and sugar with water. Add jelly powder and pineapple. Pour into sterilized jars and seal.

RHUBARB JAM NATURAL WAY

4 cups sugar	1/2 lb. figs
7 cups chopped rhubarb	1 whole orange, chopped fine

Wash and drain rhubarb well. Do not peel. Add sugar to rhubarb and mix lightly in a large bowl. Let stand overnight. In the morning, drain juice off rhubarb into a preserving kettle and simmer until it reduces by 1/4. While the juice is simmering, add figs and orange. Add the rhubarb last and boil just long enough for rhubarb to get soft, but not mushy. Seal in hot sterilized jars.

RHUBARB APRICOT JAM

4 cups sugar	1 can apricot instant pie filling
6 cups diced rhubarb	3-oz. pkg. apricot gelatin

Mix sugar and rhubarb together and let set overnight. In morning, boil 10 minutes and add pie filling. Bring to boil again. Remove from heat and stir in gelatin. Put in sterilized jars and seal. Yield: 4 pints. VARIATIONS: Strawberry pie filling with strawberry gelatin or cherry pie filling with cherry gelatin may also be used.

Georgina Taylor

PINEAPPLE RHUBARB MARMALADE

12 cups diced rhubarb	2 small oranges, ground
14-oz. can crushed pineapple	4 - 5 cups sugar

Combine all ingredients but sugar in large kettle. Put sugar on top and let stand covered overnight. In the morning, bring mixture to a boil and continue to boil for 40 minutes, stirring occasionally. Put in sterilized jars and seal.

Georgina Taylor

RHUBARB ORANGE SLICE CANDY MARMALADE

3 cups diced rhubarb	1 lb. orange slice **or**
3 cups sugar	gum candy

Combine rhubarb and sugar and let stand 1 hour. Cut up orange slice, add and boil until thick and clear. Yield: 7 pints.

Georgina Taylor

BITTER ORANGE MARMALADE

10 Seville oranges	28 cups water
2 lemons	20 cups sugar
2 sweet oranges	

Slice fruit very thinly or put through meat grinder, removing all seeds. Add water and leave to soak for 24 hours. Boil for 1 1/2 hours, leave again for 24 hours. Add sugar and boil until it jells, taking care it doesn't stick to the kettle. Pour into jars and seal.

EASY CARROT MARMALADE

2 cups grated carrots	2 oranges, sliced
2 1/2 cups rhubarb, cut small	3 cups sugar

Combine all ingredients and boil until thick. Yield: 2 pints.

Georgina Taylor

CARROT MARMALADE

12 cups carrots, put through food chopper	16-oz. can crushed pineapple
12 cups sugar	3 whole oranges, ground
3 whole lemons, ground	6-oz. jar maraschino cherries,
1 tsp. salt	chopped

Mix all ingredients except cherries and let stand overnight. Bring to a boil and boil 2 to 3 minutes. Just before putting in jars, add the cherries. Seal quickly in hot, sterilized jars.

A.F. Anderson

HEAVENLY MARMALADE

4 oranges	12 apples
2 lemons	12 pears
12 peaches	Sugar

Cut oranges and lemons into small pieces and cover with water. Let stand overnight. In the morning, cook until soft. Cut up remaining fruit and combine pound for pound of sugar. Simmer until thick. Seal quickly in hot sterilized jars.

Evelyn Davey

GRAPE JELLY

1 basket grapes	4 apples, chopped
1 cup water	Sugar

Bring grapes, water and apples to a boil and simmer 1 1/2 hours. Strain and measure. Boil 20 minutes. Add 1 cup sugar to each cup of juice. Bring to boil and bottle immediately.

Mrs. Harmon Burpee

BEET JELLY

3 cups beet juice
4 - 6 tsp. lemon juice
1 pkg. pectin crystals

4 cups sugar
1 pkg. strawberry, grape
or raspberry jello

Bring beet juice, lemon juice and pectin to a boil. Add sugar and jelly powder. Bring to boil and boil 6 to 8 minutes. Bottle while hot and seal with wax. Serve with meat dishes.

Mrs. Dorothy Hagstrom

PEPPER JELLY

1 pint vinegar
6 sweet red peppers
2 - 3 green peppers
6 cups sugar

2 lemons
6 peaches
1/2 bottle pectin

Chop peppers, scald and drain. Chop peaches and add lemon cut in thin slices. Add vinegar and half the sugar. Boil 15 to 20 minutes until it begins to thicken. Remove lemon slices and add rest of sugar and pectin. Boil 1 minute at full, rolling boil. Seal in hot sterilized jars.

Mrs. C. Blair

MINT SAUCE

1 1/2 tbsp. confectioners sugar
3 tbsp. water

1/3 cup chopped mint leaves
1/2 cup vinegar

Dissolve sugar in water. Cool. Add mint leaves and vinegar. Cool well before serving. Yield: 1 cup.

RHUBARB CONSERVE

4 cups rhubarb
4 cups sugar
2 oranges, juice and grated rind

2 lemons, juice and grated rind
1 cup walnuts, coarsely broken

Place rhubarb, sugar, orange and lemon juice and rind in a deep kettle and heat gently until juice begins to be drawn out. Then cook rapidly, stirring constantly, until the mixture is thick and clear. Remove from heat, add nuts and pour at once into hot, sterile jars and seal immediately.

B. Boutillier

For sweet fruits, use 2 cups sugar to 4 cups boiling water. For slightly acid fruit, use 4 cups sugar to 6 cups boiling water. For acid fruits use 2 cups sugar to 2 cups boiling water, and for very acid fruits use 4 cups sugar to 2 cups boiling water.

PEACH PRESERVES

12 medium, firm, ripe peaches   2 tbsp. lemon juice
3 cups sugar

Peel and quarter peaches. In processor, finely chop peaches, one-quarter at a time. Place in large pot. Add sugar and lemon juice. Bring to boil and cook rapidly until clear and thick, about 20 minutes. Stir frequently to prevent sticking. Skim off any foam. Pour into sterilized jars and seal. Yield:1 quart.

CHOKECHERRY JELLY

7 cups chokecherry juice   2 pkg. pectin crystals
Water   9 cups sugar

Make juice from chokecherries with only enough water to cover them. Boil 30 minutes. Drip through jelly bag. Place pot of juice over high heat. Add pectin crystals and stir until mixture comes to hard boil. Stir in sugar at once. Bring to full rolling boil. Boil hard for 1 1/2 minutes, stirring constantly. Skim rapidly with metal spoon and pour at once into sterilized jars and seal. Yield: 3 pints.

Mary Barrack

BLACK CURRANT JAM AND JELLY

8 cups water   8 cups sugar
4 lbs. black currants

Add 4 cups water to berries and boil for 5 minutes. Drain currants, reserving juice. Add 4 cups each of water and sugar to berries in pan and boil for 10 minutes. Pour into jars. Add pint for pint of sugar to the juice and boil for 20 minutes or until it jells. Seal tight.

Mrs. Drysdale

JELLY: Add cold water to fruit. Simmer in uncovered kettle until fruit is soft, crushing during cooking. Pour into moistened bag and allow to drain until dripping ceases. Squeezing the bag makes more liquid, but clouds jelly. Boil juice for 3 minutes. Add 3/4 cup sugar to 1 cup of juice and boil uncovered, removing scum as it forms. Allow mixture to drip off spoon. If it flows off in sheets combined from 2 or 3 drops, it is ready to bottle. Cool and bottle as for jam. To make over jelly that didn't jell, combine 3/4 cup cold water and 1 package of pectin crystals. Bring to a boil and boil hard for 1 minute. Stirring constantly, add 4 cups of unjelled jelly. Stir well and put in clean glasses. It should now set perfectly.

MISCELLANEOUS

M

HAND CREAM

3 egg whites
1 cup mutton tallow
3 oz. glycerine

3 oz. almond oil
1 oz. oil of bergamot

Beat egg whites stiff and add melted fat. Beat well. Add glycerine and almond oil and beat until creamy – about 15 minutes. Add bergamot and beat until smooth.

RENA'S HAND CREAM

1/2 oz. sodium laryl sulphate
4 oz. cetyl alcohol

63/4 oz. glycerine
1/2 oz. hydrous lanolin

Melt all together in top of double boiler. Pour 371/2 oz. boiling water into large bowl, add dissolved mixture. Beat 30 minutes at high speed with mixer. Add perfume and food coloring if desired. This is a very inexpensive way to have hand cream on hand.

Mrs. Rena Urban

CHICKADEE TREAT

1 lb. any kind of lard **or** fat
12 oz. peanut butter
2 cups sunflower seeds
4 cups water

31/2 cups cornmeal
31/2 cups oatmeal
31/2 cups cream of wheat

Mix ingredients together by hand. You may vary the amounts of cereal and some bird seed can be added. Pack the mixture into tin cans that have both ends removed. Fasten a stick through each can, so the birds have a place to stand and eat, then hang on trees or in your veranda.

Mrs. Luella Callies

FIREPLACE CAKES

2 lbs. bluestone
2 lbs. coarse salt

2 oz. salt for color
Paraffin

Combine bluestone, salt and desired color salts (red: strontium nitrate; yellow: calcium nitrate; green: borax; purple: potassium chloride) in a cardboard box. Cover and shake vigorously until chemicals are combined. With a wooden spoon, fill large colored baking cups three-quarters full. Melt wax over hot water and pour a thick layer over chemicals. Cover with sparkle or colored stars. Throw onto fire.

COPPER CLEANER

1 tsp. salt   Vinegar
1 tsp. flour

Combine salt, flour and enough vinegar to make a paste. Apply to copper utensils and rub. Repeat if necessary. NOTE: This paste may be made in a large quantity and stored in a glass jar.

BRASS, COPPER AND PEWTER CLEANER

1/4 cup salt   Flour
Vinegar

Combine salt with enough vinegar to dissolve it. Add enough flour to make a fairly dry paste.

WALL CLEANER

1 cup Spic and Span   3/4 cup milk
1/4 cup turpentine   32 cups water

Combine Spic and Span, turpentine and milk. Add to water. NOTE: This removes grease without leaving streaks.

MULTIPURPOSE CLEANER

1/4 cup baking soda   17 cups warm water
1/2 cup vinegar

Dissolve baking soda in vinegar and combine with water.

MULTIPURPOSE FURNITURE POLISH

2 tbsp. olive oil   4 cups warm water
1 tbsp. vinegar

Mix olive oil and vinegar and add to water. Mix well and use in spray bottle.

MOTOR HOME HOLDING TANK FRESHENER

16 oz. formaldahyde   1/2 cup Pine Sol
1/2 cup liquid detergent   16 cups water

When using, pour in 2 cups mixture to 1 gallon of water. Pour into toilet when tank requires it.

Christina Smith

As with commercial products, homemade cleaners should be stored in carefully labelled, well-closed containers and kept safely out of reach of children. Save your old cleaner containers to put your homemade solutions in.

TOILET BOWL CLEANER

Mix sufficient borax and lemon juice to make enough paste to clean entire ring. Swish the toilet brush around to get bowl wet. Rub on paste and let set for about 2 hours.

TUB AND TILE CLEANER

Use a combination of white distilled vinegar with washing soda to get rid of soap scum on tubs, sinks, tiles, etc. You may try straight baking soda for lighter jobs.

WINDOW CLEANER

Mix 1/4 cup vinegar with 1 cup water. Use in a spray bottle.

ENVIRONMENTALLY SAFE CLEANING SUPPLIES

STAIN REMOVER
Baking soda and vinegar
Washing soda and Borax
Lemon juice for aluminium,
   clothes and porcelin
Cornstarch

SCOURING
Baking soda and damp cloth
Damp salt
Washing soda sprinkled on for
   15 minutes and scrubbed
   with damp steel wool

SOAP SCUM
Vinegar and washing soda
Baking soda

DEODORIZER
1 cup vinegar in a bowl
Lemon juice
Baking soda and water for
   carpets, refrigerator,
   freezers, thermos bottles,
   drains and upholstery
Borax

FURNITURE POLISH
Vegetable oil
Cornstarch

FABRIC SOFTENER
Baking soda
Washing soda
Vinegar

To remove grass stains from white denim, put some wood alcohol on stain, let stand awhile and wash with detergent. Use corn syrup to remove grass stain from other fabrics. Rub, let stand until dry, brush off and rinse.

To remove a grease spot from a fabric, rub cream of tartar on spot, leave a few hours and brush off.

To remove a hot stain from wood furniture, rub with a cut raw potato dipped in baking soda.

TABLE OF MEASUREMENT
& METRIC CONVERSION
(Working Equivalent)

1/4 teaspoon		1 millilitre
1/2 teaspoon		2 millilitres
1 teaspoon		5 millilitres
2 teaspoons		10 millilitres
1 tablespoon	3 teaspoons	15 millilitres
1/8 cup	2 tbsp.	
1/4 cup	4 tablespoons	50 millilitres
1/3 cup	5 tablespoons plus 1 teaspoon	75 millilitres
1/2 cup	8 tablespoons	125 millilitres
2/3 cup	10 tablespoons plus 2 teaspoons	150 millilitres
3/4 cup		175 millilitres
1 cup	16 tablespoons	250 millilitres
2 cups	1 pint	
4 cups	2 pints or 1 quart	
4 quarts	1 gallon	
1 oz.		30 grams
2 oz.		55 grams
3 oz.		85 grams
4 oz.	1/2 cup	125 grams
5 oz.		140 grams
6 oz.		170 grams
8 oz.		250 grams
16 oz.	1 lb.	500 grams
32 oz.		1 litre

OVEN TEMPERATURES

C	F	C	F
100°	200°	190°	375°
120°	250°	200°	400°
140°	275°	220°	425°
150°	300°	230°	450°
160°	325°	240°	475°
180°	350°	260°	500°

EQUIVALENTS

Almonds, unblanched, whole
    6 oz.   1 cup
Apples
    1 lb. unpared   3 cups pared and sliced
Apricots, dried
    1 lb. $3 1/4$ cups
Brazil nuts
    1 lb. shelled   3 cups
Bread crumbs, dry
    1/4 cup   1 slice bread
Bread crumbs, soft
    1/4 cup   1 slice bread
Cheese, freshly shredded
    1/4 lb.   1 cup
Chocolate
    1 oz.   1 square
Cocoa
    3 tbsp. plus   1 oz. unsweetened
       1 tbsp. fat   chocolate
Cracker crumbs
    3/4 crumbs   1 cup bread crumbs
Cream, half & half
    1 cup $1 1/2$ tbsp. butter plus
                               7/8 cup milk, or 1/2 cup
                               coffee cream and 1/2 cup
                               milk

Dates
    1 lb. $2 1/2$ cups pitted
Figs, dried
    1 lb. $2 2/3$ cups chopped
Filberts or hazelnuts
    $2 1/4$ lb. in shell   1 lb. shelled or $3 1/3$ cups
Flour (Cake)
    1 cup sifted   7/8 cup sifted flour, or 1 cup
                               less 2 tbsp.
Flour (White)
    4 cups $3 1/2$ cups cracked wheat
Gelatin
    1/4-oz. envelope   1 tbsp.
Hazelnuts
    1 lb. shelled $3 1/3$ cups
Herbs
    1/3 to 1/2 tsp. dried   1 tbsp. fresh

Lard
    1 lb.   2 cups

Lentils
    1 lb. or 21/4 cups   5 cups cooked

Macaroni, uncooked
    1 lb.   4 to 5 cups

Macaroni, 1-inch pieces
    1 cup uncooked   2 to 21/4 cups cooked

Marshmallows
    1 cup cut up   16 large or 160 miniature

Beef, cooked
    1 lb.   3 cups minced

Beef, uncooked
    1 lb.   2 cups ground

Mustard
    1 tsp. dry or powdered   1 tbsp. prepared
                                                            mustard

Noodles, uncooked
    1 lb.   6 to 8 cups

Oatmeal
    1 cup uncooked   13/4 cups cooked

Peaches
    1 lb. or 4 medium-sized   2 cups sliced

Peanuts
    11/2 lb. unshelled, 1 lb. shelled   3 cups

Pecans
    1 lb. shelled   41/4 cups

Peppers, green
    1 large   1 cup diced

Potatoes
    1 lb. or 3 medium-sized   21/4 cups mashed

Prunes, dried
    1 lb.   21/4 cups pitted

Raisins, seedless, whole
    1 lb.   23/4 cups

To convert Fahrenheit into Centigrade, subtract 32, multiply by 5, then divide by 9. To convert Centigrade into Fahrenheit, reverse: Multiply by 9, divide by 5, and add 32.

COOKERY TERMS

BASTE: To ladle water, drippings or other liquid over food while roasting or baking.

BEAT: To mix smooth and light with a brisk, even rotary motion.

BLANCH: To submerge in boiling water for a short time and then plunge into cold water.

BRAISE: To brown meat or vegetables in a small amount of fat or salad oil, then to cover and cook slowly in the juices or a small amount of added liquid.

BREW: To cook in hot liquid until flavor is extracted.

BROIL: To cook by direct heat.

COMBINE: To mix enough to mingle ingredients.

CREAM: To make soft, smooth and creamy.

DREDGE: To coat with a dry substance.

FOLD: To combine by going vertically down through mixture with spoon, go along the bottom of bowl and continue with up and over motion.

MARINATE: To mix with oil and acid mixture and chill.

PAN BROIL: To cook, uncovered in hot skillet, pouring off fat as it accumulates.

PARBOIL: To partially cook in boiling water.

SAUTE: To cook in small amount of fat or salad oil until brown or tender.

SCALD: To bring to a temperature just below boiling point.

SCORE: To cut narrow grooves or gashes.

SIMMER: To cook in liquid just below boiling point.

CONVERTING A CONVENTIONAL RECIPE TO MICROWAVE METHOD

1. Use foods that microwave well.
2. Choose recipes with techniques similar to microwaving techniques such as covering, turning over, rearranging, stirring, shielding and standing time.

Covering: Holds in moisture and speeds heating. Lids hold in steam; tilted lets steam escape. Paper towels or napkins allow steam to escape, prevents splatters. Wax paper holds in heat while allowing some steam to escape. Plastic wrap holds in steam and heat. Pierce the top with a knife to allow excess steam to escape.

Turning Over: May be required during defrosting or when cooking foods without a cover.

Rearranging: Is done to allow for better exposure and more even cooking with microwaves.

Stirring: Is done on the top of a range to help foods heat evenly. In microwaves, it is done for the same reason, moving foods from outside to center of dish.

Shielding: Is also done in conventional cooking with foil to prevent overbrowning of thin parts, i.e. turkey wings and legs.

Standing Time: Is often done conventionally and is very important in microwave cooking. It allows food time to finish cooking.

2. Allow one-quarter to one-half of the conventional cooking time. A casserole that requires 1 hour to cook in an oven will require 15 to 30 minutes in a microwave. You may also use a microwave oven recipe as a guide. Choose a recipe using a similar quantity and type of food. Always use the shortest time, test for doneness and add more time as required. Cooking time increases as amount of food increases and time varies with wattage of oven and starting temperature. Cold foods take longer to cook.

3. You may need to reduce liquid. Evaporation is greatly decreased by the reduced cooking time. Begin by decreasing the liquid by 25 percent. Gradually add more liquid as necessary to achieve a consistency similar to the familiar product. Instead of reducing liquid in sauces and gravies, you can increase the flour and cornstarch. You might use tomato paste instead of tomato sauce. Vegetables will require little or no water. Reduce liquid in a cake mix by one-quarter. To add moisture to food, sprinkle with water, sauce or fruit juice and cover with plastic wrap, or wet paper towel with excess water squeezed out. This is good for reheating. To remove moisture from foods, microwave uncovered for a few seconds, let stand to crisp, or cover with paper napkins or towel to absorb moisture.

5. Reduce seasonings. Lack of evaporation intensifies flavor. Omit salt until after cooking. It tends to dehydrate food cooked in the microwave. Seasoning is often done near or at the end of cooking, if the food allows this, e.g. vegetables.

6. You can reduce or omit fat. If the recipe has fat for browning, omit it. If the fat is used for flavoring, reduce the amount.

7. Use low power for cooking delicate foods or for foods which require slow simmering to tenderize them. Use medium power for casseroles that cannot be stirred, for recipes using cream or sour cream and for hollandaise sauce. Use medium power or medium high power for many breads, quickbreads and cakes. Compare the amount of fat and sugar to other microwave recipes. If they are high, use a lower power. Rotating dish 1/4 turn 2 or 3 times during cooking helps food cook evenly. Shaping food in round or ring shape, or in small muffin pan sizes, allows more even cooking than square or loaf pans.

8. To blanch vegetables, add 3 to 4 tablespoons water to 1 qt. of vegetables in 2-qt. casserole and microwave on High. Stir half-way through cooking time.

Asparagus: 41/2 min.
Beans: 3 min.
Broccoli: 6 min.
Carrots: 3 min.
Cauliflower, cut into flowerettes: 6 min.
Corn, cut from cob: 4 min. (No water required)
Corn on the cob: 6 ears, 51/2 min. (No water required)
Peas: 3 min.
Snow peas, washed: 4 cups, 3 min
Spinach, washed: 4 min. (No water required)

Plunge into cold water. Dry and wrap in freezer bags and freeze immediately.

MICROWAVE TIPS

To clarify butter, let butter boil 1 minute. Clear butter may then be poured off.

A slice of pie topped with ice cream can be microwaved 30 to 45 seconds on High to heat pie without melting ice cream.

Make one large pot of coffee. Remove grounds and reheat all day as needed. Coffee won't be bitter. Reheat tea with no bitter taste.

Make extra waffles or pancakes and freeze. Reheat as needed.

Soften limes, lemons and oranges to extract more juice. Heat on High 20 to 30 seconds.

Toast almonds with butter in flat dish until lightly browned.

Warm bacon in package to separate slices easily.

Warm damp towels for use after eating finger foods.

Warm pies before serving. Melt cheese on apple pie, if desired.

Soften hard ice cream for easy scooping.

Heat brandy 10 to 15 seconds for flambeing. Warm brandy in snifters for drinking 8 seconds.

Soften frozen juice concentrate for easy combining.

Warm dog or cat food.

Rehydrate dried fruits by covering with liquid and cooking 5 to 6 minutes. Let stand 6 minutes.

Melt chocolate in wrapper in a custard cup.

Clarify liquid honey that has turned to sugar (remove metal lid).

Heat syrups for pancakes, etc. (Remove cap).

Peel peaches: Cook 15 to 20 seconds. Let stand 5 minutes.

Plump dried fruits for cakes in brandy or rum.

Freshen stale or soggy cookies. Defrost cookies.

Melt marshmallows into hot chocolate.

Sterilizing baby bottles, jam jars, etc.

Heat a damp cloth or paper towels for a minutes. The steam and warm damp towels make for any easy cleanup, especially your microwave oven.

Stiff muscles from too much exercise? Heat baby oil in microwave oven for a few seconds and then rub into sore muscles.

Plastic wrapping can be removed from frozen foods easily by heating until wrapper looks moist.

Cook too much porridge? Just refrigerate and reheat for breakfast the next day.

Even a soggy newspaper can be dried in a few seconds.

HERBS AND THEIR USES

	SOUPS APPETIZERS	SALADS	MEAT POULTRY	FISH SHELLFISH	VEGETABLES	EGGS CHEESE	BREAD
BASIL Strong enough for accent. Clove-like aroma and taste.	Seafood dips, turtle, tomato, bean, potato, vegetable and oxtail soups.	Green, vegetable, chicken, seafood, cottage or cream cheese, tomato.	Nearly all stews, liver, venison, milk gravies, stuffings, rabbit, game birds.	Baked or broiled halibut, mackerel, bluefish, all shellfish.	Asparagus, brussels sprouts, carrots, eggplant, green beans, limas, peas.	Macaroni, rice, noodles, cheese souffles, sauces, scrambled eggs and omelets.	Toasted breads, muffins.
BAY LEAF Strong enough for accent. Aromatic.	Soups, chowders.		Stews, liver, oxtail, heart.	All fish.	Potatoes, tomatoes.		
CHIVE Delicate onion flavor, especially good in blends.	Many appetizers, soup topping.	Widely-used in salads and dressings.	Meat topping.	All fish.	Potatoes, limas.	Cheese dishes, egg dishes, sauces.	Herb butter spreads.
DILL Strong enough for accent. Aromatic.	Many spreads and dips, tomato juice, tomato, bean and borscht soups.	Green, vegetable, cole slaw, potato, fish, dressings.	Fried meats, lamb, pork chops, veal, gravies, creamed chicken.	Fish, shellfish, fish sauces, herb butter.	Brussels sprouts, carrots, peas, cauliflower, cabbage, beets, beans, squash.	Cheese dishes, egg dishes.	Buns, toasted breads.
FENNEL Sweet, aromatic, anise-like flavor.	Soups. Fresh stalks may be eaten like celery.	Vegetable, fruit, seafood, dressings.	Beef, lamb, pork.	Boiled fish, shellfish, fish sauces.	Green vegetables, lentils.	Cheese dishes, egg dishes.	Breads, pastries, puddings.
MARJORAM Strong enough for accent. Aromatic, spicy.	Tomato juice, onion, oyster, chicken, clam and turtle soups,	Green, vegetable, fruit, cabbage, cheese, cole slaw, chicken, seafood, potato.	Meat, stews, game, duck, turkey, stuffings.	Baked and broiled fish, creamed crab, broiled lobster.	Asparagus, broccoli, brussels sprouts, carrots, eggplant, green beans, limas,	Cheese dishes, egg dishes.	Toasted breads, herb butter spreads.

MINT Strong enough for accent. Aromatic, tangy.	Fruit juices, many soups, especially pea or bean.	Fruit, tossed, cole slaw.	Lamb, veal sauces.	Fish, fish sauces.	Peas	Scrambled eggs, omelets.	
OREGANO Marjoram-like but more pungent.	Borscht, gumbo, chowders, , tomato and bean soups.	Fish. Shellfish. Potato. Mixed green.	Pork, veal, lamb, stews, chicken, duck, stuffings.	Fish, shellfish, fish sauces, herb butter.	Broccoli, onions, cabbage, peas, spinach, squash.		Biscuits, dumplings, herb bread.
PARSLEY Good in blends, delicate, aromatic.	Canapes, spreads, dips, many soups.	Used anywhere.	Used anywhere.	Fish, shellfish, fish sauces, herb butter.	Can be used in all according to taste.	Cheese dishes. Egg dishes.	Biscuits, corn, bread, herb butter.
ROSEMARY Pungent. Spicy odor and flavor.	Some appetizers, chicken, pea and turtle soup.	Green, vegetable, fruit, meat.	Meat, poultry, game, stews, gravies, stuffings.	Baked, broiled and fried fish, shellfish.	Cauliflower, spinach, eggplant, green beans, turnips.	Most egg dishes.	
SAGE Pungent, aromatic, strong flavor.	Used sparingly in some appetizers, soups and chowders.	Cottage or cream cheese, dressings.	Meat, poultry, game, stews, gravies, stuffing.	Fish, shellfish, fish stuffing.	Brussels sprouts, cabbage, green beans, eggplant, turnips.	Cottage cheese, casseroles, creamed eggs.	Biscuits, dumplings.
SAVORY Good in blends. Fragrant, spicy.	Vegetable juice, pea, bean, lentil, vegetable and onion soups.	Green vegetable, tomato, potato, egg, cole slaw.	Meat, poultry, game, stews, gravies, stuffing.	Baked or broiled fish.	Asparagus, cucumbers, squash, green beans, Cabbage, cauliflower.	Deviled or scrambled eggs, omelets.	
TARRAGON Strong enough for accent. Sweet, anise-scented.	Cheese spreads or dips, vegetable juice, soup, chowder.	Green, seafood, tomato aspic, dressing, vinegars.	Meat, poultry.	Fish, shellfish, fish sauces.	Broccoli, celery, cucumber, spinach, asparagus, cabbage, beets,	Cheese dishes, egg dishes.	Herb butter spread.
THYME Strong enough for accent. Aromatic.	Cheese dips, vegetable, gumbo, borscht and pea soups,	Seafood, chicken, tomato aspic.	Meat, poultry, game, stuffing.	Fish, shellfish, fish sauces.	Beets, onions, spinach, carrots, peas, asparagus.	Cheese dishes, egg dishes.	In or on corn bread, biscuits, toasted breads.

CATERING FOR A CROWD

TEA ESSENCE

1 cup tea leaves   3 cups boiling water

The essence thus made can be kept for hours and tea made by adding fresh boiling water to taste. Yield: 50 cups of tea.

COFFEE FOR 50

1 1/4 - 1 1/2 lbs. coffee   2 1/2 gallons water

Place coffee in a clean muslin bag and tie loosely to allow for swelling of the grounds. They will double in bulk.

QUANTITIES FOR SERVING 50

Soup: 12 quarts
Rolls: 75
Bread: 6 loaves
Meat loaf: 10 pounds ground steak
Baked fresh ham or veal: 15 pounds
Dressing: 5 quarts
Pot roast: 15 pounds
Roast beef: 18 pounds
Chicken (fricassee): 25 pounds
Chicken (creamed): 18 pounds
Fish: 15 pounds
Potatoes (mashed): 12 quarts
Potatoes (creamed): 8 quarts
Beans for baking: 4 quarts
Canned vegetables: 1 can for 6 people
Carrots: 10 pounds
Onions: 10 pounds
Coffee: 1 1/4 pounds
Tea: 1 cup
Cream or milk, for coffee: 1 1/2 quarts
Butter: 1 1/4 pounds
Apples for sauce: 8 quarts
Lettuce for salad: 5 heads
Fruit salad: 8 quarts
Cabbage for salad: 3 1/2 medium heads
Ice cream: 6 1/4 quarts
Cake (15 pieces to each cake): 3 1/2 cakes
Fruit punch: 10 quarts
Sugar cubes: 1 1/2 pounds
Pies: 1 pie serves 6 people

INDEX

APPETIZERS, DIPS & SPREADS

SOUPS & SANDWICHES

BEVERAGES, SAUCES & BUTTERS

VEGETABLES

MEAT, FISH & POULTRY

RICE, PIZZA & PASTA

EGGS, PANCAKES & WAFFLES

BREADS, BISCUITS & DOUGHNUTS

PIES & PASTRY

CAKES & FROSTINGS

COOKIES

DESSERTS

ALMOST DECADENT

CANNING & PRESERVING

MISCELLANEOUS

COUNTRY CLASSICS
The ideal gift for showers or to give to a friend.

Please send me _____ copies at $16.95 each $ _____

Plus $3.00 shipping and handling $ _____ 3.00

TOTAL: $ _____

Name _____

Address _____

_____

_____

Payment must accompany this
order. Make cheque or money
order payable to Plains Publishing
Inc. and mail to:
Plains Publishing Inc.
10241-123 St.
Edmonton, AB Canada T5N 1N3

- ✂

COUNTRY CLASSICS
The ideal gift for showers or to give to a friend.

Please send me _____ copies at $16.95 each $ _____

Plus $3.00 shipping and handling $ _____ 3.00

TOTAL: $ _____

Name _____

Address _____

_____

_____

Payment must accompany this
order. Make cheque or money
order payable to Plains Publishing
Inc. and mail to:
Plains Publishing Inc.
10241-123 St.
Edmonton, AB Canada T5N 1N3

- ✂

COUNTRY CLASSICS
The ideal gift for showers or to give to a friend.

Please send me _____ copies at $16.95 each $ _____

Plus $3.00 shipping and handling $ _____ 3.00

TOTAL: $ _____

Name _____

Address _____

_____

_____

Payment must accompany this
order. Make cheque or money
order payable to Plains Publishing
Inc. and mail to:
Plains Publishing Inc.
10241-123 St.
Edmonton, AB Canada T5N 1N3